Pictorial History
of the
Wild West

NOTICE!

TO THIEVES, THUGS, FAKIRS AND BUNKO-STEERERS,

Among Whom Are

J. J. HARLIN, alias "OFF WHEELER;" SAW DUST CHARLIE, WM. HEDGES, BILLY THE KID, Billy Mullin, Little Jack, The Cuter, Pock-Marked Kid, and about Twenty Others:

If Found within the Limits of this City after TEN O'CLOCK P. M., this Night, you will be Invited to attend a GRAND NECK-TIE PARTY,

The Expense of which will be borne by

100 Substantial Citizens.

Las Vegas, March 24th. 1882.

Pictorial History

OF THE

Wild West

A TRUE ACCOUNT OF THE BAD MEN,
DESPERADOES, RUSTLERS AND OUTLAWS OF
THE OLD WEST—AND THE MEN WHO
FOUGHT THEM TO ESTABLISH LAW AND ORDER

By James D. Horan and Paul Sann

SPRING BOOKS
LONDON · NEW YORK · SYDNEY · TORONTO

This edition first published 1961
Fifth impression 1970

© COPYRIGHT JAMES D. HORAN AND PAUL SANN, 1954

Published by

THE HAMLYN PUBLISHING GROUP LTD
LONDON • NEW YORK • SYDNEY • TORONTO
HAMLYN HOUSE, FELTHAM, MIDDLESEX, ENGLAND

Printed in Czechoslovakia by PZ Bratislava

T 2144

SBN 600 03103 9

FOR the officers and members of the Westerners in New York, Chicago, St. Louis, Denver, Los Angeles, Tucson, San Francisco, Wyoming, Black Hills and Portland, who so faithfully ride the trails of the Old West in their search for truth.

Acknowledgments

We can only try to thank all those who helped with this book.

First must come a gentleman known to just about every writer who ever fell in love with the Old West—Sylvester Vigilante, for forty-seven years the moving spirit of the American History Room at the New York Public Library and a walking encyclopedia on all the badmen—and the good—of a time gone by. Our debt to the ex-Sheriff of the New York Posse of The Westerners is great, for Mr. Vigilante kindly offered us the use of his remarkable Western bibliography. There are many others—East and West—who devoted many hours to our project because they liked our idea: to tell the Western story the way it really happened.

We're grateful (pay no attention to the order), to the Arizona Pioneers' Historical Society and its secretary, Eleanor B. Sloan; to the Kansas State Historical Society and its secretary, Nyle H. Miller; to the Wyoming State Historical Department and its archivist, Lola M. Homsher; to Mrs. Opal Harber of the Denver Public Library's Western History Department; to the University of Oklahoma and its acting archivist, James M. Babcock; to Mrs. C. E. Cook, curator of the Museum of the Oklahoma Historical Society; to Frances Shea, librarian of the State Historical Society of Colorado; to Dean F. Krakel, archivist of the University of Wyoming; to Winnie Allen, archivist of the University of Texas; to Allan R. Ottley of the California State Library; to John E. Pomfret, director of the Huntington Library in California, and to Mrs. Olive B. Corwin of the Museum of New Mexico at Santa Fe.

We are also indebted to Fred M. Mazzulla of Denver; Irene Simpson of the Wells Fargo Bank History Room; W. Grant Burden, assistant to general director of public relations, Union Pacific Railroad, Gene Sullivan of the Coffeyville *Daily Journal,* M. R. Cring of the Missouri-Kansas-Texas Lines, Col. Maurice Garland Fulton, Stuart Lake, Albert R. Cottle, Merrill Chilcote of the St. Joseph, Missouri, *Gazette;* to C. G. Wellington of the Kansas City *Star;* Ed Dooley of the Denver *Post* and Ray Mackland of *Life* Magazine.

The authors wish especially to thank the Pinkerton National Detective Agency for the facilities, help and many courtesies extended to them, and particularly by John O. Camden, Vice-President and General Manager; H. W. Nugent, Manager of the Department of Criminal Investigation; Frank D. Dimaio (retired); also Assistant Superintendent Charles D. Hey, Harry Rybak and George Robinson of the Department of Criminal Investigation. We are also indebted to Maurice Frink, author of *Cow Country Cavalcade,* and the Wyoming Stock Growers' Association for permission to use their rare picture of Cattle Kate.

Those three good Westerners—and Americana book dealers—Peter Decker, Fred Rosenstock and Bill Kelleher, were most helpful.

A vote of thanks is due Vincent Mercaldo in whose Mercaldo Archives of pictorial history we found some fine gems, and also to the invincible four horsemen of the American History Room in the New York Public Library, Gerald D. McDonald, James J. Heslin, Ivor D. Avellino and Mrs. Maud Cole. A special thank you must go to Percy Seibert, that extraordinary gentleman who is worth a book in himself, who contributed his pictures of Butch Cassidy and the Sundance Kid in Bolivia, along with a documented memoir of how those two outlaws brought lawlessness to the pampas.

The authors also received most generous cooperation from Floyd Shoemaker, secretary of the Missouri Historical Society, Paul Vanderbilt and his wonderful Graphic History Society of America, and Agnes Wright Spring, executive assistant of the Colorado Historical Society and Clark Kinnaird, book editor of King Features Syndicate. And we must not forget our fellow Western authors who put aside their own busy hours to help us; Merrell Kitchen, Zoe A. Tilghman, Ramon F. Adams, Burton Rascoe, Wayne Gard, Stuart Whitehouse, Lucius Beebe, Charles Clegg and Charles Kelly. We are also grateful to Ramona Javitz, curator of the Print Department of the New York Public Library and Ruth Kimball, head of the Library's publicity department; Mrs. M. Evans, director of publicity of the New York Historical Society; Josephine Cobb, Chief of the Still Pictures, National Archives, Ed Bartholomew and his well known Rose Collection of old-time photographs of the frontier; Mrs. Gertrude McDevitt of the Idaho Historical Society; Mrs. Anne McDonnell and Marguerita McDonnell, of the Montana Historical Society.

There must have been others, too—some that we talked to in our on-the-spot research in the West, some that we had letters from, some that lent a hand from the Posses of the Westerners in Denver, Chicago, Los Angeles and Wyoming. To all we humbly say "Thank you."

Table of Contents

INTRODUCTION

THE WILD West was a time as well as a place. The place was roughly from the Middle Border country of Kansas, Missouri, and the neighboring states to the Pacific. The time was roughly from the end of the Civil War to the turn of the century.

When we talk of the Wild West, we mean not wilderness wild but lawless wild—disorder, violence, fighting, and killing; we mean not the grandeur of untamed nature but the drama of undisciplined and untamed men.

What made the Wild West wild? What caused this phenomenon, unique in the world? There are, and have been always, other great wide open spaces, other vast, thinly populated areas, but nowhere else has there been the peculiar vitality, the savage turbulence, and the rip-roaring drama of the long-drawn-out struggle for law and order in the American West. Why was it so?

First, it was because of the social conditions which prevailed during the brief span of the Western frontier. Almost every man wore a six-shooter on his hip to protect his life and property. In this primitive state there were certain unwritten laws which Theodore Roosevelt called "fair play." You could not shoot a man in the back and you could not kill an unarmed man. The tacit rules of the game were these: that you serve notice of your intentions, then set out to kill your enemy or be killed. It is surprising how often these rules were observed, although there were instances of bushwhacking in the cattle and sheep wars.

In addition to the existing social conditions there was the weakness of the law. It had not been designed to fit the needs of such a wild land. Water, range, and homesteading rights were outstanding examples. These laws were inadequate and the men of the West could not abide by them and survive.

In the Middle Border states, outlawry and strife spawned by the Civil War joined forces. There was no peace at Appomattox for the men who rode under the black flag of Quantrill. The pro-Union men could not forget the murders and the looting, and for years afterward many of them rode the lonely back-roads of Missouri armed with Navy Colts.

It has been speculated that the restlessness of these wild young veterans, many like Jesse James, who had blooded his saber before he was seventeen, contributed to the lawlessness of the times. Why walk behind a ragged-eared mule and a plow when there was easier money— gold to be taken from the hated banks, railroads and express companies? If this conclusion is valid, however, what of the other men who rode under Quantrill? There were the Jameses and the Youngers, but there were others who became law officers and lawful respected citizens. One be-came a clergyman; at least two became members of the state legislature.

Just about the time the bandits of the Middle Border were subdued, there occurred the disaster that made the West truly wild. That was the great drought of the late 1870's that ruined the cattle industry, that sent thousands of young unemployed cowboys out onto the range to shift for themselves. Too many of them made the wrong shift. Yet somehow they have become heroes; they have lived on in legend and story, in ballads, on the screen, and on the airwaves.

Why? Why does the Wild West have such glamor, why do its badmen and desperadoes as well as its marshals and sheriffs capture the imagination of so many people? Why does the Wild West have such universal appeal?

This may be the answer: the timeless allure of the Wild West may rest on the inherent drama of its vast setting, the average American's assumption that any story of the West equals stirring adventure and the symbols—a fleet horse and a trusty six-shooter "who run together like molasses," as a famous captain of the Texas Rangers once said.

The West was "romantic" not to the Westerner himself but to the Easterner, who could not ride a horse across the plains, could not wear a six-shooter, herd cattle or swagger down a wooden sidewalk in high-heeled boots, colorful garb and a ten-gallon hat. As Walter Prescott Webb points out in his *Great Plains,* a superb study of the West, it was the East which set the standards, made the rules and dubbed the cowboy, bandit and marshal "romantic." As Webb says, had the West been more quickly tamed and settled, the farmer's pitchfork and the cant hook of the lumberjack might well have taken the place of the horse and the six-shooter in American folklore.

And so, having written the books and plays, the Easterner ordained the mould for the outlaw, the marshal, the cowboy, the Indian and the cattle baron. Owen Wister's *The Virginian* ("When you say that, smile," etc.) was more acceptable than the realistic view of Western life presented by Hamlin Garland, Andy Adams or Eugene Manlove Rhodes.

It is only in recent years, beginning perhaps with *The Ox-Bow Incident,* that the American public has begun to accept a more realistic view of the West. It is doubtful, however, that the phony romance surrounding those wild years will ever be completely abandoned. As long as there are the young in heart, the handsome, brave cowboy, the moustached villain in his black ten-gallon hat and Jesse James, who robs the rich only to help the poor, will ride eternally across the Western plains.

9

I. The Early Days of Outlawry in America

OUTLAWRY IN America appeared soon after the settlers had erected their first blockhouse. In New England a "Body of Laws" was enacted to combat the widespread activities of the road agents. For a first offense, a highwayman had the letter "B" branded on his forehead. The second offense brought another branding and a severe whipping; the third offense meant death. For a crime committed on the Lord's Day, his ears were cut off as additional penalty.

The Colonial landed gentry, like the ranchers and cattle barons of the West a century later, had to cope with cattle rustlers and horse thieves. While the Iroquois and their allies were still raiding the settlements on the New York-Niagara frontier and Pontiac moved among the tribes preparing the war that would bear his name, the "Grays," a fast-moving band of horse and cattle thieves, were operating in the forests near Poughkeepsie.

The Grays, however, were not the only outlaws of that period, as is shown in the Sir William Johnson Papers. Small bands were always running off stock from one pre-Revolutionary farm or another and fighting off the posses with musket fire.

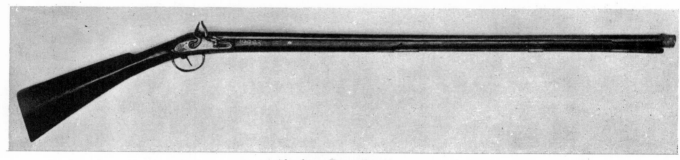

Abraham Doane's gun.

THE DOANES

Throughout the American Revolution there was widespread cattle rustling, horse stealing, and highway robbery in the struggling colonies. Perhaps most important of the outlaw gangs were the Doanes, famous in legend and story, and possibly America's first outlaw brotherhood. Moses Doane (also spelled Doan) was the leader, and his five brothers the nucleus of the band.

The Doanes pursued their career of plunder and daredeviltry for about seven years during and after the Revolutionary War before the law caught up with them. They sided with the British and helped them in many ways. Toward the end of hostilities the Doanes had thoroughly terrorized Bucks County in Pennsylvania and parts of New Jersey. To speak out against them meant certain reprisal— the burning of one's house and barns, or even death. But by 1783 the resistance against them was well organized and "Wanted" placards about them were spread over the area.

Their most important robbery took place on a windy night in October, 1781, when they raided the treasury at Newtown, Pennsylvania, which at the time was an old town in a new world. There were mansions of red and black brick, with white shutters, big brass door knobs which gleamed from the daily polishing of the neat Dutch

Lock of Abe Doane's gun.
Drawn by James M. Kane

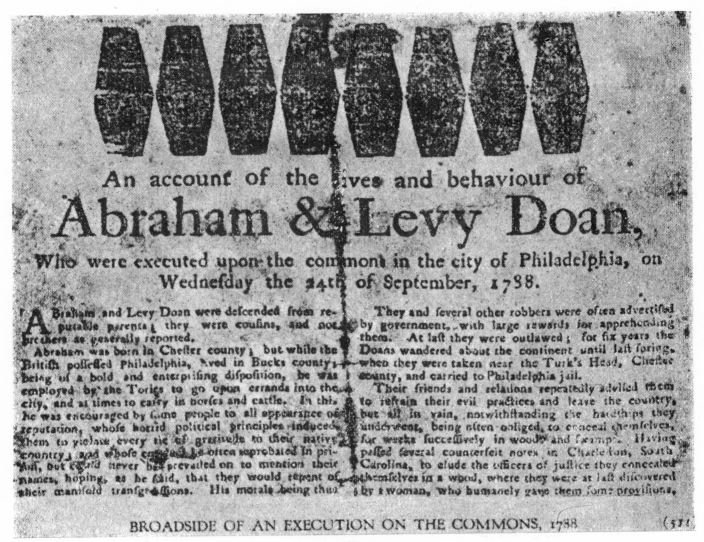

Fragment of a broadside of an execution on the Commons,
Philadelphia, 1788.

housewives, broad tiled roofs, and eaves which reached the ground.

The streets were large and orderly, and there was a public library. Here lived men famous in their time, patriot and Tory. Besides its richness and culture, Newtown was an important military center. It was the recruiting center for Bucks County and for a time there were considerable bodies of troops quartered there.

At ten o'clock on that October night, Moses Doane led his brothers and their henchmen into the quiet town. As one member of the band later said, there were sixteen riders who trotted down the moonlit street to the home of John Hart, Esq., treasurer of Bucks County, who was sitting at a table "eating his supper at an unusually late hour."

The main topic of excited discussion was Cornwallis's surrender three days before at Yorktown, and Hart was repeating the latest news he had gathered at the tavern, when the door burst open and Moses Doane, a tall, raw-boned man with a scallop-rimmed fur hat, rushed into the room followed by a number of men.

The entire house was surrounded, Moses roared in his trumpet-like voice, and with Hart staring up the barrel of his large pistol, Moses barked orders to his gang to ransack the house. They did so with an expert thoroughness. Pillow sacks of paper money—some even taken from beneath the heads of sleeping children—and a large money box were found. Then Hart and some other town leaders were marched up the main street at pistol point to the county vault, which they opened under the guns of the outlaws. The plunder was thrown into saddle bags and the gang swept out of town.

In the old Wrightstown schoolhouse the money was counted. There was £735, 17s, 9½d in silver besides the paper money—a king's ransom in those days.

It was a strange scene at the old schoolhouse; the sixteen horses, impatiently stamping at the hitching rail outside, while inside the outlaws grouped around the school desks, their eyes glittering in the candlelight as their big leader laboriously licked his fingers, counted out the bills one by one, then let the gold coins clink through his fingers.

Sixteen shares of about $280 each were issued by Moses Doane, with three young robbers who acted as pickets or horse-holders each receiving $40.

The Newtown robbery showed the outlaw band at its

peak. They had spies everywhere in Bucks County, fast horses, hideouts in caves (there are almost as many Doane caves in Pennsylvania as there are Jesse James caves in Missouri), and even a surgeon named Meyers, who worked with the gang, and of whom Moses Doane once said, "I would trust (him) with any secret."

Tax collectors were the special targets of the Doanes. Men were suddenly surrounded on the dark roads, "handled roughly," and sometimes knocked out of their saddles with a sweeping blow of a British musket. Then the outlaws, scorning masks, would be gone with a rush of horses' hooves.

"SANDY FLASH" FITZPATRICK

Once one of the Doane riders left the ranks to form his own outlaw band but without success. The handsome young Irishman, James Fitzpatrick, who emerged as "Sandy Flash" in Bayard Taylor's *Story of Kennett,* a nineteenth-century best-seller, operated mainly in Chester and Delaware Counties, Pennsylvania, preying mostly on the wealthy landowners.

In 1785, with a reward of £200 posted for him dead or alive, he calmly rode his big black stallion into Chester and dined at the Unicorn Tavern, while the posses who had chased him bragged at the bar about what they would do to the "Sandy Flash" if they captured him.

Like Jesse James after him, Fitzpatrick was a man without a face. Eventually he was captured and hanged in the Old Chester jail in January, 1787.

After the Newtown robbery, the chase closed in on the Doanes, and in a few years the brotherhood was broken up and each of the brothers sent to the gallows or to prison.

What is not generally realized is that the American Revolution also produced the original American cowboy. He was not the popularly pictured drawling, lean-shanked cowpuncher of Western lore, but a hard-riding, resourceful guerrilla fighter who operated for the British forces in the neutral ground of New York's Westchester County.

THE COWBOYS OF THE NEUTRAL GROUND

The Neutral Ground was one of the bloodiest battlegrounds in the Revolution, matched in atrocity and violence only by the Mohawk Valley. On its northern boundary were the American lines, once commanded by Aaron Burr, and on the south in New York, the British. Both sides patrolled the area but the ravaged land was usually left to the "Cowboys," who worked with the British Dragoons, or the "Skinners," who rode with the Americans. Both bands lived off the land by stealing horses or cattle and engaging in murderous forays. They were mostly farmhands who wore castoff jackets and boots of Yankee or Lobsterback cavalrymen, and carried swords, tomahawks, or the long British "bagnits." Who first named the cowboys is not known but it is generally believed they received the name from the British after the "cow boys" who tended the cattle on English farms.

A superb portrayal of the Cowboys and the Skinners can be found in *Neutral Ground* by Frank Hough, (Carrick and Evans, 1942), which unfortunately has long been out of print.

A cowboy ambush in the Neutral Ground.

THE HARPES

Another outlaw brotherhood of Revolutionary days was that of the fabled Harpe brothers, who have been the subject of several historical novels. As with the Doanes, the outlaw historian finds few facts about them, and much legend. Most of their story must come from the quaint books of reminiscences and gossip written by early settlers and regional historians, all Klondikes of anecdotes.

There were two male Harpes—"We are the Harpes," they liked to say—Micajah, or "Big" Harpe, and Wiley, "Little" Harpe. Both were born in North Carolina, one in 1768 and the other in 1770.

Like the Doanes, the Harpes were British sympathizers. After Yorktown, when their neighbors refused to forget their depredations, they fled, making their way into central Tennessee, where they settled among the Cherokees. After their first robbery, they fled to Knoxville, then the gateway to the West and as wild as any Western frontier town. After a spell at farming, they decided horse stealing was easier than following the plow. They stole a neighbor's team, were later captured by a posse, but escaped.

The next victims of the Harpe brothers were emigrants moving along the Wilderness Road. Soon more than five murders were charged to them. Finally captured, they were imprisoned in Danville, Kentucky, but the flimsy log jail was no match for their brute strength. After escaping, they resumed their activities of murder and plunder up and down the Wilderness Road. Some of their victims they disembowelled, hurling a number of the bodies, filled with gravel and stone, into the Barren River.

The terrible murders enraged the countryside. Posses formed, and "Wanted" posters—misspelling the name of the outlaws, appeared on the highways: "Three hundred dollars to any person who have apprehended and delivered into the custody of the jailer of the Danville District the said MICAJAH HARP and a like reward for the delivering as aforesaid, the said WILEY HARP alias ROBERTS, to be paid out of the PUBLIC TREASURY . . ."

The Harpes moved westward to the Ohio River, where they joined the lawless community of Cave In The Rock, a deep limestone cave with hidden subterranean passages large enough to hide an army. It was located about sixty miles below Red Bank and was long a favorite spot for the pirates and river wreckers.

So terrible was the blood lust of the Harpes that they were even driven out of the outlaw community. No torture had been too sickening for them, one account said. "They were like men turned into wild wolves."

For a year they drifted through the forest, two wild-eyed giants with tangled black beards, dressed in ragged buckskins and carrying muskets, tomahawks dangling at their sides and wicked pig stickers in their belts. By the summer of 1798 a long list of horrible murders was charged to them. However, to most people they were men without faces. Many a settler recalled hospitality given to two giant strangers, and one reported receiving from them a horn of powder to protect himself from the "Terrible Harpes."

In 1799 the Harpes' murder trail became even wilder, and they butchered a man simply " 'cause he snored too much." Posses now hunted them with dogs and skilled trappers. When they did catch up with the Harpes, the manhunters showed themselves as vicious as the hunted. Wiley (Little) Harpe escaped to reappear five years later, but a posseman shot Big Harpe in the spine, knocking him off his horse. The posseman waited, watching the big outlaw suffering a slow death. At last, tired of waiting, he sawed through Big Harpe's neck, while the criminal called out as his dying words, "You are a God damned rough butcher but cut on and be damned." Then the man "wrung off his head, in the same manner as you would a hog."

The posseman put the head in a bag and the posse set out for home. On the way they ran out of food and were forced to turn to cannibalism, boiling the outlaw's head with a pot of corn. The head was nailed to a tree—called Harpes Head to this day—and for years the gleaming white skull grinned down at frightened strangers.

SAM MASON

Mike Fink was driving nails with bullets to become a legend on the River when Sam Mason turned to outlawry. A roaring, brawling river man, Sam was one of George Rogers Clark's men. Like Hare, Mason selected the Natchez Trace for his "hunting" ground, "hunting" in this case meaning robbing, raiding, and killing. When he was captured the first time, a posse rode him out of Natchez on a rail. But Mason organized a stronger gang, to become the terror of the Mississippi. His numerous and bold crimes finally forced the governor of the Mississippi Territory and the Governor of Louisiana to join forces and hunt him down.

In March, 1803, he was captured, only to escape. Rewards were posted, and a quiet, bearded stranger named Setten offered to go out and bring him in. He did, returning with Mason's head in a ball of clay. Setten was accepting the tributes of the relieved citizens of the Trace when one man, after studying him closely, blurted out, "Why, that's Wiley Harpe!"

Harpe was arrested and identified by a scar on his breast. He was hanged in the company of one of his men on February 8, 1804.

WHOLESALE RASCAL: JOHN A. MURREL

"I have carried off more than a thousand slaves."

On a mild January day in 1834, a young man named Virgil Stewart rode leisurely along the Natchez Trace listening with horrified fascination to his older companion as he casually described the evil life of his "elder brother."

The tales were of robbery, murder, piracy, outlawry, and slave stealing. The last seemed to please the older man. He continued to dwell on the skill of his "older brother" in this "profession."

As they rode down into a quiet glen, the pale afternoon sunshine streaming down through the trees, he described how his brother took care of slaves who were apt to become "troublesome."

"He took the nigger out on the bank of a river which ran by the farm of his brother and shot him through the head and then got rid of him . . ."

Stewart, fighting down his terror, asked, "But the body? How did he get rid of it . . . ?"

His companion shrugged and carefully picked a thread from the front of his deep, rich Bolivar coat.

"Oh! That is easy. He cuts open the belly and scrapes out the guts, and then fills him full of sand and throws him into the river to feed the eels . . ."

They had come to a spot where the setting sun had turned the birches to copper bars.

"A beautiful scene," he said softly to Stewart.

Later that night, as they stopped for supper, the old man, after a long pause, said, "I might as well be out with it. I'm the elder brother I've been telling you about!"

The "elder brother" was the infamous John Murrel, later to be known as the Great Land Pirate. Young Stewart's account of his hair-raising journey with him was to form the basis for countless pre-Civil War penny dreadfuls.

Murrel had found he liked Stewart when they met on the Trace. Actually Stewart was trailing Murrel in an effort to gather evidence against him on a Negro-stealing charge. Each night he scribbled down an account of the day's conversations, sometimes even scratching names and dates on his saddle skirts. Murrel mentioned his crimes al

most casually, but his wild eyes blazed when he spoke of his Slave Revolt.

The climax of the whole wild tale was Murrel's description of the weird confederacy he had organized on the Mississippi, a black brotherhood of armed slaves who would conquer the vast frontier in an incredible blood bath. Murrel seemed to be thrilled by the very thought of the destruction and his revenge on the aristocrats who had whipped and imprisoned him. Or perhaps it was the thought of his glory and wealth as supreme ruler of the black pirate empire.

Young Stewart felt his skin crawl as the soft voice went on.

"I shall lead my men myself into New Orleans," Murrel said. "Just think, the British couldn't take it!"

He made a gesture with his thumb and Stewart saw the dull red brand mark: HT (horse-thief).

Stewart accompanied Murrel to his secret headquarters on the river, where he was accepted into the evil brotherhood. When he felt he had gathered enough evidence against Murrel, he notified the authorities, who arrested the land pirate who once boasted, "Let a man learn the use of the law and nothing can touch him . . ."

Murrel's revolt flickered briefly up and down the Natchez Trace after his arrest, by which time he had almost perfected his plans to take over Natchez on Christmas Day. One night his followers erupted out of their filthy shacks and dives, screaming their wild cries and shooting down anyone who crossed their path. But without their leader the

"They took the body . . . and heaved it over the edge of the ravine."

men milled helplessly about; the raids resulted in little more than a splatter of wild shots fired in the night. Though riot raged, it was aimless, gradually dying out. It was the end of the "revolt."

In July, 1834, Murrel was tried in Circuit Court, Jackson, and defended by no less than the Hon. Milton Brown, Esq., who ten years later found his niche in history when he introduced into Congress the bill by which Texas was annexed to the United States.

Despite Brown's oratory, Murrel was found guilty and sentenced to ten years at hard labor in the State Penitentiary at Nashville.

Back home in Lexington, Kentucky, young Stewart gathered his notes together and wrote a description of his thrilling trip along the Trace with Murrel and the long tale of robbery and violence which the Land Pirate had told him. He also added his experience in Murrel's headquarters and a detailed account of how the slave rebellion was to plunge the frontier into a blood bath. In addition he included some of the testimony from Murrel's trial and a list of the outlaw's co-conspirators. Published in pamphlet form, the story was widely read along the frontier.

Blood and thunder writers, notably those on the *Police Gazette,* rewrote Stewart's account, putting in more blood and violence than Murrel ever dreamed of. Fox's lurid pink sheet found Murrel's strange life as an outlaw leader and leader of a slave rebellion fascinating—and profitable. It was worked and reworked for years, until some weary editor topped it finally with *The Pictorial Life of the Great Western Land Pirate.*

There just didn't seem any more to go on and Murrel's name and infamy finally vanished into folklore.

JOSEPH HARE AND THE NATCHEZ TRACE

Another early American outlaw was Joseph Thompson Hare, whose specialty was holding up stagecoaches along the Natchez Trace and pirating small boats on the Mississippi.

Hare was a dapper little man who had a way with the ladies. He was born in Chester, Pennsylvania, and spent most of his life in the crowded slums of New York, Philadelphia, and Baltimore. He signed on for a year's voyage on a windjammer but jumped ship at New Orleans when that city caught his eye. Settlers carrying large money belts were leaving New Orleans for Kentucky and Tennessee. They had to go through the Choctaw and Cherokee Nations, which meant they could be easy prey for outlaws hiding along the wild trails.

The Natchez Trace, linking Natchez and Nashville, was five hundred miles of swamps, dim trails, tiny bridle paths, and twisting forest paths—an excellent territory for an outlaw gang. Hare saw the possibilities and gathered a gang together. For years he was a legend on the Trace, a will o' the wisp who robbed and plundered almost at will. Few men knew what he looked like, and Hare could easily loll in the fleshpots of New Orleans without worrying about sheriffs or posses.

When he was finally caught, he served only five years. After his release in 1818, he robbed the Baltimore night coach outside of Havre de Grace, getting $16,000, a fortune in those days. Two days later, as he was about to buy "a beautiful plaid coat," the law caught up with him. At dawn, September 10, 1818, he was hanged in the courtyard of the Baltimore jail, leaving behind his diary with the doleful warning to his readers not to embrace the highwayman's life, "as it is a desperate life, full of danger, and sooner or later it ends on the gallows."

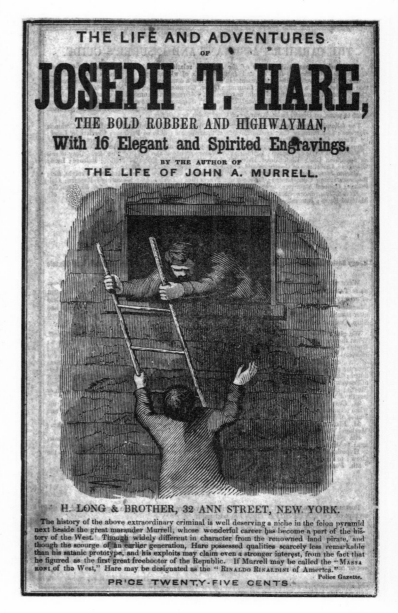

THE LIFE AND ADVENTURES OF

JOSEPH T. HARE,

THE BOLD ROBBER AND HIGHWAYMAN,

With 16 Elegant and Spirited Engravings.

BY THE AUTHOR OF

THE LIFE OF JOHN A. MURRELL.

H. LONG & BROTHER, 32 ANN STREET, NEW YORK.

The history of the above extraordinary criminal is well deserving a niche in the felon pyramid next beside the great marauder Murrell, whose wonderful career has become a part of the history of the West. Though widely different in character from the renowned land pirate, and though the scourge of an earlier generation, Hare possessed qualities scarcely less remarkable than his satanic prototype, and his exploits may claim even a stronger interest, from the fact that he figured as the first great freebooter of the Republic. If Murrell may be called the "MASSA RONI of the West," Hare may be designated as the "RINALDO RINALDINI of America."
Police Gazette.

PRICE TWENTY-FIVE CENTS.

CAPTAIN LIGHTFOOT

Michael Martin, alias Captain Lightfoot.

The most notorious post-Revolution outlaw was Irish Michael Martin, the handsome and dashing Captain Lightfoot, probably the last man hanged in Massachusetts for highway robbery.

Shortly before his execution in 1822, he dictated his memoirs to Frederick W. Waldo, a reporter for the *Columbia Sentinel*. The resulting book is one of the first published accounts of the life of an American outlaw: *Captain Lightfoot, the Last of the New England Highwaymen*. It was a great success and went into three editions within a month after Lightfoot's execution. But now it is difficult to obtain the book. A copy of the third edition can be found in the library of the Massachusetts Historical Society.

Martin was born in the parish of Connehy, about seven miles from Kilkenny, April 9, 1775. He confesses to owning a "violent temper" and a dislike for work apparently standard in successful American outlaws.

At seventeen he was a thief and a year later ran away to Dublin, where he associated with "profligate men and women." After a highly romantic interlude with a pastor's daughter, he was forced by his father to return to the farm. One day a tall, distinguished man riding a "splendid blooded horse" appeared. He was "Captain Thunderbolt," Ireland's famous highwayman, and soon young Michael was his second in command.

Captain Thunderbolt's philosophy, as his young assistant would recall many years later, "was to make property equal in this world . . . that he could get as much as he could from the rich but would never molest the poor—he would take money from those who had more than they knew how to use, but would never take life, if he could avoid it. If there was any danger of detection, or any strong opposition, he thought himself justified in taking life . . ." It was the eternal alibi of every outlaw; they were always Robin Hoods and never common thieves.

In his death cell in 1822, as he spun his tale for the young reporter, Captain Lightfoot was already laying the foundation of his own Robin Hood legend. His example would be followed down through the centuries by every other American outlaw in an attempt to justify his crimes and his way of life.

Years of outlawry in Ireland and Scotland followed for Captain Thunderbolt and young Martin, who was known as Captain Lightfoot. But in 1818 the rewards for their capture had been increased, and the countryside was alive with troops. So Martin said good-bye to his friend and left for America, on April 12, 1818, aboard the brig *Maria,* which arrived in Salem on June 17.

Some months of farming, then work as a brewer's helper followed. The next year Martin bought a small brewery in Salem, but the sharp Yankee tradespeople were too much for him. His business failed, and by the spring of 1819 he was deep in debt.

When his sweetheart spurned him, it was the last straw. Martin, the young Irish immigrant, became again the notorious Captain Lightfoot and one of America's first glamorous outlaws.

As he recalled, "to keep my hand in," he first held up a Connecticut peddler and "lifted" seventy dollars. The peddler protested and Lightfoot knocked him on the head. Lightfoot hastily excused himself to his biographer: "I took it for granted that he had been cheating some innocent person out of this money and it would be better in my keeping than his . . ."

With the seventy dollars Lightfoot bought a road agent's equipment; a fast horse, two pistols, a dark Quaker suit, a broad-brimmed hat which could be pulled over his eyes, and a sword cane. He also made a sweeping reconnaissance of the likely escape routes and the best places to ambush his victims.

On the American side of the Canadian border Lightfoot began riding. His first victims were a pair of traveling men. Lightfoot rode out of the bushes, revolver in hand.

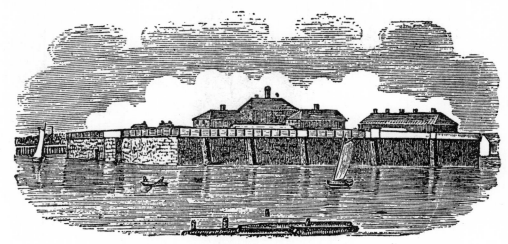

The prison in which Martin was confined.

"Shell out!" he demanded, in what sounds like modern jargon, and they did. His loot: $40 "in paper and 20 in specie."

The following day he held up an old man, "skinned him clean," and also stole the old man's horse.

"But," the old man cried, "I borrowed this horse and I'll lose my character."

"Better your character than your life," replied Captain Lightfoot, and cocked his revolver. In a few minutes he was riding off "on a fine stallion." As the weeks went by, Lightfoot became the terror of the New England roads. He was seen everywhere from Quebec to Boston. The newspapers of the time made much of him, and reward placards began to appear on the trees. Once on the way to Kingston, Upper Canada, Lightfoot held up an Indian chief who was wearing several gold and bronze ornaments. Lightfoot got $65 but almost lost his scalp when a posse of the chief's tribe started out in pursuit "setting up an Indian halloo." The chief was in the lead when Lightfoot, turning, shot him and escaped.

A few months later he returned to the United States and once again Captain Lightfoot was holding up lonely riders, stage-coaches, and travelers. Vermont and Massachusetts posted handbills in post offices and taverns, "offering $50 for the most notorious scoundrel."

Outside of Boston, Lightfoot committed his most famous robbery, holding up a chaise driven by one of the governor's aides. When a young lady tried to hide her watch, Lightfoot swept off his hat and gallantly said, "Ma'am, I do not rob ladies," thus creating another legend which soon made the rounds of the country taverns, adding a Robin Hood aura to Lightfoot.

The governor was furious that his guests could be victims of Lightfoot and ordered pursuits and alarms. On the outskirts of Medford some townspeople, suspicious of a stranger who had stopped at a tavern, challenged him, but the Captain (it was he) rode off, only to slip from his saddle when a stirrup strap broke. He dislocated his shoulder. He eluded the pursuers, but troops and civilian patrols guarded the roads to cut off his escape routes to Canada. Everywhere he stopped he saw the reward and "Wanted" posters. A few miles outside of Springfield, Lightfoot stole a horse. Horse thievery then in New England, as later in the West, was a cardinal sin, and the farmers rounded up

The execution at Letchmere Point, Cambridge.

17

their own posse which set out in pursuit. They found the horse in a stable not far from Springfield and Lightfoot asleep in a barn. The sheriff and his posse took him alive, although Lightfoot had sworn, "I will never be taken alive."

He was committed to jail in Letchmere Point, Cambridge, for highway robbery and was "rigidly watched." In October, 1821, the Supreme Judicial Court in Cambridge sentenced him to death.

When he was sentenced to the gallows, Lightfoot took off his hat, bowed, and said, "Well, that is the worst you can do for me."

The next day he made a desperate jail break, after sawing through his chains with a file smuggled in by a friend. By superhuman strength he managed to knock down a thick oak door leading to the street, but by this time the town was aroused by a deputy who ran through the streets, shouting, "Martin's gone! Martin's gone!"

A posse took out after Lightfoot and captured him in a small cornfield a hundred yards from the jail yard. This time his chains were forged on his ankles and wrists and to a ring in the floor.

Lightfoot by now was a living legend and large crowds stood in the streets, repeating, as crowds usually do, the exaggerated tales of his exploits. Ballad-makers were already at work in the country taverns composing songs of the "brave Captain Lightfoot." And even his hard-bitten jailers were telling each other that the handsome road agent was exhibiting such resignation and fortitude that he appeared "romantic and unreal," as his biographer put it.

In the December 22, 1822, issue of the *Columbian Sentinel* there is a long description of Lightfoot's execution at Cambridge, observed by a "cloud of witnesses."

He was "calm and serene" and after the death warrant had been read, he untied his neckcloth and assisted the hangman in putting the noose about his throat. He took a handkerchief out of his pocket and called out, "When shall I drop the handkerchief?"

The sheriff replied, "When you please."

Captain Lightfoot slowly raised the handkerchief, then as the crowd held its breath, let it flutter away in the warm breeze. Before it touched the ground, he was swung off into eternity.

THE LOOMIS GANG

After the death of Captain Lightfoot, the Loomis gang of New York appeared on the outlaw trail. This sinister outlaw brotherhood rode the lanes and roads of the Mohawk and Chenango Valleys, ruling the valleys with an iron hand from their robber baron's stronghold on a small rise overlooking a large desolate area known as the Nine-Mile Swamp.

The Loomis brothers formed what was probably one of the first robber empires in the United States. Their careers have been best described by George W. Walter in *The Loomis Gang*. Like the Reno brothers of Indiana, they held sections of their state in a grip of terror, intimidating the weaker law officers and bribing the stronger.

The Loomis family was large. The founder, George Washington Loomis, Sr., rode into Sangerfield Center in 1802, just two hops and a skip ahead of a posse from his native Vermont, where he had been running stolen horses to Danbury, Connecticut, much in the relay style of the later western outlaws. Just before he marched off to fight the British in the War of 1812, he married a young school teacher named Rhoda Marie Mallett. Rhoda was a slim, pretty girl whose only beauty secret, as one of her friends later recalled, "was to wash her face every day with a fine linen handkerchief soaked in dew."

Rhoda, whose father had been a distiller and forger, mothered twelve children, for whom she was a female Fagin. As Washington, Jr.—"Wash" to outlaw history—recalled, his mother approved of their "stealing little things —and as long as we were not caught it was all right. If we got caught we got licked."

Wash was the leader, followed by Grove, Bill, Wheller, Plumb, Denio, and their sister Cornelia, who loved to steal expensive muffs by putting them on her legs under her billowing party dresses.

The Loomis boys were educated in the county schools and the girls, of whom there were three besides Cornelia, in private seminaries. Mostly dark, they favored their

Waterville, as the Loomis gang knew it.

mother, who was half-French, with thick black hair, black eyes, and chiseled features. They were all daredevil riders, prepared at any time to jump their fast horses over the tallest rail fence. Also excellent shots with both the rifle and pistol, they were shrewd, arrogant, fearless, and ready to close ranks against anyone who tried to trespass on their land.

The miasmal Nine-Mile Swamp was their favorite hiding place. Before they reached their teens they all knew it as well as the backs of their own hands. They grew up in the golden age of New York's hop-growing era, and by the time a vigilante movement of honest citizens smashed their power, they had controlled large sections of upstate New York by terror, committed many murders, burnings, and highway robberies, and flooded the countryside with counterfeit money.

Facts substantiate the stories of double-paneled rooms and double garrets in which they hid loot and men in the rambling house looking out over the valley.

If Wash was the leader of the gang, Maria Cornelia was the "outlaw queen." She was a slim, pretty girl as wild as her brothers. Her three sisters married young and left home. But Cornelia never married, seeming to prefer the company of her brothers, for whom she would fight like a wildcat when the occasion demanded.

She was a familiar sight in the small towns as she rode in astride in a low-necked gown and without the shawl fashionable at the time. With a contemptuous look on her cold face and a riding crop dangling from her hand, she looked oblivious of the frankly admiring stares of the loungers.

By 1847 the Loomis brothers had built up a strong gang of escaped convicts, fugitives from other states, and runaway slaves. They stole sheep, cattle, and horses, and openly assaulted local citizens, once almost stomping a man to death at a dance, but seemingly they themselves led charmed lives.

Their crimes grew so bold that in 1857 a posse of outraged citizens surrounded the Loomis house on a winter night and broke in. Behind concealed trap doors they found great quantities of clothes, skins, food, and farm equipment. Sleighs loaded down with stolen material were taken to Waterville, N. Y., where a Court of Oyer and Terminer indicted the gang for grand larceny. But as in all the other cases, the indictments dragged on and were mysteriously quashed.

That same year counterfeiting swept the northern section of the United States, and the Loomis gang promptly staked out its territory in upstate New York. Grove Loomis went to Utica, returning with thousands of dollars in counterfeit bills drawn on Oneida County's Onondaga Bank. When Grove was arrested, the Utica newspapers pointed out that the local District Attorney carried the evidence with him. Thereupon the rest of the gang kidnapped the prosecutor, stole the evidence, and Grove went free.

Sheep stealing and horse stealing were next in the Loomis program. After one of the brothers was arrested—to be freed as usual—for sheep stealing, they formed a horse-stealing syndicate with relays and hideouts in various parts of New York, New Jersey, Pennsylvania, Connecticut, and parts of Canada.

The principal point was the swamp near the Loomis home, where the gang made a huge horse-stealing center, complete with barns and corrals. Grove was the salesman, traveling about the eastern seaboard creating markets. When a particularly outraged farmer who had lost a favorite horse began rounding up his family and friends to start a search, Wash would offer to "find" the animal—usually collecting a $50 fee for doing so—rather than risk a shooting engagement.

In 1858 James L. Filkins, a blacksmith, was elected constable of the town of Brookfield. He became the nemesis of the gang, a plodding little village officer who almost singlehandedly broke up one of the strongest outlaw gangs in America. When his fellow-citizens refused to help him, he "went in alone," armed only with iron nerve and a big horse pistol.

Four months after he was appointed, Filkins received his first assignment of serving a warrant on Plumb Loomis. He marched up to the forbidden farmhouse, knocked on the door, and asked for Plumb.

"Plumb isn't here," a feminine voice replied.

Just then Plumb jumped out of a rear window and headed for the swamp. Filkins chased and caught him. When Plumb started to bluster and threaten the little law officer, Filkins slashed him across the nose with a revolver butt.

"Shut up or I'll brain you," Filkins snarled.

Plumb held his bleeding nose and gave the constable a look of surprise. It was the first time anyone had struck one of the dread Loomis boys!

By 1858 the Loomis gang controlled the Chenango Valley. On Saturday nights they would ride into small

Constable Filkins' home.

19

Bissell's store, where the vigilantes met.

valley villages like Hamilton, take over the community for their drunken parties, and beat up or shoot down the officers who tried to arrest them. The horse-stealing syndicate was also operating full blast and Wash later boasted he knew where every horse stolen in the valley could be found. Counterfeiting was rampant, too, along with sheep stealing, highway robbery, assault, and murder.

During the Civil War years, the Loomis brothers robbed at will. Their only opponent was the rotund little marshal, Filkins. More than once he raided the big farmhouse to drag out the brothers on one charge or another.

When the Union forces called for horses, Wash sent Grove out to increase their stolen horse market. The ring became more widespread than ever, and farmers had to protect their stock by standing guard with muskets at night. Hundreds of disguised horses were sold in the Albany market and others were driven to Scranton, Pennsylvania, where the brothers established another farmhouse station. Still others were driven north and sold in Canadian markets. The routes were also used by the gang to dispose of stolen goods, farm wagons, and equipment.

To expedite the shipment of their loot, "thief boats" were organized on the Erie Canal and the goods sent down into New York City where a Thieves' Market operated from dawn to dusk at Chatham Square, under the cold eye of Maw Mandelbaum, one of the most remarkable thieves in our history.

When witnesses threatened to testify against them, the Loomises would mutter, "You'll get smoked for that," and fire bells would ring in the night. Once when they were infuriated at a deputy for bringing them to justice, they supposedly set fire to the North Brookfield Courthouse and cut the fire hoses. However, there were no witnesses and no evidence to connect them with the fire, so no action was taken against them.

Next, six years of indictments against the Loomis brothers, all stored in a safety vault in the town clerk's office in Morrisville, were burglarized and burned in the clerk's pot-bellied stove.

When by 1865 all legal means to wipe out the gang had failed, Constable Filkins decided that vigilantes were the only solution. In the fall of 1865, the Sangerfield Vigilante Committee met for the first time in a store in Waterville, N. Y., and rode for the Loomis farmhouse. The password, appropriately enough, was "hops."

During the raid Wash was beaten to death and Plumb, also beaten and believed dead, was thrown into a fire. Although critically burned, he was saved by his mother.

Wash's death failed to halt the gang. Twice they tried to assassinate Filkins, wounding him severely both times, but the little deputy swore he would break up the gang. In 1867, after the brutal murder of a farmer during a robbery and another attempt to kill Filkins, the vigilantes again sounded a call to arms. Thundering along the back roads of the valley to Nine-Mile Swamp, they surrounded the house and put it to the torch.

While the flames pinked the warm June sky, Plumb and Grove were put to the dread "hanging torture"—hung until they almost strangled—to make them confess to their crimes. As the once proud house tumbled into a bed of coals, Plumb was marched to jail and Grove managed to crawl away into the darkness of the swamp.

Despite the raid, the gang, now a pale ghost, continued to ride the outlaw trail, with Denio taking Wash's place as its leader. By 1870, when Grove Loomis died, they were still stealing horses on a wide scale and shipping them to the Albany and Pennsylvania markets.

Plumb, who had been shot, thrown from horses, beaten up, burned by vigilantes, and hanged three times, lived to a ripe old age. The wild and pretty Cornelia died in 1897, a short time before James Filkins, her brothers' bitter foe, died in his sleep. By 1911 the last of the Loomises had vanished from the valley, which returned to its pastoral quiet.

II. Overture: The Forty-Niners and the California Vigilantes

The first California jail, Monterey.

IN 1848, when James W. Marshall discovered gold at Sutter's Mill in California, he also unwittingly set the stage for a preview of the great Wild West drama.

From all over the country, from Australia, England, and other lands, men rushed in droves—some 75,000 came in 1849—to the California goldfields. Inevitably the criminal elements and the more reckless and adventurous constituted a large proportion of the new population, which in any case was infected with mob fever. The struggle for accommodations, food, and facilities in the enormously overcrowded boom towns caused great disorder, if not actual chaos.

The law was a puny thing, for it was only in 1842— eleven days after the discovery of gold—that California was ceded by Mexico and became part of the Union. The system was Mexican and quite ineffective even for the sparse pre-gold rush population. Of course it could not begin to handle the tremendous new problem. The people had to make and enforce their own law as they saw it, had to maintain order the best way they could, by cooperation and common consent. Emotion colored justice, which had to be administered directly.

News of big strikes spread like a prairie fire across the country, attracting criminals of all types to the goldfields. The criminals robbed defenseless miners of their dust, jumped claims, killed, looted, and even stole mining equipment to sell to the newcomers pouring into the fields. The whipping post, banishment, tar and feathers were adopted by the miners at first, but as the crimes became more numerous and terrible, more drastic action seemed necessary.

In January, 1849, five bandits were hanged without ceremony for robbing a gambler named Lopez, giving the mining camp its name of Hangtown, later changed to Placerville. As the gold rush continued, such hangings became commonplace.

The brig *Euphemia*, San Francisco's first jail.

Site of San Francisco, 1848.

in *Eldorado, or Adventures in the Path of Empire,* the "only sure means of administrating Justice."

San Francisco soon became the mecca of hardened criminals. The gold rush had turned it into a boom town filled with gold-mad men and women, and for a time outlaws ran the city. At times the town itself seemed to have gone berserk; tents, rickety shacks, brawling men and men rolling in the muddy streets, drunken miners waving bags of gold dust, while bandits robbed men in broad daylight. In the early summer of 1849, an outlaw band known as the Hounds terrorized the city. Composed of New York's East Side toughs, army deserters, and fugitives from other states, they brazenly swaggered up and down the streets, openly brandishing six shooters and blackjacks. Mexicans, Negroes, and Chinese were their special victims, subjected to unspeakable outrages.

One summer's night after the Hounds had bullied the city and its citizens, a young newspaper editor, Sam Brannan, roused the citizens of San Francisco to action. An army of four hundred vigilantes tore apart the Hounds' tent city and arrested them. There were no jails, and a miners' court ordered them driven out of San Francisco. Soon after this incident taxes were imposed to pay for a jail, lights, and a police force.

The city's first jail was the hulk of an old windjammer named *Euphemia,* and its first sheriff a tough old Texas ranger, Colonel John C. Hays. But the bandits and outlaws continued to rob, steal, and kill. By 1850 large gangs virtually controlled the city's streets at night. In 1851

Miners' courts, with justice distributed on the barrelhead, sprang up throughout the diggings to decide not only criminal but also civil cases. Decisions were rendered by popular acclaim, with the "judge" usually the most popular man in the camp, and the jury the camp itself.

Vigilance committees were formed in a few camps, and the idea spread all over the fields. This vigilante movement was not mob violence but, as Bayard Taylor pointed out

A photograph of San Francisco in 1865.   An amazing contrast to the drawing above.

Brannan again called for a Vigilante Committee, which was finally formed. The manhunters gave notice they would "respect the law" but would not stand for legal dilly-dallying. A firebell convened the miners' court.

The clanging bell soon sent the Vigilantes into action. An Australian highwayman, captured while trying to rob a safe, was strung up without ceremony after conclusive evidence of his guilt had been presented before a crowd of several thousand citizens who jammed the streets. The police chief made a move to try to rescue the bandit, but the Vigilantes pushed him to one side.

"Every lover of Liberty lay hold the rope," Brannan shouted, and as the contemporary newspaper reports show, there were more than ample hands to swing the Australian outlaw off into eternity.

In July, 1850, the firebell clanged again and the citizens shouted their approval when James Stuart, a young English thief convicted and sentenced to hang for robbery, was strung up on Market Street wharf. In August, the Vigilantes stormed the city's jail, kidnapped two confessed, habitual prisoners, and hanged them on Battery Street.

There was a lull in Vigilante justice until 1855, when corrupt officials turned the city over to the lawless. The Vigilantes again swung into action, raiding the city prison and removing two killers of a United States Marshal. After an "orderly and dignified trial," both were hanged from the second story of the Vigilante headquarters.

In August two more lynchings followed when the Vigilantes, under the command of the fiery Sam Brannan, hanged the English outlaw, Joseph Hetherington, and the New York thug, Philander Brace. Following the election of honest city officials, the Vigilantes disbanded after a final triumphant review in which more than 5,000 citizens marched through San Francisco's streets.

The California Vigilante Committee was now inter-

The hanging of Hetherington and Brace, San Francisco, July 29, 1856.

nationally known, and perhaps for the first time in the violent history of the American frontier Vigilante law was honored.

The *London Times* observed that it was "seldom self-constituted authorities retire with grace and dignity, but it is due to the vigilante committee to say that they have done so."

Lola Montez

Lola Montez was one of the more flamboyant figures of the gold rush days. She came to California by way of Ireland (where she was born), the music halls of London and Paris (where she danced), and the castle of Louis I of Bavaria, which she had to vacate in '48 when the revolution drove Louis off the throne. The dark-haired beauty set herself up in royal style in Grass Valley, but the more conservative elements in the mining center rebelled against the soirées the ex-royal mistress ran. Lola, who was also a princess, courtesy of Louis, threatened to horsewhip an overcritical editor and then packed up and decided to try Australia. She spent her last days in New York saving the souls of lost women. It was a field she knew well.

WILL BE
EXHIBITED
FOR ONE DAY ONLY!
AT THE STOCKTON HOUSE!
THIS DAY, AUG. 12, FROM 9 A. M., UNTIL 6. P. M.

THE HEAD
Of the renowned Bandit!
JOAQUIN!
AND THE
HAND OF THREE FINGERED JACK!
THE NOTORIOUS ROBBER AND MURDERER.

"JOAQUIN" and "THREE-FINGERED JACK" were captured by the State Rangers, under the command of Capt. Harry Love, at the Arroya Cantina, July 24th. No reasonable doubt can be entertained in regard to the identification of the head now on exhibition, as being that of the notorious robber, Joaquin Murietta, as it has been recognised by hundreds of persons who have formerly seen him.

Murieta—An artist's conception and a showman's eulogy.

CALIFORNIA BADMAN: JOAQUIN MURIETA

John Rollin Ridge, part-Cherokee, part-writer, and part-broke, started it all. Out of the wafer-thin facts available to a hurry-up researcher in 1854, he fashioned himself a pot-boiler called *The Life and Adventures of Joaquin Murieta, Celebrated California Bandit*. It was quite a touching item, though spattered with blood. Joaquin was a perfectly good kid, the idol of his playmates in Sonora, Mexico. He came into the golden hills with the Forty-Niners. He, too, would dig in the wonderful earth that had belonged a few years earlier to his own people. Then cruel fate struck: American miners ravished his bride, Rosita, hanged his brother, whipped Joaquin. That was the way Ridge told the story.

From the simple "celebrated bandit" of Ridge's paperback Murieta became the *Brigand Chief of California*, courtesy of an anonymous word-merchant in the pay of the *Police Gazette* out there; *The Saddle King*, in the Beadle Dime Library; *The Claude Duval of California*, in the DeWitt 15-Cent Library; *The Marauder of the Mines*, in a 25-cent edition, and then *The Terror of the Stanislaus*, out of the pen of Hubert Howe Bancroft, an otherwise respectable historian having an off-day. And then, three-quarters of a century later, Walter Noble Burns put the icing on the cake. Having heated up his writing machine with his vastly overdrawn *Saga of Billy the Kid*, Burns brought out Murieta as *The Robin Hood of El Dorado*.

It remained for Joseph Henry Jackson, dean of the West Coast book critics and a man with a lusty appetite for the truth, to re-examine the Murieta legend. Step by step, he traced it all back to the imaginative John Rollin Ridge, who had only done it because he needed the money (and who made a good deal less than all the Murieta "biographers" who came after him).

There *was* a man named Joaquin Murieta. He was an outlaw. He *did* prey on the miners in the time of the gold rush. He *was* an authentic desperado. But no one knew how he got that way—or why. For that matter, no one knew precisely what criminal deeds Murieta perpetrated. No one can know, for in his time there were five different Joaquins terrorizing the goldfields.

Commissioned by the California Legislature, Captain Harry Love of Texas rode out with a company of rangers in '53 to bring in any or all of the Joaquins. They came back with the head of a Mexican pickled in a bottle and they said it was Murieta and let's have that $1000 reward, please. Whether it was Murieta or any other bad Joaquin is still a matter of debate. It was the head of a Mexican; only that much was sure.

And as noted here, there was a Murieta, although a great shortage of facts surrounds the man. In his excellent study of the Far West's early robber fraternity, *Bad Company*, Jackson imposed only a light sentence on the fellow who adorned the Murieta story in the first place. "It is Ridge's justification that, since there wasn't a Murieta—at any rate not much of a Murieta—it was necessary to create one."

THE MONTANA VIGILANTES

The vigilante movement in Montana is another vivid example of how the American frontiersman stamped out lawlessness with swift justice until orderly, honest legal procedures could be established. Before it had finished its work, the Montana committee had broken up the Plummer Gang, one of the most deadly in Western outlaw history.

Henry Plummer, leader of the gang, was a handsome man of imposing stature who started his criminal career in Nevada City, California, where he killed the husband of a woman with whom he was having an affair. He was convicted for the shooting, but powerful friends interceded with the Governor to pardon him. After his release he joined a stage-coach gang operating in Nevada City, killed another man, broke out of jail, and fled to Idaho's rich gold camps.

By 1861 Plummer was planning all the robberies and killings for his gang while posing as a respectable citizen of Lewiston. Once when one of his riders killed a man and there was talk of mob action, Plummer made such an impassioned speech for "Justice" that the citizens voted to do nothing. When a courageous storekeeper spoke out against such "cowardice," Plummer had his men kill him.

By 1862 he commanded a story-book outlaw gang of a hundred highwaymen who terrorized stage-coaches and miners traveling in and out of Bannack. Spies and secret agents on his payroll chalked code symbols on the coaches to be robbed, while his henchmen wore special sailor knots in their ties to identify them to other members. Among themselves Plummer's riders ironically called themselves "The Innocents."

But his crimes at last caught up with him, and Plummer dangled on the end of a vigilante's noose, dying "without

Vigilante headquarters.

a struggle" on a cold January afternoon.

Within six weeks the Montana vigilantes had hanged twenty-six outlaws. As Wayne Gard points out in his excellent *Frontier Justice,* "their work had made it easier to set up effective courts and law enforcement agencies when the territorial government was formed a few months later."

But although Plummer was dead, the vigilantes soon discovered their work was far from finished. Joseph A. Slade, head of one of the divisions of the Overland Stage Company, was engaged "in terroristic activities." Once after a quarrel he cut off his victim's ears, using them as watch charms.

When he scorned the warning to get out of Virginia City by stopping in at a bar to get drunk, the vigilantes escorted him to the nearest corral gate, where, after tightening a rope around his neck, they pushed him off a box.

In Montana the vigilantes were less formal but just as effective as their California brothers. Their leaders were cool-headed men and not rabid inciters to violence. Often they gave their defendants a far greater opportunity to clear themselves than did the California groups. They seldom used masks and cannot be classed as night riders.

Like the California organizations, they passed into history when orderly communities came into existence.

John X. Beidler, leader of the Montana vigilantes.

The gallows built by Plummer and on which he was hung January 10, 1864.

III. The Violent West

Theodore Roosevelt made the point, in the *Century Magazine* of 1880, that the phenomenon of Western outlaws and gunfighters and their ability to ply their trade with impunity for so long could be understood only if the virtually absolute wilderness of the plains during the frontier period was taken into account.

Gamblers, swindlers, prostitutes, and criminals of all kinds drifted about the frontier, and almost every road was infested with road agents. From 1845 to 1885 outlawry was one of the gravest problems in the West because law and order could not keep in step with the rapid strides of the growing settlements.

In the National Archives are vivid records which show how the Southwest, about 1877, was completely in the grip of the lawless. The state adjutant general of Texas, in that year alone, posted descriptions of 5,000 outlaws and bandits in the Rio Grande district, and asked Congress to compel Mexico to stop shielding American outlaws from justice.

Northern Texas and Kansas were the wildest of the wild, and as Edward King, the English writer, said in his book, *Southern States of North America,* describing his tour in 1875, every small town "had hundreds of saloons populated by depraved people who used whiskey."

Another reason for the rapid growth of outlawry in the West was the attitude of most men toward the law. They were too busy with their own survival to bother much with politics or law enforcement. Few cared for the career of law enforcement. Other opportunities were more promising. In most frontier towns it was difficult to find a man to wear the "tin badge" and stand up to outlaws noted for fast draw.

Many times the law was a six gun on a man's own hip. Bob Wright, one of the founders of Dodge City and historian of that town, recalled in his memoirs that Hays City, ninety-five miles to the northwest of Dodge, was the nearest point where formal justice could be found, and so the citizens of Dodge had to settle their differences "with a gun or with a rifle—and settle we did."

By 1880 the violence in the West was such that Charles M. Hager's statement, "There is no Sunday west of Newton and no God west of Pueblo,"[1] was accepted as a fair summary of the situation.

What type of men were these gunfighters, outlaws, and road agents, some of whose names are more familiar to our young than the names of patriots and honored soldiers? The truth is they were mostly illiterates, sometimes morons. Some, like Jesse James, were products of a violent Civil War of neighbor against neighbor, and others, like the cowboy Wild Bunch, found their way into outlawry because of a depression in the cattle country.

None of them was a Robin Hood. All of them spent their money for wine, women, and song, and there is no evidence that any one of them gave a cent to a weeping widow or a helpless old man, despite the memoirs of senile old men, some of which have been accepted by historians.

---

[1] "Cattle Trails of the Plains," *Scribner's Magazine,* 1880.

THE BLOODIEST MAN IN AMERICA

Charles Quantrill truly earned his title of the "bloodiest man in American history." A slim, handsome man, former teacher and superintendent of a small Bible school, he was Jesse James' teacher in the art of murder, horse stealing, arson, and butchery.

Quantrill was the leader of Missouri's largest guerrilla band during the Civil War. Jesse James, before he was sixteen, was one of his best riders. Harrison Trow, in his autobiography, *I Rode with Quantrill,* recalled that Jesse was a slim, handsome beardless boy possessed with a cold courage that made many of the elder and more experienced guerrillas respect him and give him a wide berth. On more than one occasion Jesse was dressed in women's clothes to lure Federal officers to "a meeting" where the other guerrillas cut their throats.

Frank James and the Youngers also rode with Quantrill. They were at the Lawrence, Kansas, massacre, but despite legend there is no evidence that Jesse was there. The future outlaw leader had his blood bath at Centralia, where he helped to kill seventy-five Federal soldiers.

The troops had ridden out after receiving news of the massacre of the citizens of Lawrence, Kansas. Their major had foolishly dismounted them and marched them up a hill "behind Singleton's barn," where, outlined against the sky on a ridge, were the mounted guerrillas, with Jesse second in command. With a wild scream he led a charge against the dismounted Federal troops, who were cut to pieces. Jesse raced after three survivors and killed them all. The wounded were shot and the bodies buried in a common grave by citizens forced to dig under the Navy Colts of the guerrillas. Now, beyond question, Jesse had tasted blood and seemed to like it.

But in 1864 he refused to join Quantrill on his trip to Kentucky, which proved wise for Jesse, fatal to Quantrill. Instead he formed his own command, riding as far west as Texas and back to Missouri, fighting and looting all the way. He was shot down in Lexington, as he rode in holding aloft a flag of surrender.

For a time it seemed that the bullet through his right lung would be fatal, but Jesse survived, through the efforts of his first cousin, pretty Zerelda Mimms, of Kansas City, later his wife.

DINGUS JAMES AND HIS MEN

Outlawry became a crucial part of the nineteenth-century American scene with the rise and fall of the James-Younger gang. The Reno brothers and the Harpe brothers had played their violent roles years before the gang led by Jesse ever took to horse. But they lacked the elusive ingredient that makes one man, good or evil, stand out among many. Their fame, despite their startling exploits, remained only regional.

Jesse James, however, became a national figure; no one else will ever fill his niche in American folklore. Now, some seventy years since Bob Ford's bullet cut him down in St. Joseph, Missouri, books are still being written about his life and times.

It is apparent that he is timeless. Despite world wars, the atom bomb, the jet age, he will never die. To most Americans he will always remain the eternally handsome youth who rides across the western plains into the golden sunset, the bag of gold—stolen, of course, from the hated railroads—tied to the pommel of his saddle, while far behind, hidden by the towering wall of dust, come his hopelessly outclassed pursuers.

He is America's Robin Hood. His yew bow is a Navy Colt; his jerkin a faded blue coat. He never fails to distribute his stolen loot among weeping widows about to lose their homesteads. Old men receive his coat in the freezing cold with tearful thanks. He reduces to a bloody hulk the bully torturing the frail young farmer, recently arrived from the East to till the soil.

Incredible as it may seem, this is the way most Americans view Jesse James, who was called Dingus by his friends. Nothing that is said about him will change their view.

Now what is the true story of Jesse James? The answer is simply that he was a cold-blooded killer and a thief. There is no credible evidence that he ever gave one cent to a widow, or anyone else in need, or took up arms for the helpless or the downtrodden.

For most of his life he was hunted like a wild animal. He survived for sixteen years only because he and his gang could intimidate weak-spined county officials, and could count on the affection of his kissing kinfolk who hid him out.

Exactly how many banks or trains he robbed will never be known. But the rough score is seventeen and the total loot about $200,000. He is said to have "invented" train robbery and bank robbery. That is just another legend. The Reno brothers of Indiana were the first to rob trains in this country, if not in the entire world, and two years before Jesse stepped into the Liberty, Missouri, First National Bank to rob it of $17,000, a handsome young Confederate officer had robbed three banks in St. Albans, Vermont, of $170,000 in the record time of fifteen minutes. His name was Lieutenant Bennett H. Young, and his

Dingus James, as a guerrilla with Quantrill.

raid included all the elements that would be a feature of western outlaw raids for the next twenty years, including fighting off a posse in a running gun battle, separating after the robbery, and joining up at a previously selected rendezvous.

But Jesse and his men cannot be dismissed as nothing more than outlaws. Their lives and times are too complex to wave them so lightly from history's scenes. At one time they were the center of one of the most violent battles in the political history of the Middle Border. There is evidence that their train robberies had an adverse effect on the movement of immigrants to the West and on the development of their own state.

Jesse and his gang, whose depredations had aroused the state, rode into Missouri's political picture in 1874. They stayed there for ten years, fanning the hates and feuds spawned in that bloody ground by the Civil War.

When Jesse appeared on the political horizon, the state was divided into two factions: those who had fought in the Confederate Army or were Southern sympathizers, and those who had fought for the Union Army or had been violent abolitionists. With each new robbery the pro-Confederates would insist "the boys" had been driven to their crimes by the relentless persecution of the Northerners. The ex-Union men countered with the cry that the James and the Youngers were bandits and killers and should be sent to the gallows.

The leading newspapers of the state added fuel to the bitter controversy. The powerful *St. Louis Democrat* thundered that the James-Younger reign of terror had halted immigration into the Middle Border and to points in the state used by the immigrants as jump-off spots for their trip west, and had also shut off the flow of untold millions of dollars into the state from new industries.

That same year the *Democrat* coined the phrase, "Poor Old Missouri," which was to echo for years in newspaper editorials and in the convention halls of both parties.

The Republican Party adopted a resolution in 1874, condemning the policy of the Democratic Party "which has led to the insecurity of persons and property, the prevention of immigration, the ruination of business and the ruinous depreciation of all values of property."

The political pot boiled over on March 23, 1874, when Missouri's Democratic Governor Silas Woodson, in a dramatic meeting of both houses, denounced the lawlessness of the Jameses and the Youngers. He warned his state that the time had come for a reckoning.

Frank James.

His voice echoing through the domed hall, he listed the crimes and killings attributed to Jesse and his riders and lashed out at the law enforcement officers who had let themselves be intimidated by the gang.

Two days after Woodson's message the legislature voted $10,000 for a secret body of investigators to track down the gang. But the bill was declared "out of order" by the presiding members of the legislature.

The speech started a furious battle of the editorial pages, dividing the state more violently than ever. The James-Younger issue became so grave that in its 1874 state convention the Republican Party did not nominate a ticket. Instead it voted "almost to a man" to support the People's Party's candidates, whose plank was "suppression of outlawry in Missouri in order that capital and immigration can once again enter our state." This plank was the highlight of the acceptance speech of William Gentry, the gubernatorial candidate.

The Democratic convention, meeting a few weeks later, carefully ignored the issue of Jesse and his hard-riding bravos.

The outlaw question rocked not only the state, but the country, when that same year a Pinkerton operative, Louis Lull, was killed in a gun duel with two of the Younger brothers. Jim Younger was shot out of his saddle, and also a local peace officer was killed. A short time later another Pinkerton man, John W. Wischer, was found riddled with bullets on a lonely Clay County road, his body torn by wild hogs.

In the winter of 1875 there occurred the famous "night of blood" when the Pinkertons and a posse of local men raided the Samuel farmhouse. A "bomb"—actually an iron pot of Greek fire which was used by spies in the Civil War to start incendiary fires—was hurled through a window. The explosion tore off the right arm of Jesse's mother and killed his young stepbrother.

The story made headlines throughout the country. Popular opinion, always in favor of "the boys," was now intensified. It was impossible for peace officers to enter Clay County. There was no need for Jesse and his gang to hide out now; they had their own "iron curtain" of sympathizers, frightened sheriffs who were often in their pay, and kinfolk.

As a correspondent for the *Missouri World* wrote under an Appleton City, Missouri, dateline: "So great is the terror that the Jameses and Youngers have instilled in Clay County that their names are never mentioned save in back rooms and then only in a whisper. Clay County has a population of 15,000."

While the state simmered with hate, Jesse and his men roamed south and west, robbing trains, stage-coaches, and banks.

Lawrence, Kansas, in 1867.

JESSE'S TECHNIQUE

It is interesting to study the technique he developed, used for years by outlaw bands in another time and another part of the country.

Jesse's gang was seldom large. He preferred a small, tightly knit group. He usually knew each man intimately; some were kin. The scene of every robbery was carefully reconnoitered before he struck. He knew the layout of the town or village, the number and caliber of the peace officers, the getaway routes, the total assets of the bank or train to be robbed, and exactly how much he could afford for "expenses" for each robbery.

His men were all superb riders, and experts, from their guerrilla tactics, at "busting a town." But the legend of their marksmanship is doubtful. They would not have been a match for some of the later western outlaws like Harry Longbaugh, "the Sundance Kid," who had a draw as fast as a snake's tongue. In his time sixteen men rode with Jesse. Some appeared briefly, then vanished.

But the Jameses and the Youngers were the principals. This can be said of them: they rose from the dark complexities of the terrible border war between Missouri and Kansas, where it was son against father and brother against brother. They were schooled by the bloody hand of Quan-trill and their friendship was cemented, as in the case of the Doanes, by the clannish hatred of outsiders. Of the personal ties which bound them together we do not know. But this we do know: they pursued their godless, goalless circle of robbery and violence, until at last, gradually seeing the bonds which originally bound them together in trust—perhaps even in rough affection—burst asunder by the inexpiable crimes they perpetrated, they turned, betrayed and killed each other.

They were not only outlaws, but symbols of an era in our history.

Old home of Zerelda Samuel, mother of Frank and Jesse James.

29

AMERICA'S ROBIN HOOD: JESSE JAMES

LET US look at our American Robin Hood. In his maturity Jesse was about 5′11″ tall, with a solid, compact build. He was fair complexioned with blinking blue eyes—he had had granulated eyelids since childhood—and a carefully trimmed dark beard, which sometimes when he was on the run grew thick and straggly. So say the "Wanted" posters. He was a born organizer and a leader of men. He demonstrated these qualities during his leadership of the gang. His courage cannot be questioned, but a hidden streak of cruelty and dark violence marked him. It showed up more and more as the years went by. He was psychically lonely. As the old ballad goes: "He was born one day in the County of Clay and came from a solitary race."

He revealed sometimes a wry sense of humor, usually when relieving a man of his watch or when he was robbing a train. Once he interrupted an express car robbery casually to introduce each member of his gang to the engineer, conductor, and expressman.

He justified his crimes with the hackneyed phrase, "They drove us to it," or by glibly explaining that the victims were "Yankees" and as such not entitled to any consideration. "They" was popularly interpreted as the North. This was carried over in numerous legends and stories about Jesse, a great many written by former Confederate soldiers or Southern sympathizers.

"He Was Always Quotin' Shakespeare"

The second member of the James gang was Jesse's brother, Frank. He was duller than his slimmer and more handsome brother, plodding and cautious where Jesse was swift and decisive. He tried to maintain the role of aloofness because of what he believed was a higher intellect, but actually he was a sanctimonious, hypocritical man, equipped with an education that was superficial, to say the least. He was prepared to quote Shakespeare or the Bible on any occasion. He liked to write long and indignant letters to editors and must have bored Jesse in the later years. There is evidence that on at least one occasion Jesse turned on Frank with a gun.

"WE ARE ROUGH MEN"

THE YOUNGERS

Stirrup to stirrup with Jesse until the very end of their long stretch on the outlaw trail rode the Younger brothers, a strange clan of handsome, laughing men whose blood lines reveal peculiar ties. Among their relatives were sheriffs and legislators.

In 1830 Charles Younger, the father of the famous outlaws, married Miss Busheba Fristo. The union produced fourteen children, eight boys and six girls. By a strange coincidence Cole and Jim had the same birthday—January 15. Cole was born in 1844 and Jim in 1848.

In 1861 Younger opened a livery stable in Harrisonville, Cass County, Missouri. He was fairly prosperous and soon bought two farms, one in Jackson County, ten miles from Independence, and the other in nearby Harrisonville.

The most likable member of the gang was Coleman ("Cole") Younger. A huge man of two hundred pounds, with a fleshy, handsome face, sharp, laughing eyes, and a wonderful sense of humor, he was a complete extrovert. When the posses were hunting the gang all over the border states, it was Cole's idea to hide out in Texas, where he sang in the choir and accepted a job with the government census takers.

Sometimes he adopted a brooding, melancholy air, which made him appear like a clergyman meditating on his next week's sermon for the faithful. But Cole was never solemn for long. He loved the dramatic and the flamboyant. That is best demonstrated in one remarkable scene. After the debacle at Northfield, where the citizens rose to wipe out his gang with shotguns, revolvers, pitchforks, and even rocks, the gang scattered. Cole was captured with eleven bullets in his body. As the rickety haywagon carrying him and his brothers entered Madelia, Minnesota, he could not resist rising to his feet and sweeping off his hat to the flustered ladies who stood on the wooden sidewalks watching the posse escort the celebrated prisoners to jail.

Jim Younger, like Cole, was big and good-humored. He was easily swayed by Jesse, but at Northfield he stuck it out until the bitter end. His short life ended on a tragic note. Jim committed suicide after his release from prison because the family of the girl with whom he was in love refused to let her marry him.

Bob Younger was the baby of the gang. He was only twelve when Quantrill's raiders sacked Lawrence. He was

The Youngers (*left to right*) Bob, Rhetta, James, Cole.

Cole Younger in his later years.

31

James Younger.

Bob Younger (from a photograph taken at the time of his capture at Northfield).

twenty-three when he knelt behind the outside wooden staircase at Northfield to trade shots with a cool and very brave hardware merchant. To a reporter for the *St. Paul, Minnesota, Press*, he tersely summed up what could have been the philosophy of all of them: "We are rough men and used to rough ways."

John Younger was a surly gun-slinger at an early age. When he was fifteen, he killed his first man (who had hit him over the head with a dead fish). His one-day trial ended in an acquittal on the grounds of "self-defense."

AN OUTLAW IS BORN

Like better men, Jesse James was a son of the Middle Border. The pressures, the dreams, and the tides of land hunger which brought the Grants, Lincoln, the father of Hamlin Garland, and the other homesteaders west, brought the James family to help open the frontier and break the virgin soil.

Jesse's parents were Robert James of Logan County and Miss Zerelda Cole of Lexington, both in Kentucky. Their families were of frontier stock and can be traced back to Revolutionary days. The senior James was twenty-three, a third-term student preparing for the Baptist min-

istry at Georgetown Academy, Georgetown, Kentucky, when he met Zerelda Cole, then seventeen. It was a short courtship.

Jesse's mother was a strong, dominating woman with a sharp tongue and a quick temper. She had a fanatical love of family. In her eyes her sons could do no wrong. It was not they but the rest of the world which was out of step with life. In Jesse's father there were strange strains of avarice and restlessness. After ten years of married life, he left for the California goldfields to scoop up the riches which everyone was saying could be had just by breaking

Mrs. Samuel.*

Mrs. Jesse James.

the clay with a sharp pick. He left behind him two sons. The elder, Alexander Franklin James, had been born on January 10, 1843, in the new James cabin in Clay County, Missouri. The second son, born September 5, 1847, was listed in the family Bible as Jesse Woodson James.

The frail constitution of Robert James could not withstand the rough life of a forty-niner. He died, possibly of pneumonia, after only three weeks in the goldfields.

In 1851, Mrs. James married a second time. The bridegroom was a fifty-six-year-old farmer named Simms, "a widower with children." The union was an unhappy one,

ending in divorce. One version of the split has Simms refusing to stand the two young hellions who were his stepsons. In 1857 Mrs. James married Dr. Reuben Samuel, a farmer-physician. This marriage apparently was a happy one.

Samuel will always remain a shadowy man, tall and stooped, who remained loyal—at least outwardly—to his bandit stepsons. Mrs. James always defended the actions of her sons, but Dr. Samuel never made known his own feelings.

The two boys spent their formative years on the Samuel place, a few miles from Lee's Summit, the family home of the Youngers.

* Without the final s. Marriage certificate, as well as gravestone, have no final s. Homer Croy, neighbor of the Jameses, confirms this spelling.

The James' homestead, near Kearney, Missouri. The rear portion is the original house in which Frank and Jesse were born.

The James children.

THE OUTLAW AND HIS LADY

In bright contrast to his dark and violent life is the love story of Jesse James and pretty Zerelda Mimms. Jesse fell in love with Zerelda, his first cousin, during the time she nursed him back to health in 1865, when physicians said his war wounds would be fatal. But Zerelda, who had been named after Jesse's mother, stayed by his bedside day and night for several weeks until Jesse was out of danger.

On an April morning in 1875, Jesse left Kearney for his wedding, riding his favorite bay. His boots glistened, his beard was trimmed, and his cold blue eyes, usually filled with animal shyness and ferocity, were this time almost merry. Some citizens of Kearney later recalled how he waved a cheery greeting. But they also recalled the bulge of his Colts under his long frock coat and the gleaming new Winchester tied to the saddle.

On April 24, 1875, in the cold, stiff parlor of his sister-in-law to be, Jesse and his sweetheart were married by a clergyman relative.

After the ceremony in Kansas City, Jesse and Zerelda slipped out of the city. Where they spent their wedding night no one knows. Legend has had it in a hotel in New York City, a relative's farmhouse, and with kinfolk.

Two children were to be born of this strange union—Jesse, Jr. and Mary. (Note the resemblance of Jesse, Jr., to Jesse.) Zerelda's love, though tested by violence, gunfire, and madness, never faltered. After seven years of flight and sadness, Zerelda stroked the bloody head of the man she loved in "the house on the hill" in St. Joseph, after Bob Ford had fired his fatal shot.

She did not weep—there were probably no more tears to shed.

34

BANK ROBBERIES

Cole Younger covering cashier Long.

On March 20, 1868, Jesse and his men raided the quiet little town of Russelville, in the heart of Logan County, Kentucky. The local bank, run by Nimrod Long and George W. Norton, was their target.

The raiders numbered about seven, and the battle started after one of them, believed to be Cole Younger, tried to cash a counterfeit bill. Long made a dash for the rear door, but a slug creased his head, spinning him around. Jesse tried to chop him down with the long barrel of his Navy Colt, but Long fought him toe to toe, then managed to push Jesse aside and made another leap for the door as the Colts roared. But the marksmanship of Jesse and the Youngers was miserable, and Long broke through the door to give the alarm.

Five thousand dollars in cash and nine thousand in bonds was the loot, but the raiders found they had a fight on their hands when they ran for their horses. Rifles and revolvers blazed at them from housetops, from behind hedges and trees. Jesse led his men, in a Quantrill-style charge, up and down the street, but the heavy fire of the townspeople finally forced the gang to retreat. The famous Yankee Bligh and the Pinkerton man eventually arrested Big George Shepherd, one of the gang, and sent him to prison for his part in the robbery.

MANHUNTERS . . .

William A. Pinkerton, flanked by two express agents, Pat Connell (*left*)
and Sam Finley (*right*).

In the days when Jesse rode the outlaw trail, there were no FBI agents, interlocking police alarms covering blocks of whole states in a matter of minutes, or large municipal police forces. There were county sheriffs, some utter cowards or easy to bribe, and makeshift posses, usually formed on the spot and deputized by the sheriff. The most vigorous manhunters were the Pinkerton operatives and the express company detectives.

It was Allan Pinkerton, founder of the famous agency, who first devised what was the forerunner of today's Rogues' Gallery. Pinkerton made it an iron-clad rule of his organization to list every important physical item about a criminal, his background, companions, hideouts, and so on. A case was never closed until the criminal was officially declared dead. In the case of Harvey Logan, vicious killer of the Wild Bunch, Operative Spence dug up a corpse in Colorado and ended a Western mystery. Several law officers had insisted the body was that of an unknown train robber. Spence proved it was Logan.

There was constant danger for operatives chasing Jesse.

... AND REWARDS

$500 REWARD

For the Arrest and Conviction of

JESSE JAMES

St. Louis Midland Railroad

$25,000 REWARD

JESSE JAMES

DEAD OR ALIVE

$15,000 REWARD FOR FRANK JAMES

$5000 Reward for any Known Member of the James Band

SIGNED:

ST. LOUIS MIDLAND RAILROAD

These posters, only a few years apart, tell their own story about the effectiveness of rewards.

To catch him meant going into Clay County. Two died in their attempt to do so, one a local peace officer.

The hatred Jesse James felt for the Pinkertons, especially Allan and his son William, remained at white heat for years. On one occasion James trailed Pinkerton to Chicago, where he had planned to kill him. But at the last moment he decided "to shoot him down would be too swift."

"I want him to feel it . . . I want to watch him," Jesse told his friend and rider, Wood Hite, upon his return to Missouri.

The Death of John Younger, Pinkerton Man Lull, and Sheriff Daniels

A gun duel that shocked Missouri and had repercussions all over the country occurred on March 16, 1874, when Jim and John Younger tangled with three lawmen. Pinkerton captain of detectives Louis J. Lull of Chicago, Sheriff Ed Daniels of Osceola, and John Younger were killed, and Jim Younger was wounded in a gun battle that took place on Chalk Level Road nearby. Lull and Daniels, dying, were taken to the cabin near Monegaw Springs, (see page 39) where they were treated by Dr. D. C. McNeil, who tried unsuccessfully to save the lives of the two officers.

37

NORTHFIELD AND DISASTER

First National Bank of Northfield, Minnesota.
Holdup and Murders by the James and Younger Brothers' gang, September 7, 1876.
Citizens killed: J. L. Heywood, cashier, and Nicholas Gustafson, a pedestrian. *Robbers killed:* Bill Stiles alias Chadwell, Clell Miller, and Charlie Pitts. *Robbers captured:* Cole, James, and Robert Younger.

In September, 1876, the James-Younger gang was blasted to pieces at Northfield, Minnesota, by honest citizens who refused to be intimidated by the so-called "greatest revolver fighters in the West."

On the afternoon of the 7th, Jesse led his men into Northfield and started to rob the First National Bank. One of the bandits, believed to be Jesse, shot down Joseph Lee Heywood, the cashier. But by this time the town had been roused. Henry M. Wheeler, a young student, grabbed a rifle and ran to the second floor of the Dampier Hotel. When Clell Miller, one of Jesse's riders, passed by, young Wheeler killed him with one shot.

In the street a hardware merchant, A. E. Manning, killed Bill Chadwell. Bob Younger's horse went down, cracking its front legs. Bob rolled free of the screaming mount and took refuge behind an outside staircase. He fought a duel

Joseph L. Heywood,
the murdered cashier.

Henry M. Wheeler
(photograph taken years later).

A. E. Manning,
the hardware merchant.

Northfield, Minnesota, some seventy years later.

with Manning, then leaped up behind one of his brothers. For thirty minutes the citizens fought the gang with rocks, rifles, and revolvers. When the fight grew too hot, Jesse ordered a retreat.

The whole Northwest was aroused this time, and the gang was hard-pressed. Jesse adopted guerrilla tactics and broke up his command in small parties. He and Frank got through the informal lines around the town, but the rest of his men, Cole, James, and Bob Younger were badly wounded and captured. Charlie Pitts, who was with them, was killed on his feet and died still holding his Colt.

The farmers and former Union soldiers who made up the posse returned their prisoners to a local hotel at Madelia, in Watonwan County, Minnesota. It was on the way into the small, peaceful town that big Cole, punctured with eleven bullets, rose to take off his hat and bow to the startled ladies on the sidewalk.

On November 9, sixty-three days after their guns had shattered the quiet of Northfield, the three Youngers were sentenced to life imprisonment in the state prison at Stillwater.

Cabin near Monegaw Springs, Missouri, where fatally wounded Pinkerton Detective Captain Louis Lull of Chicago and Deputy Sheriff Ed B. Daniels of Osceola, Missouri, were carried after their gun fight with the bandit brothers, Jim and John Younger, March 16, 1874, in which John Younger was killed and Jim Younger wounded.

Dr. D. C. McNeil, who attended detective Louis Lull.

39

Good Bye, Jesse

GOOD-BYE, JESSE!

The Notorious Outlaw and Bandit, Jesse James, Killed at St. Joseph

BY R. FORD, OF RAY COUNTY,

A Young Man but Twenty-one Years of Age.

THE DEADLY WEAPON USED

Presented to His Slayer by His Victim but a Short Time Since.

A ROBBERY CONTEMPLATED

Of a Bank at Platte City—To Have Taken Place Last Night.

JESSE IN KANSAS CITY

During the Past Year and Residing on One of the Principal Streets.

KANSAS CITY EXCITED

Over the Receipt of the News—Talks with People— Life of the Dead Man.

An item from the front page of the *Kansas City Daily Journal* of Tuesday, April 4, 1882. Many columns were devoted to the story in this newspaper and in almost all papers throughout the country.

"I saw the Governor (Crittenden) and he said $10,000 had been offered for Jesse's death. I went back and told Bob and he said that if I was willing to go, all right. Then we saddled up and rode to the Samuel place . . ."

In this laconic fashion Charles Ford later told how the assassination of Jesse James was planned. The state of Missouri had not enough funds to post a reward large enough to tempt some of the James gang to turn on their leader. So in 1882 the railroads, Jesse's favorite targets for many years, made up a fund of $10,000 for the capture of Jesse James. Charlie Ford, after his talk with Crittenden, planned the murder of their friend and leader with his brother Bob.

Meanwhile the gang was breaking up fast. Wood Hite, one of Jesse's favorite riders, fled back to Kentucky. Dead men came to haunt him and he became so jittery he shot an innocent Negro on a fence, "because he looked at me." In a farmhouse in Ray County, Missouri, where he hid out, he thought Dick Liddell, another of Jesse's riders, was giving him strange looks and he went for his gun. But Dick was faster and shot him through the heart. Another rider, Jim Cummings, who witnessed the scene, wisely decided to abandon outlawry and rode off, later to write his memoirs.

Shortly after eight o'clock on the morning of April 3,

1882, Bob Ford fired his famous shot, killing Jesse as he stood on a chair to straighten a picture.

The tragic figure in the scene was his wife, Zerelda, who rushed from the kitchen to cradle the bloody head of her husband, as Ford mumbled, "The gun went off accidentally."

"Yes, I guess it did," she murmured brokenly.

The posse rushed up to the house on the hill as the news spread through St. Jo with the speed of a prairie grass fire. The Fords, who sent a telegram to Crittenden ("I have killed Jesse James. St. Joseph. Bob Ford") had to run to catch up with the posse.

"I'm Bob Ford," gasped Bob. "I shot him."

"I'm Charlie Ford," blurted out his brother. "I saw him."

Thus they officially staked out their claim for the blood money. The classic headlines of the day are well known. The *St. Joseph Gazette* cried: "Jesse By Jehovah." The *Kansas City Journal*: "Good-Bye, Jesse!" The *St. Joseph Evening News*: "The Notorious Bandit at Last Meets His Fate and Dies with His Boots On." The accounts of the assassination ran for columns. Each edition was sold out. Even in New York the story was Page One.

There was a dramatic coroner's jury inquest at which Mrs. Samuel identified the body as that of her son, as did Dick Liddell and Charles Alderman, the latter a livery man in St. Jo who had known Jesse for years. To clinch the identification, Crittenden wired Captain Harrison Trow, who had ridden with Jesse as a guerrilla, to come to St. Jo to view the body.

Trow, then living in Texas, recalled, "I was playing safety first." He arrived with several hard-eyed and well-armed cowhands. He went to the funeral parlor and took one look.

"That's Jesse," he said, and walked out.

Even in death Jesse was wanted by the law. There was a dispute between the St. Jo authorities and those from Clay County. While a large crowd looked on in silence, the coffin was slid into the baggage car. Someone tried to break through the lines. There were several shots, and a man fled, followed by Sheriff Timberlake's officers. It was a fitting requiem for Jesse.

The coffin cost five hundred dollars, causing a reporter for the *Ralls County Herald* to write:

"When he gets across the creek, the folks there will take him for a banker."

In Kearney, Dr. Reuben Samuel paced slowly up and down the windy platform. Violence had been added to violence that very day with John, Jesse's half-brother, wounded in a gun fight at a dance. For a time it seemed as if he would die.

While John fought to live, the funeral ceremonies for Jesse were held in the Kearney House. Long lines of men, women, and children passed the coffin. Some in amazement looked down at the calm, bearded face. They had seen this man ride in and out of Kearney and never knew who he was!

In the quiet of the dying afternoon the coffin was lowered into the deep grave at the foot of a coffee bean tree in the corner of the Samuel yard. Later a white shaft was erected with the inscription:

Jesse W. James,
Died April 3, 1882.
Aged 34 years, six months, 28 days.
Murdered by a coward whose name is not worthy to appear here.

Jesse James had come home.

Jesse James in death (picture taken just before he was placed in his $500 coffin).

The house at St. Joseph in which Jesse James was killed (from a drawing made the day after the shooting).

THE TRAITOR'S TRIUMPH

A Day of Excitement and Turmoil in St. Joseph—Is it Jesse? the Question on Every Tongue.

Continuation of the Coroner's Inquest—Highly Dramatic Scenes at Dick Little's Appearance.

Mrs. Samuels and Mrs. James Break Out in Fierce Invectives—Gossip Around the City.

A Talk With Little—Cole Younger Interviewed—Governor Crittenden's Expressed Satisfaction.

Identification of the Remains—The Burial at Kearney To-Day—The Trials at Independence.

The Day's Developments.

[Special to the Kansas City Times.]

St. Joseph, Mo., April 4—At a very early hour this morning, hundreds of people, men, women and children began to wend their way toward the undertaker's establishment, where the dead body of the outlaw had been placed in a cooler, eager for a look at the noted train robber, and so dense was the throng at 9 o'clock that the doors had to be closed and a special detail of police called in to keep the tide of humanity back. The morbid curiosity of all classes was never more plainly shown than on this occasion, and as one man said: I believe they would all come in the same way to see the devil. About the establishment, the long watches of the night had been to many any thing but wakeful ones, and for several hours the members of the Kansas City police force—Sergeant Ditsch and Policeman Nugent—were the only officers on guard, and the suspicion entertained late last evening that an attempt might be made to steal the body of Jesse from the hands of the officers, was a false one. To be sure, there were many persons in St. Joseph who

TALKED OPENLY

of such a move, but no sane man could have had a like idea in his head. Sheriff Timberlake and Captain Craig, who have really had all arrangements touching the future disposition of the body and of the Ford boys in their hands, did not retire to their quarters at the Pacific house until a very early hour this morning, but at 8 o'clock were on the streets again, and the

the room and passed by Little he covered his face with a hat and said to The Times reporter, I don't know but she will slap me in the face.

Arrival of Mrs. Samuels.

Mrs. Samuels did not arrive from Kearney until 3 o'clock this morning, and at once she was driven to the residence of her daughter-in-law, Mrs. Jesse James, where her son had been killed. Not until after she had asked many questions would she think it was Jesse who had been shot, and would not believe it until she had seen him. Shortly after 9 o'clock she drove to the undertaker's establishment, with the widow of Jesse and the two children, and it being known who she was, every one was made to leave the building, and she entered and looked at the body. After a long look, she exclaimed: Oh, yes, it is my poor boy, would to God that it was not. Why was he killed? The traitors, to kill such a good man. Mrs. James tried to quiet her, and for a time succeeded, but the mother broke out several times, and remained in the room with the body for about half an hour before she could be induced to leave for the court house, where she gave her testimony. After the coroner's inquest a Times reporter met Mrs. Samuels in the prosecuting attorney's room, and was granted an extended interview.

WHAT SHE SAID.

Of course, Mrs. Samuels, you believe the dead body to be that of your son?

Why, of course, it is; wouldn't a mother know her own boy?

You have seen the remains then?

Yes, I came from there a short time ago. Oh, my poor boy, to be shot down so.

You do not believe him guilty of all that has been charged?

I know he has not done it all. He never told me when he robbed a bank or train, if he ever did those things as has been charged.

When did you get the news that he had been shot?

It came to me at Kearney from his wife. I could not believe it at first.

You came at once upon receipt of the news?

Yes, and when I met Zee she said it was Jesse. He was so good to us all. Why wouldn't they leave him alone?

Do you believe he wanted to reform?

Of course he did, but the officers and newspaper men would not let him, and at the close of the war they made him take to the brush.

Do you remember the report that George Shepherd had killed Jesse at Joplin?

I remember he said so, but George Shepherd is a lying scoundrel and always was. Jesse never did trust him, and he knows it. No one will believe him, and all the officers know how he has lied about Jesse, and when he said he

back of the head, except made by the bullet which killed the man; all reports to the contrary are false.

Dick Little Talks.

Dick Little, the former train robber and companion of Jesse James, has attracted more attention and talk in St. Joe than any of the hundreds of strangers drawn to this point by the death of the great leader, during the past twenty-four hours. When he arrived on the special train with Sheriff Timberlake Monday afternoon, he was unknown, save to the officials and two or three newspaper correspondents, but now nearly every able bodied man of the town has had a look at his features, which are of the pleasantest character, and if one did not know he had been a train robber, the fact would be hard to believe from his face and actions. When he surrendered to Sheriff Timberlake he had been "out in the bush," as the saying goes, for three or four years, but now that he has come to town and taken to civilized habits once more he is an entirely different person. At St. Joseph yesterday Little allowed himself to be interviewed by the Times, but said to begin with that it was not at his request. He stated that his first joining the James boys was when he

believe Mattie ever saw Governor Crittenden to know him.

"Are you going back to Clay county to live?"

"I am going back there this afternoon with Mr. Wymore."

Arrival of Identifiers.

There was considerable excitement to-night when the Kansas City parties, who came up on the Missouri Pacific train, went to the undertaking establishment for the purpose of identifying the remains of the dead man. As is well known, there have been many persons here in St. Joseph who scoffed at the thought of its being Jesse James, and declared it to be some "put up job" to obtain the $10,000 reward offered by Governor Crittenden. The names of those who arrived were Prosecuting Attorney Wallace, Harrison Trow, James Wilkinson, J. Clay, Mattie Collins Little, Mr. Mimms, Mr. James and C. D. Axman. About midnight the above named party were driven to the undertakers and the body was positively identified as that of Jesse James, some of the men having known him for years. Mattie Collins, who is registered at the World's hotel, was terribly excited as she viewed the remains and in the strongest language denounced the parties who brought it all about. She cried and talked loud for awhile, but at last

JESSE W. JAMES.

[From a photograph taken March 13, 1882, and furnished The Times by his wife.]

From the *Kansas City Daily Times.*

HE CAME IN

On October 5, 1882, while the state still boiled over with violent discussions of the "manner of the way" the bandit leader had been murdered, Frank James, weary and tired of running, gave himself up. Characteristically, he stalked into the governor's office, unstrapped his guns, and announced that this was the first time he had done so since his days with Quantrill.

He was already a living legend, and the people of the state treated him as one. Mobs cheered him as he stood on train platforms on his way back to Clay County to stand trial for the double murder of the conductor and a passenger named McMillan in a train robbery.

On August 21, 1883, his trial began. So great were the crowds that it was held in the Opera House at Gallatin, Missouri, instead of the County Courthouse. The defense contended that the fifth man on that robbery had been Jim Cummings and not Frank James.

Thomas T. Crittenden.

The power the gang still had over the citizens of Missouri was demonstrated when the railroad refused to allow one of its employees, a vital witness, to appear for the state. Prosecutor Wallace, enraged at the railroad's refusal, threatened to subpoena the whole line, from the president down. The employee was produced in a hurry, but on the stand proved useless. Under the steady gaze of Frank James he was struck dumb. Wallace, in disgust, had to dismiss him. He went "scooting down the street to the depot, and that's the last we saw of him," Wallace later reported.

James was acquitted and the crowd went wild trying to get to shake his hand.

William H. Wallace.

END OF AN ERA

Bob Ford, the James' cousin who shot poor Jesse in the back.

There is little doubt that the vigorous war they had waged against the James gang helped to end the political careers of Prosecutor William Wallace and Governor Crittenden. Wallace, the following year, was refused the Congressional nomination and Crittenden "was refused his party" for the gubernatorial nomination. The election that year was bitter; old scars were rubbed raw; there was gunfire and violence. Again the state was divided: pro-Confederate Democrats, pro-Union Republicans.

But the James gang could not rest in peace. It was reported that Minnesota was dusting off the Northfield indictments but nothing came of it. During Teddy Roosevelt's campaign, Frank James announced his support of the "Rough Rider," and the Missouri papers "made much of it." The sensation lasted only a few days this time. Outlaws, at the turn of the century, were becoming outdated, even Frank James.

On July 10, 1901, Coleman and James Younger were released from Stillwater Penitentiary. Bob had died of tuberculosis on September 16, 1889, slightly under thirty-three years of age.

An impressive list of names of state and government officials had been signed to many appeals petitioning their parole. The Robin Hood legend was never so bright.

Cole and Jim worked for a time—and it is fitting—as salesmen for tombstones. In 1902 Jim Younger committed suicide over an unrequited love affair. Later Cole and Frank James joined a Wild West show, but quit after a short time. Frank finally wound up as a starter for a racetrack. He died February 18, 1915, in his old bedroom at the Samuel place. A year later on March 21, big Cole passed away at Lee's Summit, Missouri. To the neighborhood children he was "Uncle Cole." When he was lowered into his grave he still had seventeen bullets in his big body. He was then seventy-two years of age.

Not only a man but an era had been laid to rest.

JESSE RIDES AGAIN

Scarcely a decade passes that an old, white-bearded man does not appear to claim he is "the real Jesse James." The first one appeared in 1901 when the remains of Jesse were being disinterred from the front yard of the Samuel place to be buried beside Zerelda's in the Kearney, Missouri, family plot. That morning the sheriff of Kearney received a postcard which said, "I will not be buried in Carny next week. I am not dead. I was not shot by Bobie Ford. I wasn't there, so you can't bury me. Signed, the real Jesse James."

The last of the "real Jesse Jameses" appeared in 1948. There are many who still believe he really was Jesse. Nothing could be further from the truth. Homer Croy, one of Jesse's better biographers, paid the old man, Frank Dalton, a visit before he really became acquainted with Jesse's life and could answer all the questions of the unbelievers. When Homer asked "Jesse"—then curing a bile attack with whiskey and doughnuts—what "Red Fox" meant to him, the old gentleman quickly replied he was a scout for Quantrill, part Indian. Red Fox, of course, was Jesse's race horse.

The old fellow really was surprised by Homer's next question of how he happened to grow a new tip for the finger of his left hand, which Jesse had accidentally shot off when a young boy. The old gent simply took another slug and offered Homer a doughnut.

Al Jennings, the most overrated bandit in western out-

Al Jennings (*left*), early-day Oklahoma train robber, looking at J. Frank Dalton (*right*), who called himself Jesse James, said, "Boys, there isn't a bit of doubt on earth. It's him. It's Jesse James." In this photo Jennings is 85, Dalton 101 years old.

law history, took one look at the old man and said—according to Associated Press—"It's him. It's Jesse." As the AP reporter wrote, "It was a touching scene and the tears flowed."

The place where Jesse died, as it is today.

The Man Who Killed The Man
Who Killed Jesse James

Bob Ford's funeral procession, Creede, Colorado, June 25, 1892.

There was never any peace for Bob Ford, the man who killed Jesse James. Instead of being acclaimed as a hero, he was cursed, reviled, and threatened. The glory he had sought turned to ashes in his mouth. After Jesse's death, Ford was put on trial for the murder of Wood Hite and found guilty. But the governor kept faith with his ace informer and pardoned him.

After that he became a wanderer. For a time he stayed in Richmond with his parents, but the cold eyes, sneers, and whispers of his friends and neighbors turned him surly and arrogant. He liked to boast of how he shot Jesse down, but a contemptuous silence always greeted him when he had finished.

Then Bob took to the stage—*The Outlaws of Missouri,* they called the act. His chore was to come out between curtain drops and tell how he shot down his outlaw chief. Boos and jeers were the usual reaction. Then romance bloomed. A girl in the chorus named Nellie Waterson fell for Bob's good looks, and they were married.

After two seasons Bob went to bigger things—a spot in P. T. Barnum's freak show. But he couldn't shake the shadow which seemed to hover over his life. Jesse was always there. He began to drink heavily and to gamble. He and Dick Liddell bought a saloon in Las Vegas, New Mexico, but the customers didn't pour in as the ex-outlaws had expected. Even the rough frontier town objected to

a Judas drawing its beer or pouring its shots of whiskey.

N. C. Creede found two silver mines in Colorado and had a tough, roaring town named after him. In the mad stampede Bob Ford went along, sized up the wild town, and opened a saloon. He wore a diamond stickpin, smoked a big cigar, and enjoyed leaning on the bar telling the miners how he shot Jesse down. For a time business boomed. One of the first things Ford did was to buy a diamond brooch for Nellie.

One night on a visit to Pueblo, Ford agreed to share a room in the local hotel with another boarder. The other tenant was Ed Kelly from Harrisonville, Missouri. Kelly, by marriage, was kin of the Youngers. When Ford walked into the room, they stared at each other, nodded, then had a drink. In the morning Ford's diamond ring was missing and he accused Kelly of the theft. Kelly, who had a bad past himself, brooded over the accusation. When he heard from friends that Ford was repeating his accusations in Creede, Kelly went there and tried to kill him. Thrown out of Ford's saloon once, he returned. The second time he killed Ford with a shotgun blast of slugs. The court found him guilty and sentenced him to the Colorado pen for twenty years. Meanwhile Nellie took her husband's body back to Richmond to be buried. It was just eleven years after he had killed Jesse James.

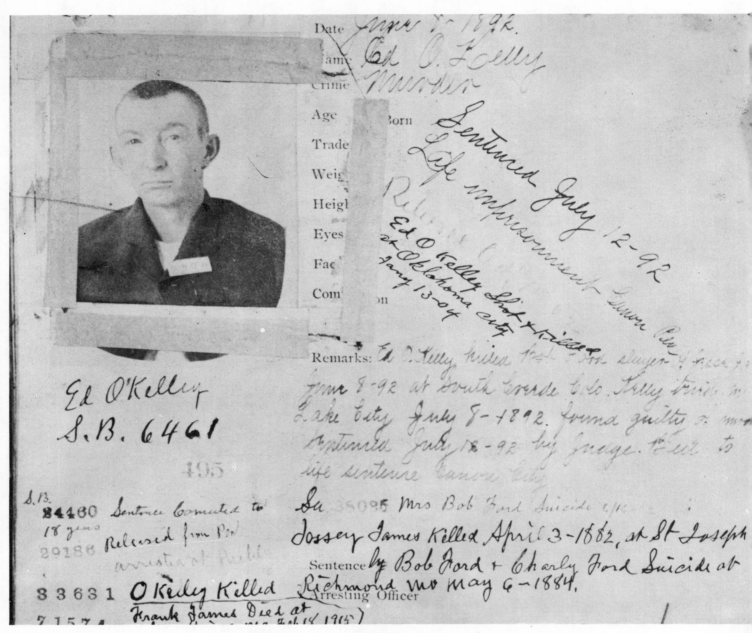

The blotter on the man who killed Bob Ford.

Charles Ford, Bob's brother.

Mrs. Ford, mother of Bob and Charles.

WILD BILL HICKOK *(and the wilder stories)*

It wasn't love at first sight. It was just a case of goggle-eyed, moon-struck hero worship. Colonel George Ward Nichols, an Eastern galoot, couldn't help himself. He was simply set back on his high heels that day in Springfield, Missouri, when he was privileged to look upon this marvelous specimen: 6'2", long flowing hair, chest like a barrel, thin waist adorned by twin Colts, graceful, dignified bearing. And under a sweeping sombrero a "quiet, manly face; so gentle in its expression as to utterly belie the history of its owner. And eyes as gentle as a woman's," so gentle that "you would not believe that you were looking into eyes that have pointed the way to death for hundreds of men."

"Yes," the Colonel went on in his reverie, "Wild Bill with his own hands has killed hundreds of men. Of that I haven't a doubt. 'He shoots to kill,' as they say on the border."

Nichols' flowery prose appeared in *Harper's Monthly* in February, 1867. That was the introduction of Wild Bill to the multitudes east of the Mississippi and west of the Rockies. Before then his fame was limited to the Great Plains. He had ridden with General Jim Lane's Free State forces in Kansas against the Border Ruffians in '56. He had done a hitch or two on the Santa Fe Trail as a wagon driver. He had spent some time in Nebraska, where he figured in a shooting fray—the McCanles Affair, it was called. He had won his spurs as a Union Scout during the war. And when Nichols dropped in on him, he was something of a celebrity in Missouri because he had just killed gambler Dave Tutt in a fair 'n square duel in the sun. Now the saga of Wild Bill would span the nation in the pages of *Harper's*.

Hickok and his camp-followers in Springfield told the Colonel stories of one death-defying adventure after another—on the trail, in the border towns, behind the Confederate lines. Wild Bill fought his way past whole companies of rebel troops time after time, the way he told it, but the story he relished the most was the one about Dave McCanles and his "gang of desperadoes, horse-thieves, and murderers." He said he slew McCanles and five henchmen with his only six bullets, cut four more to death in hand-to-hand combat, and walked away from the carnage in fair health except for eleven buckshot holes and thirteen stab wounds. But that wasn't the most glorious afternoon of his young manhood, either . . .

"In all your wild, perilous adventures," the Colonel asked, begging that the question wouldn't be misunderstood, "have you ever been afraid?"

"I think I know what you mean, sir," Wild Bill replied, recalling a wartime escapade, "and I'm not ashamed to say that I have been so frightened that it 'peared as if all the strength and blood had gone out of my body, and my face was as white as chalk. It was the Wilson Creek fight.

Wild Bill Hickok, 1873.

I had fired more than fifty cartridges and, I think, fetched my man every time . . ."

The Colonel put down every little word just the way Bill told it, and he was positively staggered. Samson, slaying a thousand men with the jawbone of an ass, and Hercules, for all his superhuman feats, paled before Hickok's "grand heroism and deeds of prowess." Why, the Colonel's hero not only enjoyed "the power of a Samson and Hercules combined," but also made Jack the Giant-Killer and Sinbad the Sailor look like craven weaklings.

Nichols was only the first in a long line. J. W. Buel, in *Heroes of the Plains*, vintage 1882, poured more star-touched prose into the heady Hickok mixture. He had his mustached idol picking off thirty-five rebels single-handed in the Battle of Pea Ridge in '62 and strewing the plains with dead Indians in his spare time. Sir Henry Morton Stanley, the man the *New York Herald* once sent into darkest Africa to find Dr. Livingstone, penetrated the western wilds and nudged the Hickok saga along. His opus, *My Early Travels and Adventures in America,* (1895) carried these lines:

STANLEY: I say, Mr. Hickok, how many white men have you killed to your certain knowledge?

HICKOK: I suppose I have killed considerably over a hundred.

47

STANLEY: What made you kill those men? Did you kill them without cause or provocation?

HICKOK: No, by heaven, I never killed one man without good cause.

There were other scribblers waiting in the wings—General and Mrs. Custer, Buffalo Bill Cody, Emerson Hough, Frank J. Wilstach, Wilbert E. Eisele, William Elsey Connelly (the most critical). And there are some even now, walking in Colonel Nichols' purple path almost a century later. Indeed, it is a curious commentary on the movie-TV age that Wild Bill is one fabled character out of the Old West whose reputed deeds have to be under-written and underplayed. Nobody dares to ask the kids to swallow the more epic tales about the man. In the celluloid flesh today, he's just a hard-bitten frontier marshal, struck from the familiar Hollywood mould. He's the garden variety law 'n order man. Just Plain Wild Bill.

Somewhere between the two images lies the elusive truth. . . .

William F. Cody (Buffalo Bill).

IF YOU HAD TWO HEADS, IT WAS EASY

It happened during the Civil War, so we're told, in wide-open North Platte, Nebraska.

Bill Hickok, Union Scout, Indian fighter and dead shot (with a lightnin'-quick draw, of course) hitched Black Nell to a post and went into a restaurant for supper. A waitress approached him nervously and whispered that she had heard two men plotting to kill him. One was going to come in the front door and the other the rear, guns blazing before Mr. Hickok could whip out his Colt Dragoon .44's.

The gentleman pistoleer swept a lock of golden brown tresses off his shoulder and chucked the trembling bearer of Death's tidings under her chin. "Little girl," he said softly, "you get to one side. You might get hurt in the overflow." The waitress fled to the kitchen. Moments later,

it says here, the Western badmen were stretched out cold on the floor. Here is the way the carnage was described by O. W. Coursey, one of the more open-mouthed Hickok biographers:

"Wild Bill, facing the desperate character who entered the front door, had shot him with a revolver in his left hand, while with the right hand he had thrown the other gun over his left shoulder and shot the man coming in from the rear. History does not record a more daredevil act, a more astute piece of gun work."

The episode fits nicely into Wild Bill's self-portrait as the shy, fearless, square-shootin' hero who triumphs over the damnedest odds. The only trouble with it is that there isn't a shred of evidence that it ever happened.

48

HICKOK AND McCANLES

William Alonzo Hickok, the good Presbyterian deacon who ran the general store in Troy Grove, Illinois, was wiped out in the business panic of 1837. Otherwise it was the most noteworthy of all his years. Polly, his wife, bore him a fourth son. The boy, called James Butler Hickok, ran away and became Wild Bill Hickok, and in time brought everlasting renown on the family. William Alonzo Hickok didn't live to see the days of glory when the name blazed across the Western frontier, but Polly Hickok did. Right to the end, even after he himself perished at an assassin's hands, Polly Hickok heard wondrous accounts of her far-off son's deeds of daring.

And Wild Bill remembered Mama.

"I have a mother back there in Illinois who is old and feeble," he told an interviewer in 1865. "I haven't seen her these many years and I haven't been a good son to her, yet I love her better than anything in life. It doesn't matter much what they say about me here. But I'm not a cutthroat and vagabond, and I'd like the old woman to know what'll make her proud. I'd like her to hear that her runaway boy has fought through the war for the Union like a true man."

Bill left home in his teens and sampled all the varieties of violence then in style. As a Redleg in Kansas, he took up arms against the Border Ruffians. Then, driving stage, he fought Indians on the plains. Then, so the story goes, he tangled with a grizzly bear which shook off his pistol fire and had to be subdued with a knife in man-to-man (or bear-to-man) combat. And then, in Nebraska, came the first of his celebrated gun battles—the McCanles Affair.

Hickok said that he alone slew ten men in that encounter, suffering twenty-four buckshot and knife wounds, but that was a very tall tale. That warn't the way it happened at all.

David C. McCanles, a settler from North Carolina, sold some property along Rock Creek in Jefferson County to Russell, Majors and Waddell's Overland Stage Company for a pony express station. Hickok, supposedly sent there to recuperate from the wounds the durable bear had inflicted, was a stablehand for J. W. (Dock) Brink, the stockkeeper. Horace Wellman managed the place.

On July 21, 1862, McCanles went to the station either to press a demand for an overdue installment on the property, "clean up" Wellman and his helpers, or settle an affair of honor; some historians said the dashing Hickok had slipped out of the stable to purloin the affections of beautiful Sarah Shull (Kate Shell), a lass upon whom McCanles supposedly had put his brand. McCanles took along his twelve-year-old son, Monroe, and two neighbors, M. R. Gordon and James Woods.

Only the boy came back. In the story he gave to the Nebraska Historical Society years later, he said that when his father came into the Wellman house, Hickok turned a rifle on him from behind a curtain. Then, he said, Hickok shot Woods and Wellman crushed the wounded man's skull with a hoe, while the fleeing Gordon was tracked into the underbrush and killed with a shotgun; it's not clear who did that.

Monroe McCanles' death toll squares with court records dug up in 1927. Three men died, not the ten-man band of "desperadoes" and "cutthroats" Wild Bill described. There was also a large disparity between Hickok's box score on his assorted wounds and Monroe McCanles' statement that neither his father, Gordon nor Woods was armed. Hickok partisans always point out that the trio must have been "heeled," because Wild Bill, Wellman, and Brink escaped prosecution on a plea of self-defense, as the long-missing records showed. Of course legal processes in Jefferson County, Nebraska, were not too stuffy back in '61.

After the McCanles episode, Hickok served as a scout in the Civil War, and later, in the Indian campaigns, with

David C. McCanles.

Custer. He did his share of damage behind the Confederate lines, but did he pick off 50 rebels with 50 shots in one day, as he said? Did he send another 35 to their doom in another hectic afternoon's sharpshooting? ("It was like shooting buffalo for him," one writer said.) There's no support for that kind of story. Nor can it be shown that it was Wild Bill, with his trusty Bowie knife, who destroyed Black Kettle. It appears that he was some place else the day Custer's troops did in the Cheyenne chief in the Battle of the Washita. But let's get on to some gunfightin' that really happened.

A Matter of Honor

There was a story that Wild Bill Hickok once took up with an eighteen-year-old Sioux maiden named Mary Logan. They were very close, but let's not have any idle gossip. Frank J. Wilstach cleared the matter up in *Wild Bill Hickok: The Prince of Pistoleers:*

"Notwithstanding this remarkable intimacy, Bill always declared that he left the girl as he found her and that she would readily have sacrificed her life rather than forfeit the jewel of her chastity."

In fact, after a while the dashing frontiersman and the nicely-curved Indian lass even stopped living together. Mary Logan got married, and one day she put poison in her husband's coffee because he said bad things about her old alliance with Wild Bill. After the husband drank the bitter brew, there was nothing for him to do but die.

Wild Bill in buckskins (from a photograph taken at Fort McPherson in 1871, when he was scouting for General Penrose).

Kate Shell

Sarah Shull (Kate Shell) was the feminine interest in the Hickok-McCanles mystery. She knew both men. Before she died she told Frank J. Wilstach that on the morning of the great Nebraska shooting fray she heard Dave McCanles say that "he was going to clean up on the people" at the Rock Creek Station. But McCanles partisans always insisted that he went to the station unarmed and full of peaceable intentions, only to be shot dead by Wild Bill.

THE OTHER MAN FROM ABILENE

If you were a boy in Abilene at the turn of the century, you would have heard wonderful stories about a stern and fearless giant who had left his mark on that cow camp when it was the wildest town in all of Kansas: a man named Hickok. You would have heard about it from men who were there when it happened in '71 and remembered —or thought they remembered—every incident, every splendid detail. Dwight D. Eisenhower grew up in Abilene, and he heard the stories. He would never forget Mr. Hickok. Indeed, after he became President of the United States, he publicly threw a garland in Wild Bill's direction. In an attack on the character assassins among us, the President recalled the Western tradition of face-to-face, fair 'n square fightin' and urged for our troubled times the code of honor exemplified by Hickok when he was Marshal of Abilene.

But Wild Bill was only an angel in the bedtime stories Ike heard, as he is today in the TV hoss operas about him. In Abilene during his lifetime, he was something less than a six-foot tower of virtue. He didn't wear down the two-inch heels on his sixty-dollar boots patrolling the streets to make law 'n order stick. He spent most of his time bucking the cards in the saloons, or lolling around the cribs where the town's fallen women sold what was left of their charms. He didn't tame Abilene. He found it tamed—by Tom Smith, a fighting, two-fisted Marshal gone from the town in a breach of the face-to-face tradition. Somebody shot Tom Smith in the back because he was too rough on the outlaws. Mayor Joseph G. McCoy, the pioneer cattleman who had opened the market at Abilene, turned to Wild Bill when Smith was murdered.

McCoy thought he had solid reasons. The Hickok name was something to reckon with in the West. On top of the vastly overdrawn *Harper's* article recounting his wartime exploits and his lurid version of the McCanles killing, among other deeds, Hickok had added some luster as Sheriff in Fort Riley and City Marshal in Hays City, Kansas. The Fort Riley record is skimpy, but Wild Bill got credit for cooling off the drunken soldiers who were trampling on the little military post. In Hays, lusty, brawling terminus of the Union Pacific in '69, Hickok added at least two cadavers to his score. He was there only a month when, on October 19, the guns went off.

Jack Strawhorn (also Strawhan) started the play in Drum's Saloon. He had had trouble with Hickok in Ellsworth and came into Drum's with mayhem on his mind. Miguel Antonio Otero, ex-Governor of New Mexico, who used to trail around after Wild Bill in Hays when he was a boy, recorded the encounter in his book, *My Life on the Frontier*:

"Strawhorn entered the saloon and walked carelessly toward the bar. On getting within a few feet of Wild Bill, he attempted to draw his gun, but Wild Bill was too quick

Hickok, "Prince of Pistoleers."

for him . . . he dropped dead with a bullet through his brain."

Hickok set up a round of drinks, the town band offered up a serenade in his honor, and a coroner's jury wrote a brief and dispassionate epitaph for the departed badman: "Served him right, and so we declare."

Bill Mulvey, a brawler of some note, tangled with Wild Bill in December when the Marshal tried to arrest him for "hurrahing" the town, a form of pleasure now called disorderly conduct. Mulvey got the drop on Wild Bill and smugly announced that he held the winning hand. "I can't beat that pair," the Marshal said. Then he looked past the badman and called out, "Don't shoot him, boys, he is drunk." The ruse worked. Mulvey turned and Wild Bill killed him.

Hickok left Hays after a brush with a large and playful segment of the Seventh Cavalry. It was said that he had

Mayor Joseph G. McCoy.   Marshal Thomas J. Smith.

to kill three or four troopers to put down their rebellion, turning on some fancy over-the-shoulder shooting when he was outflanked, but the record is cloudy and the dead nameless.

In Abilene a rather expensive error in judgment—suggesting that the "beau ideal" of the Western gunfighters could get as nervous as any dude—tarnished Wild Bill's one display of marksmanship. The Marshal shot Mike Williams, another lawman, when he came on the run to help out as Bill was throwing lead at gambler Phil Coe. It happened outside the Alamo, Wild Bill's hangout, and it came down in history in the usual two versions, pro and con.

Coe, a Texan, ran the Bull's Head Saloon with Ben Thompson and had all kinds of trouble with Wild Bill. The showdown came on October 5, 1871, on the long end of a day of liquid farewells. Coe was bidding good-by to a bunch of Texans who were going back to the Chisholm Trail, and the celebrants wound up in front of the Alamo. Coe fired a shot and Wild Bill hurried out of the saloon, because there was an ordinance against toting six-guns within the town limits. This is where the road forks: the Texans said that when Hickok reprimanded him, Coe explained that he had only fired at a stray dog. Then he put his pistol away and turned, whereupon the Marshal whipped out a pair of derringers and shot him. The other story is that Wild Bill didn't shoot until Coe had fired point-blank at him. Then, hearing the clatter of boots behind, he whirled and fired again (there went Williams) because he thought he was being attacked from the rear.

Coe lingered for a few days. The faithful Williams, who had dashed to the scene with guns drawn, died on a poker

table in the Alamo as the crestfallen Marshal stood beside him. One Hickok drum-beater, perhaps overwrought himself, described the scene this way: "Tears are the safety valves of a woman's soul. Without them she could not survive. Sometimes they aid strong men also. 'Jesus wept,' declares the Gospel. So did Wild Bill."

What was the trouble between Coe and Hickok? We're told that Coe had charged that fellow-Texans were being fleeced at the Alamo tables because the Marshal was looking the other way, while Hickok had accused Coe of running a crooked game at the Bull's Head. And we're told that Coe had pirated one of Wild Bill's lady friends—possibly from the part of town called "The Devil's Half-Acre." That kind of lapse in social etiquette could be fatal, then as now. One of Hickok's earliest gun duels, with Dave Tutt, was traced to the same sort of thing. Their fight in the public square at Springfield, Missouri, in '65, followed a quarrel over a gambling debt. But the real bitterness apparently set in when Tutt tampered with Susanna Moore, an item that had come into Wild Bill's life by way of the Ozarks. Bill put a bullet in his heart at 75 yards. Susanna went back to Hickok after Tutt was deposited in the earth. She was with him in Abilene, but let it not be said that her skirts lay behind the unpleasantness with Coe; if it was a woman, it was some other frontier Jezebel. The Marshal, a fashion-plate out of the Prince Albert mould, checkered trousers 'n silk waistcoat 'n all, was never accused of being a one-woman guy.

The Wages of Sin

In Wild Bill Hickok's time—not that it was his fault—Hays City, Kansas, must have been somewhat loose. An eyewitness set down this heavens-to-Betsy description of the town in '69:

"Hays City by lamplight was remarkably lively, but not very moral. The streets blazed with the reflection from saloons, and a glance within showed floors crowded with dancers, the gaily dressed women striving to hide with ribbons and paint the terrible lines which that grim artist, Dissipation, loves to draw upon such faces. With a heartless humor he daubs the noses of the sterner sex a cherry red, but paints under the once bright eyes of women a shade as dark as the night in the cave of despair. To the music of violins and the stamping of feet the dance went on, and we saw in the giddy maze old men who must have been pirouetting on the very edge of their graves."

Wild Bill Hickok. Texas Jack Omohundro. Buffalo Bill Cody.

Buffalo Bill

William Frederick Cody was just another Indian Scout (as shown right) when Ned Buntline (Edward Z. C. Judson) came out West in '69 looking for the stuff of dime novels. After their meeting, a series of cliff-hanging "true" stories began to appear in the *New York Weekly*, followed by a torrent of paperbacks. Buntline invented the dime novel and "Buffalo Bill"—nemesis of the marauding redskin and defender of frontier womanhood—with the same sweep of his swift pen. After a while even Cody began to see himself as the terror of the plains. Actually the unschooled Iowa farm boy had served as Union soldier (in '64), bison hunter, and scout without ever shedding much human blood in anger.

Now his fame spread. Fred Meader fashioned a hair-raising drama, *Buffalo Bill, the King of the Border Men*, out of Buntline's fiction. Cody saw it at the Bowery Theater in New York, took a bow, and savored the taste of the footlights. In '72 Buntline got his overdressed frontiersman to star in *Scouts of the Plains*, a thin rewrite of the Meader hash. Later Bill brought in Texas Jack Omo-

hundro, an ex-scout from Jeb Stuart's Confederate Cavalry, and the already-famous Wild Bill Hickok, who couldn't stomach the thing and faded out quickly. In time Cody got talked into taking his act into a tent. That was the beginning of Buffalo Bill's Original Wild West Show, which ran for some thirty years and made Cody ample money to keep his appetite for wine, women, and song sharp at all times. He died during World War I in Denver, broke and alone. He was buried atop Lookout Mountain and became in death one of Colorado's biggest tourist draws. For that, Ned Buntline could take a bow if he were alive today.

Annie Oakley

Phoebe Anne Oakley Mozee learned to shoot with a clumsy muzzle-loader in the Ohio backwoods in the '60's. She was still in her teens when she beat Frank Butler, the celebrated marksman, in an all-comers challenge match in Cincinnati. Butler married the girl, trimmed her name to Annie Oakley, and took her into Buffalo Bill's Original Wild West Show. Billed as "Little Sure Shot," she was an instant hit. When she toured Europe, her wonderful feats with a rifle entranced royalty. Once she shot the ashes off a cigarette held in young Kaiser Wilhelm's mouth—a stunt which was a standard bit in her act with Butler. A headliner for seventeen years, she was all but forgotten by the time she died in 1926, at 67. Ethel Merman revived her fame in our time in the Broadway musical hit, *Annie, Get Your Gun*, but the name would have lived on in any case. In American slang an Annie Oakley is a free pass or ticket, so identified by the holes punched through it, just the way Annie plugged playing cards in the old days.

MISS ANNIE OAKLEY,
(LITTLE SURE SHOT.)
BUFFALO BILL'S WILD WEST.

THE DEAD MAN'S HAND

Wild Wild Hickok lasted only eight months as Marshal of Abilene. Not long after he killed Phil Coe and his own deputy, Mike Williams (Whoops, sorry!), the Town Council let him go "for the reason that the city is no longer in need of his services." It is also possible that his services, such as they were, had become embarrassing. Some citizens of the Kansas cattle town frowned on the fact that Williams had been cut down while rushing bravely to Wild Bill's side to help him. It was an accident that ill-befitted the Hickok reputation for icy calm under fire.

The road from Abilene was all downhill for Hickok. He wandered around the West for a while and then went into Buffalo Bill Cody's touring theatrical troupe, an all-time low on the American stage. In Ned Buntline's blood-soaked Indian drama called *Scouts of the Plains*, Hickok became a seedy caricature of the Wild Bill portrayed in the dime novels and yellow journals of the time. It was a pathetic thing for a man who had a legitimate claim to glory as scout, Indian fighter, and gunslinger with or without the more fanciful legends he himself helped circulate. Hickok couldn't play with any conviction the role of the gallant hero plucking the lovely, pale-faced heroine from the steel grip of the villainous redskin. "When he went on the stage before an audience," Buffalo Bill wrote sadly, "it was almost impossible for him to utter a word."

Buffalo Bill's lament is easier to understand when you consider the lines Hickok had. In one scene, clasping the heroine to his breast as his pistols barked out sudden death for a small army of Indian warriors, he was supposed to say, "Fear not, fair maid; by heavens you are safe at last with Wild Bill, who is ever ready to risk his life and die if need be in defense of weak and helpless womanhood." Naturally it came hard. It was an altogether unhappy experience both for the paying public and the man sweating it out under the lights in heavy buckskins and a Stetson the size of a small tepee. In Buffalo one night, Wild Bill called a halt to the "right foolish" business of play-acting with a terse and utterly final pronouncement. "I ain't going to do it any more," he said. There was a gold strike in the Black Hills. He would be more at home there.

When he was Marshal of Hays City, Kansas, in his better days, Wild Bill had met Mrs. Agnes Thatcher Lake, the famous equestrienne who ran her own Wild West show. She was eleven years older than he, and her mature charms evidently left a mark. The two met again in Rochester when Hickok was touring New York with Cody. Wild Bill proposed, but Mrs. Lake turned him down. Two years later, in the spring of 1876, their paths crossed for a third time in Cheyenne, Wyoming, and the pretty widow gave in. They were married in March and went to Cincinnati, the bride's home, for a brief honeymoon. Then Bill left for St. Louis to organize a gold-hunting expedi-

tion to the Dakotas. It wasn't Hickok's purpose to soil his own elegant hands, of course. He would only lead the fortune hunters over the crude trails to the promised land.

While the prospectors ventured out into the rich hills, the roving groom tried his luck in the gambling halls of Deadwood City, South Dakota. As the *Deadwood Telegram* once noted, "Wild Bill sought to accumulate gold by manipulating the picture cards rather than by digging in the earth for it."

Hickok, then 39, was neither happy nor well. His eyes were troubling him. He had reason to believe that he was going blind, and he began to talk about approaching death. Colorado Charley Utter, his friend, used to chide him about it, but Deadwood was a paradise for desperadoes, and Wild Bill may have had the feeling that he couldn't take care of himself in a fight any more. His letters to Agnes Lake talked longingly of his hopes for the future and how much he wanted to have a home with her, but there was a note of despondency in his words.

The end came on the afternoon of August 2, 1876.

Wild Bill was playing poker in Carl Mann's Saloon with his back to the open door when Jack McCall, a cross-eyed, broken-nosed whiskey-head, came in and blew out his brains as he slowly pondered his cards—aces and eights, of course, thereafter *"The Dead Man's Hand."*

Emma Hickok, famous Wild West show rider and stepdaughter of Wild Bill.

55

Hickok slumped to the floor as the cowardly McCall backed out of the gambling parlor.

It was never quite clear why the deed was done. McCall said that Hickok had killed his brother in Hays City in 1869 (it was not true) and had threatened him, too. Another story was that Hickok had cussed out McCall the night before because he was $3.50 short in a card game. Another was that outlaw elements in Deadwood had heard that Wild Bill was going to become Marshal and hired McCall to get rid of him. It was just as likely that McCall was simply drunk and overplayful that day.

There was a story about Calamity Jane tracking the assassin to a nearby butcher shop and manhandling him with a meat cleaver, but that ain't what happened. McCall was caught and tried by a miners' court which, strangely, found him not guilty by a vote of 11 to 1. It was an odd verdict, considering that the man had shot Wild Bill in the back of the head, but justice had its way in time. McCall was tried again in a more formal kind of court in Yankton. Asked why he didn't face Hickok in a fair fight if he fancied he had a reason for killing him, he said: "I didn't want to commit suicide." It was a nice sporting tribute to the deceased, but the court found McCall guilty anyway. He was hanged on March 1, 1877.

Don Roberto Brady sits beneath portrait of his father, Sheriff William Brady, who was murdered by Billy the Kid during the Lincoln County War. Peter Stackpole of *Life* magazine made this photograph in 1941.

BILLY THE KID

Homicide and Folklore

It happened on April 1, 1878, under a broiling New Mexican sky. Sheriff William Brady and three deputies walked down the main street of Lincoln toward the courthouse. Behind them, from an adobe wall in the rear of the McSween & Tunstall store, a volley of rifle bursts rang out.

Brady fell dead in the morning sun, his back riddled. George Hindman staggered forward a few feet and collapsed into the parched earth outside the Church of San Juan, pleading for water with his last breath. Unhurt, the other two deputies—Billy Matthews and George W. (Dad) Peppin—fled to cover.

The band of assassins behind the wall kept their ground, not knowing whether Matthews and Peppin would open fire, but from among them a slim little boy of eighteen dashed out into the Plaza. He wanted Brady's weapons, but as he picked up the sheriff's Winchester a slug tore into his hand. Matthews, hidden in a doorway, was shooting at him.

If it happened in the movies or on your TV screen, the kneeling boy would yank his .45 with his good hand and fight it out, there in the open. Not this boy. He had staged the murderous ambush. He didn't always fight the way they do in the Westerns. So he ran. He ran for his life, as he had been doing since he was twelve when (they tell us), he killed his first man.

The boy was Billy the Kid. This is his story.

*   *   *

William H. Bonney, II, was born in a tenement in New York on November 23, 1859. When he was three, his parents left the slums and went out West to Coffeyville, Kansas. Mr. Bonney died and his pretty Irish widow moved on to Colorado. There she married William Antrim, who worked in the mines and dreamed of a strike of his own, and they settled in Silver City, New Mexico.

There were no schools in the raw boom town in 1871. Left to himself while his mother ran a boarding house, Billy got his education in the mud-caked streets. Wide-eyed, the little boy heard men talking in awed tones about somebody named Jesse James, the Border Bandit. There were remarkable stories coming out of war-torn Missouri about the young desperado's bank raids. The most magnificent of the outlaw sagas was solidly on its way as young Bonney took the plunge that in time would place his name alongside the James boys' in American folklore.

The only account of Billy's introduction to violence comes out of Pat F. Garrett's *Authentic Life of Billy the Kid*, published one year after the lanky sheriff had killed

Billy the Kid.
He was right handed and carried his
pistol on his right hip.

Mrs. William Antrim, mother of Billy the Kid.

William Henry Harrison Antrim, stepfather of Billy (from a photograph taken at the portal of the Confidence Mine in New Mexico in the 1890's).

the boy. Ash Upson, the itinerant newspaperman who wrote the 25-cent pamphlet for Garrett, roomed with the Antrims in New Mexico, and this is the way he described the incident that set Billy among the frontier's castoffs:

A street-corner 'blackguard' insulted Mrs. Antrim. Billy punched him and reached for a rock. The man set out after him, but Ed Moulton stepped in and floored the bully. Three weeks later Moulton was fighting two men in a saloon when the bully went for him with a bar stool. Armed with a pen knife, Billy rushed in, leaped on the bully's back, and stabbed him to death. Then he fled— the beginning of the long flight that didn't end until he walked into Garrett's ambush in Pete Maxwell's darkened bedroom in Fort Sumner nine years later.

There is no way to find out what really happened between then and the time the ungainly, buck-toothed boy turned up in Lincoln County to play out the flamboyant role upon which his real celebrity rests. The legend that Billy killed at least one man for each of his twenty-one years ("not counting Indians and Mexicans") springs entirely from the Garrett-Upson accounts of his feats during the missing years. Upson was an imaginative writer, and Garrett had an understandable reason for investing Billy with all kinds of derring-do. The more garish the youth's skills and the more notches on his guns, the more bold would seem the sheriff's act of killing him. Garrett was sensitive; people were saying he had shot down a mere boy. He made the boy a man of massive stature as outlaws go.

"The truth, in the life of young Bonney, needs no pen dipped in blood to thrill the heart and stay its pulsations," said Garrett's introduction. ". . . This verified history of the Kid's exploits, with all the exaggeration removed, will exhibit him as the peer of any fabled brigand on record, unequaled in desperate courage, presence of mind in danger, devotion to his allies, generosity to his foes,

gallantry, and all the elements which appeal to the holier emotions . . ."

Gaudy as it was, Garrett's portrait was topped almost half a century later by Walter Noble Burns in *The Saga of Billy the Kid,* a piece of purple prose that made the slumbering legend soar. Burns embellished the boy's more dubious exploits and put some frills on the real ones.

The legend of the earlier years sets Billy forth as a fearless gunslinger, dead shot, superb horseman, and polished gambler—all in the knee-pants stage. Three weeks out of Silver City, he massacres a trio of Apaches from the Chiracahua Reservation in Arizona for their mounts, weapons, and furs. In Camp Bowie, he kills a Negro blacksmith either for holding out on card losses or calling him "Billy Goat." His "lightning-rapidity, iron nerve and marvelous skill" account for the sudden exits of Mexican monte dealers in Sonora and Chihuahua; they tried to cheat him. Teamed with Jesse Evans—"young knights," in Upson's words—he rescues a party of Texans beleaguered by Mescalero Apaches. The score: eight dead Indians, our wounded hero destroying some of them with a prairie ax after his shooting iron is blasted out of his hand. In the Guadalupe Mountains, Billy takes on "twenty well-armed savages" with only a six-gun and a dirk between himself and eternity. He sends two Indians to the Happy Hunting Grounds, outwits the rest, and comes away without a hair out of place.

Is all this good or bad? In the Garrett-Upson chronicle, none of the bloodletting alters the fact that Billy was ever "polite, cordial and gentlemanly," wore a smile even in his "most savage and dangerous moods" and cursed only in "the most elegant phraseology."

So there is Garrett's Billy in the lost years—a curious mixture of darling and desperado of the Old West. Only seventeen, he had fifteen supposed killings to his credit when he made his triumphant return to New Mexico.

John Chisum.

WAR IN LINCOLN COUNTY

Lincoln County in the '70's covered 27,000 square miles of rich grazing land untouched by the railroad, the barbed-wire fence, or effective law 'n order. Most of it was in the public domain. Cattlemen flocked to the free grass. So did the badmen whom neighboring Texas was driving out—rustlers, gamblers, thieves, and murderers. Thus, typically, southeastern New Mexico became a last outpost for the honest settler and the gunslinger at the same moment.

The trouble started in the summer of 1876. The nesters and small cowmen charged that John S. Chisum, called the Cattle King of New Mexico, was monopolizing the great Pecos Valley range. They said his vast herds, up from Texas, were enveloping their stock. Chisum in turn accused the independents of rustling. In time the long-simmering conflict burst into a much broader fight, with control of the territorial county seat at stake as the winning faction's prize.

When the battle lines finally were drawn, there were on one side Major L. G. Murphy and J. J. Dolan, backed by United States Attorney Thomas B. Catron and the so-called "Santa Fe Ring," and on the other hand Alexander A. McSween and his British partner, John H. Tunstall, backed by Chisum. The sprawling Murphy & Dolan mercantile and banking operation dominated Lincoln until McSween and Tunstall set up the only rival enterprises.

Billy the Kid alternately hired out to each side. The deeper implications of the struggle had no meaning for him. He came in with the Murphy-Dolan forces, recruited by Jesse Evans, Jim McDaniels, Billy Morton, and Frank Baker—the "Seven Rivers Warriors." They used to raid Chisum's Jinglebob brand for some of the beef Murphy needed to furnish the Indians under the fat government contracts he held through his political connections.

THE GUNS GO OFF

Somewhere along the line, when he was riding for Major Murphy in the Lincoln County War, Billy the Kid met John Tunstall and switched to his side. Picture the pair: a rough, untamed, homeless child of the frontier in dusty cowpuncher's gear; a cultured English gentleman in imported tweeds. A boy wrangling a living as a paid gunhand; a man of genteel origin come West to invest his capital. Adventurer and entrepreneur from worlds apart, cast together in a strange alliance in strife-torn, turbulent New Mexico.

The Kid went to work on Tunstall's ranch on the Rio Feliz. A strong bond developed between them, and then—heralded by gunfire—the great drama began.

On February 18, 1878, Tunstall was murdered by a posse led by Billy Morton and Frank Baker. The posse, deputized by Sheriff William Brady to seize some Tunstall stock claimed by Murphy, intercepted the Englishman on the road between his ranch and Lincoln. Evans shot him as he dismounted and tendered his pistol and Morton fired another bullet into his head as he hit the ground. It was a senseless deed.

The Kid was deeply affected. Tunstall was the one influence-for-good in his life. "He was the only man that ever treated me like I was free-born and white," Billy had said. And Tunstall had told George Coe, who rode with the Kid: "That's the finest lad I ever met. He's a revelation to me every day and would do anything on earth to please me. I'm going to make a man out of that boy yet."

Curiously, Tunstall did make a man of Billy—by dying, that is, for his violent exit marked the Kid's transformation from rustler to killer in Lincoln. Miguel Antonio Otero, one-time territorial governor who wrote *The Real Billy the Kid*, said that as the Englishman's body was lowered into the grave, Billy swore: "I'll get every son-of-a-bitch who helped kill John if it's the last thing I do." Coe was more genteel. He quoted Billy: "I never expect

John Tunstall.

to let up until I kill the last man who helped kill Tunstall, or die in the act myself."

Lincoln County had a shooting war on its hands from that moment on.

Morton and Baker were dead within a month. Captured by a posse led by Tunstall's foreman, Dick Brewer, who had been sworn in as a special constable on the insistence of Alexander McSween, the slain cattleman's partner, they bit the dust at Dead Man's Hole on the road from Roswell to Lincoln. Pat Garrett said that Billy the Kid shot his old playmates for trying to escape. In this version, Billy's vaunted marksmanship is again underscored: "Twice only his revolver spoke, and a life sped at each report."

There was one other casualty—soft-hearted William McCloskey, a Brewer lieutenant, who had told Morton and Baker that "they will have to kill me first if they kill you two boys." Frank McNab, another posseman, obligingly met that condition and Billy did the rest in his self-appointed role as Tunstall's avenger, as Garrett told it.

Brewer himself was next. He died leading his braves in an effort to haul in a one-man regiment known as Andrew L. (Buckshot) Roberts, a suspected Murphy-Dolan partisan. The doughty Roberts, badly wounded by the posse but blasting away with a powerful Sharp's buffalo rifle from the unwholesome sanctuary of an outhouse at Blazer's Sawmill, shot Charlie Bowdre and George Coe, killed Brewer, and routed the whole delegation, including Billy, before he cashed in.

Now in charge, with Brewer gone, the Kid's first order of business was the assassination of Sheriff Brady, a Murphy man, and his deputy, George Hindman. This deed aroused the whole state. Within a week, the Kid was indicted for murder and Dad Peppin, who succeeded Brady, sent a posse after him.

Sue McSween.

THE THREE-DAY BATTLE

Sheriff Peppin's posse didn't bring in the Kid. Billy came back to Lincoln on his own and barricaded his fourteen-man outlaw force in the Alexander McSween mansion for what turned out to be the climactic fight of the Lincoln County War. On July 17, 1878, Dad Peppin and his deputy, Marion Turner, mounted their attack from

The McSween store.

the "Big House," as the Murphy-Dolan store was called. Both sides blasted away from their fortresses across the broiling Plaza for three days and nights without much damage. Then, from nearby Fort Stanton, Lt. Col. Nathan A. M. Dudley marched his troops on the New Mexico county seat, planted a still-shiny Civil War cannon in the road, pointed it at the Kid's weary and greatly outnumbered band—and called on both sides to cease fire.

Billy's side always maintained that this was a partisan gesture (the Colonel was court-martialed for it but cleared) because it enabled the enemy to slip up behind the McSween mansion and set the torch to it. As the fire spread, Billy ordered his men to run for it. Emerging into the night, they faced a withering fire (what was Colonel Dudley doing?). The Bible-toting McSween, unarmed, was killed by cattleman Robert W. Beckwith. Billy in turn killed Beckwith before he himself escaped. In all, there were five casualties on the McSween side and two on the other, but in a way Billy himself was a casualty—deferred, let's say—because the three-day battle set in motion the events that put the relentless Pat Garrett on his trail.

Governor Lew Wallace.

FATEFUL MEETING:

GOVERNOR AND DESPERADO

Echoes of the gunfire in Lincoln Plaza reached all the way to the White House. President Rutherford B. Hayes deposed Samuel B. Axtell and named Lew Wallace Governor of New Mexico. Wallace, whose larger fame was to rest on *Ben Hur,* then in the writing, was sent in to sweep the territory free of political dirty-dealing and outlawry. The Governor declared an amnesty for the warriors in embattled Lincoln, provided that every man lay down his arms, but it wasn't quite broad enough to take in Billy the Kid. The amnesty excluded persons then under indictment. Billy had the murder of Sheriff Brady hanging over his head, and a new one, too. Morris J. Bernstein, government clerk on the Mescalero Reservation, had been cut down trying to stop the Kid from appropriating some choice steeds when he turned horse-thief after the Three-Day Battle drove him out of Lincoln.

Billy didn't wait for a fresh manhunt to form under Wallace's rule. He had an idea. On a night's excursion into Lincoln early in '79, he had seen Jim Dolan, Billy Matthews, and William Campbell taunt and finally kill Huston I. Chapman, a one-armed lawyer called into town by Susan McSween to help settle her husband's estate. Now, while it was hardly in the tradition of the Western desperado, the Kid composed a note to the Governor offering to testify against Chapman's slayers in return for his own freedom. Wallace arranged a rendezvous for March 17 at the home of John B. Wilson. This is the way Irving McKee described the opening of the oddly historic session in his biography, *"Ben Hur" Wallace:*

At 9 P.M., the time designated, Wallace heard a knock and called out, "Come in." The door swung slowly open and there stood the Kid, a Winchester in his right hand and a revolver in his left. He was a mere boy in years and appearance—nineteen, five feet seven, thin, light-haired, blue-eyed. This was the terrible Kid, companion of thieves and murderers . . . ruthless killer . . .

"I was sent for," said the Kid pleasantly, "to meet the Governor at nine o'clock. Is he here?"

"I am Governor Wallace."

"Your note gave me a promise of absolute protection."

"Yes, and I have been true to my promise." Wallace pointed to Wilson and added: "This man (Wilson), whom of course you know, and I are the only persons in the house."

The Kid put down his arms and a fast deal was made. Billy would submit to a fake arrest, so it would not look like a surrender. He would testify in the Chapman case. And the Governor would let him go "scot free with a pardon in your pocket for all your misdeeds."

Before the month was out, Billy strolled into Lincoln, laid aside his armor, and got arrested. He was confined in the cellar-like jail but, much in the manner of the big-city prosecutor, the Governor reasoned that his star witness might talk more freely in more pleasant surroundings. Thereafter the Kid was kept in the Patron store. Handcuffs rattled on his thin wrists but he had a nice choice of foods, cigars, liquors, and other diversions to help him while away the hours. This tasty recipe, then as now, usually works.

The Kid not only went before the Grand Jury in the Chapman slaying but also developed such a wagging tongue that he was able to furnish the Governor with "the names and misdeeds of numerous badmen," as Wallace recalled it. This is an item never mentioned by the writers of dime novels, TV and movie thrillers, or other forms of spotless folklore about W. H. Bonney, for it hardly befits the gay young desperado to turn state's evidence in high, piping tones. It spoils the script.

As it happened, nothing came of the deal. With his own trial near, Billy lost faith in Wallace's promises and rode off as casually as he had come in. He went back to the sanctuary of Fort Sumner, ninety miles away, where he had many friends.

BILLY THE KID.

$500 REWARD.

I will pay $500 reward to any person or persons who will capture William Bonny, alias The Kid, and deliver him to any sheriff of New Mexico. Satisfactory proofs of identity will be required.

LEW. WALLACE,
Governor of New Mexico.

PAT GARRETT ON THE TRAIL

Patrick Floyd Garrett was born in Alabama and brought up in Louisiana. He quit school in his late teens —they said he couldn't get his gangling legs under the low desks—and headed for the Western plains. He worked as a cowhand in Texas, hunted buffalo in the Panhandle, and then drifted into New Mexico. In Fort Sumner he wrangled horses for Pete Maxwell, son of the great landholder, Lucien B. Maxwell, and came to know a lad named W. H. Bonney, now and then a Maxwell hand himself.

Pat, twenty-eight, and Billy, nineteen, did some drinking and gambling together and came to be known as "Big Casino" and "Little Casino." The Mexicans had another name for Garrett. They called him "Juan Largo" (Long John), for he looked like a giant to them with his 6'4" frame stretched skyward by high-heeled boots and sombrero. The mustached Southerner's charms did not elude the native girls, either. He married Polinaria Guiterrez and she bore him seven children.

The Kid went off and took up arms in the Lincoln County War while Garrett had a brief experience in a grocery-and-saloon business before law 'n order beck-

oned and he was elected sheriff of Lincoln County late in 1880. The decent elements, tasting peace, reform, and prosperity with Lew Wallace on hand as Governor, deemed Garrett the man most likely to succeed in the hazardous task of turning "Little Casino" face down. Billy supposedly had added two cadavers—Joe Grant and Jimmy Carlyle—to his collection after departing from the Governor's custody while awaiting trial for earlier homicides.

The story of Grant's demise went this way: Grant announced that he had come up from Texas to rid Fort Sumner of the Kid. He let Billy examine his .45 in a moment of drunken exuberance. Billy spun the barrel around to an empty chamber. When it came time to start shooting, Grant's gun didn't go off; the sober Billy's did.

Carlyle's sudden exit came against even greater odds.

Trapped on the Greathouse ranch by a posse hunting his band for stealing some horses from the gold rush town of White Oaks, Billy offered to negotiate a surrender. Carlyle, who knew the Kid, volunteered for the dangerous mission. He died in a hail of lead as he bolted out through a window some hours later. It was never quite clear why he was executed, for there were no further negotiations that day. The posse left without taking Billy, but the more formidable Garrett was looking for him now.

Garrett set a trap in Fort Sumner one night, but the only casualty was the Kid's lieutenant, Tom O'Folliard. Riding at the head of the outlaw band, O'Folliard was killed by the sheriff's posse. Billy and the others got away —until December 21, 1880, when Garrett trailed them

Pat Garrett.

Garrett brings in Billy the Kid.

to Stinking Spring. Barricaded in a deserted farmhouse, the Kid elected to shoot it out. Charlie Bowre was badly hit. Billy pushed him out the door, saying:

"They have murdered you, Charlie, but you can get revenge. Kill some of the sons of b's before you go."

Bowdre never carried out the order. He lunged forward, muttering, "I wish . . . I wish," and then died. In time, starved out and inhaling the sweet aroma of fresh beef frying on Garrett's fire nearby, the Kid surrendered, along with Dave Rudabaugh, Tom Pickett, and Billy Wilson. Rudabaugh, a badman of some note in his own right, was wanted for killing a jailer in Las Vegas, New Mexico. Garrett passed through there with his prisoners on the way to Santa Fe and had to face down an angry mob at the depot, come to collect Mr. Rudabaugh. Here again the Garrett-Upson book points up the Kid's cold courage. It says that when the sheriff warned him that the crowd was in a mood for lynching, the "unconcerned" Kid simply said, "All right, Pat, all I want is a six-shooter."

So there is Billy casually prepared to take on a whole raving-mad mob, armed to the teeth. Does it square with the surrender at Stinking Spring with the hangman's noose surely awaiting him?

"... Until Dead, Dead, Dead"

When Pat Garrett deposited him in Santa Fe's lock-up, Billy the Kid penned a letter to another old friend, Lew Wallace:

"I expect you have forgotten what you promised me, this month two years ago, but I have not, and I think you had ought to come and see me," the boy wrote. "I have done everything that I promised you I would, and you have done nothing that you promised me. . . . I can explain everything to you. . . . I am not treated right by (U. S. Marshal) Sherman. He lets every stranger that comes to see me through Curiosity (sic) in to see me, but will not let a single one of my friends in, not even an Attorney. I guess they mean to send me up without giving me any show, but they will have a nice time doing it. I am not intirely (sic) without friends.

The Governor was unmoved. He simply called in the press and released his earlier correspondence with the Kid. The deal they had made in '79 called for Billy to turn state's evidence in a murder case against some of his enemies in Lincoln and then go "scot free" after standing trial himself. The Kid had neglected to wait for his own day in court. Wallace put it all on the record lest loose charges of double-dealing fill the New Mexican air. He said he would do nothing to help Billy now.

Shackled in a cart, the outlaw was taken to Mesilla to stand trial in the death of Buckshot Roberts, but that indictment was thrown out on a technicality and he was tried instead for the ambush murder of Sheriff William Brady. George R. Bowman, clerk of the court, left this vivid account of the proceedings:

Tom Pickett, who with Billy and two others surrendered to Pat Garrett at Stinking Spring (as he appeared 65 years later).

In the squalid little adobe courthouse of La Mesilla the trial began. Day after day it dragged out until a week had passed. The courtroom was crowded with a motley array of spectators, blanketed Indians, swarthy Mexicans and cowpunchers, rough and unshaven, from the wind-swept mesas of New Mexico. In the back of the room sat the judge, behind an old fashioned flat-top desk which was on a raised platform. In front of the desk was a small clearance where the lawyers came to make their pleas. Rough wooden benches were provided for the spectators. And there, sitting a little to one side of the judge's desk, was Billy the Kid.

Rather pleasant looking was Billy, wavy hair, dark eyes, sullen and defiant, but looking as though they were made for laughter and sunshine and the reflection of the happy smiles of children. There was the mark of a keen intellect in the forehead and the clean cut sweep of the jaw, but there was the mark of brutishness in his face, too, a coarseness stamped across his features.

There was Billy the Kid, on trial for his life—twenty-one and proudly boasting he had killed twenty-one men. And all about him sat men with guns on their hips. It looked almost ridiculous, all those armed men sitting around a harmless looking youth with the down still on his chin.

As a further precaution, Billy the Kid was kept handcuffed during the trial. He was a dangerous man and the court was taking no chances.

Billy was found guilty on April 8. In one version of the story, as Judge Warren Bristol condemned him to be hanged by the neck until "you are dead, dead, dead," the Kid in turn angrily suggested that the jurist "go to hell, hell, hell." The chances are that Billy didn't say that but he was bitter. The *Mesilla News* quoted him:

"If mob law is going to rule, better dismiss judge, sheriff, etc., and take all chances alike. I expect to be lynched."

He said he felt the governor should pardon him because "it's wrong that I should be the only one to suffer the extreme penalties of the law." Nobody else ever had faced the gallows in the multitude of crimes committed under the banners of the Lincoln County War. Indeed Billy and Jim Dolan—declared innocent in the wanton murder of Huston I. Chapman—were the only ones to face a jury.

BILLY BREAKS OUT

Pat Garrett delegated deputies J. W. Bell and Robert W. Ollinger to deliver Billy the Kid from Mesilla to Lincoln to keep his date on the gallows. Bell was a kindly man. Ollinger, a gunthrower in his own right before pinning on the star, had fought on the Murphy-Dolan side in New Mexico's darker days, so he could hardly be expected to strain himself to make his shackled prisoner comfortable. He went right out and bought a splendid new breech-loading shotgun and taunted the condemned youth with suggestions that if he'd just make a run for it, one quick load of buckshot would spare him the long, agonizing ordeal that lay ahead. Billy preferred to wait for the hangman, no doubt a nicer fellow than Ollinger in his view.

Since the rickety Lincoln jail had never been able to hold the strong-minded youth against his will, the Kid was installed on the upper floor of the old Murphy store, then used as a courthouse, but that bastion couldn't keep him either. On April 28, 1881, while the hulking Ollinger was at La Rue's Bar across the street, Billy got a revolver and killed Bell. Garrett, who was away that day shopping for wood for the gallows, said that Billy got Bell to take him down to the latrine, bolted away from him on the stairs going back (this is while wearing leg irons!), shouldered his way into a small room used as an arsenal, armed himself, and shot the deputy as he turned to run for help. Another version is that Billy slipped Bell's Colt out of his holster when he stooped for a card while they were playing casino. A more romantic story is that a Mexican girl who loved him somehow planted the weapon in the outhouse for her "Bilito."

When Ollinger heard the shot, he dashed back to the courthouse. Billy, waiting at a window with the big officer's own shotgun caressed in his manacled hands, called out a cheerful "Hello, Bob!" and let go with both barrels. Ollinger pitched into the dirt and died. The Kid hurled the gun at the body, got a Winchester and two revolvers from the ample Garrett stock, ordered the jail handyman to saddle him up a mount, hacked his leg shackles in two, called out a gay *"Adios, compadres,"* and rode off. Nobody tried to stop him.

The break—fifteen days ahead of the hangman's rope—was the Kid's supreme moment. The *Santa Fe New Mexican,* which had never given Billy a rave notice before,

observed that it was "as bold a deed as those versed in the annals of crime can recall. . . . Never before has he faced death boldly or run any great risk in the perpetration of his bloody deeds. Bob Ollinger used to say that he was a cur, and that every man he had killed had been murdered in cold blood and without the slightest chance of defending himself. The Kid displayed no disposition to correct this until this last act of his when he taught Ollinger by bitter experience that his theory was anything but correct."

Whatever they demonstrated, the twin killings were Billy's last. He had only 77 more days to live.

Lincoln County Courthouse.

THE AMBUSH AT MIDNIGHT

Pat Garrett always spoke of the "glorious moonlight" over New Mexico on July 14, 1881. For the lanky sheriff it was indeed glorious. For Billy the Kid, only twenty-one, it was a blazing neon hung in the heavens to light the way to whatever hell awaited the badmen of the West.

When Billy shot his way out of Garrett's improvised Lincoln jail, the big man with the badge lost large chunks of his prestige along with the two deputies cut down in the remarkable break. So Garrett was deadly earnest when he took to the trail again.

For nearly three months, the hunt led nowhere. Then the scant leads pointed to Fort Sumner and the sheriff rode there with two deputies, John W. Poe and Thomas K. (Tip) McKinney. Garrett reasoned that Pete Maxwell

might know where the Kid was hiding out. He got to the Maxwell place at midnight, stationed Poe and McKinney on the porch outside the bedroom, and went inside.

A moment later, wearing neither hat nor shoes and only half-dressed, a slight, thin-waisted figure came out of the darkness toward the porch. The burly, square-jawed Poe, a bank president in his later years, told it this way in his book, *The Death of Billy the Kid.*

Upon his seeing me, he covered me with his six-shooter as quick as lightning, sprang onto the porch, calling out in Spanish, *"Quien es?"* (Who is it?)— at the same time backing away from me toward the door through which Garrett only a few seconds before had passed . . . I stood up and advanced

The fence which shields Billy's grave.

toward him, telling him not to be alarmed, that he should not be hurt; and still without the least suspicion that this was the very man we were looking for. As I moved toward him trying to reassure him, he backed into the doorway of Maxwell's room, where he halted for a moment . . . and asked in Spanish for the fourth or fifth time who I was . . .

Billy was turning and still calling out *"Quien es?"*—now addressing the urgent inquiry to Maxwell—when Garrett's Colt exploded twice. The first bullet crashed into the Kid just above his heart. The second went wild. Garrett had carried out the execution from a sitting position at the head of the terrified rancher's bed. The chances are that Billy never saw the big peace officer in the pitch black chamber. For that matter, Garrett couldn't be sure he was shooting at the boy he wanted. He conceded that later, although he emerged from the room shouting, "I killed the Kid! I killed the Kid!"

Maxwell bolted out, brushing past Poe. Deluvina Maxwell, the Indian servant girl who was devoted to Billy, was the first to reach the lifeless form on the stone floor. "You didn't have the nerve to kill him face to face!" she screamed at Garrett. The Sheriff's answer, if any, is unrecorded, but he told Emerson Hough twenty-five years later that "I knew now (after Billy broke jail) that I would have to kill the Kid. We both knew that it must be one or the other of us if we ever met." But Deluvina and Jesus Silva, who built the plain wooden coffin for Billy, always insisted that the Kid had nothing but a knife on him. Garrett's story was that Billy was spending the night with a Mexican friend—was it a girl-friend?—and had taken care to fortify himself with a six-gun as well as the necessary silverware when he came over to Maxwell's to cut himself a piece of beef for a midnight snack.

But for the formal record, Garrett added some details. His report to Governor Wallace said:

It was my desire to have been able to take him alive, but his coming upon me so suddenly and unexpectedly leads me to believe that he had seen me enter the room, or had been informed by someone of the fact; and that he came there armed with a pistol and knife expressly to kill me if he could. Under that impression I had no alternative but to kill him, or suffer death at his hands.

(*If Billy knew his mortal enemy was in the bedroom, would he back into the trap, a perfect target framed in a full moon? Would he go in after encountering two armed strangers on the porch? Would he take them all on?*)

The coroner's jury called Garrett's act "justifiable homicide."

Deluvina and the others dressed Billy in a borrowed white shirt that was much too big for him and buried him. The Indian girl put a wooden cross over the grave and scrawled on it the legend: *"Duerme bien, Querido"* (Sleep well, beloved).

The cross with the eloquent farewell didn't last long. Souvenir hunters carried it away. Now Billy lies in a common grave between farmers' fields in Old Fort Sumner with Tom O'Folliard and Charlie Bowdre alongside him. A stone marker bearing the inscription, "Pals," and the names and dates, identifies the grave and a high wire fence protects it against the raids of the curious. It is the only enclosure that ever held the Kid.

Sallie Chisum, daughter of John Chisum.

66

Billy.

THE BOY WHO NEVER GREW OLD

How bad was Billy? If John Tunstall hadn't been murdered, would the Kid have turned out differently? Padre Redin, in Anton Chico, said that "Billy didn't have a bad heart; most of his crimes were crimes of vengeance." Sallie Chisum, John Chisum's daughter, remembered Billy as "the pink of politeness . . . as courteous a little gentleman as I ever met." George Coe said Billy was as nice as any "college-bred youth and with his humorous and pleasing personality got to be a community favorite. In fact, Billy was so popular there wasn't enough of him to go around."

Indeed, there isn't enough of him to go around now.

He is Billy the Kid, killer, and Billy the Kid, avenging angel. He is Billy the Kid, desperado, and Billy the Kid, pride of the Southwest. He is Billy the Kid, filled with hate, and Billy the Kid, singer of sad ballads (they said "Silver Threads among the Gold" was his favorite). He is Billy the Kid, lying in ambush, and Billy the Kid, afraid of no man and gaily dancing under the bright stars with his favorite señorita. He is Billy the Kid, handsome, dashing and manly, and Billy the Kid, ugly, weasel-eyed, and effeminate.

What was he, really?

He was a runaway boy on a man's frontier in a brawling, lusty time. His father faded out of the picture when he was an infant. His stepfather was a stranger. His mother, laden with care, couldn't have showered much attention on him. He grew up—if you can say that—by himself. He must have known real hardship in the years he roamed the plains, from twelve to seventeen, before he came to Lincoln County. He had no roots . . . New York, Kansas, Colorado, New Mexico, Arizona, Texas, Mexico, and back to New Mexico . . . He had been everywhere and nowhere and only once came close to finding the father he must have missed. "John Tunstall always treated me fair," he said.

A case can be made for the argument that Billy was nothing more than a delinquent, Wild West style, before the murder of Tunstall by Murphy-Dolan gunmen touched off Lincoln County's shooting war. You start by throwing out the dead Indians and Mexicans strewn through the hair-raising paperback that Ash Upson ghosted for Pat Garrett. *The Authentic Life of Billy the Kid,* springboard

for the whole legend, would have us believe that even in his early teens the boy possessed the necessary skills to roam the plains nonchalantly killing grown men. The Indians were crafty fighters. As for Billy's Mexican victims, it is hard to imagine an adolescent so richly endowed that he deals monte to seasoned gamblers below the border, wins at will, and casually shoots down the bad losers who cheat.

What's left in the portrait of the Kid? Garrett put down as his first victims a street-corner bully in Silver City (when Billy was twelve) and then a Negro soldier in Camp Bowie. No verification exists in either case. For the four violent years after the fugitive's return to New Mexico, Garrett named eleven men as having fallen before Billy's blazing six-gun. The preceding pages recite each of these episodes. Let's examine the collection more critically now.

We don't know about Joe Grant, the Fort Sumner casualty. That could have been an invention. We don't know about Joe Bernstein, the Indian Agency clerk who perished trying to stop Billy from stealing some government horses. Maurice Garland Fulton, the leading authority on Lincoln County's history, says the evidence indicates that a trigger-happy Mexican in Billy's band shot Bernstein. We don't know about Jimmy Carlyle, Sheriff William Brady, Deputy George Hindman, or Buckshot Roberts, because they all died in the fire from many weapons; it is too much to believe that it was always Billy's unerring eye that guided the fatal bullet.

You come down, then, to five—Billy Morton and Frank Baker, who paid with their young lives for the Tunstall slaying; Bob Beckwith, a casualty of the Three-Day Battle at Lincoln; and Deputies J. W. Bell and Bob Ollinger, Billy's jail guards. But if Morton and Baker did try to escape when they were being brought in after Tunstall's death, wouldn't the whole posse have opened fire on them? Would Billy, on a bucking pony, be able to

put two fatal slugs into two plunging horsemen with but two shots from the clumsy, erratic firearm of the '70's? It is unlikely. In Beckwith's case, the evidence indicates that Billy did kill him, although there were other guns blazing the night the Kid's band burst out of the flaming McSween mansion. As for Bell and Ollinger, there's no doubt at all: Billy had no help when he laid them out to break his date with the hangman.

What's left? You have three sure kills among the **eleven** fatalities in which Billy was demonstrably involved. The Kid's true toll lies somewhere between those two **numbers**.

So the legend of twenty-one men for his twenty-one years ("not counting Indians and Mexicans") **doesn't** wear well at all on the boy who never grew old. **He did** spill his share of blood into the soil of the Wild West. Say that for the maverick called Billy the Kid.

POSTSCRIPT: NO GLORY FOR GARRETT

What happened to Pat Garrett after his smoking Colt put away Billy the Kid?

First, he lost his badge. The Democratic political powers in Lincoln County, perhaps not happy about the way the sheriff had killed Billy in ambush, denied Garrett renomination. John W. Poe, who had helped him track Billy down, was elected in his place.

Then there was the unfinished business of the $500 reward. Governor Lew Wallace's proclamation had offered the bounty to "any person or persons who will capture William Bonny (the poster spelled the name wrong), alias The Kid, and deliver him to any sheriff of New Mexico." Having delivered Billy dead, Garrett had to hire a lawyer and finally go to Santa Fe and do his own lobbying to get the State Legislature to pass a special act so he could collect.

Garrett's career thereafter was spotty. He went into the cattle business in Fort Stanton for a while. Then Sheriff Jim East of Tascosa asked him to head a company of Home Rangers hunting down rustlers in the Canadian River country. Garrett served a year and left to become cattle boss for Captain Brandon Kirby, an English stockman in Lincoln County.

In this interlude a sudden distaste for gunplay showed itself. Garrett ruled that no Kirby hand could carry a six-shooter. The men resented the order. There were suggestions that the ex-sheriff was afraid some cowboy with a sentimental attachment for the long-gone Billy might take a shot at him.

Garrett quit Kirby in '86 and went into ranching in Roswell. Then he failed in a land irrigation project in the Pecos Valley, ran for sheriff of Chaves County, lost, and

William Antrim, in his later years.

George Coe, who rode with Billy the Kid in New Mexico, shown as he appeared in 1941.

Pat Garrett, John W. Poe, James Brent, sheriffs of Lincoln County, 1877 to 1881.

Theodore Roosevelt, who appointed Garrett Collector of Customs at El Paso.

decided to try his hand at breeding horses in Uvalde, Texas. There he became friendly with John Nance (Cactus Jack) Garner, then in his thirties and a long way from the political prominence that was to make him Vice-President in the first two White House terms of Franklin Delano Roosevelt. With Garner's help, Garrett got elected a County Commissioner and settled down for a long, uneventful stay in Uvalde. In '97 friends in Dona Ana County got him to come back to New Mexico and run for sheriff. He served one term, turned to ranching at Las Cruces, and then wangled an appointment from President Teddy Roosevelt—TR adored the Western law 'n order breed—as collector of the customs at El Paso. He served four years and went back to raising blooded horses again.

Then came the row that cost him his life. Garrett leased his property in the Organ Mountains to a young rancher, Wayne Brazil, and then tried to get him off the property. Brazil wouldn't go. On February 29, 1908, the two met on the road to Las Cruces. There was a fierce argument and Garrett, fifty-four and gray-haired, started to get out of his wagon. Brazil shot him in the head. Carl Adamson, who was with Garrett, pleaded "Don't shoot him again," but Brazil fired another bullet into the dying man's stomach as the giant form tumbled into a sand pit.

The rancher's defense was that Garrett was coming at him with a shotgun and he had to fire to save himself. It was a half-hearted prosecution and he was speedily acquitted.

Garrett was buried in Las Cruces as one friend intoned the celebrated eulogy the agnostic Robert Green Ingersoll had written for his own brother and another kept the balance by reading from a deeply religious oration by William Jennings Bryan. The famous sheriff's grave is unmarked today. There is no tombstone and no monument and no steel fence to keep away the souvenir hunters —the way it is with Billy the Kid over in Old Fort Sumner.

John N. (Cactus Jack) Garner, friend of Pat Garrett.

CLAY ALLISON, FOR REAL

One of the TV and comic-book heroes today is Clay Allison, hard-ridin', square-dealin' frontier marshal. He reaches for his .45 only when some damn fool outlaw has "drawed" on him. He prefers to use his own two fists and bring the culprit in and let the courts in their wisdom deal with him.

What are the facts? Clay Allison was a quick-tempered, quick-triggered, hell-raising alcoholic killer. He left a trail of men dead in senseless gunplay in the West. *That* was the real Clay Allison.

Tennessee-born, our hero turned up on the Washita in New Mexico in the '70's as a cowman. In the towns he terrorized thereafter he was a striking figure: 6' tall, black frock-coat with tails, white shirt with shoe-string tie, gleaming black boots, wide-brimmed sombrero, chin whiskers, and the usual square jaw and steel blue eyes credited to all the he-men of the West. In no time at all, people took note of Clay Allison. There were some awesome stories.

Clay Allison dispenses his own prairie justice: two brothers suspected of rustling his steers vanish from the range. "No horse or cattle-thief could live within reach of Clay's gun," a biographer said. And there's some social justice, too: a Las Vegas quack pulls the wrong aching tooth. The pain only mildly soothed with whiskey, Allison goes back and extracts four of the quack's molars.

Then there's some plain harmless horseplay in Texas and nobody hurt. Naked but for boots, ten-gallon hat, and gunbelt, Allison charges down from College Hill on a black steed and shoots up the little town of Canadian. Then he sobers up and dresses.

There's some brawling, too. In Las Animas, Colorado, Clay and his brother John "hurrah" the local dance emporium. Sheriff John Spear and Deputy Charles Faber arrive to restore order. The Allisons won't put down their .45's. Faber unloads a shotgun burst into John Allison's arm, whereupon Clay kills the deputy.

And there's some sporting fun: over on the Red River station, Chunk Colbert lets it be known that he means to destroy Allison. The two meet at the Clifton House for dinner. The coffee is stirred with the muzzles of their .45's (it says here). Colbert's right hand comes off the table. Allison tips his chair backward, firing as he drops out of range. The bullet strikes Colbert between the eyes. Allison rights his chair and finishes his dinner—so the tale goes—as the body is removed.

And there's the sudden death of Francisco (Pancho) Griego in Cimarron. In the familiar pattern, he boasts that he will kill Allison. Pancho dies over a friendly drink in Lambert's Bar, shot three times as he fans himself with his sombrero. Why? Well, it was winter and no time for fanning; Clay suspected Pancho was going for his revolver with his free hand.

There are other stories, too, some perhaps doubtful, some clearly wearing too much Sunday prose. There are stories of Clay Allison "facing down" Bat Masterson and tangling with Wyatt Earp. Well, the bad boy from the Washita might have taken on anyone in the West—so long as the liquor supply held out.

In time Allison was credited with fifteen victims, but by then this kind of fame appalled him. When a St. Louis newspaper cited his string in 1880, Allison protested that the report was "extremely false" and added that any blood he did spill was for the purpose of "protecting the property holders and substantial men of the country from thieves, outlaws, and murderers . . ." Once before he had said, "I never killed nary a feller what didn't need it."

Allison died with his boots on, but not in the story-book way. Riding to his ranch, roaring drunk, he fell out of his buckboard and a rear wheel broke his neck. The accident probably saved a life, because Clay had written his brother that he was coming out to kill an in-law, John McCullough, for saying some nasty things about him. The end came on a bright July day in '77. Allison was thirty-seven. The *Ford County Globe* gave him a nice send-off:

> *Clay Allison knew no fear. To incur his enmity was equivalent to a death sentence. He contended that he never killed a man willingly but out of necessity.*

Maybe that's where the writin' fellas of our time got the idea that "Marshal" Clay Allison was a model citizen of the frontier.

Clay Allison at 26.

THE RENO BROTHERS

Frank Reno.

It was bitterly cold that night of December 11, 1868, and the good people of Seymour, Indiana, burrowed sleepily under their blankets as the wind rushed through the streets. At midnight men suddenly began to appear singly and in pairs. They hurried on their way, disappearing now and then in the shadows cast by the bare-branched trees in the front yards. Each man carried a six-shooter, a rifle, club, or Navy Six strapped to his middle, and wore a long flapping scarlet mask. A few, obviously leaders, with numbers chalked on their jackets turned inside out, lined the men up in single file as they arrived at the Seymour depot where a train had just arrived. Then the men entered the coaches, one by one.

The last man climbed the telegraph pole. Moonlight glinted on his shears. There was a loud twang as the wires were cut. In his cab, the engineer was given his orders: "No headlights. Disconnect the bell cord and whistle."

In a few minutes the train chugged out of the Seymour depot to stop fifty miles south of Seymour at the Jeffersonville station. There the engineer of another train was overpowered and the masked men took over the train and continued their journey. At 3:20 A.M. the train pulled into the New Albany, Indiana, station, and the leaders with the chalked numbers whispered the orders to their men, to line up, close up, and march up the street.

A rider rode up to the depot to report: "The lines are cut."

"Number One" replied: "Good." Then, raising his voice slightly, he called out, *Salus Populi Suprema Lex!*

The masked men echoed him. Then Number One raised his hand and pointed up the street. The strange army of men with long, flapping scarlet masks marched briskly up the street.

They were on their way to lynch the Reno gang, imprisoned in the stout New Albany, Indiana, jail. One of the bloodiest incidents in American history was about to begin.

* * *

The plan of the Indiana vigilante movement to lynch the Reno brothers was a coldly calculated scheme to eliminate one of America's worst bands of outlaws. It was the climax of a steady war fought between honest men and outlaws who had terrorized, murdered, plundered, and corrupted the state.

The Reno brothers, Frank, John, Simeon, Clinton, and William Reno, had begun their career in outlawry immediately after the Civil War, from which they had emerged as expert bounty jumpers. When the Renos returned home to Jackson County, they found that the burned-out town of Rockford had become a hangout for the lawless. In Seymour confidence men swindled returning veterans of their pay, while armed bands of murderers and outlaws rode the countryside, killing, looting, and plundering at will. The Renos consolidated the individual gangs in an organized band which soon controlled the southern part of the state. The state attorney admitted it was an "alarming" situation but did nothing about it. Counterfeiting became a sideline for the gang and Peter McCartney, one of the most skillful of all counterfeiters, supplied the Renos with spurious bills, which soon flooded the countryside.

As the *Seymour Times* sadly commented, "Seymour has a carnival of crime." As the months passed, honest citizens began to murmur and there was talk of forming vigilante committees.

On October 6, 1866, the Reno gang, led by John Reno, committed the first train robbery in America, if not the world, a few miles from Seymour, Indiana, when they held up the wood-burning Ohio and Mississippi Railroad

Michael Rogers.

71

Adams Express Company advertisement showing a train typical of the period when the Reno Brothers operated.

and robbed the Adams Express car of $10,000. They tried to break open the safe, but were forced to abandon it.

Encouraged by the Renos' success, the other young bandits held up another train, getting $8,000 from the Adams Express car, but this trespassing enraged the Renos, who organized their own posse of outlaws and captured the two rivals, whom they turned over to the law.

A short time later the Renos moved into Jesse James' home state of Missouri to rob the Daviess County Treasury of $22,065. The Pinkertons, who protected the Adams Express Company, then took up the trail of the Reno gang. Through a ruse, Allan Pinkerton and "six muscular men from Cincinnati" whisked John Reno off the Seymour railroad depot platform under the eyes of his men and took him to Missouri to stand trial for the robbery.

Frank Reno commandeered a special train, loaded his outlaws aboard, and attempted to head off Pinkerton's train, but at Quincy, Illinois, he "missed connections" and failed to save his brother, who was convicted and sentenced to forty years at hard labor.

The rest of the brotherhood continued their lawless way, and in the winter of 1868 Frank led his riders in a raid on the Harrison County Bank in Magnolia, Iowa, stealing $14,000, which the local newspaper called a "public calamity."

Pinkerton, through dogged police work, managed to capture the entire gang at Council Bluffs, but they escaped from jail on the morning of April, 1868, leaving behind a large hole in the wall of the cell, over which they had written in chalk: "April Fool."

The Renos' most famous train robbery took place near Marshfield, south of Seymour, when they held up the Jefferson, Missouri and Indianapolis Railroad train on Friday, May 22, 1868, getting $96,000 in gold and government bonds. The loot almost tripled the proceeds of any train or bank robbery committed by the James-Younger gang.

Pinkerton again took the battle to the outlaw band after he had received information that the gang intended to rob another train near Seymour. Pinkerton juggled the railroad schedules so that the Adams Express car, instead of holding $100,000 in gold as the gang had been informed, held Pinkerton and his posse.

When the robbers forced open the car door, they were hit by revolver fire. The wounded outlaws fled into a swamp and were hunted down by a posse in carriages and on horseback. Mob violence took over the countryside and two members of the gang were lynched after they had been removed from the cells by masked vigilantes.

Shortly after, three more of the outlaw band were taken from the Pinkertons when they missed their special train through circumstances never explained. Forced to transport their prisoners by wagon, the Pinkertons were overpowered by a mob of masked men a few miles west of Seymour. The prisoners were quickly hanged.

William and Simeon Reno were arrested by Pinkerton operatives a few months later, while Allan Pinkerton himself trailed and arrested Frank Reno, Michael Rogers, Miles Ogle, Albert Perkins, and Charles Spencer in Windsor, Canada, which was then as wild and lawless as any Western town.

A bitter international extradition fight followed, while members of other gangs took turns trying to assassinate

Cell block of the New Albany jail from which the Renos and Charlie Anderson were taken to be lynched.

Laura Ellen Reno, who had no part in her infamous brothers' crimes.

Pinkerton. One attempt took place on the Windsor ferry platform. Pinkerton leaped at the hired killer, wrested the six-shooter out of his hand, knocked him unconscious, handcuffed him, carried him onto the ferry boat, and later delivered him to the Detroit police headquarters.

The extradition struggle was marked with several sensational disclosures. Once the Governor-General of Canada announced that Frank Reno had **tried** to bribe his sixteen-year-old son with $6,000 to "influence his father in their behalf."

After weeks of international bickering, President Andrew Johnson signed the extradition documents, which were approved by the British authorities.

Pinkerton and his prisoners in irons started across the river to Detroit in a hired tug, but halfway across to the American side, a steamer cut the tug in two. Outlaws and detectives were thrown into the water. The prisoners, weighed down by their irons and handcuffs, almost drowned, but were supported in the water by the detectives until another tug picked them up.

When the gang finally arrived at the New Albany jail, the vigilantes openly declared they would storm the jail,

while in return the remnants of the Reno gang replied they would "lay Seymour in ashes" if the Renos were lynched.

By October, 1868, the fugitive members of the gang had declared open warfare against the suspected leaders of the Southern Indiana Vigilance Committee. Men were ambushed at night, shot, beaten, horribly mutilated, or subjected to the dread "hanging torture," while messages, "If the Renos are lynched you die," tied to rocks, were flung through the windows of the homes of state and county officials. The whole county was in a state of terror and, as one newspaper said, it was "worth a man's life to be abroad at night with these murderers lurking at every turn."

The incidents increased. On December 7, an engineer who had been shot by the Renos in a July train holdup died of his injuries. The vigilante leaders then acted. Riders pounded along the back roads, men whispered instructions to other men, small scarlet-masked groups gathered by lantern light in barns and sheds. Finally the last orders were passed: December 11, 1868, would be the "night of blood."

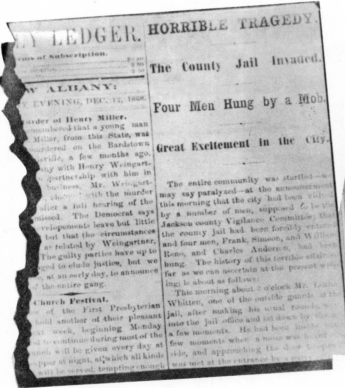

The Reno lynching as reported in the local papers.

Sheriff Fullenlove.

THE NIGHT OF BLOOD

As the scarlet-masked army marched up the street of New Albany in the December moonlight, men designated as flankers and provost marshals hurried through the city picking up citizens on their way home or on the way to work.

After an explanation, they were searched, then escorted

under guard to the darkened train coaches. If they attempted an outcry, they were slugged into unconsciousness.

Meanwhile the masked mob reached the jail. They rushed into the yard, wounding Sheriff Fullenlove and forcing two county commissioners to turn over their cell keys. Ropes were passed from hand to hand to the men who ran up to the second floor. Frank Reno was dragged out, pleading and crying. The noose was slipped over his head and one end tied to an iron beam, and the screaming outlaw tossed into the air. He fell like a stone until the rope jerked tight. There was a loud snap like a man breaking a dry stick over his knee. His body twisted slowly in the light of the lantern held high by the men with the horrible scarlet masks. Frank Reno was dead.

"Number Three and Five get William Reno," Number One shouted.

Cell Seven was opened, and the second brother was dragged out.

"Gentlemen . . . my father . . . oh, protect . . . ," he begged.

The noose choked off his last words. He was hurled over the second-floor rail. His body flopped pitifully, his eyes threatened to pop from his skull as he slowly strangled to death. Then he, too, swung in silence.

Simeon Reno fought to the end. He had wrenched the iron sink from the wall in his cell, with the ferocity of a madman, and used one of its legs as a club. Finally he was

HEADQUARTERS SOUTHERN INDIANA,
VIGILANCE COMMITTEE.
TO THE PEOPLE OF THE UNITED STATES!

"SALUS POPULI SUPREMA LEX."

WHEREAS, it became necessary for this organization to meet out summary punishment to the leaders of the thieves, robbers, murderers and desperadoes, who for many years defied law and order, and threatened the lives and property of honest citizens of this portion of Indiana, and as the late fearful tragedy at New Albany testifies that justice is slow, but sure, we promulgate this our pronunciamento, for the purpose of justifying to the world, and particularly to the people of the State of Indiana, any future action which we may take.

We deeply deplore the necessity which called our organization into existence; but the laws of our State are so defective that as they now stand on the Statute Books, they all favor criminals going unwhipt of justice; a retrospective view will show that in this respect we speak only the truth.

Having first lopped off the branches, and finally uprooted the tree of evil which was in our midst, in defiance of us and our laws, we beg to be allowed to rest here, and be not forced again to take the law into our own hands. We are very loth to shed blood again, and will not do so unless compelled in defence of our lives.

A WARNING,

We are well aware that at the present time, a combination of the few remaining thieves, their friends and sympathizers, has been formed against us, and have threatened all kinds of vengeance against persons whom they suppose to belong to this organization. They threaten assassination in every form, and that they will commit arson in such ways as will defy legal detection. The carrying out in whole, or in part, of each or any of these designs, is the only thing that will again cause us to rise in our own defence. The following named persons are solemnly warned, that their designs and opinions are known, and that they cannot, unknown to us, make a move toward retaliation.

Wilk Reno, Clinton Reno, Trick Reno, James Greer, Stephen Greer, Fee Johnson, Chris. Price, Harvey Needham, Meade Fislar, Mart Lowe, Roland Lee, William Sparks, Jesse Thompson, William Hare, William Biggers, James Fislar, Pollard Able.

If the above named individuals desire to remain in our midst, to pursue honest callings, and otherwise conduct themselves as law abiding citizens, we will protect them always.— If however, they commence their devilish designs against us, our property, or any good citizen of this district, we will rise but *once* more ; do not trifle with us ; for if you do, we will follow you to the bitter end; and give you a "short shrift and a hempen collar." As to this, our actions in the past, will be a guarantee for our conduct in the future.

We trust this will have a good effect. We repeat, we are very loth again to take life, and hope we shall never more be necessitated to take the law into our own hands.

By order of the Committee.

Dec. 21, 1868.

Warning published by the Southern Indiana Vigilance Committee.

clubbed unconscious to the floor, bound, dragged from the cell, and thrown into space.

Charlie Anderson wept and pleaded as the vigilantes dragged him out. He, too, was thrown high in the air, but the noose snapped and he sprawled on the floor, screaming and crying. A second time he was held up to allow another noose to be put about his neck; then he was lowered to strangle slowly to death.

"Any more?" Number One shouted.

"Let's hang them all," someone said.

"No," the leader said. "We did what we came for. Now let us go."

The vigilantes hurried from the jail. Behind them the bodies of the four outlaws slowly twisted in the air.

As the horrified prisoners watched, the body of Simeon Reno came to life. As he opened his bulging eyes, his body began jerking at the end of the rope like a hooked fish. The other prisoners began banging on their cell doors and screaming as Reno fought for his life. As he swayed back and forth his toes barely touched the stone floor. Gradually the pandemonium ceased and with hor-

rified fascination the prisoners watched Reno die b inches. It lasted a half hour; then the twitching body wa quiet.

In the town the mob-army marched to the depot wi perfect military precision, prodding before them one the county commissioners, who was barefoot with an ove coat over his shoulders. As they passed street corners, th makeshift provost patrols fell into line. They all enter the coaches in silence. As the train began moving out the depot, the leader threw the ring of keys to the com missioner.

"Here are your keys. We are sorry we had to shoot th sheriff. Go back and get him a doctor."

Salus Populi Suprema Lex, echoed through the col night as the darkened coaches disappeared down th tracks, leaving the frightened barefoot commission shivering in the bitter cold. Back in the New Albany ja the four bodies were still, and in their cells the othe prisoners pressed their faces to the bars and stared i silence at the dead outlaws.

The Night of Blood was over.

THE FARRINGTON BROTHERS

There is no doubt that the adulation and hero worship bestowed on Jesse James and his gang helped to start at least twenty-five young Missourians on a life of outlawry. Some, like Jesse, were former guerrilla fighters who found the good life after the war too peaceful for their wild ways and, like the James-Younger gang, terrorized small towns on Saturday nights, splintering the store signs with their gunfire and sending the "charcoals," as they called the Republicans, scurrying for cover.

Among the first groups to follow Jesse on the outlaw trail were the Farrington brothers. Levi and Hilary Far-

rington had taken part in the Lawrence, Kansas, massacr with Quantrill and later fought under the Black Flag wit George Todd. They were superb riders, excellent revolve fighters, handsome and daring. Both were bearded, semi illiterate giants.

In 1870 they made their biggest strike when the stopped the Mobile and Ohio Railroad at Union City Tennessee, and robbed the Southern Express Company c $20,000 in cash.

Pat O'Connell, one of the best express company detec tives of his time, and William Pinkerton found the gang i

William Barton and William Taylor, two of the Farrington Brothers' gang.

The fight at Lester's Landing.

heir hideout at Lester's Landing on the Mississippi, a lonely wood-chopping depot deep in the canebreaks. O'Connell was shot in the leg when he and Pinkerton broke into the cabin. The two law officers captured five horse-thieves and fugitives only to learn the Farringtons had left two hours before they arrived.

Pinkerton trailed Hilary to a farmhouse in Verona, Missouri, where the outlaw had holed up, armed with three rifles and enough ammunition for a long siege. Pinkerton, O'Connell, and the county sheriff led a posse to Verona and surrounded the farmhouse. The siege began shortly after dawn.

All day the gunfire echoed in the hills. Farrington ran from window to window, keeping the possemen at a distance. Several were nicked but not seriously wounded. In the end it was a young farm girl, cousin of the outlaw, who persuaded him to surrender.

William Pinkerton and O'Connell handcuffed the outlaw between them and booked passage aboard the stern-wheeler *Illinois* for Union City, Tennessee. But during the night Farrington broke loose and, in a dramatic scene in the moonlight on the deck of the steamboat, fought a fight to the death with Pinkerton. O'Connell, who heard the shouting, ran out in his underwear to see the giant outlaw lose his balance as he tried to brain Pinkerton with the butt of a gun, and slip over the side to be crushed to death in the stern paddle.

Meanwhile other operatives located Levi Farrington in Farmingdale, Illinois, where he had terrorized the town. With two Colts on his hip he swaggered up and down the town square, challenging the townspeople to throw a six-shooter on him. A Pinkerton operative named Brown fought a hand-to-hand battle with him in the square and finally knocked him out. The townspeople wanted to lynch Levi, but Brown held them off at pistol point to save the man he had just knocked out and bring him back to justice.

Levi was delivered safely to Union City, but never stood trial. Night riders broke into the hotel room where the sheriff was guarding him, and lynched him on an elm tree overlooking the main gate of the county cemetery.

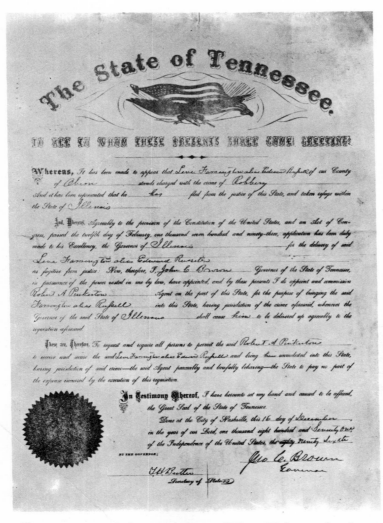

Tennessee governor's commission to Robert Pinkerton for the extradition of Levi Farrington.

HANGOVERS FROM THE GOLD RUSH

While the nation watched the Jesse James saga unfold on the Middle Border, California doggedly hunted down the last of the bandit marauders spawned by the Gold Rush. Tiburcio Vasquez, Dick Barter, Bill Miner and Black Bart deserve some notice here.

Tiburcio Vasquez.

VASQUEZ

Tiburcio Vasquez was small and swarthy and, for a man of his calling, durable. A horse-thief from his teens, he came out of San Quentin in 1870 a veteran of three prison terms determined to enjoy some easy living before the Far West's relentless lawmen caught up with him again.

Vasquez and a ragged assortment of recruits who had managed to escape vigilante nooses robbed stages, stores and wayfarers with fair if not spectacular success, not stirring up too much excitement in their early forays. Then the band wantonly killed three innocent bystanders during a holdup in Tres Pinos, and manhunters spurred by big rewards took out after them.

Bold if not brilliant, Vasquez pressed his reign of terror even while the trail was hot. He took his men into Fresno County and cleaned out a hotel and several stores in Kingston, first taking care to tie up all the male citizens found idling on the main street. This outing was followed by some scattered stage robberies before the outlaws were trailed to a hideaway in the Cahuengas.

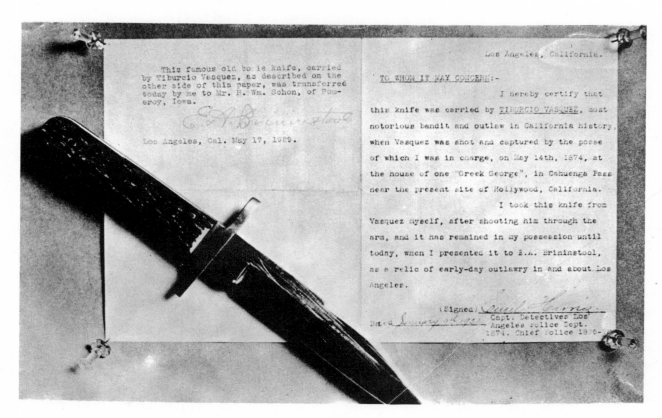

This famous old bowie knife, carried by Tiburcio Vasquez, as described on the other side of this paper, was transferred today by me to Mr. H. Wm. Schon, of Pomeroy, Iowa.

E. A. Brininstool

Los Angeles, Cal. May 17, 1929.

Los Angeles, California.

TO WHOM IT MAY CONCERN:-

I hereby certify that this knife was carried by TIBURCIO VASQUEZ, most notorious bandit and outlaw in California history, when Vasquez was shot and captured by the posse of which I was in charge, on May 14th, 1874, at the house of one "Greek George", in Cahuenga Pass near the present site of Hollywood, California.

I took this knife from Vasquez myself, after shooting him through the arm, and it has remained in my possession until today, when I presented it to E.A. Brininstool, as a relic of early-day outlawry in and about Los Angeles.

(Signed) _____
Date _____ Capt. Detectives Los Angeles Police Dept. 1874. Chief Police 1876-

The delegation that set out to collar the fierce Mexican included George A. Beers, a sharp-shooting reporter from the *San Francisco Chronicle*. Beers fired the shotgun blast that brought the much-wanted bandit down. Justice was swift. Vasquez was tried in San José in January, '75; two months later his life was snuffed out on a gallows imported for that special purpose from Sacramento.

The usual raft of Robin Hood stories flowed from the presses before the body was cold, as with the bloodthirsty Joaquin Murieta before Vasquez, but in our time Joseph Henry Jackson, toiling over the murky record, found nothing in it to bear out the virtues dreamed up for the man. Vasquez was all bad.

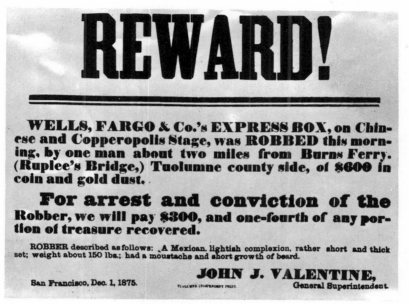

REWARD!

WELLS, FARGO & Co.'s EXPRESS BOX, on Chinese and Copperopolis Stage, was **ROBBED** this morning, by one man about two miles from Burns Ferry, (Ruplee's Bridge,) Tuolumne county side, of **$600** in coin and gold dust.

For arrest and conviction of the Robber, we will pay **$300,** and one-fourth of any portion of treasure recovered.

ROBBER described as follows: A Mexican, lightish complexion, rather short and thick set; weight about 150 lbs.; had a moustache and short growth of beard.

San Francisco, Dec. 1, 1875.   TUOLUMNE INDEPENDENT PRINT.

JOHN J. VALENTINE,
General Superintendent.

From a Wells Fargo reward circular.

RATTLESNAKE DICK

Before the violent Vasquez, California had to dispose of British-born Richard Barter—called Rattlesnake Dick because he prospected briefly at Rattlesnake Bar in the Northern Mines—in the process of maintaining peace and quiet in the gold boom.

While Rattlesnake Dick never made a dime digging for gold or chasing it in the streams, he did dope out a way to pick up $80,000 in one quick stroke. He simply sent George Skinner and some confederates out to intercept a mule train carrying gold down Trinity Mountain from the mines near Yreka. The little band surprised the convoy, disarmed the guards, removed the cumbersome bullion treasure, and set out to keep a rendezvous with Dick and Cy Skinner, who were to meet them with a fresh pack of mules to lug the gold to a safe haven. As it happened, Dick and his sidekick didn't keep the date: they were in the Auburn jail, having got caught stealing some mules!

Without the fresh animals, George Skinner couldn't get all of the treasure down the mountain. He buried half of it —is it still there?—and started for Folsom with the other half. There Wells Fargo sleuths killed him and captured his companions. Thus Rattlesnake Dick never tasted the fruits of his gaudiest accomplishment. After he broke out of jail, he devoted three years to robbing stages, never coming up with anything even faintly resembling $80,000 in bullion. In the summer of '59 he died shooting it out with a trio of lawmen outside of Auburn.

Canada Bill

William Jones, alias Canada Bill, was a swindler and three-card monte shark who operated in California and the Northwest during the 60's and 70's. He worked the Union Pacific trains, but the Pinkertons finally drove him off.

OLD BILL

William ("Old Bill") Miner.

Who used the first recorded command of "Hands up!" in a Western holdup? The man who is supposed to have invented the usage is little known and most bibliographes fail to list him. His name was Bill Miner, "Old Bill," and he held up stage-coaches and trains from Civil War days to as late as 1911, when Pinkerton operative Minster captured him in a Georgia forest. Shortly before his death, he dictated a 30,000-word memoir of his life and adventures, a copy of which is now in the possession of the authors.

The strange story has Miner embarking on a grand tour of Europe, during which he worked with a slave trader supplying women to a Turkish harem, operated as a gun smuggler, as a revolutionist, and one time, in Capetown, South Africa, attempted to hold up a diamond train transporting millions of dollars in gems.

Miner was born in Jackson, Kentucky, in 1847, of a schoolteacher mother and a mining, footloose father who deserted his family before the boy was ten. Bill inherited his father's restlessness. When he was just past thirteen, he ran away to California "to become a cowboy."

He drifted from ranch to ranch working as a cowpuncher and a bullwhacker. In his late years he liked to brag of his skill with a mule team when he was a youngster working in the tough California mining towns.

In 1863 he was in San Diego when the Apaches were on the warpath. General Wright, commanding the Division of the Pacific, announced he would pay $100 to any man who would ride through the Apache-infested country to deliver a message to a Colonel Corner who was stationed in a fort on the Gile River.

Miner, then as thin and slender as a jockey, volunteered and was given a "fast horse and General Wright's God speed." He rode all night, stopping off at the Tehone Ranch near Salt Lake to rest and feed his horse. Then he took off, swimming his horse across the Colorado, to reach the colonel without incident. Within the hour he was back in the saddle, and the following morning rode up to General Wright's headquarters to receive $100 in gold and the general's thanks.

When Miner had set out, several residents of San Diego gave him letters to be delivered to the fort and when Miner reported back that they had been delivered, some gave him $5 and $10 pieces for his trouble. This gave Miner an idea, and with General Wright's blessing he began a one-man mail service from San Diego to the Gile River fort and other points, charging $5, $10, and $25. But as fast as he earned the money, Miner spent it, and before long he was forced to turn over his horses and equipment to creditors.

By this time he had acquired a taste for high living, and the precarious life of a road agent appealed to him. In 1869 he robbed his first stage-coach, near Sonora, getting a few hundred dollars, but a posse captured him when his horse dropped in its tracks. He was convicted of highway robbery and sentenced to fifteen years in San Quentin. Released in 1879, for good behavior, he went to Colorado, where he met Bill Leroy, one of the most daring of Rocky Mountain highwaymen. Together they carried out several train and stage-coach robberies, but then vigilantes set out after them, capturing and hanging Leroy. Miner, however, escaped after shooting three possemen. With the proceeds of the robberies, Miner traveled to San Francisco, where he embarked for London. For several months he toured Europe. Though he denied holding up any trains there, American style, he recalled that he thought about it more than once. In Turkey, he fell in with a sinister-looking Turk who confided to Miner that he was in the slave trade, abducting women of desert tribes and selling them for use in harems. When the Turk asked Miner to become his partner, the Western outlaw agreed and spent several months as a desert raider and slave trader.

After several adventures with desert bandits, Miner left Turkey and continued his travels to North Africa. In Capetown he got the idea of holding up a diamond train, but his better sense prevailed "when I saw they (the guards) would be too much for me."

Reluctantly he left the diamond fields and sailed for South America, settling for a time in Rio de Janeiro, where he engaged in gun running. A South American tour followed, but Miner yearned for the West and in about 1880 he returned to the United States.

It wasn't long before he was back in business as a road agent. On November 8, 1881, he held up the Sonora, California, stage, getting $3,000. When the posses grew hot on his trail, he fled to Colorado, and in November, 1881, held up the Del Norte stage, stealing several thousand dollars in gold dust.

He next appeared in Chicago, where, as a Pinkerton report revealed, "he purchased an outfit of fashionable clothing, and in a few days went to Onondaga, Michigan, under the name of W. A. Morgan, a wealthy man from California.

After losing most of his money across the faro table,

Miner returned to the outlaw trail, this time in the company of a young gunfighter named Stanton T. Jones of Chillicothe, Ohio, "who was the same type as myself."

In March, 1881, they again stopped the Del Norte stage, but the loot this time was only a few hundred dollars. A posse took up the chase and for four days it was a run-and-fight battle through the canyons and gullies. Miner and Jones were excellent shots, and the possemen turned back after three had been shot out of their saddles.

On November 7, 1881, Miner and three other outlaws held up the Sonora stage again. Possemen surrounded the area and despite Miner's fast shooting, the gang was captured. Miner was convicted and sentenced to twenty-five years in San Quentin prison.

On June 17, 1901, he was released for good behavior. But on September 23, 1903, he single-handedly held up a train near Corbett, Oregon. A year later almost to the day, he held up the Canadian Pacific, near Mission Junction, British Columbia, securing $10,000. Rewards totaling $15,500 were offered for Bill, "dead or alive," by the Canadian Pacific, the Canadian government, and the Province of British Columbia. For three years he played his favorite role of "a wealthy man from California," returning to outlawry on May 8, 1906, to hold up the Transcontinental Express of the Canadian Pacific, at Furrer, British Columbia. The Northwest Mounted Police set out to get him, and true to their tradition they brought Old Bill back two months later. On June 1, 1906, he was sentenced to life, and the Canadian Pacific gave a sigh of relief.

"No jail can hold me, sir," Old Bill told the sentencing judge. On the morning of August 9, 1907, he made good his boast by crawling through a thirty-five-foot tunnel under the fence surrounding the brick yard where he was working.

Bill had had enough of Canada and returned to the States. In July, 1909, he held up the Portland, Oregon, Bank, getting $12,000, and three years later, on February 18, 1911, led a five-man gang in a hold-up of the Southern Railroad Express, near White Sulphur, Georgia, to get $3,500.

Bill was now a stoop-shouldered old gentleman with snow-white hair, a large mustache, and a friendly smile. Despite his age, he was still an expert horseman and had retained his shooting eye.

But progress had caught up with Old Bill. News of the robbery clicked out over the telegraph wires to the Pinkerton office and to the local marshals. A posse was organized and Pinkerton operative W. H. Minster, using a map, ringed several swampy areas with possemen, gradually closing in.

Miner and his men were nodding over a small fire when the possemen crawled through the brush.

"Rouse, boys, the law is on us," he shouted to his men as he suddenly jerked awake, alerted by a sense of alarm sharpened by years of practice in eluding the chase.

His men scrambled to their feet. Miner began firing from a kneeling position. The forest echoed with gunfire. Two of Miner's men went down under the fusillade, but Miner kept working his rifle. At last he realized the game was up, and throwing down his rifle, he surrendered.

"Well, I guess you got me, boys," was his comment as Minster snapped on the handcuffs.

"What's your name?" asked the Pinkerton man.

"William Morgan," was the prompt reply.

Minster studied the weatherbeaten old face. "You look familiar to me," he said.

After questioning Miner, he sent the train robber's picture to the main office in Chicago with the notation that the name Morgan was obviously false. William Pinkerton took one look at the picture, then sent a reply back to his operative in Georgia:

"Morgan is Bill Miner, California's train and stage robber. Alias William Morgan, George Anderson, Sam Anderson, California Billy, Old Bill, Budd and G. W. Edwards. Escaped from New Westminster Penitentiary, Victoria, British Columbia."

When Minster showed him the wire, Miner grinned. "That's me," he said.

He was convicted of train robbery and sentenced to life in the Georgia State Penitentiary at Milledgeville. But three times in as many years the old-time outlaw proved that, at least for him, iron bars did not a prison make.

Each time he escaped he was recaptured only a few days later. The last time, after he had walked miles through swamps in waist-deep water, he confided to the guards who had hunted him down with dogs:

"I guess I'm getting too old for this sort of thing."

Miner returned to prison to spend the last three years of his life tending a flower garden and dictating his adventures to a friendly detective who got to like the old thief.

In 1913 he died quietly in his sleep. Newspaper obituaries judged his age anywhere from sixty-five to seventy-five.

BLACK BART:
POET LAUREATE OF OUTLAWRY

A typical example of the world-renowned Concord coach, made in Concord, N. H. This was one of thirty made for the Wells Fargo Company for the Rockies-California service in the 70's and 80's.

Black Bart (Charles E. Bolton).

It was dawn on a June day about 1877. More than thirty stage-coaches were lined up before the stage office in the small California town, the teams stamping impatiently, hides shivering off the vicious flies. Also impatient were the waiting passengers—a cold-eyed gambler in shiny top-hat and checkered vest, a rouged "fancy" lady, miners in mud-splattered shoes and pants, mountain men in fringed buckskin, sleepy-eyed drummers, a drunken cowhand, a whole theatrical troupe, Chinese who chattered like magpies. Hired hands loaded down with carpet-bags, cheap suitcases, canvas bags, loads of miners' picks, shovels, bags of cattle feed, hurried in and out of the office, stopping for a moment at the doorway where the harried manager checked off the items on the long list he held.

Finally all the passengers were aboard. After asking permission of the lady, the gambler took a long cigar from a silver box, lighted it, and settled back, his face impassive. The lady stared ahead. The drunken cowboy snored, the drummer picked his teeth reflectively, while the travel-experienced drummer, who had pushed his way in first to grab the far corner seat despite the gambler's frown, settled down for a nap.

The drivers picked up their "ribbons," and the messenger, "ridin' shotgun," hooked a high-heeled boot over the seat and cradled his weapon. The dispatcher shouted through a speaking trumpet: "All aboard for Mormon, Brighton, Usley, and Hangtown . . . all aboard . . ." The manager waved at one driver, then another and another. Whips cracked like exploding firecrackers. Teams leaped into their collars and big wheels turned, as the drivers cursed automatically at their teams. Dust billowed in the fresh morning breeze, the shrill cries and the sound of the wheels growing fainter and fainter and at last dying away. The manager wiped his forehead, looked swiftly down his list for the last time, then went inside.

This was a scene at a California stage depot, from which coaches spanned hundreds of miles to link towns, villages, hamlets, states, and territories. For more than half a century the coach was the only form of transportation on the frontier. Before it became extinct, it had rumbled into American legend to become an inseparable symbol of our wild West, as important in our folklore as the Indian, the cowboy, the longhorn, and the outlaw.

That was before the railroads snaked their way across the plains. But even after the majority of the main stage lines had been transplanted by the transcontinental railroad, stages still operated as connecting links, or feeder lines to the railroads, in the more remote areas on the frontier. The Globe stage was still active as late as 1900 in Arizona and had the dubious honor of being one of the last held up in this country, and by a female road agent at that.

A ride on a frontier stage-coach was something to be remembered as a back-breaking, bone-twisting experience. "I felt like a mess of eggs being scrambled," one traveler described the trip. "I was bounced and tossed all over and despite our discomfort the driver never paid us any heed."

That traveler, of course, wasn't experiencing anything unusual. Most early stage-coach rides were bumpy, for obvious reasons. The roads were primitive, and the driver, or "ribbon handler," as he was sometimes called, with one eye cocked for hostiles and highwaymen and the other on the uncertain road, had no time for a complaining tenderfoot.

The stage-coach was the principal target of the early western outlaw, and it was only after the Reno brothers invented train robbery, later perfected by Jesse James, that the railroad express car took its place as the outlaw's ideal target.

It is impossible to list all the West's stage-coach robbers. In 1877 in one month alone, Wells Fargo listed more than two hundred, and about 1900 William Pinkerton, in addressing the Police Chiefs' Association, said he had lost count of how many road agents his agency had arrested and sent to prison for robbing stage-coaches.

The most colorful, however, was undoubtedly Charles E. Bolton, alias Black Bart, who can rightly be called the poet laureate of outlawry. Bart was not only an expert stage-coach robber but an amateur poet who left his verses in the empty express boxes. By far the best accounts of Bart's career are in Joseph Henry Jackson's *Tintypes in Gold* and *Bad Company*.

A faded clipping in the Pinkerton archives quotes Bart as saying he was born in Jefferson County, N. Y., and came West when he was about ten years old. The *San Francisco Bulletin* of November 14, 1883, in its account of his capture, describes him as a "dapper man with a penchant for diamonds." As invariably happened when a newspaper of that time covered the activity of outlaws, reporters, perhaps reflecting the sentimental mood of the frontier, let slip into their stories about Black Bart paragraphs which later became the basis for strange legends.

The *Bulletin* reporter described Bart as a man "of gentle birth with the manners of a perfect gentleman" and another account pictured him as a highwayman "but never a killer." All accounts underscored the fact that Bart "scorned" to shed blood.

Bart's first holdup was reported in August, 1877, when he held up the stage running from Fort Ross to the Russian River. His loot was $300 and a check for $305.52. He was dressed as he always would be, in a long linen duster and a flour sack with eyeholes over his head. He was armed with a rifle and uttered his command to "throw down the box" in a voice described as "deep and hollow."

After each holdup the drivers and detectives found scraps of doggerel left behind and signed "Black Bart, PO-8."

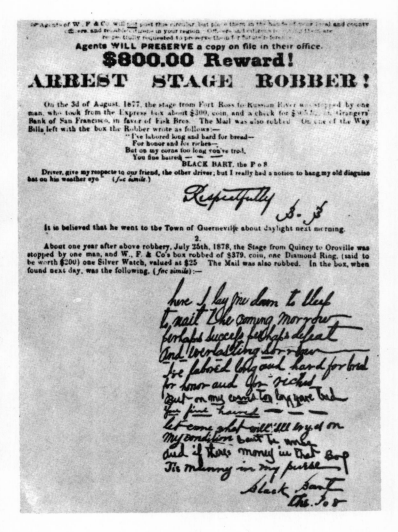

Here is one example of his verse:

> *Here I lay me down to sleep*
> *To wait the coming morrow,*
> *Perhaps success, perhaps defeat*
> *And everlasting sorrow.*
> *Yet come what will, I'll try it once,*
> *My condition can't be worse,*
> *And if there's money in that box,*
> *'Tis munney in my purse.*

And another:

> *I've labored long and hard for bread,*
> *For honor and for riches,*
> *But on my corns too long you've tred,*
> *You fine-haired sons of bitches . . .*

Each line of the first poem was carefully disguised as if written by a different hand, and the second verse was scrawled on the back of a waybill.

83

Bart's last holdup was the stage from Sonora for Milton, near Copperopolis. The road agent in his weird garb stepped from behind a rock, leveled his rifle, and in that "deep and hollow" voice gave his command to throw down the box. This time he got $4,800 after working on the lock of the box some time and cutting his right hand. But before he could get away, a rider came up, and the driver borrowed his gun and fired at Bart, who scooped up the money and fled, leaving his handkerchief behind.

Detectives traced the laundry mark, "F.O.X. 7," through ninety-one laundries and finally came up with the name of Charles E. Bolton, "a distinguished-looking gentleman who walked erect as a soldier and carried a gold-knobbed cane."

When they questioned him, Bart drew himself erect and said, "Sir, I am a gentleman . . ."

"Not with that voice you're not," the detective said, and arrested him. Bart confessed, adding, "I never robbed a passenger, or ill-treated a human being." When Bart came out of prison, he vanished. Some reports had him settling in Nevada, "where he became a peaceful tiller of the soil."

SAM BASS:

'I've Got the World by the Tail, with a Downward Pull'*

The best day in the life of happy-go-lucky Sam Bass was Tuesday, September 18, 1877. The Hoosier orphan started out as poor as a buzzard in a bone-yard and wound up tethering his pony with a bag of gold. And it was fresh-minted gold with the big eagle on it, not the skimpy dust you had to scrape out of the hills or pan out of the streams. It was gold you could go right out and buy things with, and all Sam Bass had to do to get it was go out with Joel Collins and four other playmates and stick up the Union Pacific express when it stopped to take on water at Big Springs, Nebraska.

Joel Collins planned the whole thing, and it came out just like he said. It would have been a lark from start to finish except for the stubborn behavior of Charley Miller, the Wells Fargo messenger on the train. Miller wouldn't open the "through" safe. He said the time lock on it had been set at San Francisco not to open before Omaha. Nobody had thought to bring along any dynamite, this being the band's first venture in train robbery after a flock of stage raids in the Black Hills had produced something less than a bare living.

Sam Bass attacked the safe with an axe, but the blade bounced harmlessly off the iron. Then somebody noticed three little boxes on the floor. Miller managed a look of childlike innocence and said he thought there was some kind of hardware in them. The bandits smashed one open just to be sure. The boxes turned out to be the snug little home of $60,000 in $20 gold pieces consigned to Wells Fargo and the National Bank of Commerce in New York. Collins and Bass managed to contain their elation long enough to proceed with the remaining business at hand. Jim Berry and Tom Nixon were delegated to stand guard over the golden treasure trove while Collins and Bill Heffridge kept an eye on the coaches and Bass and Jack Davis shook out whatever stray dollars the coach passengers had neglected to hide as the drama played itself out in the express car.

Nobody ever toted up the net on the evening's labors at Big Springs, the gold blinding a succession of historians. One estimate was that the passengers gave up $1,300 in jewelry and cash. Collins' lads also swept $458 in currency out of Miller's small safe, so it was a splendid haul by any standards. Bass at least could look upon even his one-sixth share of it and compare himself favorably with the idols of his meager Indiana boyhood, the Reno Brothers, who invented and perfected the Western industry known as organized train robbery.

---

* From a letter someone helped the illiterate Sam Bass write from the Black Hills once when things seemed very bright.

Sam Bass, in his twenties.

$1,000 Reward!

WE WILL PAY FIVE HUNDRED DOLLARS FOR THE
Arrest and Detention
UNTIL HE CAN BE REACHED, OF
Tom Nixon,

Alias TOM BARNES, five feet seven or eight inches high, 145 to 150 lbs. weight, 25 years of age, blue-gray eyes, light hair and whiskers; beard not heavy or long; mustache older and longer than beard. He is a blacksmith, and worked at that trade in the Black Hills, last summer; has friends in Minnesota and Indiana. He was one of the robbers of the Union Pacific Train, at Big Springs, Nebraska, on September 18, 1877.

He had about $10,000 in $20 Gold pieces of the stolen money in his possession, of the coinage of the San Francisco Mint of 1877. The above reward will be paid for his arrest and detention, and 10 per cent. of all moneys recovered; previous rewards as regards him are withdrawn.

ANY INFORMATION LEADING TO HIS APPREHENSION WILL BE REWARDED. Address,

ALLAN PINKERTON,
191 and 193 Fifth Avenue, CHICAGO, ILLINOIS.

Or, **E. M. MORSMAN,**
Supt. U. P. R. R. Express, OMAHA, NEBRASKA.

Sam Bass, when he was 16.

Sam Bass was born in Indiana, it was his native home;
At the age of seventeen young Sam began to roam.
Sam first came out to Texas, a cowboy for to be—
A kinder-hearted fellow you seldom ever see.
                                          —FROM THE BALLAD

Sam Bass had a good Christian beginning, but he got a bad break. Elizabeth Jane Sheeks Bass died on the little Woodville farm having her tenth child. Sam was only ten then, and three years later illness took his father, Daniel, and he had to go with some of the other children to be brought up by his uncle, Dave Sheeks. In his tender account of those days in the biography, *Sam Bass*, Wayne Gard said that all the boy owned in the world were the two precious possessions he was able to salvage from the auction of his father's effects: a $7 saddle and a $4 bull calf.

Uncle Dave was a stern taskmaster and Sam ran away when he was just past eighteen. He worked in a Mississippi sawmill for a year, so he could get a stake to go West and be a cowboy, just as the ballad said not too many years later. Then he hitched a ride with a wagon train going to Denton in southeast Texas. There he worked on a ranch for a while, tended the stock at the Lacy House, and finally went to work as a hired hand for Sheriff William F. (Dad) Egan. He was not a deputy, as the more romantic accounts say. Egan did entrust the youth with frequent missions in a freighting business he ran, and Sam was so cautious with his expense money that other Denton boys began to call him "Honest Eph."

The horse races accounted for Sam's first troubles. He got so wrapped up in the ponies, betting on them and finally acquiring a mare of his own, that Egan finally fired him in the spring of '75. Sam, a solid youth of medium height and better-than-medium confidence in Sam Bass and a fleet little pony called Jenny, began to race with the help of Henry Underwood, who was not one of Denton's better boys. Jenny beat all the ponies in sight and when there were none left to run against, Sam and Henry took her into the Indian Territory to fleece the Cherokees and Choctaws and across the border to take the Mexicans. It was on one of those trips that Sam encountered Joel Collins, in San Antonio, and turned to bigger things than horse racing.

ROAMING—AND ROBBING

Sam Bass and Joel Collins, two bright and adventurous hustlers in their mid-twenties, arrived in the Black Hills in '76 with nothing but money and high hopes of getting more. They were carrying thousands of dollars that belonged to ranchers who had entrusted their steers to them to take up the trail from Texas and sell in Kansas. Joel Collins thought the thing to do was to push on to Deadwood to fatten up the small fortune so they'd have some money of their own when they got home, but the mining

But Mr. Reno's four bad boys had a four-year run before Missouri clamped John into jail and vigilantes strung up the other three in Indiana in '68. Collins' band of amateurs didn't even survive its first and only big strike. The leader himself, a Texas boy who tended saloon and drove cattle before he went into horse-racing and then outlawry with Bass, was dead in no time at all. Pushing toward home with Heffridge, he ran into a smart sheriff and a squad of soldiers near Fort Hays, Kansas. The bandit pair, readily identified, was riddled after Collins announced that he meant to go down fighting. Their $20,000 split of the gold was found tied up in an old pair of levis.

Jim Berry, for his part, never had a whisper of a chance. Before the raid he had stopped in nearby Ogallala to buy six red bandanas from a storekeeper who knew him: a piece of one of them was found in the little water station after the robbery. So Berry only got as far as the town of Mexico, Missouri, and there a charge of pellets from Sheriff Walter Glasscock's shotgun proved fatal. Less than $3,000 was recovered from Berry. Nixon, who had left the band with him, presumably got away with the healthier share.

Sam Bass made out fine. He rode as far as Fort Worth with Davis and then headed for Denton County, the part of Texas he liked to call home. He would go back there and call on his old friends and spread some of his gold around and maybe take some time out to dwell on what a lucky fellow he had been since he shook off that Hoosier dust . . .

capital enjoyed an abundance of card sharks and cut-throats drawn from all over the United States. The boys from Texas went broke in the sin dens in no time at all—broke in the midst of the most wondrous gold boom since '49.

Jack Davis knew a way out. A Virginia City gambler who had done time for sticking up a Central Pacific train in Nevada, he had helped preside over the collapse of a freighting business that Collins and Bass had tried briefly, and now he had an idea. He suggested that the coin of the realm was moving in two ways all around them—coming in by stage in the bulging money belts of late-arriving prospectors, and going out from the big mines in solid gold chunks headed for the home offices. The thing to do was to rob the Deadwood coach.

Collins, Bass, and three confederates made a mess of their first venture as highwaymen. The stage from Cheyenne, intercepted in Whitewood Canyon outside of Deadwood, never even stopped in response to their command even though a shotgun charge killed the driver, Johnny Slaughter. The bandit who fired the blast was banished from the masked band; Collins wanted no gunplay.

The raids that followed, while less bloody, only barely made the history books. As Wayne Gard reconstructed the comic opera of the road, the first two coaches that did stop for the band proved to be fresh out of passengers, currency, or gold; the next one yielded up $30 from among four penny-poor travelers, and the road agents gave them back $1 apiece for breakfast money; the next one was only good for a gold watch and chain and $3 (minus $1 for eating money); and the one after that produced a total of $6. Obviously the boys were stopping the wrong stages. Since nothing succeeds like failure, it occurred to Collins

that they should turn their still latent talents to the greener fields of train robbery.

It turned out to be a happy thought, because the train the six-man band then descended on in the Nebraska waterhole called Big Springs happened to be carrying $60,000 in brand new $20 gold pieces from the San Francisco mint to the money temples in New York. We have related how Collins and two of his confederates were cut down by the law soon afterward and how two others, including Jack Davis, vanished into the open spaces.

Sam Bass went on to make the stuff of legends.

Back in Denton with the shiny coins jingling in his patched pants, Bass collected Henry Underwood and Frank Jackson and set up camp in Cove Hollow, a six-mile ravine complete with caves and so much wild growth that someone once remarked that the daylight never got in before high noon. It was a splendid refuge. For want of something to do, the trio went north now and then to rob a stage or a bank, sometimes drafting other cast-offs from Denton to help. But as a road agent in Texas, Bass only made out a little bit better than he had in the Black Hills. He got $11 off the Fort Worth coach in December of '77, and $70 and a pair of watches from another coach two months later.

And as a train robber Bass would never again know the lush good fortune of Big Springs. The next best haul added up to only $1,280, taken off a Houston and Texas Central express at the Allen station on Feb. 23, 1878, and split four ways between Bass, Jackson, Seaborn Barnes, and Tom Spotswood. Another choo-choo on the same line yielded only $400 the next month, and then in April two Texas Pacific trains turned out to be good for $200 between them. Somehow, Bass and his helpmates never

Deadwood, South Dakota, in 1876.

managed to stumble over any great caches of gold or currency.

The result, as tabulated by Eugene Cunningham in *Triggernometry,* hardly matched the portrait of Sam Bass as one of the West's more celebrated highwaymen. The forays Bass master-minded himself after Joel Collins was deposited in the earth showed a net take of $1,961. The rewards on the outlaw and his amiable but not-too-bright lieutenants were much higher than that.

Thus the fame of Sam Bass rests more securely on his remarkable if brief success in eluding capture than on his accomplishments as a brigand in command of his own force. When he came back to Texas from the big strike in Nebraska, he was trailed by hordes of Texas Rangers, railroad detectives, Pinkertons and sheriffs' deputies. But around Denton no one felt an overwhelming impulse to bring him in. He was a pretty good kid in the town before he went bad; even Sheriff Egan conceded that. Better still, Cove Hollow was an all-but-impenetrable fortress. The minions of the law assailed it time and time again only to be driven off more by its great natural defenses than by the marksmanship of Bass and his ragged band. It was a common thing for the manhunters to come in force, pour fire into the murk that surrounded the ravine, and go away angry. In one case, a delegation of Rangers assembled by Captain Junius Peak wouldn't even go that far; they said they had enlisted to fight Indians and not to hunt down fellow Texans.

When Sam Bass did meet his doom, it was through a betrayal that has come down in folklore along with the saga of Jesse James' downfall. James was to be done in by Bob Ford—"the dirty little coward that shot Mr. Howard and laid Jesse James in his grave." Sam Bass preceded the great Border Bandit to the grave because weak-willed Jim Murphy put the finger on him.

Murphy, a long-standing Denton chum, lived near Cove Hollow and was at first impressed into the Bass service just for the sake of stashing away some surplus $20 gold pieces—the outlaw only got to San Antonio a couple of times to spend some of his riches on the pleasures of the flesh.

Jim and Bob Murphy and their father were swept into the dragnet in April of '78 when the railroads put the heat on Governor Hubbard to put a stop to the raids on their trains. The Murphys were charged with harboring the outlaws. Those arrests proved to be the beginning of the end for Sam Bass.

Major John B. Jones of the Frontier Battalion entered into an arrangement to let the Murphys beat the case against them if Jim would help trap the bandit chief. But it is hard to say whether the major can be credited with engineering the sellout. Ranger Captain Lee Hall described Jim Murphy as a "veritable Judas in every sense of the word," and Dora Neill Raymond, Hall's biographer, said that Bass's old friend had made six different offers to the law 'n order side to turn in his friend Bass for a consideration.

Let out to do the devil's work, Jim Murphy joined the Cove Hollow fugitives at a time when fresh hands were sorely needed. Bass had only Barnes and Jackson with him and wanted to rob the bank at Round Rock. Barnes was suspicious of Murphy, but the leader would tolerate no aspersions on the new recruit. On the way south to Round Rock, Murphy managed to slip into a telegraph office and wire Major Jones: "We are on our way to Round Rock to rob the bank. For God's sake get there." The major ordered Rangers Dick Ware, George Herold, Chris Connor, and Vernon Wilson into town. He also asked Deputy Sheriff Morris Moore of Travis County and Deputy Sheriff A. W. Grimes of Williamson County to go there, but he didn't tell them what was stirring.

The Bass gang came in on the sweltering afternoon of July 19. The outlaws meant to get the feel of the town and raid the bank the next day. As they headed for Henry Koppel's store to get some tobacco and pass the time of day, Murphy asked leave to roam around and see if he could find out whether there were any Rangers around. Bass thought that was a good idea.

Moore and Grimes, idling on the corner, saw Bass, Barnes, and Jackson go into Koppel's, noted that they were wearing revolvers, agreed that where they came from gun-toting was not allowed in town, and went in after the trio. Grimes had barely managed a question about the matter of firearms when the bullets began to fly. He was hit six times before he could draw. Moore was able to fire five times before he fell with a bullet in his lung. Rangers Ware, Connor, and Herold, hearing gunfire, came on the run and opened fire as the bandits fled. Major Jones rushed

A disputed photograph. Whether the seated gunman was Sam Bass is the subject of hot debate. There is no clear documentation.

to the scene from the telegraph station and got in a few shots, as did Captain Hall, who had reached Round Rock that morning for the showdown.

Barnes pitched dead into an alley before he could mount his horse. Bass, hit, managed to ride out the ambush with Jackson's help. Huddled in a doorway, Jim Murphy saw them clatter past toward Bushy Creek. The pair got away, but that night a farmer came into town and said that Sam Bass was dying outside of his cabin, and the Rangers went and collected their man. The outlaw had a serious body wound and a shattered right hand. He had lost so much blood that the doctors said he couldn't live long and Major Jones pleaded with him to name his confederates in the raids of the past year.

"It is agin my profession to blow on my pals," Sam Bass replied. "If a man knows anything, he ought to die with it in him."

The Ranger officer persisted. On and off for three days the gentle, futile questioning continued. Finally a doctor named Cochran asked the dying man to help the authorities.

"Let me go," Sam Bass said. "The world is bobbing around."

Then he died. It was his twenty-seventh birthday.

Jim Murphy was to follow Sam Bass to the grave eleven months later. When he went home to Denton, the charges against all the Murphys were dismissed, but Jim found no acclaim among the populace. Indeed, it was the other way around. The air in Denton was charged with bitterness. There were nights when Jim Murphy was so overcome with fear that he asked if he could sleep in Dad Egan's little jail for safety's sake. And then some medicine meant for his ailing eyes somehow found its way into his mouth and Jim Murphy died in convulsions. A ballad writer composed his epitaph years later:

> And so he sold out Sam and Barnes and left
> their friends to mourn,
> Oh, what a scorching Jim will get when Gabriel
> blows his horn!
> Perhaps he's got to heaven, there's none of us
> can say;
> But if I'm right in my surmise, he's gone the
> other way.

89

IV. The Wild West

"They were a different breed of men. They dressed differently, they had their own language, code and costume. They lived by the gun and they died by the gun. There were seldom any cowards among them. They loved best the open range, the sky, the mountains and the breathless expanse of their wild, untamed land . . ."

From *An Old Timer Remembers,* Inter-Ocean, February, 1899.

. . . where the buffalo roam . . .

Rounding up the cattle on the way north. *Frederic Remington.*

POINT 'EM NORTH!

As far as the eye could see, the broad wavering river of cattle moved north, bawling, grunting, munching the lush grass, their hoofs raising a pillar of dust which seemed to reach the sky. On either side of the column, cowpunchers waved their hats, shouted curses, snapped long rawhide whips, or whistled shrilly at the plodding steers.

Far up ahead of the seemingly endless column, the foreman of the outfit pointed north with one hand and made a hand trumpet with the other.

"Point 'em north," his voice echoed faintly above the bawling herd. "Point 'em north."

His punchers heard him. They made motions with their hands that they understood. And all down the column the cry went up: "Point 'em north . . . point 'em north . . ."

It was the year 1866. The great herds from Texas were on the move north to railheads of Kansas. One of the world's last frontiers, America's Wild West, was opening. In the short span of its violence, it was to produce legends, heroes, heroines, and villains who have become as much a part of America's history as Valley Forge and George

Washington, creating also two of the most romantic figures in our history—the outlaw and the cowboy.

Both are inseparable from the story of the cattle industry in the West. To understand them, we must first understand the opening of the West immediately after the Civil War.

After Appomattox, Lee's soldiers, still wearing their side-arms and riding their scarecrow mounts, returned home. In Texas, the returning veterans found their ranches in ruins, and the entire state seemingly running wild with unbranded longhorns, the tough, ugly-tempered steers descended from the herds imported to America earlier from England and Ireland.

Most small ranchers, after making repairs to their homes, banded together in what were the first roundups, to corral the wild steers and count what remained of their own stock.

Meanwhile, in the cattle-hungry north, beef was selling at fifty dollars a head. In Texas a steer brought five dollars. As the saying went, any Texan with a pencil and paper

91

A street in Abilene (from an old woodcut).

could be a millionaire. The cattlemen looked north to where the railroads were now nosing their way across the prairie. The Missouri Pacific already had reached Sedalia, Missouri, which offered rail facilities to St. Louis and other cities.

The first cattle drive began in 1866. In that year more than 260,000 head splashed across the Red River, bound for the northern railheads, beginning one of the most thrilling chapters in American history: the grunting tough steers, with their magnificent spread of horns—"glistening in the sun as though they had been polished," one old cow-puncher recalled years later; the towering pillar of dust the cowhands on their cattle-wise ponies, whooping and shouting as they rode the fringe of the herd; and the lonely campfires, tiny torches in an endless night.

The first drives were bitter ones. Kansas farmers drove back the herds because their own cattle had become infected with a fever brought north by the herds. The tough longhorns were impervious to the disease.

There were also outlaw bands to fight. Former Quantrill riders and Jim Lane's Redlegs, with watchers on the hills, swooped out of Baxter Springs, and either stampeded the

Ellsworth, Kansas, 1865-66.

herds, stole the remudas, groups of extra mounts, or killed the cowboys.

It was a bad year or two. The drovers turned east, moving along the Missouri-Arkansas border in the Indian territory, heading for a railhead east of Sedalia. It was a rough stretch of land and hard on the cattle. The western drovers took the cattle along the south border of Kansas, into the grassy plains and shipping points from St. Jo, Missouri, to Chicago. Other drovers moved their longhorns as far as Iowa and Illinois.

Within one year the trial and error, the fighting off of the robbers, and the terrible strain of moving virtually armies of cattle across more than 1,200 miles of wild territory, had finally linked the beef-hungry North and cattle-stocked Texas.

But one man, more than any other, had made the permanent contact between the Texas ranchers and the northern buyers. He was Joe G. McCoy, one of the unsung heroes of the West. McCoy established the cowtown of Abilene, Kansas, signed contracts with the Hannibal and St. Jo Railroad, and, with extraordinary foresight, single-handedly swung the booming cattle trade from St. Louis to Chicago, where it has remained ever since.

Abilene, McCoy said in his memoirs, was selected because "it was entirely unsettled, well watered and had excellent grass."

Despite the fact that the season was late when Abilene opened for business in 1867, more than 35,000 head arrived on the Abilene Trail and were shipped out of the cowtown.

The cattle kingdom spread rapidly out of Texas. It was like an ever-spreading blot of ink on the western map. The United States census of 1880 showed that in fifteen years, from 1866 to 1880, a total of 4,223,397 head of cattle moved out of the Lone Star State.

As the railroads moved west, the cattle business followed. But it was always Abilene that was the jumping-off place, the goal of the Texas drover, the cowboy, and the gambler. It was a rough, tough town with gunfire and violence commonplace.

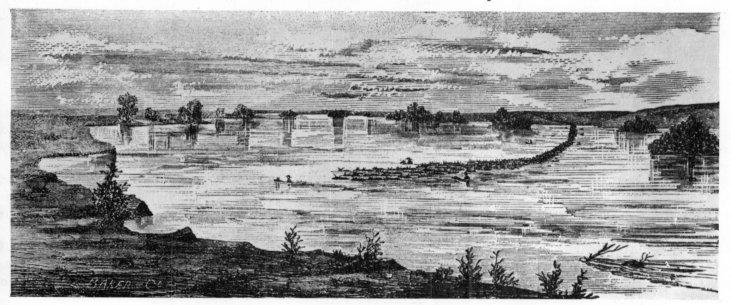

Herds swimming a river on the way north (from an old woodcut).

THE CHISHOLM TRAIL

After the establishment of the Abilene Trail, there was a succession of other trails and cattle paths; some were named, many were not. It is the Chisholm Trail which is the best known. Exactly who laid out the trail, and its exact location, are academic questions still debated whenever two Texas cattlemen meet.

West of the Chisholm Trail was the Panhandle Trail, leading into Kansas and Colorado, and the Pecos Trail, up the Pecos River Valley into New Mexico and on to Colorado and Wyoming.

The main root of the Chisholm Trail began on the Rio Grande. Drovers swam their herds across and pointed them north on a beaten trail which was then known as the Old Beef Trail. This led to Austin. One part of the trail forked east to San Antonio, a rough frontier town where the drovers could stock up. After a day or two they usually continued north, then swung east again to Austin and picked up the Chisholm Trail.

Just above Austin, the herds swam the Colorado. They moved northward, past the rolling pastures, the cotton-fields, and Edwards Plateau, green with oak, cedar, and mesquite. The San Gabriel and the Lampases were crossed next. It was the reddish, muddy Brazos that gave the herds their first difficulty. Sometimes cowpunchers were drowned and cattle lost in the fast-moving river.

Fort Worth was the next stop on the trail. There the drover could replenish his foodstuffs, six-shooters, and saddles. After the herds grazed a day on the edge of town, they were again pointed northward. The trail crossed the West Fork of the Trinity, then veered to the northwest and north along the Wise-Denton line. Here were the great stretches of open prairie and creeks for watering.

The valley of the Red River, one of the high points of the long march, was next. Like the Brazos, the Red River was difficult to cross. Here, too, stock and men were often lost. But after the crossing the drive became easier. Fifteen miles north of the Red River was deep Indian territory and usually the first stop after the crossing. There was plenty of grass and water. Near this point was Monument Hill, a tower of flat rocks used as a marker which could be seen ten to fifteen miles in either direction.

Beaver Creek, then Rush Creek, sixty miles north of Red River, and the Little Washita came next. Indians usually were met, some on the warpath, some just begging for a cow. There were skirmishes and lonely burials, indicated along the trail by the headstones made of slabs of board into which had been burned or carved the legend, "Killed by Indians."

Thirteen miles north of the Washita crossing came the North Canadian, Kingfisher Creek, and then the Cimarron. Along the Cimarron game was plentiful, and the cowboys would augment their sourdough biscuits with venison and buffalo. Several more small creeks, then Nine-Mile Creek, and again the open prairie with countless prairie dog towns.

At a point called Polecat Creek the trail entered Kansas. There were only the River Chikaskia, Slate Creek, a few smaller ones, then the Arkansas River to cross. The cowpunchers could now be cheerful. Abilene, with its saloons, dancing girls in spangled dresses, and red light districts, was not too many days ahead.

THE LONE COWHAND

It was lonely on the prairies at night. The cowpuncher on his horse would move slowly about the herd, which slumbered in the moonlight. He knew that any sudden, unexpected move might cause the herd to stampede. The steers, when they first bedded down for the night, were always restless until the night guards appeared. Then they slumped down and slept. They sensed that the cowhands were their protectors.

As he rode about the herd, the cowpuncher, thinking perhaps of Abilene, or of home, sang softly to the steers. If he were tired of beans and bacon, he put it into song...

> *"Oh, it's bacon and beans, 'most every day—*
> *I'd as soon be eatin' prairie hay."*

They sang other songs, some which they had brought home from the war, others learned at their mothers' knees. Still others they made up. If their friends liked them, they sang them. Thus were born our western ballads of lonely men in a lonely land.

It was not only important to have the night guard soothe the herd by his presence and his lyrics; he was also im-

The herd at night.

portant as a lookout ready to rouse the camp. Comanche were notorious for their ability to steal horses from the remuda, and more than once outlaws had made midnight attacks on the cowcamps.

The night guard was usually taken in shifts. Everyone with the outfit had a turn. There was always a pot of hot black coffee simmering on the coals of the supper fire. When a man came in, he first called softly to the relief, then had a cup of coffee before "hitting the hay," as they said in those days.

As Wayne Gard points out in his splendid *Chisholm Trail*, a night watcher seldom touched the body of the man who was to relieve him. There was always the danger that the sleeping man might spring up with a six-shooter in one hand and begin blazing away.

Night attacks were not uncommon. Outlaw bands waited until the early hours of the morning before they rode out of the darkness, reins in their teeth and revolvers blazing as they did when they rode under the black flag of Quantrill.

The herds were stampeded, the guards died in their saddles, and the horses were stolen. Sometimes there were running gunfights. There were no posses or marshals to run to on the open prairie. The law was the six-shooter at a cowpuncher's belt.

But most nights were peaceful. Men who experienced the nights on the lonely trail could never forget them. They would always recall for their grandchildren the awesome feeling that crept over them as the night closed in and the cookie started his fire. There was a feeling of comradeship which was never lost. Those who had banjos or guitars would begin strumming. Rough voices would lift in song. Far out on the prairie the lonely watcher would listen and begin humming to the steers as they slept under the black bowl of the night sky.

"Oh, it's beans and bacon, 'most every day . . ."

STAMPEDE!

This one word, more than the warning cry that Indians or outlaws were attacking, made any cowpuncher's blood turn cold. There was no way of foretelling it; the sudden bark of a coyote, a rumble of a summer storm, lightning, the rearing of a horse, or the scream of a panther could all start a disastrous stampede. Sometimes there was no apparent reason; it seemed as though a half-wild but dormant instinct of flight had suddenly flared up in the brain of one of the steers.

As many memoirs recall, it was a terrifying experience. There would be a sudden rumble like that of a far-off cannon; then the herd would bolt. Like an army of modern steam-rollers, the steers would move across the open prairie with the speed of an express train. No one could tell what direction they would take. Sometimes they plunged off cliffs, filling whole canyons with their broken bodies, or choked a river with their thrashing.

The task of the cowpunchers was to divert that terrifying, fast-moving animal mass into a gigantic circle. To do that, cowboy and pony became as one.

Sometimes the stampede went on for days. No one got any sleep. There was only time for a quick drink of scalding hot coffee and then back into the saddle.

"I didn't sleep for three days," one puncher recalled. "The herd ran for miles . . ."

Cattle in a storm.

THE AMERICAN COWBOY

There is probably no more romantic figure in American history than the cowboy of the Wild West. As a symbol of eternal youth and adventure, he occupies a permanent spot in our nation's heart from which he is not likely to be unseated, not even by the space man of the atomic age.

The cowboy was a breed far different from the sullen desperado of Jesse James' Middle Border country. Gay and carefree, these men loved song and story. They had a wealth of vitality and lived a reckless, exuberant life. They were ready to sing, fight, or make love at the slightest provocation.

In appearance also they were different. Most of them were lean and sinewy, with faces burned by the sun to the color of old leather. They were born to the saddle and were, in most instances, bowlegged. In 1907 in faraway Bolivia, Clement Reese Glass, manager of the Concordia Tin Mines, spotted Butch Cassidy as he rode up the trail for his first job, while "on the dodge" from the Bolivian Army.

"He had a look about him that stamped him a man from the West," he later recalled. "He was on a mule, but I knew from the way he handled him, he had been a puncher. And he was bowlegged as hell."

Those men of the western range were inseparable from their six-shooters and their horses. Their dress seems destined to remain a part of the American scene: flannel shirt, loose handkerchief about the neck, broad hat, jingling spurs, leather chaps, denim trousers or levis, and high-heeled boots.

Jesse and his gang have been described as expert shots in legend—not in fact. The western outlaws, like Cassidy, or the Sundance Kid, could have outgunned them easily.

Only last year Percy Seibert, in telling author Horan about the end of the Cassidy saga in South America, recalled the swiftness of the Sundance Kid in drawing his single-shot .45 Colt (the peacemaker of the frontier).

"He was as fast as a snake's tongue," he said.

Another old Westerner in Wyoming told how Cassidy and Elza Lay, the "educated member" of the Wild Bunch, tested their marksmanship by shooting the heads off chickens. For every chicken he killed, one of the gang would toss a five-dollar gold piece in a pot. The landlady of the boarding house where they were staying—she is still living —said they missed but once or twice.

A major part of the cowboy's life centered about his horse. It was not only his means of transportation, but also the horse was his friend. Cattle-wise horses were almost human in intelligence. It is not unusual, in the memoirs of a former cowpuncher on the Chisholm Trail, to read of how, awakened by a stampede, he found his horse standing over him ready to protect him from the terrified animals moving across the plains.

Cow ponies varied in color and build, but all had to be trained and broken before they were taken on the trail. A common phrase on the range was "smart as a cutting horse." A good trail horse might be part mustang blood, or a quarter horse whose forefathers had been raised in the Blue Grass.

Bronc busting was both fun and work. A good bronc buster was invaluable to any outfit. It took enormous endurance, a backbone made of steel, and a grip as well as a will of iron.

Nearly all of the western outlaws had been cowboys. Ironically, many of them were not born in the West. For example, Billy the Kid was born on New York's East Side and the Sundance Kid was raised in Plainfield, New Jersey.

Bill Doolin was a puncher on the XL ranch in Wyoming. Cassidy was a cowhand on ranches from Utah to Alma, New Mexico. So was Black Jack Ketchum. Harry Tracy had his own ranch on the Red River, where his wife was killed by a posse. Elza Lay worked on the Calvert ranch in Baggs, Wyoming. The Logans, Bob Lee, and all the rest ran away from home to work as cowpunchers on ranches.

The Jameses and Youngers were products of a terrible Civil War. But as we shall see, many of the outlaws and the gunfighters of the Wild West were born of a great depression in the cattle country.

Cowboys had to be ready always to shoot it out with Indians or outlaw bands.

Breaking in broncos was the part of the cowhands' job that many cowboys liked best. What they all liked least was herd riding across the howling prairie in winter. A good cowhand had not only to ride well and shoot well, but also had to be good with a lasso, fast at cutting out and throwing a steer or calf, competent at driving the steers to the roundup, branding and all the rest.

The roundup (*above*). Throwing a steer (*below*).

COWBOY CAPERS

There was fun, too, for the cowboy. There was singing and story-telling, of course, and always a little horseplay. But the real excitement came when the boys went to town for a little drinking or gambling. There was almost always shooting and violence. Some-times it was harmless, as when some lively vaqueros would ride hell-for-leather through the town, yipping and yelling and firing their six-guns. This was called hurrahing a town and almost every-body enjoyed it. But often enough there was trouble and tragedy.

A row in a cattle town.

What happened when a gambler cheated a cowboy. Remington titled this
picture "A Miss Deal."

COWTOWNS OF THE OLD WEST

San Antonio, 1876.

Wichita, 1873.

Dodge City, 1878.

Nebraska City, 1865.

Ellsworth, 1873.

Helena, 1869.

The Story-book Marshal: Wyatt Earp

The big guy, rail-thin but strong, stood under the canvas shading Beebe's General Store and Brennan's Saloon in the Kansas cattle town of Ellsworth. He wore no guns. A white linen shirt set off his bronzed features and his broadcloth trousers were tucked into short boots. He was twenty-five years old and his name was Wyatt Earp. He came from Scotch stock out of Monmouth, Illinois. The family went west by wagon train in '64 and young Wyatt, hardened by the journey across the plains, took a man's job as a stage driver on the run between San Bernardino and the pueblo of Los Angeles. Then he ran mule and wagon teams in the Wyoming railway construction camps, signed on as guard with a government surveying party going from Missouri into the Indian Nations, and turned to buffalo hunting when Wild Bill Hickok told him in Kansas City that there were lush profits in the skin of the bison. A good shot, he made a fair stake and then followed the trek to the prospering cowcamps. That was the way of the West in that time.

In the summer of '73, when Wyatt Earp got there, Ellsworth was a rollicking, riotous trail-end town in its last fling. There were 1,500 parched and well-heeled cowboys on the premises on the end of the long, weary haul up the Chisholm Trail from Texas with great herds awaiting shipment to the new markets in the North. So there was much hell-raising in Ellsworth. Ben and Bill Thompson were right in the thick of it and, quite by accident, it was this much-feared pair of Texans that launched Wyatt Earp on his brief but remarkable career as a lawman.

It happened on a sweltering August day. The Thompsons checked their shooting irons at the Grand Central Hotel, as local ordinance required, and joined some idlers heckling a poker game in one of the saloons. An argument started and a hardy gentleman named John Sterling slapped Bill around, whereupon the brothers immediately reclaimed their artillery and took up battle stations behind a hay wagon outside the saloon. Sheriff Chauncey B. Whitney got them to come into Brennan's in the hopes that some whiskey would cool them off. But when the sheriff came out later, Bill Thompson fired a fatal load of buckshot into him from Brennan's doorway.

Muttering drunken curses, Bill then rode slowly out of town while his squat older brother and a delegation of Texans held off the outraged citizenry. Marshal J. W. (Brocky Jack) Norton and his deputies, Charlie Brown and Ed Crawford, assembled in the Kansas Pacific depot across the Plaza but made no move when Mayor Jim Miller ordered them into action, whereupon Wyatt Earp remarked: "It's none of my business, but if it was me I'd get me a gun and arrest Ben Thompson or kill him." The mayor tore the badge from Norton's shirt. "I'll make this your business," he told the lanky stranger. "Here's your

badge. Go into Beebe's and get some guns. I order you to arrest Ben Thompson." Earp picked up two second-hand .45's and a gun belt and set out across the Plaza. Thompson, who knew him, called out, "What do you want, Wyatt?" Still walking, Earp replied, "I want you, Ben." As he told it to Stuart N. Lake for his biography, *Wyatt Earp: Frontier Marshal,* this exchange followed:

THOMPSON: I'd rather talk than fight.

EARP: I'll get you either way, Ben.

THOMPSON: Wait a minute. What do you want me to do?

EARP: Throw your shotgun in the road, put up your hands, and tell your friends to stay out of this play.

THOMPSON: Will you stop and let me talk to you? (Earp stopped.) What are you going to do with me?

EARP: Kill you or take you to jail.

THOMPSON: Brown's over there by the depot with a rifle. The minute I give up my guns he'll cut loose at me.

EARP: If he does, I'll give you back your guns and we'll shoot it out with him. As long as you're my prisoner, the man that gets you will have to get me.

THOMPSON: You win.

Sheriff Chauncey B. Whitney.

There followed a tense procession to Judge V. B. Osborne's court, Earp and his celebrated prisoner trailed by the Texans with Cad Pierce, George Peshaur, Neil Kane, and John Good marching at the head of the angry band.

The end of the episode was anti-climactic. The Texas badman was fined $25 for disturbing the peace. (Well, *he* hadn't shot the sheriff.) Thompson left to follow his quick-tempered brother out of Ellsworth. The mayor asked Earp to stay on as marshal at $125 a month. Earp turned it down. The trail-herds would be stopping at Wichita now that the railroad had reached that town. He wanted to go into the cattle business there and maybe live less dangerously and somewhat longer than a lawman could expect to in the West's bloody decades.

EVERYTHING GOES IN WICHITA*

Wyatt Earp came into Wichita in '74 preceded by accounts of his quick touch of glory in Ellsworth. "You the fellow that run it over Ben Thompson?" Mayor Jim Hope asked him. Earp scarcely had time to answer before the deputy marshal's star was pinned on his narrow chest.

The Wichita interlude was comparatively peaceful, although the fun-loving Texans were there now. Ben Thompson was on hand. So was George Peshaur, the Clements brothers—Manning, Gyp, Joe, and Jim—and a galaxy of other gun-throwers. The Marshal kept them all in line most of the time. The only serious shooting scrape took place one night when the cowboys got a youth of eighteen drunk and suggested that he could get himself famous by

* From a highway sign outside of town in the '70's.

blowing some daylight into the law officer's six-foot frame. The boy got the drop on Earp but a gesture of unwise gallantry spoiled his evening's play. He offered his intended victim a chance to jerk his .45 and Earp put a slug in his arm. Then he banished Peshaur from Wichita for staging the near-bushwhacking and told the Clements they could stay only if they stopped toting six-shooters within the town limits.

Between times, Earp had some light chores: throwing the fabulous Shanghai Pierce into the calaboose for "hurrahing" the town, flattening the brawny Peshaur in a fistfight, reclaiming from Ida May's house of shame a lavish piano the madam had imported from Kansas City but neglected to pay for, and cuffing around assorted badmen for disturbing the peace. In '76, with Wichita not only tame but following Ellsworth into oblivion as a cowtown because the longhorns were being driven up the Jones and Plummer Trail to Dodge City, Earp moved on.

He came West from the peaceful North with the name of Abel Head Pierce. He went into cattle-breeding in Texas and was soon known in all the cowtowns as Shanghai Pierce, which also spelled trouble. A fun-loving giant, he could raise as much hell as the wildest range hand coming off the trail into such Kansas camps as Dodge City or Wichita. He had several run-ins with Wyatt Earp for conduct unbecoming a cattle king. He made more money than he could spend on drink or otherwise. One idle inspiration led to the monument shown here—a 40-foot pillar of solid bronze with Shanghai Pierce astride it in full cowboy regalia. He built the thing on his ranch on Tres Palacios Creek in Bay City, Texas, so that he wouldn't be forgotten when he died. It cost $10,000—and Shanghai Pierce was not forgotten.

104

Wyatt Earp and Company: (*standing*) W. H. Harris, Luke Short, Bat Masterson; (*sitting*) Charles E. Bassett, Wyatt Earp, M. C. Clark and Neil Brown.

GOMORRAH OF THE PLAINS

When the Santa Fe came to Dodge City on its glorious push southwest across the barren wastes to the Rio Grande, the little outpost consisted of a sod-house and two tent saloons living off the bad whiskey sopped up by the soldiers from Fort Dodge. The railroad gangs turned it from a hole-in-the-ground oasis into a big bawdy, brawling camp. Then the buffalo hunters made Dodge their headquarters, and finally the trail herders came.

Dodge became the "Queen of the Cowtowns," the "wickedest little city in America," the "beautiful, bibulous Babylon of the frontier," and the "Gomorrah of the plains," all rolled into one throbbing package. It was a paradise for gamblers, girls, and gunmen. A hell-bent cowpuncher could get loaded in the Lady Gay Saloon, cool off in Big Nose Kate Fisher's place with some fallen flower of the Old West, lose what was left of his roll in the sky's-the-limit game at the Alhambra, and then empty his six-shooter in the direction of some kindred soul's guts before bedding down for some shut-eye in the Cosmopolitan Hotel.

Dodge gave the West one popular term—Boot Hill—and the world another. Boot Hill was what the cowpunchers called the cemetery, because it was said that most men died with their boots on. The other term—Red Light District—derived from a two-story pleasure dome that had a red glass pane in its front door as a beacon in the night for the lusty cowboys off the lonesome trail. The

editor of *The Hays City Sentinel* took note of this sort of thing after inspecting Dodge. "No restriction is placed on licentiousness," he wrote. "The town is full of prostitutes and brothels." An early settler put it more vividly. "All they raise around Dodge City," he said, "is cattle and hell." Someone else observed that every man in Dodge was a "walking howitzer"—but there were no more than twenty-five violent deaths in the first year.

A succession of law 'n order men tried to tame Dodge. William (Buffalo Bill) Brooks gave it a big try but he had to be spirited aboard an outbound Santa Fe coach after backing down in a fight. Jack Allen, serving as Marshal Larry Deger's deputy, went out the same way under the insistent prodding of an exuberant band of trail drivers. When that happened, Mayor George M. Hoover sent for Wyatt Earp because of the name he had made in Wichita's turbulent time. The job of chief deputy paid $250 a month and Dodge added a bonus of $2.50 per arrest. Earp and his three sturdy lieutenants, Bat and Jim Masterson and Joe Mason, relied on brute force to subdue the town. "As practically every prisoner heaved into the calaboose was thoroughly buffaloed (crowned with a revolver barrel) in the process, we made quite a dent in cowboy conceit," Earp recalled.

In the fall of '76 Dodge's rustlers and more playful elements got a reprieve. Earp turned in his star and headed for Deadwood, South Dakota, to cash in on the gold strike. He was barely out of town before the Texans were ignoring the Dead Line he had set—no gun-toting north of the railroad tracks. Earp found the Black Hills overrun with prospectors and came back to Dodge the following July when the new mayor, James H. (Dog) Kelley, wired him that .45's were exploding again on Front Street.

Dog Kelly owned pieces of both the Alhambra Saloon and Gambling House and the Dodge City Opera, a dance hall, but he wasn't for coddling the visiting Texans. He wanted a law-abiding town. "I'll back you in any play you make," he told Earp. A fresh clean-up was launched and the outlaws reacted bitterly. Word went out that a $1,000 bounty awaited anyone who would kill Earp. Two attempts missed fire because of bad marksmanship. The next summer George R. Hoyt, a cowboy, rode into the Plaza and wildly emptied his six-gun at Earp while the marshal was standing outside the jammed Comique Theater, where Eddie Foy was doing his act. Hoyt's mount bucked frantically, making the would-be assassin an elusive target, but Earp's third shot spilled him into the dirt. Hoyt died of his wound a month later. He was the only man Wyatt Earp killed in Dodge, although you would imagine from some of the tales told about him that he had filled Boot Hill all by himself.

Rowdy Joe Lowe and his wife, Rowdy Kate, ran dance-halls and saloons in the trail-end towns in the days of the cattle drives, but their main business was peddling girls. Kate has been pictured as a tender, soft-hearted madame who occasionally sent a stray maiden home to escape a life of sin. The same nice things were never said about Joe. He was killed in a brawl in Denver some time after his heyday in the cowcamps had passed.

Queen of the cowtowns: Dodge, Front Street.

Chalk Beeson (*below*) owned the Long Branch Saloon (*above*) in Dodge City with Bill Harris. The Long Branch was one of the cowtown's tamer resorts, because Beeson always asked overheated cowboys or hotheaded gamblers to step outside so the place wouldn't get messed up when the guns went off. But Beeson could not move fast enough the night Levi Richardson, a buffalo hunter, came in to kill Cockeyed Frank Loving, one of the Long Branch dealers. Richardson emptied his revolver at Loving from a distance almost close enough to pick his pocket but all the shots missed. Loving then fired three times and the hunter was dead. The nickname obviously had been fastened on the wrong man. Loving was not locked up. It was an open and shut case of self-defense by any standards.

MURDER BY MISTAKE: Dodge's "First Lady" Dies

Her name was Dora Hand or Fannie Keenan. Dodge City knew her under both names and, indeed, under two wholly different identities. Stuart Lake put it this way:

Saint or sinner, Dora Hand was the most graciously beautiful woman to reach the camp in the heyday of its iniquity. . . . By night, she was the Queen of the Fairybelles, as old Dodge termed its dance-hall women, entertaining drunken cowhands after all the fashions that her calling demanded. By day, she was the Lady Bountiful of the prairie settlement, a demurely clad, generous woman to whom no appeal would go unheeded.

Once, Dora Hand had been a singer in Grand Opera. In Dodge, she sang of nights in the bars and honkey-tonks. On Sundays, clad in simple black, she crossed the Dead Line to the little church on the North Side to lead the hymns and anthems in a voice at which those who heard her forever marvelled. A quick change of attire after the Sunday evening service, and she was back at her trade in the dance hall . . .

Before Dodge, earlier cowtowns had known Dora Hand's stimulating presence. She had been in Abilene and Hays in their hell-roaring prime. Before that? The word was that she had come out of a genteel Boston home, studied voice abroad, and made good in the opera before turning up on the frontier. Was she an alluring woman? They said that twelve men died in the West in warfare over her charms. It may have been this kind of warfare that led to Dora Hand's own death.

In the summer of '78, Mayor James H. (Dog) Kelley and James W. (Spike) Kennedy, errant son of a wealthy Texas cattleman, got into a fight. Kelley was a partner in the Alhambra and Dora Hand was the star attraction among the belles on the premises. Kelley threw Kennedy out one night, presumably for lavishing too much attention on Dora. The Texan left Dodge, but he meant to come back and square accounts.

On a dark October morning before dawn, Kennedy stole up on Kelley's two-room frame house and fired two shots through the front door in the direction of the mayor's bedroom. The first slug passed over Fannie Garretson, one of the Alhambra girls. The second went through a partition and killed Dora Hand, asleep in the other room. Kelley wasn't even there, but the Texan didn't wait to inspect the fruits of his murderous adventure. He rode wildly out of town.

Marshal Wyatt Earp set out with Bat Masterson, Charlie Bassett, and Bill Tilghman to bring Kennedy back. The quartet pounded across a hundred miles of prairie before running down the fugitive at Cimarron Crossing near Meade City. The Texan spurred for flight but a slug from Masterson's rifle tore into his right arm while Earp brought his horse down. "You sons of bitches, I will get even with you for this," Kennedy greeted his captors. When they told him that he had shot Dora Hand instead of Dog Kelley, he grew morose and said he wished they had killed him. Back in Dodge, doctors took four inches of bone out of his shattered arm—and that was the only price he paid. He was freed for lack of evidence and his father took him home.

And Dora Hand, or Fannie Keenan, slept eternally in the new Prairie Grove cemetery north of town. She had the biggest and finest funeral in Dodge's history. A remarkable procession followed the coffin: dance-hall girls, gamblers, gunslingers, saloon-keepers, cattlemen, and even some of the town's respectable ladies, wearing their Sunday bonnets. And a minister hardened to the ways of the frontier intoned the words, for everyone to hear, "He that is without sin among you, let him first cast a stone at her."

Bat Masterson.

James H. (Dog) Kelley.

Bird's eye view of Tombstone, Arizona, 1880.

THE SILVER HILLS

Ed Schieffelin's black hair hung in wild array on his broad shoulders. The dust-caked clothes that covered his big frame were patched with rabbit skins. His beard was matted and soiled. He made an odd sight as the scouts from Fort Huachuca in the Apache country came upon him in the foothills of the Dragoon Mountains in southeastern Arizona. "Whaddya doin?" the riders asked. "Prospectin'," Schieffelin said, and a soldier laughed. "All you'll ever find in them hills," he said, "is your tombstone." But Schieffelin found silver-bearing ore, vein upon wonderful vein, and when he staked his claim he could think of no better name for the place than Tombstone. There, on the borders of the Grand Canyon in the endless, lonely desert, a town sprang up on the bedrock and men stripped $30,000,000 in silver from the magical hills before the veins were spent and they went away.

When Wyatt Earp appeared in Tombstone as 1879 drew to a close, it was hell's last wide open resort under the western sky. The Kansas cowtowns, all but Dodge, had been tamed. Missouri had Jesse James and the tattered remnants of his band on the run. The Rangers were chasing the outlaws out of Texas, and in New Mexico Billy the Kid and his murderous men were about to be ground into the dust by Pat Garrett. There were desperadoes, to be sure, and they had a while to go on the frontier, but Tombstone was the last big one-tent arena to play in.

Earp, thirty-one and wearing a drooping mustache, came into Tombstone with his older brothers, Jim and Virgil, and Doc Holliday, the dentist-gambler and gunfighter who had backed him in some tight spots in Dodge. Morgan Earp, who was twenty-eight, got there in January from Montana, where he had killed Billy Brooks in a six-shooter duel. Crippled by Civil War wounds, Jim Earp was no hand for gunplay, but the other four made up a most formidable quartet in Tombstone's time of blood and glory.

The battle lines were quickly drawn. Wyatt Earp came in as a deputy under Sheriff John E. Behan, but they couldn't get along. Behan had a remarkably tolerant attitude toward the Arizona rustlers who made the mining town their base. The outlaw faction was led by N. H. (Old Man) Clanton, who contributed three sons to frontier warfare; Frank and Tom McLowery, Curly Bill Brocius (William B. Graham), and John Ringo (Ringgold). Behan wasn't above deputizing gentlemen such as these for tax collections and other special missions. (In time, Tombstone's lawless ways developed such deep implications that President Chester A. Arthur sent two special messages to Congress on conditions in the Territory of Arizona.)

The first bloodletting between the two factions came in October, 1880. Ike and Billy Clanton, Curly Bill, the McLowerys, Frank Patterson, and Pony Deal set out to shoot up Allen Street. Since Behan usually looked the other way on nights like that, Town Marshal Fred White and Wyatt Earp undertook to stop the whiskey-sodden outlaws. White was wounded fatally when Curly Bill's hair-trigger Colt went off as he tried to take it from him. Earp floored Curly Bill by crashing a gun barrel against his head. Then he threw all the other merrymakers into jail.

The rustlers, bloodied but hardly contrite, were let out the next day. The bigger showdown was a year away. For Wyatt Earp it was both a busy and highly profitable year. Between occasional flare-ups with Clanton & Company, he had his hands full as deputy U. S. Marshal, shotgun messenger for Wells Fargo—and quarter-owner of the Oriental Saloon and Gambling Hall.

You may wonder how a police officer turned up with a piece of a legal den of sin. The answer comes wrapped in a word more familiar in today's society than it was in the Old West: protection. Rival interests in Tombstone hired professional fighting men to mess up the Oriental because it was doing too well, so the proprietors invited Earp in as

Wyatt Earp, 1885.

James Earp, 1881.

a partner. He called his share, worth $1,000 or more a month, the "fighting interest" in the pleasure palace. As dealers, the Oriental imported such accomplished gunfighters as Luke Short and Bat Masterson, and the Marshal himself handled the cards occasionally. So while there were some brushes with the old-time muscle men, Earp in the double role of gambler and law officer provided the Oriental with a nice immunity against trouble. In our day, undercover arrangements between police and racketeers accomplish the same miracle of immunity for illegal gambling operations.

*   *   *

In the spring of '81, the Wells Fargo stage was held up outside of Contention. The bandits didn't get the $80,000 bullion shipment it carried, but before they were outrun they killed the driver, Bud Philpot, and a passenger. Bob Paul, riding shotgun, brought the stage back to Tombstone. Clanton men were suspected and Wyatt Earp had four names to go on—Bill Leonard, Jim Crane, Harry Head, and Luther King—when he hit the trail. King, speedily captured, admitted his role but managed to escape after Behan claimed him as his prisoner. *The Nugget,* which always sided with Behan and the Clantons, charged that Doc Holliday had led the bandits on the fatal raid and that the Earps had masterminded it. Big-Nosed Kate Fisher, the dance-hall girl and sweetheart of Holliday, pitched in with an affidavit supporting the newspaper's sensational charge but later admitted that she had signed it during a spell of drinking with Behan. Holliday submitted that he had been playing faro at the Alhambra when Philpot was killed. The Doc added a characteristic comment. "If I had pulled that job," he said, "I'd have gotten the eighty thousand."

In time a curious deal muddied the situation. Wells Fargo put up a $6,000 reward for the capture of Leonard, Head, and Crane, dead or alive. Wyatt Earp told Lake that he had offered to pay the reward over to the outlaw leaders if they would turn in the fugitives. He said that Ike Clanton agreed to the betrayal but that nothing came of it because Crane was killed in Guadalupe Canyon when a band of Mexicans ambushed Old Man Clanton and four of his men for rustling a herd of their steers, and Leonard and Head were cut down trying to rob a store in Huachita, New Mexico. Later Ike Clanton accused Earp of having told others about their deal. Clashes and near gunfights between members of both factions followed, and the marshal had occasion to bend his .45 over the heads of both the graying Clanton and Tom McLowery. Then the lid blew off . . .

DEATH IN THE CORRAL

It was October 26, 1881. The outlaws were lined up along the 'dobe wall of the Assay Office backing on the corral, spread out so they wouldn't make a bunched target when it came time to fight. Tom McLowery was the nearest to the street. Then came his brother Frank, the most dangerout gunslinger in the lot, and teen-aged Billy Clanton and his brother Ike. Billy Claiborne, wearing a Colt on either hip, was on the other end of the line. The quintet stood tense and alert, eyes glued on the point where the corral opened into Tombstone's Fremont Street.

In a moment the men they were waiting for came into view. Wyatt and Virgil Earp turned the corner first, then Morgan Earp and Doc Holliday. The tall, handsome Earps wore black from head to foot, the somber design broken only by their white shirts. Holliday had on a black frock coat—aside from the chill weather, he had tuberculosis—and under it bulged a sawed-off shotgun. "You men are under arrest," Virgil Earp sang out as his party moved within eight feet of the lean, desert-hardened outlaws. "Throw up your hands."

Billy Clanton and Frank McLowery put their hands on their six-guns, and Virgil, who was Town Marshal, called to them again: "Hold, I don't mean that. I have come to disarm you." Tom McLowery, springing behind his pony, reached for a .45 jammed into his waistband.

Suddenly guns roared in the crisp, bright afternoon, as the greatest face-to-face, wide-open gunfight in the history of the West—the Battle of the O. K. Corral—got under way.

Frank McLowery fell first. A slug from Wyatt Earp's Buntline Special tore into him just above his gunbelt. Morgan Earp, his coat singed by a bullet from Tom McLowery's .45, put a shot into Billy Clanton's gun hand as the youth poured fire at Wyatt. Billy Claiborne fired wildly at Virgil and then fled in panic into the safe sanctuary of C. S. Fly's photograph studio, the door conveniently held open for the twenty-one-year-old rustler by sheriff Johnny Behan, an intensely interested ringside spectator.

Claiborne's flight from the carnage suggested something to Ike Clanton. He rushed up to Wyatt Earp. "Don't kill me! Don't kill me! I'm not shooting," he pleaded. "This fight's commenced," Earp answered. "Get to fighting or get out." So Clanton got out, ducking into Fly's.

Now Tom McLowery's .45 found a mark. A slug ripped into Morgan Earp's left shoulder but he kept fighting. As Billy Clanton shifted his gun from his shattered right hand to his left, Morgan hit him in the chest and Virgil sent a bullet into his lower ribs. Wyatt concentrated on Tom McLowery, who had fired at him from behind the pony even as Clanton clung to his arm begging for mercy. The horse bolted. McLowery lunged for a Winchester slung in the saddle-boot but missed and started to run. Both Holliday

Virgil Earp, 1885.

Morgan Earp, 1881.

111

and Wyatt Earp hit him and he fell dead. His brother Frank, staggering toward Fremont Street as his life ebbed away, turned on Holliday. Morgan Earp saw it. Three pistols exploded at once. McLowery fell with bullets in his head and heart. His shot creased Holliday's back.

The dying Billy Clanton, left to fight it out alone, shot Virgil through the leg before Wyatt's gun brought him down. Billy worked himself upright, trying to balance his 45 on his knees and pleading, "Just one more shot, God, just one more shot." Then the courageous boy pitched back into the dirt, too weak to hold his shooting iron. The lawmen held their fire.

The Battle of the O. K. Corral was over.

It had taken less than thirty seconds. In that time the outlaws had fired seventeen shots, only three scoring. The Earps and Holliday had fired seventeen shots, too, but they hit Frank McLowery three times, Tom twice, and little Billy six times. The boy lingered half an hour. He died with his boots on, the way he wanted.

*　　*　　*

When they laid out the dead outlaws at the undertaker's, a large sign was hung over the caskets:

MURDERED IN THE STREETS OF TOMBSTONE

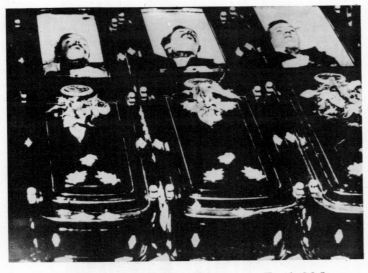

Reading from left to right: Tom McLowery, Frank McLowery, Billie Clanton.

The murder theme was pushed hard by *The Nugget*, Tombstone's anti-Earp newspaper. But *The Epitaph*, published by John P. Clum, quoted eyewitness accounts which described the fight in the O. K. Corral as an even gun duel. The Cochise County Grand Jury heard the evidence and found no cause to indict anyone, but Sheriff Johnny Behan and Ike Clanton swore out warrants charging the Earp brothers and Doc Holliday with murder. Judge Wells Spicer ordered a hearing.

Behan, the soul of law 'n order on the stand, testified that he had tried to disarm the cowboys and head off the fight but they "demurred." He said that when the Earps marched on the corral, ignoring his pleas to stay out, he heard Wyatt say, "You s . . . of b . . . . . s, you have been looking for a fight and now you can have it." Then he said somebody— "I think Doc Holliday"—blasted away at Billy Clanton with a nickel-plated pistol even as the boy pleaded, "Don't shoot me. I don't want to fight." The sheriff passed over the brief exchange that occurred when he tried to take Wyatt Earp into custody after the fight:

BEHAN: I'll have to arrest you.

EARP: I won't be arrested today. You have deceived me. You told me these men were disarmed; I want to disarm them.

Ike Clanton, the flannel-mouth who promoted the battle—he had announced that his band was in town to shoot it out with the Earps—and then fled when the guns started to roar, told much the same story as his friend Behan. "We threw up our hands and they commenced shooting," Clanton testified. He swore that the Clantons and McLowerys had been marked for death because they knew (1) that the Earps had plotted the Wells Fargo holdup the preceding March and (2) that it was Doc Holliday who had killed the stage driver, Bud Philpot. Clanton asked the court to believe that Wyatt Earp had confided this to him in the course of offering him the full $6,000 reward if he would turn in three members of his own gang as the highwaymen. When he threw the case out, Judge Spicer noted crisply that the trouble with this story was that Ike Clanton was still very much alive whereas the Earps could have killed him at will in the Corral if that was their purpose.

The court ruled that the law 'n order party had acted "wisely, discreetly and prudentially to secure their own preservation" and "were fully justified in comitting these homicides" as a "necessary act done in the discharge of official duty."

So ended the legal wrangling, but there was more blood to be shed in the San Pedro Valley—much more—before the book could be closed on the terrible saga of Tombstone.

THE MIDNIGHT ASSASSINS

Virgil Earp, Town Marshal of Tombstone, left the Oriental toward midnight on December 28, 1881. As he crossed Fifth Street, his big frame silhouetted in the lights of the Eagle Brewery Saloon, five shotguns roared. Just recovered from the leg wound he suffered in the Battle of the O. K. Corral, Earp took one load of buckshot in the side and another in the left arm. He staggered back to the Oriental just as his brother Wyatt burst through the swinging door. "They got me," Virgil gasped. He was crippled for life.

Ike Clanton, Frank Stilwell, Hank Swilling, and John Ringo, all toting shotguns, had been seen in the town that night. Sheriff Johnny Behan, who had such a soft spot for the outlaws that he had tried to build a murder case against the Earps and Doc Holliday for killing the McLowery brothers and Billy Clanton in the gun duel in the corral, did not organize a posse to hunt down the suspects. He must have been embarrassed, because Stilwell was one of his deputies.

Outraged, the Citizens' Safety Committee, Tombstone's vigilantes, swore out warrants against Clanton, Stilwell, and Swilling. The trio promptly swaggered into the cozy custody of Behan—and walked out after an array of friendly witnesses testified that they were miles away when Virgil was bushwhacked.

On a Saturday night in March, assassins firing through a window shot Morgan Earp as he played pool with Bob Hatch in the Campbell & Hatch Billiard Parlor on Allen Street. A second bullet lodged in the low ceiling over the head of Wyatt Earp, who had been watching the game. Morgan died in his older brother's arms, whispering, " . . . I can't stand it." Earlier that day, the Earps had heard that Stilwell, Swilling, Pete Spence, and Florentino (Indian Charlie) Cruz had slipped into Tombstone. Wyatt and Morgan couldn't find them. Now Wyatt would resume the quest. Now it would be a manhunt.

The body of Morgan Earp was put aboard a train for burial in California. The crippled Virgil and his wife went along. So did Wyatt, Doc Holliday, Sherman McMasters, Texas Jack Vermillion, Turkey Creek Jack Johnson, and Warren Earp, who had come to Tombstone after Virgil was shot. All but Virgil and his wife left the train at Tucson. There, the next dawn, Frank Stilwell was found sprawled on the railroad tracks with four rifle slugs and two loads of buckshot in his cold body.

In Tombstone, a coroner's jury ruled that Stilwell, Spence, and Indian Charlie had murdered Morgan Earp. In Tucson, a coroner's jury held that Stilwell had died at the hands of Wyatt and Warren Earp, Holliday, and Texas Jack. Wyatt didn't tell it that way to Stuart Lake. He said he made out four figures crouched in a flatcar up ahead on an adjoining track, got off the train, ducked two shots that whizzed over his head, and then got to Stilwell as he was crossing the roadbed. . . .

Peter Spence.

Sheriff Johnny Behan.

113

"Stilwell caught the barrel of my Wells Fargo gun with both hands . . . I forced the gun down until the muzzle of the right barrel was just underneath Stilwell's heart. . . . (then he) found his voice. 'Morg!' he said, and then a second time, 'Morg!' I've often wondered what made him say that."

"What happened then?" Lake asked.

"I let him have it," Earp replied. "The muzzle of one barrel . . . was just underneath the heart. He got the second before he hit the ground."

There was no explanation of the four rifle slugs in the slain outlaw's body.

Back in Tombstone, Sheriff Behan thought he ought to arrest Earp. All that came out of it was this exchange:

> BEHAN: Wyatt, I want to see you.
>
> EARP: Behan, if you're not careful, you'll see me once too often.

John P. Clum and his bodyguard.

Earp and four of his men rode out of Tombstone—for the last time, it developed—to complete his unfinished business. He found Indian Charlie first and left him dead in a gulch. He said he gave the half-breed a count of three in which to draw first after Charlie confessed that he had stood watch for $25 the night Morgan was murdered. "That twenty-five dollar business just about burned me up," Earp told Lake in 1927.

So two of Morgan Earp's accused assassins were dead long before his body reached his parents' home. Wyatt never caught up with Swilling, and Spence put himself under Behan's very safe custody until the avenger was no longer around to hunt him down.

The last to go was Curly Bill Brocius, ally of the Clantons and McLowerys and long-time enemy of the Earps. Curly Bill and his men, curiously, formed a posse of "hon-est ranchmen" sent out by Behan to bring in the Earp posse. The two bands met at Iron Springs, a waterhole in the Whetstone Mountains outside of Tombstone. Earp said he killed Curly Bill there. The outlaw faction never conceded this and you can still get an argument over it in the ghost town of Tombstone.

After the battle at Iron Springs, Earp and his men scoured the desert country for a month and then headed for Colorado. Governor Pitkin refused to extradite the Marshal to face trial in the Stilwell case. The Governor wasn't too worried about what might happen in Tucson but he had an idea that Arizona—and particularly the town so aptly called Tombstone—was simply overrun with gunmen who seemed to be desperately intent on killing everybody named Earp.

A Wells Fargo chest, typical of those in use in Earp's time.

DOC HOLLIDAY: THE DEADLY DENTIST

It is impossible to view the history of Dodge City and Tombstone without running across the emaciated, overcoat-clad ghost of Doc Holliday, the murderous dentist.

Holliday, a graduate of the Baltimore College of Dentistry, was the son of a Confederate officer who had been killed in the war. His family, though impoverished, somehow scraped together enough money to send him to college. Holliday hated Negroes, and when the sons of former slaves insisted on sharing a swimming hole near his home, Holliday killed two and wounded two others with a shotgun blast. "Nigras must be taught their place," he said.

He fled to Dallas, Texas, where early in the '70's he put on his shingle, "J. H. Holliday, Dentist." Holliday loved poker more than dentistry and usually his patients had to seek him out in the gaming rooms. When a rancher accused him of cheating, Holliday killed him. The dead man had powerful friends and Doc was forced to flee to Jacksboro, near the Fort Richardson Military Reservation, where he killed a soldier a few months later. With a posse at his heels he rode 800 miles alone through the Texas Panhandle and No Man's Land to Denver, where he hid out. After only a few weeks there, he carved up a young man named Bud Ryan, who somehow lived to tell of it and show the long jagged scar on his cheek. Following the stabbing Holliday rode to Dodge City, then Tombstone, where he met Wyatt Earp. The rest of his life was devoted to Earp, and according to Bat Masterson, "Doc idolized him."

He was a familiar figure in the roaring days of Tombstone, a tiny man in an overcoat who constantly coughed blood into a dark blue handkerchief. He carried a nickel-plated six-shooter, a bowie knife tied around his neck by a string, and sometimes a sawed-off shotgun stuck in his belt. He had pale blue eyes, a wispy, sandy mustache, and blond hair.

His sweetheart, Big Nose Kate, once burned down a hotel in Texas to rescue him after he had been held for a killing.

Doc died in the Glenwood Springs, Colorado, sanitarium in 1885, at the age of thirty-five. On his deathbed he asked for a last drink of whiskey, then raised his head, looked down at his feet, and whispered: "Well, I'll be damned."

Doc had always sworn he would die with his boots on. They were off.

Holliday, D. D. S.

Kate Fisher, better known as Big Nose Kate.

115

TEMPLE HOUSTON: OKLAHOMA LAWMAN

One of the most popular and also one of the most eccentric characters of the Oklahoma Territory's early days was Temple Houston, son of the famous General Sam Houston. He wore his hair long—down to his shoulders—used a rattlesnake skin for a tie, and employed very unusual tactics when defending clients in court. Once, to demonstrate a point about the dangers of a quick draw, he whipped out his .45, fired several times at the jury and at the judge. When the excitement was over, Houston explained that the cartridges were blanks. The stunt was effective, but the jury found Houston's client guilty anyway.

Houston was well-known through the Southwest as a crackerjack shot with pistol and rifle. He fought and was feared by outlaws, who got as far away as they could when they knew Houston was on the trail. When things got more orderly, Houston settled down as a criminal lawyer and won new fame as the fightingest and greatest orator in the Territory.

Temple Houston, posse leader (third from left, the only man without a hat).

TERROR FROM TEXAS: JOHN WESLEY HARDIN

The Rev. Mr. J. G. Hardin rode circuit in Bonham County, Texas, in the '50's. In a time when a man of God had to be able to brandish a six-gun as skillfully as his Bible, Mr. Hardin pounded across the lonely frontier and spread the Gospel.

Elizabeth, the preacher's wife, bore two of his sons in Bonham. He called the first after himself, Joseph, but the second he named for another circuit rider, across the seas, whose flaming spirit had forged the Methodist Church in England in the previous century.

The boy so reverently christened, John Wesley Hardin, grew up to be a killer, the worst in the whole history of Texas.

Another miscast son of a preacher, Jesse James, the desperado sprung from the Border Wars, deservedly won greater notoriety, but not for the havoc wrought by his shooting irons. James was the classic bandit, Hardin the story-book gunfighter. In his domain he inspired such terror that during the '70's Texans in the great open spaces taunted unruly children with the warning that "Wes Hardin will git ya if ya don't watch out." That's how terrible Mr. Hardin's boy turned out to be—and nobody could account for it.

Wes was only twelve when the South's tattered legions came home from the Civil War, but he was a fierce rebel. Thus the freed Negro and the soldier who enforced the victors' military rule, plus the inevitable "good Injuns" and Mexicans, were the favorite targets of his unbridled youth. The first blood he spilled issued from a Negro who "came at me with a big stick." The stick proved no match at all for the Colt wielded by Hardin, then fifteen. Wes chose a curious way to describe his parents' reaction to his deed. "It nearly distracted them," he wrote, adding:

> To be tried at that time for the killing of a negro meant certain death at the hands of a court backed by Northern bayonets . . . thus, unwillingly, I became a fugitive not from justice, be it known, but from the injustice and misrule of the people who had subjugated the South.

Now, just as in the case of Billy the Kid's earlier years, you have to skip quickly over Hardin's boyish feats. *The Life of John Wesley Hardin,* by himself, told the story in dime-novel fashion:

Our hero slays three soldiers who track him down fleeing his first killing. Then he turns up in Navarro County as a school teacher, no less, but switches to driving cattle and mastering the arts of poker, euchre, and seven-up. He tames (but spares) a Negro bully who calls him "white trash." He teams up with Cousin Simp Dixon to knock off a couple of Yankee soldiers trying to take them in tow. He kills Jim Bradley in a gambling row. He puts a bullet

through the head of a quarrelsome circus hand—and then he falls afoul of that old devil, sex.

It happened in Kosse, Texas, when it was spring and Wes was eighteen and a moonlight made for lovers hung over Texas. An easy mark, the youth let himself get lured to a pretty girl's room only to have a man identified as her sweetheart come panting in just a step behind him. Let Wes tell it:

> The fellow told me he would kill me if I did not give him $100. I told him that I only had about $50 or $60 in my pocket but if he would go with me to the stable I would give him more, as I had the money in my saddle pocket . . . He said, "Give me what you have first." I told him all right, and in so doing, dropped some of it on the floor. He stooped down to pick it up and as he was straightening up I pulled my pistol and fired. The ball struck him between the eyes and he fell over, a dead robber.

Later the youth found himself jailed in Longview for a murder which he modestly disclaimed. On the way to Waco for trial, he escaped by killing a half-breed assigned

117

to guard him, having taken the precaution to buy a Colt from a curiously well-supplied cell mate before the journey began. After that Wes whittled down the Union ranks again by slaying three soldiers who had recaptured him. Army records do not list the triple fatality, but Texas newspapers carried accounts of it long before Hardin's own book came out in 1896, so maybe it happened.

In any case, Wes claimed twelve notches even before he started to shave. Then he added a whole mess of Indians and Mexicans wiped out in warfare on the plains when he joined the Clements brothers in a cattle drive from Texas to Abilene in 1871. You have to allow for some loose reporting from the explosive Texan, of course, but he did proceed to make a demonstrable record as a gunslinger . . .

Manning Clements.

BUCKSHOT AND GROWING PAINS

"You can't hurrah me," said the tall, dark 'n handsome Wild Bill Hickok. "I won't have it."

"I haven't come to hurrah you," answered John Wesley Hardin, aged eighteen, "but I'm going to stay in Abilene."

The boy, wanted in his native Texas for a variety of killings, gave away sixteen years and a couple of inches to the much-touted Marshal. In his trail-dusty pants and worn flannel shirt, he looked like an undergrown urchin alongside the long-haired clothes-horse who was the law in the Kansas cattle town.

It was a scene packed with the live drama of the Old West, but no blood was shed that day in '71. Hickok allowed that the boy could stay in the longhorn capital if he behaved himself and kept away from such bad influences as Ben Thompson, the easily inflamed Texan who was running the Bull's Head Saloon and Gambling House. Wes did steer clear of Thompson. He said that Ben asked him please to turn his .45s on the Marshal but that he replied, "If Bill needs killin' why don't you do it yourself?"

But behaving was something else. Hardin wasn't in Abilene long before he was in trouble again. You might say the kid was provoked. He was drinking with a friend in a saloon when a loud-mouth pounded on the bar and proclaimed that he didn't like Texans. "Two Texans present," Wes announced. When the smoke cleared, seconds later, the man who didn't like Texans was stretched out on the floor and John Wesley Hardin was riding hell-for-leather out of the town.

He got himself a ticket back to Abilene, his memoirs went on, by tracking down and slaying a Mexican who had murdered Billy Coran, a trailhand. Wes said that Hickok not only welcomed him as a returning hero but even arranged to let off Manning and Gyp Clements, his cousins, when they came into town after killing Joe and Dolph Shadden for shirking their labors on a cattle drive from Texas. Biographers or Hickok naturally take offense at suggestions that their hero would write off a murder rap that way, even as they've always laughed off Hardin's story that he got the drop on Bill with the "border roll" the one time the Marshal tried to take his guns away from him. The notion that a mere boy could fool Hickok by whirling two shooting irons into firing position while surrendering them, butts forward, always appalled the Marshal's more ardent admirers. At that, they were probably right.

Who was the more skillful gunslinger? You can't tell because no showdown ever occurred between Hickok and Hardin, on account of the Texan made another hasty exit from Abilene one midnight after pouring four slugs into a prowler in his room at the American Hotel. He left in his shirt and drawers on a commandeered pony. "I was a sorry spectacle," Wes recalled, " . . . bareheaded, unarmed, red-faced and in my night clothes."

Back in Texas, Hardin recovered his composure rapidly. He killed one Negro policeman, Green Paramoor, and wounded another, John Lackey, in Gonzales County when they came to collect the price on his head. Then, as he told it, he took on a whole posse of Negro policemen, leaving three dead. Between the two encounters, he married Jane Bowen, "one of the prettiest and sweetest girls in the country," and set himself up as a horse-trader.

In the summer of '72 Hardin, never badly nicked in gunplay before, was filled with buckshot by Phil Sublet following an argument over a bet on a game of ten pins in John Gates' place in Trinity City. The doctor barely had time to probe for the pellets before the much-hunted Hardin had to hit the saddle again. Then a posse put a bullet in his thigh, and after that close call he decided to surrender himself to Sheriff Dick Reagan of Cherokee County. Even the act of laying down his arms produced violence: a nervous Reagan deputy shot Hardin in the knee. The prisoner was installed in the jail at Gonzales but after a while a thoughtful friend brought him a saw and he cut his way out and limped home to his loving wife to get his health back.

THE SUTTON-TAYLOR FEUD: HARDIN TAKES A HAND

DeWitt County, halfway between San Antonio and the Gulf Coast, was noted for two things in the turbulent days after the Civil War. It was good country for cattle and good country for feudin'. Everybody raised cattle. The Suttons and the Taylors did the feudin'. The Suttons said it all began in the spring of '68 when William E. Sutton, leading a band of indignant citizens, killed Charley Taylor for the high crime of rustling. The Taylors always rejected that notion, even denying that the slain thief was kin to them. They said the trouble began on Christmas Eve in '68 when Buck Taylor—son of William, brother to Creed, Pitkin, Josiah, and Rufus Taylor—was ambushed in Clinton by Bill Sutton and a delegation of riflemen. The Suttons said hell, Buck Taylor started that one and everybody opened up at once and it was a fair 'n square fight. Lee Hall, the famous Texas Ranger captain, submitted that the feud actually dipped back a couple of decades into history. He said it started in the Carolinas, moved to Georgia, and settled down for its violent third act finale in DeWitt County when the surviving Suttons and Taylors elected to settle there, curiously, as neighbors.

The Suttons' band of "Regulators," 200 strong, boasted such stalwarts as Old Joe Tumlinson, ex-Indian fighter, Shanghai Pierce, the hard-drinking, hard-fighting cattleman, and Jack Helm, police captain, sheriff, and vigilante rider. Helm headed the informal frontier battalion.

The Taylors fought under the inspiration of a family motto burned into their minds in the cradle: "Who sheds a Taylor's blood, by a Taylor's hand must fall." They had on their side the clans Kelley and Clements and, come '73, John Wesley Hardin. The Clements were Hardin's cousins and another cousin had married Creed Taylor's daughter Mary. So the terrible Texan had no trouble choosing sides when he arrived in DeWitt County after breaking out of jail in Gonzales and nursing the wounds suffered in the gunplay there.

Hardin's role in the Sutton-Taylor feud was entirely in character. His first victim was J. B. Morgan, a Helm deputy. Wes said Morgan bothered him in a saloon in Cuero and drew on him when he tried to shake him off: "I pulled my pistol and fired, the ball striking him just above the left eye. He fell dead. I went to the stable, got my horse, and left town unmolested."

The tempo of the feud picked up one summer when Bill Kelley and his brother Henry, a son-in-law of Pitkin Taylor, shot up what seemed to them an indecent performance by a traveling troupe in a little community

Captain Creed Taylor.

Pitkin and Susan Taylor.

Judge Henry Clay Pleasants.

Joe Clements.

which happened to be called Sweet Home. After that lark, the Kelley boys were plucked from the hearth by Helm's State Police, presumably to stand trial for disturbing the peace.

The prisoners never got to town. They were found shot to pieces in a clearing near their ranch. John Meador and Doc White were identified as the executioners. Jack Helm said he was out looking for two other Kelley brothers when Bill and Henry perished. His deputies were freed after saying they had to kill the Kelleys because they tried to escape. The newspapers raised so much fuss that Governor E. J. Davis ousted Helm from the State Police force, but he was able to stay in the thick of things because he was also sheriff of DeWitt County.

Pitkin Taylor was the next casualty. Lured outdoors by the tinkling of a bell on one of his own oxen, which he had tied up for the night, he was cut down by Sutton warriors. Jack Hays Day's account of the funeral has a tender scene between the old man's wife and his son, Jim, twenty-one. "Do not weep, Mother," Day quoted the boy. "I will wash my hands in old Bill Sutton's blood!"

That turned out to be a hard trick to turn in a hurry. Jim and some confederates poked their shooting irons through the door of Bank's Saloon and Billiard Parlor in the direction of Bill Sutton on April Fool's Day in '73, but he survived his wounds. In May, Captain Jim Cox and Jake Chrisman, Sutton men, were mowed down. Hardin

John Gipson (Gyp) Clements at the age of 18.

120

said they died when a peace meeting between the two factions turned into a free-for-all; with uncommon modesty, he said he had done no shooting that day. He was in fine fighting trim two days later, however.

Hardin met Helm in a blacksmith's shop, presumably for some more peace talk, but took the precaution to bring Jim Taylor along. When the session ended, the sheriff was dead. Hardin said Helm went after Taylor with a knife and he (Hardin) had to turn his shotgun on him, whereupon Jim made the deed secure by emptying his six-gun into the fallen sheriff's head. Thus, wrote Hardin, died a man "whose name was a horror to all law-abiding citizens . . ."

Wes had no time to bask in the plaudits of the "law abiding," because the next day a pitched battle between the warring sides, both in full force, opened on the Tumlinson place outside of Clinton. A hardy group of citizens effected a truce after two days of cat-and-mouse warfare, but it didn't last long.

Wiley Pridgen, a Taylor man, was ambushed in December in a Thomaston drug store, and again the two sides lined up to shoot it out. The Taylors besieged the Suttons in the Clinton Courthouse but let them go when Judge

H. Clay Pleasants submitted with some force that he wouldn't stand for it if innocent people got hurt when the guns went off. The fight was quickly shifted to the Gulf Hotel at Cuero. Neutral citizens brought about a fresh armistice before any blood was shed, but there was a loophole in it big enough to push some shooting irons through: Jim Taylor allowed that he couldn't include that varmint Bill Sutton in his half of the peace pact.

The exception was written more formally into the records on March 11, 1874, when Jim Taylor trailed Bill Sutton to a steamer about to cut off from Indianola for New Orleans and shot him through the head and heart before he could draw. Gabe Slaughter, who was with Sutton, dropped with a bullet in his brain—fired by Bill Taylor. Sutton's young wife and child witnessed the encounter in stark horror on the ship's deck.

Hardin took the credit for tipping off the Taylors to Sutton's presence on the boat. Then, evidently feeling that his guns were no longer needed, with both Sutton and Helm dead, he settled down to dealing in cattle again and enjoying a brief peace in Comanche with his wife and newborn daughter, Molly.

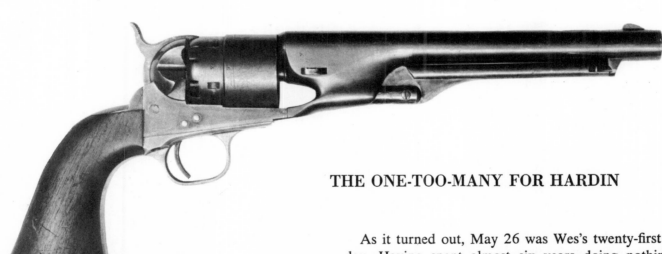

THE ONE-TOO-MANY FOR HARDIN

Charlie Webb was the law, and lots of it, in Brown County, Texas, and he wasn't one to shrink from the idea of going outside his own precincts to haul in a badman who needed taming.

On May 26, 1874, Sheriff Webb strapped on two guns, slid a Winchester into his saddle boot, and rode his big bay over the line into Comanche. He had heard that John Wesley Hardin and Jim Taylor were there and that the town's easy-going lawman, John Karnes, wasn't doing anything about it. There was a price on Taylor's head for deeds committed under the bloody banners of the Sutton-Taylor feud, and Hardin, of course, was the most wanted Texan of them all.

As it turned out, May 26 was Wes's twenty-first birthday. Having spent almost six years doing nothing but blowing other men's brains out, he was now settled down with his wife and baby, trading in cattle and hardly ever firing his guns in anger. You might say he was coming into his manhood in a peace-abiding manner. Anyway, he was a model of behavior in Comanche that day and had himself a jolly time at the races.

It was also highly profitable. "I and my friends won everything in sight," Hardin's memoirs said. "I won about $3,000 in cash, fifty head of cattle, a wagon or two, and fifteen head of saddle horses. I set more than one man afoot and then loaned them the horses to ride home on."

Comanche was only a dot on the map of Texas but it had six saloons. Wes made the grand tour when the races were over, setting up the hangers-on and bar-flies in one oasis after another. Toward dusk he sent his little brother Jeff for a horse and buggy to take him to his father's place

121

two miles out of town. While waiting for the chariot, he elected to have one more drink in Jack Wright's place. Outside the saloon Deputy Sheriff Frank Wilson and Jim Taylor begged him to go home.

"Wes, you have drank enough," Taylor said. "Let us go home; here is Jeff with the buggy."

Just at that moment someone observed: "Here comes that damned Brown County sheriff."

Let Hardin pick it up here:

I turned and faced the man whom I had seen coming up the street. He had on two six-shooters and was about fifteen steps from me, advancing. He stopped when he got to within five steps of me . . . and scrutinized me closely, with his hands behind him. I asked him:

"Have you any papers for my arrest?"

He said: "I don't know you."

I said: "My name is John Wesley Hardin."

He said, "Now I know you, but have no papers for your arrest."

"Well," said I, "I have been informed that the Sheriff of Brown County has said that Sheriff Karnes of this County was no sheriff or he would not allow me to stay around Comanche with my murdering pals."

Webb disowned all such unneighborly declarations and accepted an invitation for a drink. Now hear Hardin again:

As I turned around to go in the door, I heard someone say, "Look out, Jack." It was Bud Dixon, and

as I turned around I saw Charles Webb drawing his pistol. He was in the act of presenting it when I jumped to one side, drew my pistol and fired.

In the meantime Webb had fired, hitting me in the left side, cutting the length of it, inflicting an ugly and painful wound. My aim was good and a bullet hole in the left cheek did the work. He fell against the wall and as he fell he fired a second shot, which went into the air.

Jim Taylor and Bud Dixon put some slugs into the sheriff for insurance, but he was already dead—set down in the loosely-kept records as No. 40 for the quick Hardin triggers. Of course this count included all the anonymous Negroes, Yankee soldier-police, and Indians and Mexicans, with no corpus delicti to prove the conquests, but the roster of identifiable dead was imposing enough.

Charlie Webb, however, was the one-too-many in the violent time of John Wesley Hardin. The Texan would have to pay dearly for that one.

Voice of Experience

John Wesley Hardin, something less than a model son of the Old West, left this piece of personal philosophy for generations to come:

"If you wish to be successful in life, be temperate and control your passions; if you don't, ruin and death is the inevitable result."

Somehow, he knew.

"ROBBERS! PROTECT ME!"

Wes Hardin made the hills outside of Comanche only a few paces ahead of a lynch mob, but in the next nine days his killing of Sheriff Webb was avenged many times over. Hardin's brother Joe was strung to a telegraph pole. Then his cousins, Tom and Bud Dixon, died on a posse's noose, and Alex Barrickman and Ham Anderson, deemed his allies, were executed by gunfire.

Now Texas was too hot for its wildest son—for the first time. He had moved around with remarkable immunity during most of his one-man, six-year wave of destruction. Now the word was out: *Get Hardin*. Now there was a $4,000 price on his handsome head—a new high. Now he had not only the mob and an occasional brash sheriff to deal with, but also the Pinkertons and the Texas Rangers, plus any damn fool with enough lust for gold and glory to tangle with a killer of his repute.

So, hunted day and night, Wes ran for his life. By rail, riverboat, stage, and steed, the twenty-one-year-old outlaw ran for three years . . . New Orleans . . . Florida . . . Georgia . . . Alabama . . . back to Florida.

Lieutenant John B. Armstrong of the Texas Rangers brought the three-year masquerade and flight to an end in Pensacola after trailing Hardin all through the South. Armstrong won his spurs serving under L. H. McNelly, the celebrated Ranger captain who had swept the badmen out of southwest Texas, and volunteered to go after Hardin. While he moved in the killer's wake, Special Ranger John Duncan played out the role of a farmer in Gonzales County, Texas, and kept an eye on Hardin's kin. A letter intercepted by Duncan set Armstrong on the way to Florida.

The lieutenant was waiting in the Pensacola depot on August 23, 1877, when John Wesley Hardin, now "J. H. Swain," came in from Alabama on a mission connected with a logging enterprise in which he had an interest. The way Hardin told it, Armstrong needed a whole platoon of local officers to take him. He said that two deputies rushed into the car and seized him—he was screaming, "Robbers! Protect me!"—and then reinforcements poured in and helped wrestle him into the narrow aisle, where he

Captain John Armstrong.

This was a thoroughly bad son of Texas—William P. Longley. Like the contemporary John Wesley Hardin, his distaste for the "upstart Negro" got him into trouble with the law after the Civil War. He had to go "on the dodge" in his teens after some senseless (and fatal) shooting scrapes around Evergreen. Then he ranged the Southwest and death moved in his wake. So many Negro police, Federal soldiers, occasional possemen, and just-plain-quarrelsome folk dropped before his quick triggers that within ten years the papers back home were charging more than 30 cadavers to the Bill Longley account. In April of '75, while a much-hunted man, the Texan slipped back to Evergreen to kill Wilson Anderson, who he believed had murdered a cousin of his. Caught two years later, he was doomed to the gallows at Giddings, Texas. One of his last acts in prison was to write a letter to the authorities bitterly protesting that Wes Hardin had gotten "only twenty-five years" for all his misdeeds and why were they hanging Bill Longley? But he died bravely. "I deserve this fate," he said on the scaffold. "It is a debt I owe for my wild, reckless life . . . Goodbye, everybody." Then the trap was sprung and frontier Texas closed its books on the wild and handsome 27-year-old gunslinger.

ound himself staring up into the long barrel of Armstrong's Colt:

I said: "Blow away. You will never blow a more innocent man's brains out, or one that will care less."

Someone else was trying to strike me over the head with a revolver when Armstrong called out:

"Men, we have him now; don't hurt him; he is too brave to kill and the first man that shoots him I'll kill him."

The other story is that the Ranger's local helpmates went the other way when the showdown came. In that version, Armstrong—hobbling on a cane because of a recent bullet wound—went into the car alone, killed a young companion of Hardin's who had sent a slug whistling through his hat, and then slammed his six-gun against the fugitive's head. The Texan woke up two hours later, shook his battered head, and insisted that he was not Hardin but J. H. Swain and besides, did the lieutenant have any papers for his arrest? Armstrong said no but he'd get some.

All the way back to Texas delegations assembled at the railroad stations. Nobody tried to take Hardin away from his doughty captor by force, but lawyers got him out of Armstrong's custody in Montgomery, Alabama, on a writ of habeas corpus. A wire from Governor R. B. Hubbard of Texas straightened that out.

When he got to Austin, Hardin told a reporter for the *Statesman* that he had killed Charlie Webb in a fair fight and wanted to be vindicated. "I am a prisoner and must stand trial," he said. "All I want is to be allowed to appeal to the law of the land. I am sick and tired of fleeing from it, and I would not go away if I could."

Wes didn't want for company in Austin. The jail was well supplied with friends, relatives, and kindred souls. Bill Taylor, buddy-in-arms during the Sutton-Taylor feud, was there. So was Brown Bowen, Hardin's no-love-lost brother-in-law, and Manning Clements, his cousin. John Ringo, later one of the outlaw gang in Tombstone, Arizona, also was on the premises, along with assorted gunmen from the Sam Bass gang. It was quite a collection to be housed under one roof, but the Rangers outnumbered them.

In September, Hardin was shackled in irons and hauled to Gonzales in a wagon for his trial. It was brief. Wes was the only witness for the defense, and he addressed the jurors with much emotion:

"Gentlemen, I swear before God that I never shot a man except in self-defense. Sheriff Webb came to Comanche for the purpose of arresting me, and I knew it. I met him and defied him to arrest me, but I did not threaten him . . .

I knew it was in his mind to kill me, not arrest me . . . Everybody knows that he was a dangerous man with a pistol . . . I know I haven't any friends here (in the courtroom) but I don't blame them for being afraid to come out for me. My father is a good man, and my brother who was lynched never harmed a man in his life. People will call me a killer, but I swear to you, gentlemen, that

I have shot only in defense of myself. And when Sheriff Webb drew his pistol I had to draw mine. Anybody else would have done the same thing. Sheriff Webb had shot a lot of men. That's all, gentlemen."

The jurors deliberated ninety minutes and found Hardin guilty of murder in the second degree. The punishment was fixed at twenty-five years' hard labor.

In gambling parlance the "man in the white hat" is the marked man, the sucker who is going to be fleeced. In this photo, the man in the white hat (seated at left) is Jim Miller, who was vaguely related to John Wesley Hardin by marriage but very much akin to the wild Texan as a thoroughly antisocial citizen of the West. It was a shooting scrape of Miller's that brought Hardin to El Paso, where he was slain. Miller is shown here in a quiet moment in the gambling room of a saloon in Pecos, Texas, in the 80's.

. . . WITH HIS BOOTS ON

The gates of Rusk Prison in Huntsville opened on a cold February afternoon in 1894 and Convict No. 7109 stepped out into a brisk Texas wind. He was forty-one years old. He had been behind bars for sixteen years. He went in a killer; by his own account he had slain men by the score, and he wouldn't be tamed in a penitentiary. He would fight back. Time after time, he was spread-eagled on the floor, flogged, and thrown into the "dark cell"— solitary. But between escape plots, rebellion, and defiance, he turned to the twin callings of his father—theology and law. Once they let him teach Sunday school in the prison. And other times, when he was behaving and there were no lashings and he had the run of the place, he pored over Blackstone and the statute books. When he got out, he went back to Gonzales. His pretty wife, Jane, had died two years earlier, but his children were there, grown now. He finished his law studies and wrangled a full pardon

from Governor Jim Hogg. He was a free white citizen of Texas again, and he hung out a shingle:

JOHN WESLEY HARDIN, ESQ.
Attorney-at-Law

He was not the same Hardin the state had locked away for killing Sheriff Charlie Webb. He was a somewhat milder man, not quite as quick to take offense, but no meek either. The rebel inside, who loved a fight, was still there, and in no time at all Hardin was in the thick of a bitter political battle over the office of sheriff. The man he backed lost, perhaps understandably, and Hardin left Gonzales. In London, Texas, he married Callie Lewis who was much younger than he, but the union soon broke up.

El Paso was his next stop—and his last.

* * *

Jeff Milton.

George Scarborough.

The *El Paso Times* carried this genteel item on April 7, 1895:

> Among the leading citizens of Pecos City now in El Paso is John Wesley Hardin, a leading member of the Pecos City bar. In his younger days he was as wild as the broad western plains on which he was raised. But he was a generous, brave-hearted youth and got into no small amount of trouble for the sake of his friends, and soon gained the reputation for being quick-tempered and a dead shot.
>
> In those days when one man insulted another, one of the two of them died then and there. Young Hardin, having a reputation for being a very brave man who never took water, was picked out by every bad man who wanted to make a reputation, and that was where the "bad men" made their mistake, for the young westerner still survives many warm and tragic encounters.
>
> Forty-one years has steadied the impetuous cowboy down to a peaceable, dignified, quiet man of business. But underneath his dignity is a firmness that never yields except to reason and law. He is a man who makes friends of all who come into close contact with him.
>
> He is here as associate attorney for the persecution in the case of the State of Texas vs Bud Frazer, charged with assault with intent to kill. Mr. Hardin is known all over Texas. He was born and raised in this state.

If that sounds like the sort of rave which Mr. Hardin might have written himself, well, it was the day of the paid news notice, so draw your own conclusions.

Bud Frazer had shot and crippled Jim Miller, who was a brother-in-law of Hardin's cousin, Manning Clements.

Miller was something less than a model citizen himself, so Frazer beat the case, but Hardin elected to stay in El Paso. Among other inducements, he had been smitten by the charms of a luscious blonde whose husband, Martin McRose, couldn't come into town because the authorities wanted to talk to him about some large deeds of cattle rustling and a little matter of murder. McRose and his partner, Vic Queen, along with Tom Finnessy and an army of their riders, were holed up across the border in Juarez.

Martin McRose and Tom Finnessy.

Mrs. McRose preferred the bright lights and roaring saloons of El Paso.

McRose and Queen ventured across the border one night—either to stick up the Sunset Line or keep a rendezvous with El Paso peace officers to talk surrender. Whatever they came over for, they didn't get very far before guns started to go off. McRose went down fighting; Queen fled. Special Ranger Jeff Milton and Deputy U. S. Marshals George Scarborough and Frank McMahon were indicted in the killing of the outlaw leader.

Hardin, now taken to heavy drinking as his heavy romance proceeded, boasted that he had hired Milton and Scarborough to kill McRose so that he could inherit the rustler's fun-loving wife. Milton encountered Hardin one night in a crowd in front of Con Ryan's Parlor Saloon—

> MILTON: Hardin, you've been telling people you paid me to kill McRose. You're a goddamned liar.
> HARDIN: You can talk to me like that when I'm not armed.
> MILTON: You're lying again. You're always armed. And you can go for your gun right now or tell all these men here and out loud that you lied.
> HARDIN: Gentlemen, when I said that about Captain Milton I lied.

Scarborough got a written apology from Hardin. Evidently the lawmen felt strongly about (a) being indicted for killing the fugitive McRose in the line of what they thought was their duty and (b) having it said that they were paid assassins in the employ of a man like Hardin.

Wes next got into trouble with the Selmans, father and son. Young John Selman, a policeman, tossed Mrs. McRose into jail one night on a charge of vagrancy. Hardin bailed out his buxom lady fair and then cussed out Old John Selman as the sire of a monstrous offspring. Old John, who had played both sides of the law in his time and was now constable of El Paso, elected not to have it out at that moment. But he did brood over the things Wes had said about his son, and he let it be known that he'd kill him if he heard any more, whereupon Hardin started to brush up on his draw, dryly commenting: "Old John better go fixed at all times." Old John took the advice. On the night of August 19, 1895, he came into the Acme Saloon not only "fixed" but with mayhem on his mind.

Hardin was shaking dice with Henry Brown, the bartender, for drinks. He rolled, handed the box to Brown, and, looking down at the dice, said, "four sixes to beat." At that moment a bullet crashed into the back of his head. Old John stood a few feet away, smoke curling out of his pistol. Hardin sank to the floor and died.

Albert Fall, decades later a central figure in the Teapot Dome Scandal that rocked the administration of President Warren G. Harding, served as Selman's lawyer. He outlined a simple defense: Old John thought Hardin had spotted him in the mirror behind the bar. And when Hardin tendered the dice box to Brown, Old John thought

Old John Selman.

he was reaching for the gun he always kept in the shoulder holster he himself had fashioned. Naturally, Old John had to throw lead to save himself.

Ironically, George Scarborough settled the score for Wes before the case got to court. He cut Old John down in a gun duel the next April, punctuating an evening of drinking and good fellowship in the Wigwam Saloon.

There were some skeptics who termed it an odd "duel" because no gun was found on the body when, having assured the assembled throng that he had really been a substantial citizen and always meant well, Old John finally expired of his wounds. Others submitted that he did have a revolver but that a collector of trophies of that kind had walked off with it while Old John was making his belated overtures to the Maker. In any event, the man who sent the great John Wesley Hardin to hell was at least facing his assailant when he bit the dust of Texas.

The Loser Wins

John Wesley Hardin lost his roll shooting dice in the Gem Saloon in El Paso one night in 1895. For a while he watched the game, brooding. Then he drew a pistol and demanded his money back.

"Take it all, Mr. Hardin," said the timid soul handling the cash for the house. "It belongs to you."

Hardin got arrested for it the next day but nobody thought to ask him to return the money. He did get told not to play that way any more.

CALAMITY JANE

A WOMAN LOW DOWN

There is no doubt that the woman most popularly associated with the western frontier is Calamity Jane. As long as books on the West are written, Jane will be a part of them. She has no middle-of-the-road critics; they are either pro-Calamity Jane or anti-Calamity Jane.

For example, Doane Robinson, South Dakota historian, says of her, "She was a woman low down, even in her class . . ."

Dr. W. A. Allen of Billings, Montana, who knew Jane, says, "She swore, she drank, she wore men's clothing. Where can you find a woman today who doesn't do such things? She was just fifty years ahead of her time."

There is no doubt Jane was tragically miscast by nature. She should have been a man. Her figure was definitely not feminine. She was a good rider and could handle a mule team with ease. An old cowhand once said "she gave the finest demonstration of firearms" he had ever witnessed.

She had an impressive vocabulary of cuss words, using them senselessly, automatically as any mule-skinner. She lived to drink, and lived her short and merry life with a rowdy sort of happiness.

Her birth and birthplace are still debated. The best guess is Princeton, Missouri, about 1848. The United States census of 1860 lists a Martha Jane Canarray, of Marion Township, and that may have been Calamity. In 1863, the family left the two-hundred-acre farm and rolled west. There is a blank here in the known record of Jane's life, but many legends. She is supposed to have been married, lived for a while in Virginia City, and from her own story, stopped in Alder Gulch.

She drifted from town to town, once working as a laborer on the Union Pacific. By her account, she drifted to Cheyenne in 1869. She was already wearing men's pants, chewing tobacco, and drinking heavily. Two years later she was working as a mule skinner or in a cattle-driving train.

Abilene and Hays City knew her, also Livingston, Montana. She claimed she joined the army in 1872 in its fight against the Indians. Her "autobiography" gives a dramatic account of saving a young cavalryman's life, but that is nonsense.

However, it was about this time that Jane got her nickname. It had a special ring of doom which appealed to the crowds in the rough frontier saloons.

"Here's Calamity!" they would shout as Martha Jane would swagger toward the bar. Sometimes she fired off her six-shooter and shattered a mirror. The crowds loved it. The bartenders grinned. It was good for business.

In 1875 she joined Crook's expedition against the Sioux

Calamity Jane, General Crook's scout.

as a mule-skinner but was sent back after her sex was discovered. Jane had gone swimming with some of the skinners and a horrified colonel fired her on the spot.

127

The famous Deadwood coach. Bill McCune driving, Johnny Nelson riding "shotgun," Johnny Baker and Della Farrell in front, Buck Taylor and Mitchell in rear.

JANE MEETS WILD BILL

In the '70's Jane was roaming the Black Hills and there her legend grew bright. Bill Hickok rode into her life. It will always be debated whether Bill was her lover. It's doubtful he considered her anything more than a humorous addition to his entourage. But whatever Hickok thought of her, Jane was enjoying her most triumphant hour when she rode into Deadwood at Bill's side while the miners, gamblers, and dance-hall girls whooped and shouted as the Great Hickok rode down Main Street. They all wore creamy new Stetsons, brand-new fringed buckskins, and shiny boots. Revolver butts gleamed and the silver decorations on their saddles and rifles flashed in the sun.

Deadwood, which always loved a good show, whooped in glee. Calamity Jane shone in Hickok's reflected glory all the summer. But then Jack McCall shot Hickok in the back of the head and Calamity was bereft. She rolled from saloon to saloon, spicing her beer with bitter tears. The great days were gone. Jane was skidding downhill. But when the smallpox plague swept Deadwood, she regained some of her lost glory. Doctor Babcock, the town's only physician, told how Jane risked her life to care for some of the dying miners. One of her patients was a small boy named Robinson. Jane was an efficient if rough nurse. She was apt to growl, "Here, drink this, you little bastard," or "Damn you, sit still until I can wash your face . . ."

The Robinson boy recovered and appeared again in Jane's life.

Calamity Jane at Hickok's grave in Mount Moriah Cemetery, just a few years before she died.

128

JANE IN DEADWOOD

The tales of Jane in Deadwood are many. In 1930 an old man recalled how Jane dangled him on her knee when she found him weeping with loneliness. Another recalled how Jane won a fifty-dollar bet for shooting a hole in the top of a hat hanging in the rear of a saloon. The most hilarious story comes from Charles E. Chaplin, whose account is in the Montana Historical Society. In about 1880, when he was playing with the Lard Players at the East Lynne Opera House, Jane and Arkansas Tom, a notorious gunfighter, were in the audience. Jane soon grew indignant at the conduct of Lady Isobel, who, in the play, elopes with Sir Francis. At a crucial moment Jane stood up and let fly a stream of tobacco juice. Her marksmanship was good. The juice hit the actress and splattered her long pink dress. As the house went into an uproar and the actress screamed with indignation at her, Jane calmly stood up, threw a gold piece on the stage, and said in a loud voice, "That's for your damn dress."

Then, with Arkansas Tom gallantly offering his arm, she strode up the aisle and out into the night. Two days later Tom was killed in a raid on a small Dakota town bank.

Jane and friend enjoy a few beers.

Kohl & Middleton's
PALACE MUSEUM
Week Beginning Monday, Jan. 20.

CALAMITY JANE!

The Famous Woman Scout of the Wild West! Heroine of a Thousand Thrilling Adventures! The Terror of Evildoers in the Black Hills! The Comrade of Buffalo Bill and Wild Bill! See this Famous Woman and Hear Her Graphic Description of Her Daring Exploits!

A HOST OF OTHER ATTRACTIONS

Two Big Stage Shows!

that's all ONE DIME! that's all

A poster advertising Jane's show.

DRIFTING

Jane continued to drift about the West. She was now a living legend—"White Devil of the Yellowstone," one dime novel called her. In 1885 she is said to have married a man named Burke in California. In 1887 she turned up in Gilt Edge, Montana, her hair gray, the years of dissipation showing plainly in her face. In 1889 she turned up in Rawlins, Wyoming, and the following year Ben Arnold, the Indian fighter, saw her in a small South Dakota town. She was so old and haggard he didn't recognize her at first.

In 1896 she joined the Palace Museum at Minneapolis. She toured Chicago, St. Louis, and Kansas City. She was expected to play her flamboyant role and she did. But she got drunk once too often and was fired. Now she could cadge drinks by giving the bartenders a copy of her tiny "autobiography" which sold by the thousands.

Estelline Bennett, in her *Deadwood Days,* recalled that in 1899 Jane came back for a visit to the scene of her greatest triumph. She shuffled down Main Street dragging along a girl about seven years old. According to the *New Northwest,* a newspaper of Deer Lodge, Montana, she had been married twice, "once to a young man named Washburne who entered the Army, and also to a Lt. Summers, who apparently fathered her daughter," the young seven-year-old. Curious townspeople watched the grotesque figure and shook their heads. Was this the glamorous Calamity Jane?

A benefit was played for her and her child. But Jane forgot her child and blew the money across the bar the same night. Miss Bennett heard her coming home, howling like a wolf and offering to give battle to anyone at all in Deadwood.

In May, 1900, the editor of the *Livingston Post* found Jane in a bawdy house and nursed her back to health. She was hired by the Pan-American Exposition, but she went on "a high lonesome," wrecked a bar, blackened the eyes of two policemen, and was fired. Two years later the *Daily Yellowstone* located her in Billings, Montana, where she had shot up a bar. The next morning she was ordered out of town.

Louis Freeman, the noted American explorer, met her in 1902 in Yellowstone. He bought her several pails of beer and took some pictures of Jane smoking a cigar. As he recalls, she looked like a woman of seventy.

In July, 1903, Jane appeared at the Calloway Hotel in Terry, a short distance from Deadwood. She was dying. On August 2, 1903, she opened her eyes and whispered, "What's the date?"

When they told her, she nodded and replied, "It's the twenty-seventh anniversary of Bill's (Hickok) death." Then, "Bury me next to Bill."

At five her breathing became labored. A short time later she died. Her funeral was one of the largest in the history of Deadwood. There was one last wonderful touch. The man who closed the coffin was C. H. Robinson, rector of the Mt. Moriah Cemetery. He was the little boy Calamity Jane had nursed during the smallpox plague.

SCOUT OF THE CUMBERLAND

The most glamorous and in a way the most tragic of the "celebrated" women of the western frontier was beautiful Pauline Cushman, who served in the Tennessee campaign as a Union spy. General John Hunt Morgan, the Rebel raider, found her so attractive he set her free even though she had been arrested as a spy.

Pauline's pictures show she possessed a gypsy-like beauty. Her hair was long and black as a raven's wing. Her voice was remembered by one New York theatrical critic as "lark-like."

Pauline was born in New Orleans on June 10, 1833. Her father was a Spanish dry goods merchant and her mother a New Orleans beauty. In the 1840's the family moved to Michigan, where Pauline's father opened a frontier trading post. Her formative years were spent on the open prairie among the Chippewas, who called her Laughing Breeze.

At eighteen she ran away from home to join a theatrical group. Before she was nineteen she was playing leading roles, once opposite John McDonough, the matinee idol of his day.

In 1863, while starring in Wood's Theatre, Louisville, Tennessee, she agreed to serve as a Union agent for William Truesdail, chief of the Army of the Cumberland's secret police. Some of the reports she sent to him during the Tennessee campaign were smuggled past Confederate lines in loaves of bread.

After several admiring Confederate officers took her on a tour of Shelbyville, she foolishly made a series of sketches of the fortifications and hid them in a boot. On the way to Nashville, she was picked up by a Rebel scouting party belonging to Morgan's command. Morgan freed her and she started out again. She was recaptured by some of Forrest's men and the sketches were found.

She was court-martialed at Shelbyville and found guilty. While she was awaiting sentence, Rosecrans launched his attack on Shelbyville, Wartrace, and Tullahoma. On the twenty-seventh the Federal cavalry drove in the pickets and the Rebels evacuated Shelbyville. Union symphathizers brought Pauline from the prison to a boarding house and General Rosecrans ordered that she be given the best of care.

In 1864 she embarked on a triumphant theatrical career. In September the *New York Herald* said hundreds stood for hours to buy tickets to hear her "recite her narrative," a dramatic version of her adventures.

Pauline and her troupe toured the country from New York to San Francisco. She played to the wildest audiences on the frontier, who fired six-shooters at the ceiling instead of applauding.

In a small town south of San Francisco, Pauline again stole the headlines. She was part owner of the well-known La Honda Hotel, and had stopped off to manage it for a while between engagements. When she heard that another hotel manager was making remarks about her virtue, she grabbed a stage-coach driver's whip and flogged the "traducer" unmercifully.

Another time in a California hotel she broke a soup plate over a man, who later said he had been "hypnotized" by her swarthy beauty.

In 1879 she married Jere Fryer and settled with him in Casa Grande, Arizona. Fryer, handsome and wild, had a roving eye and broke Pauline's heart several times. But she loved him dearly and tried to overlook his wanderings.

In Casa Grande she became unofficial referee of six-gun battles. On one occasion, as a diary of one of her friends tells it, she stood in the center of the dirt street, six-shooter in hand, while the leaders of two rival factions fought to the death. After one fighter had drawn too slow and died on his feet, Pauline dressed the corpse, said the prayers for the dead, and buried him.

In 1880 Casa Grande, with the Southern Pacific terminal nearby, was a booming town. Outlaws, fugitives, drunken cowhands, and mule skinners crowded the narrow walks. On one occasion Pauline, armed with a rifle, climbed to the top of the corral fence adjacent to the hotel she owned and ordered one of the skinners to "cut out" a sick animal in his team. When the skinner indignantly told her to go to hell, Pauline aimed her rifle at his heart and told him she was going to count to three. At two, the skinner surrendered and substituted another mule.

The great tragedy in her life occurred when she attempted to hold her husband's love by substituting an infant born to a prostitute as her own. The handsome Jere, proud of his fatherhood, forgot his roving eye. But the child was sickly and died during a fit before it was two. Then the real mother appeared and the plot was exposed. Pauline, broken-hearted and ashamed, left town to return to the stage. But nobody was interested in the Civil War, the producers told her. She was already a legend, and no manager wanted to hire legends, especially old ones. As the diary of her friend, Mike Sears, recalls, by 1880 she was a tall hoarse-voiced woman with gray-streaked hair and skin dried by the desert sun, and usually dressed in a fashion outdated by twenty years.

Pauline Cushman.

Mike sat with her in a box through an unforgettable performance of *Julius Caesar* in San Francisco. During the evening Pauline drank long slugs of whiskey, bellowing comments to the leading man, James Ward, one of the finest actors of his time. Ward bowed and waved several times. He had reason to be gracious. Twenty years earlier Pauline had given him his first stage job, and what was more, had recognized and encouraged his talent.

In 1892 Pauline was reduced to scrubbing floors in the San Francisco theatres where once men had fired six-shooters in tribute to her. On December 7, 1893, her landlady forced in the door of her tiny bedroom and kitchen apartment at 1118 Market Street. Pauline Cushman, Federal spy, theatrical great, frontier woman who had refereed gun battles alone and unafraid, who had horse-whipped a scandal-monger and made a tough mule skinner treat an animal kindly, had died quietly during the night.

She was saved from potter's field by the Grand Army of the Republic, who gave her an enormous funeral. The plaque they mounted above her grave, still on view today, reads, "Pauline Cushman, Federal Spy and Scout of the Cumberland."

THE NOTORIOUS BELLE STARR

Belle Starr.

Belle Starr shares equal billing with Calamity Jane in frontier history as one of the glamour girls of the Old West. But as in the case of Jane, the facts of her life give the lie to the legend. Belle was a hatchet-faced woman with the disposition of a tantalized rattlesnake. She was far from being a "bandit queen" but, as a Federal indictment handed down against her in Fort Smith charged, she was "the leader of a band of notorious horse thieves . . ."

Calamity Jane preferred the fringed buckskin coat and trousers, but Belle adopted a long velvet gown and a plumed hat. Time and again she has been confused with Belle Boyd, the truly glamorous Confederate spy.

The hack writers for Richard Fox's *Police Gazette* planted and nourished the legend that Belle Starr was a "female Robin Hood and a Jesse James." In reality Belle was a horse-thief and perhaps a frontier fence. But unlike Jesse, she never held up a stage-coach or a train or a bank.

It is generally accepted that Myra Belle Shirley was born on February 5, 1848, in a log cabin somewhere along the Missouri frontier. We know nothing of her mother, Elizabeth, but her father, John, is said to have been from "an aristocratic" Virginia family. Tradition has given him the title of "Judge," but there is no evidence that he ever presided over a court of law.

In 1848 his homestead consisted of 800 acres ten miles northwest of Carthage, Missouri. When she was eight, Belle became a pupil of the Carthage Female Academy, board and lodging ten dollars a month. The curriculum included reading, writing, spelling, grammar, deportment,

Greek, Latin, and Hebrew. Instruction in painting, piano, and organ were extra.

When the Kansas-Missouri border war broke out, Belle's brother joined Jim Lane's Redlegs. He was killed at Sarcoxie, Missouri. The continuous raids ruined Starr's tavern business and he moved his family to Scyene, Texas (ten miles east of Dallas).

In 1866 the James-Younger gang robbed their first bank in Liberty, Missouri, and fled with $6,000 in cash and bonds. They broke up, Jesse and the Youngers going to Texas, where Cole met Belle and probably—there is no positive evidence—fathered her firstborn, a daughter she named Pearl.

The bandit queen.

132

The cabin at Younger's Bend.

Jim Reed, a bank and train robber from Vernon County, Missouri, was her next lover. With the law hot on Jim's trail, he and Belle fled to California, where she presented him with a son named Edward. In 1869 Belle, Reed, and two other outlaws rode to the North Canadian river country, where they tortured an old Creek Indian until he told them where he had hidden $30,000 in gold. With their share of the loot, Jim and Belle returned to Texas, where she played the role of "Bandit Queen" to the hilt. At the turn of the century there were still old residents of Scyene who remembered Belle in her velvet gown, shiny boots, and six-shooters riding her black mare, "Venus," into town, a riding crop dangling from her right wrist.

In August, 1874, Reed was killed by one of his gang. Belle left her children with her mother while she rode the Outlaw Trail.

BELLE ON THE OUTLAW TRAIL

From 1875 to 1880, Belle was the undisputed leader of a band of cattle- and horse-thieves who made their headquarters in "The Nations," or Indian-held sections of Oklahoma. Some she accepted as lovers, but Cole Younger still occupied, as he always would, the choice spot in her heart.

In 1876 another "husband" appeared on the scene. He was a flat-faced Indian with the odd name of "Blue Duck."

Blue Duck and Belle.

REWARD
$10,000
IN GOLD COIN
Will be paid by the U. S. Government
for the apprehension
DEAD OR ALIVE
of
SAM and BELLE STARR
Wanted for Robbery, Murder, Treason
and other acts against the peace
and dignity of the U. S.
THOMAS CRAIL
Major, 8th Missouri Cavalry, Commanding

He lasted only a short time, after which his place was taken by Sam Starr, a tall, slim Cherokee. Belle was twenty-eight, Sam thirty-two. The honeymooners settled down on Sam's sixty-two acres on the north side of the Canadian River, near Briartown. Belle named the place Younger's Bend, after her first love. Belle was now surrounded by members of the Starr clan, presided over by "Uncle Tom" Starr, an incredibly vicious old man who had burned a whole family to death in 1843.

Belle herself told a story of how a slim man with blinking blue eyes once visited her and Sam at Younger's Bend. Starr was suspicious of the cold and silent man who refused to hang up his guns, but Belle told him he was an "old friend from Missouri." Sam Starr never knew the blinking blue-eyed man was Jesse James on the dodge from the posses.

In 1883 Belle made her appearance as the first female ever tried for a major crime in the courtroom of the celebrated "Hanging Judge" Parker in the Federal Court of the Western District of Arkansas. The indictment charged her with being the leader of a band of horse-thieves.

Pearl Starr (*right*), Belle's daughter, with two friends.

"THE PETTICOAT OF THE PLAINS"

The trial provided much lurid copy and Belle was dubbed "The Petticoat of the Plains," "Queen of the Bandits," and "The Lady Desperado" by Fox's writers in the *Police Gazette*.

She was found guilty and Parker sentenced her to six months and Sam to a year in the Federal Prison in Detroit. Both were model prisoners. After serving their time, Belle and Sam returned to Younger's Bend. In the fall of 1884 Belle, as legend has it, took part in a Wild West show in the role of an outlaw. She held up a stage-coach. One of the passengers was Judge Parker.

Sam Starr vanished temporarily in 1885, and accounts vary as to why. John Middleton, wanted for a cold-blooded murder in Texas, had been hanging around Belle and there were plenty who said this fast-drawing outlaw had killed Sam and then claimed Belle. But Sam had simply taken a vacation back in the hills.

That spring Middleton himself was bushwhacked and killed. Belle wept and put a handsome marker over his grave. But when Sam Starr reappeared, she forgot her tears in housekeeping and stealing horses again at Younger's Bend.

In 1886 Belle and Sam were arrested by United States marshals, who brought them to Fort Smith on charges of robbery and horse-stealing. Belle was more mellow than ever before and granted long interviews to local editors. The Starrs were arraigned the following day before Judge Parker, who was forced to dismiss the charges for lack of evidence. With her "jolly lads" and Sam at her side, Belle rode out of town, smiling graciously at the townspeople.

It was near Christmas when Sam was killed by a dying Indian deputy whom he had shot down in a drunken argu-

ment. Belle, once again a widow, did not remain alone for long. Several months after Starr's death, Jim July came into her life. The *Dallas News* described him as "a tall, well formed Creek Indian with long black hair falling to his shoulders." In a short time the marshals of Fort Smith were looking for July on a larceny charge. When Belle pointed out to Jim that the government had little or no evidence to support its case, he agreed to surrender. On a hot July day in 1889 Belle rode halfway to Fort Smith with him. At San Bois they stayed overnight, and the following morning after breakfast July set out alone.

Somewhere along the lonely road back to Younger's Bend a bushwhacker did in Belle Starr. She was found dying by a passerby. Her daughter Pearl came up on a gallop when she heard the news, flinging herself out of the saddle to reach her mother as she whispered a few dying words. Pearl never disclosed what they were.

Belle was buried on February 3, 1889, in the front yard of the cabin at Younger's Bend. Months later Pearl hired a stonecutter to mount a monument over her mother's grave. On the top of the stone was carved an image of her favorite mare, "Venus." On the stone was this inscription:

Belle Starr
Born in Carthage, Missouri, February 5, 1848.
Died February 3, 1889.

    Shed not for her the bitter tear,
    Nor give the heart to vain regret,
    'Tis but the casket that lies here,
    The gem that fills it sparkles yet.

Belle herself had supplied a more fitting inscription a few months before. "I regard myself," she had said, "as a woman who has seen much of life."

CHINA POLLY: A LEGEND COME TRUE

As they say, it was like a scene in the movies. The saloon in the booming town of Warren, Idaho, was packed to its swinging doors. The tinny piano had been stilled; there was a hush over the smoky room.

Two men sat at a table, an island in the crowded room. One was tall, good-looking, and bronzed by the sun; the other was a pigtailed Chinese, with skin yellow and tight as old parchment drawn over the high cheek-bones. His face was impassive; his eyes beady black.

The white man, Johnny Bemis, slid out the four aces. The Chinaman made a slight bow of defeat.

"Bring the girl," he said in a low voice.

Another Chinese standing behind him disappeared. In a few moments he reappeared holding the arm of a young and pretty Chinese girl.

Johnny scratched his head. "Now I got you, I don't know what the hell to do with you," he said, and laughed.

A moment later he walked out, followed by the slender girl in the yellow gown slit at the knee. Johnny Bemis had won the girl, later to be known in Idaho's frontier history as China Polly. Their true story, strangely enough, has been overlooked by Hollywood and the legend-makers.

Polly was a Cantonese slave girl who had been shipped to the United States in 1871, when she was eighteen. She was sent to Warren to be the wife of the rich Chinese gambler. On the night she arrived, Johnny and the gambler played for high stakes—the highest was Polly—and Johnny won.

Later, in another game, he was shot but Polly put him on a horse, got him away safely, and nursed him back to health. During his recovery Johnny realized he was deeply in love with this pretty, slight Chinese girl, and married her.

Johnny, who is described in a letter from an old friend of his to one of the authors as "no better or no worse—who took his pleasures as did his friends," deserted the gambling tables after his marriage. He and Polly settled at the mouth of Cripple Creek, "to rock some gold," and to live a peaceful, lawful life.

PEARL HART:

America's Last Stage-Coach Robbery

The slim young man nervously fingered his six-shooter, turned to his heavier, older companion, and cried, "Here comes the stage, Joe. Let's go!"

They spurred their horses through the brush onto the highway as the Globe, Arizona, stage swept around a bend, the driver's whip cracking over the ears of his team. When he saw the two riders, the driver pulled back on his reins "with a tug that set them on their haunches," he reported.

His three passengers, who had been dozing, flew across the coach, landing in a heap. One of them, a drummer, looked up through the tangle of legs and arms into the barrel of a six-shooter held by a young road agent.

"Get up and line up."

The short fat drummer and the other two passengers— a dude with his hair parted in the middle and a pigtailed Chinaman—tumbled out. At the order to "shell out," they emptied their pockets. The drummer "contributed" $390, the dude $36, and the Chinese $5.

Joe waved his six-shooter. "Get back in the coach," he roared, "and if one of you looks back . . ."

The passengers jumped for the coach. The driver cracked his whip and, with a rattle of trace chains, the stage rumbled down the road.

The younger road agent took off "his" hat, long brunette locks tumbled down, and "he" was revealed as a young woman. Pearl Hart, a pretty young boarding-school student who had pulled off what was to be the last stage-coach robbery in the West, slapped Joe Boot, a one-time miner, on the shoulder.

"Guess we did it, Joe," she cried.

"You're a smart 'un, Pearl," replied the admiring Boot.

Pearl was to discover she had not only committed the last stage-coach robbery in the West, but probably the most bizarre. Joe and Pearl got lost! They rode around for three nights. Then, completely exhausted and soaked by the storm that had plagued them all day, they lay down in the rain and fell asleep. A passing rancher saw them and, recalling the alarm which had been sent out, notified Sheriff William Truman. The law officer who woke them up brought them to Florence, where a huge crowd greeted the prisoners.

"Would you do it again?" a reporter asked Pearl.

She gave him a "savage look" and snarled, "Damn right, podner."

The student was now talking like a Zane Grey character.

Pearl was finally sentenced to five years in the Yuma Territorial Prison, where she became a western curiosity. Sunday visitors never failed to ask her to pose for a picture in the jail yard. Pearl always obliged.

Yuma was not built to accommodate female prisoners, and the warden and the governor were only too glad to parole Pearl. She traveled about the country, swaggering on the stage as the "Arizona bandit." Her glory lasted for about a year before she gradually slipped into obscurity.

In 1924 a tiny, white-haired old lady visited the Pima County courthouse and asked to look over the building. When the chief clerk asked why, she replied, "Well, I lived around here in the old days and would like to see if the place is the same."

After the curious clerk took her on a tour of the building, he asked her name. She hesitated, then said, "Pearl Hart," and hurried out. She was never heard from again.

ROY BEAN: Judge, Bartender, and Jury

Judge Roy Bean was a soiled and bewhiskered fat man who had three passions. One was the law; he loved to fine people. Another was hard whiskey in adult portions. And the third was Lily Langtry, the celebrated English actress. The Jersey Lily was his idea of a lot of woman, even at great distances. He named a saloon after her. The saloon was also his courtroom. It was a cozy arrangement; a man only had to cross the hardwood floor to spend what was left of his roll after a run-in with the "Law West of the Pecos," otherwise known as Roy Bean, a figure of comic relief in Texas history.

His beginnings are rather cloudy. The Judge liked to talk, but he was apt to alter the script as he went along. Born to a poor but large family in Mason County, Kentucky, around 1825, he turned up in Mexico as a strapping youth, and in Chihuahua killed a home-grown badman who liked to pick fights with gringos. He shoved on to San Diego, California, on the heels of the Gold Rush, and did a month in jail for shooting a man in a perfectly proper duel on horseback. Then, in the Mission of San Gabriel, outside Los Angeles, he acquired rope burns on his neck after destroying a Mexican Lothario in a row over a girl; he said the señorita cut him down after her boy friend's chums strung him up and left him for dead.

The Civil War found Bean in Old Mesilla, New Mexico, hungering to advance the Southern cause and his own fortunes at the same time. He organized a guerrilla band called the Free Rovers, known to more critical observers as the Forty Thieves. Then he shifted to San Antonio, Texas, hauling goods from Mexico to run the Northern blockade. There again his dedication to the Confederacy was called into question, because he had trouble over financial dealings and had to spend much time in the courts defending his assets and his reputation. He also acquired a child bride, Virginia Chavez, who bore him two sons and two daughters before quitting his company. After that twenty years passed without event before the man got himself famous in the Pecos country.

Pressing sixty, gray, portly, whiskey-sodden and short on ready cash, Roy Bean moved into west Texas because the Southern Pacific was pushing west from New Orleans to the Gold Coast and railroad towns were prospering. In the tent town of Vinegaroon Bean managed to get himself appointed Justice of the Peace in 1882. He had been in and out of enough courtrooms to qualify as a man possessed of much legal lore even if he wasn't too strong on readin' and writin' and that sort of nonsense. Vinegaroon withered as fast as the road gangs departed and Roy followed the rails to Langtry, a stop-over point on the Southern Pacific. The Judge said he named the town after the girl of his wildest dreams; the railroad said the little oasis actually was named for one of its own dignitaries. A fine coincidence, the matter is still in dispute.

Roy Bean.

THE LAW WEST OF THE PECOS

Roy Bean set himself up in business with a copy of th Revised Statutes of Texas for 1879, a strong will, and 14' by 20' shack complete with bar, poker tables, jury bo and bench. He ruled over Langtry for twenty years, fir by appointment, then by election (held in his saloon). H hated rival, Jesus P. Torres, won the office away from hi in 1896 because of a lapse in the Bean electioneerir technique—a count of the 100-odd ballots showed th the foxy old Judge had more votes than there were peopl so the office was awarded to Torres. Bean was unmove by this foul device. He went right on handling cases orig nating on his side of town, so there was no break in h hard and fast practice of dispensing justice along wi other brands of watered hootch in the Jersey Lilly Saloo (Lily was spelled wrong, the fault of the drunk-and-di orderly sign-painter sentenced to paint the name on th porch to work off a fine.)

The Judge had a variety of profitable lines. He got $ a head for officiating at inquests and $2 to $5 for presidi

138

at weddings and divorces. When his love-'em-and-leave-'em mill drew the disfavor of the nearest district court, Bean had an answer ready. "I guess I got a right to unmarry 'em if it don't take," he said. His marriage ceremonies always ended with a pronouncement used by more orthodox jurists in levying death sentences: "May God have mercy on your soul."

While he liked the feel of money and may have been guilty of excessive fines in the case of minor disorders, such as getting drunk on the wrong side of the Jersey Lilly, Roy Bean was also capable of unusual tolerance. When a railroad hand who was a good customer at the liquor end of the bar got hauled in for killing a Chinese laborer, the Judge leafed through his dog-eared law book and solemnly ruled that "there ain't a damn line here no-wheres that makes it illegal to kill a Chinaman. The defendant is discharged." When another kindred soul was charged with blowing daylight into a Mexican, the Judge ruled that "it served the deceased right for getting in front of a gun." Court opened in the same light spirit: "Hear Ye! Hear Ye! This honorable court's now in session and if any galoot wants a snort before we start, let him step up and name his pizen."

But the "Law West of the Pecos" could be harsh, too. The story is told of a cattle rustler brought before the Judge to hear this sentence:

"You have been tried by twelve good men and true, not of your peers but as high above you as heaven is of hell, and they have said you are guilty. Time will pass and seasons will come and go. Spring with its wavin' green grass and heaps of sweet-smellin' flowers on every hill and

Lily Langtry.

Roy Bean holds court.

139

in every dale. Then sultry Summer, with her shimmerin' heat-waves on the baked horizon. And Fall, with her yeller harvest moon and the hills growin' brown and golden under a sinkin' sun. And finally Winter, with its bitin', whinin' wind, and all the land will be mantled with snow. But you won't be here to see any of 'em; not by a damn sight, because it's the order of this court that you be took to the nearest tree and hanged by the neck till you're dead, dead, dead, you olive-colored son of a billy goat."

If Roy Bean said it that way, it shows how far a man could have gone without book-larnin' in the flowery old days out west.

The Judge sometimes dealt as harshly with the dead as with the living. When a stranger made the mistake of expiring in his bailiwick, he inspected the corpse and found it to contain a revolver and $40, whereupon he fined the deceased $40 for illegally carrying a weapon. He was equally firm with offenders brought in drunk on red-eye bought on other premises. They were sometimes sentenced to buy a round for the whole house, including the twelve good men and true, who were also thirsty at times.

Roy Bean only got one look at the lady he had worshipped for years from a yellow magazine photo. ("By gobs, by ziggity, what a purty critter!") Lily Langtry played San Antonio on her American tour in the spring of '88. The Judge got his Prince Albert out of his trunk, wiggled his beer-barrel midriff into the striped trousers, journeyed to San Antonio, bought a front-row seat, and feasted bloodshot eyes on his statuesque beauty all through the one enchanted evening of his life.

The actress made a trip to Langtry in 1903 but Roy Bean had died eight months before from the combined effects of old age—he was about eighty—and a prolonged battle with his own rum. Like so many other tourists, Lily picked her way from the depot over the sagebrush and prickly cactus to the now-famous saloon-courtroom. It was the Judge's habit, down through the years, to short-change curious railroad passengers stopping in for a quick drink and a look at the "Law West of the Pecos." The Jersey Lily was not short-changed. Far from it, the townspeople gave her the Judge's pet bear, which he had kept chained to his bedpost for years. And when the bear ran away, not knowing the lady, they gave Lily the Judge's revolver. She hung it in what she called a "place of honour" in her home in England—a reminder of the funny old secret lover she never knew at all.

THE HANGING JUDGE

On the edge of the Indian Territory, in Fort Smith, Arkansas, things got much too frisky in the '70s. Horse-stealing and whiskey-running flourished, along with a touch of murder now and then, while the only judge, a tolerant man, looked the other way. Hardly anybody behaved except the girls in "The Row." They always quit walking the mud-caked streets at 9 P.M., the lawful curfew for their trade, and never ventured into the wild town's thirty saloons, all off-limits to the fair sex.

To tame the men, President Grant sent in Isaac Charles Parker, lawyer, ex-judge, and ex-Congressman out of Ohio by way of St. Joseph, Missouri. A stern, stiff-backed, be-whiskered giant of thirty-six, Parker eased himself into the high-backed chair in the United States Court for the Western District of Arkansas with Grant's parting words fresh in his mind: "Stay a year and get things straightened out."

The devout, Bible-slinging Judge stayed on the raw frontier many years and straightened out many things—mostly necks, including those of the homicidal Cherokee Bill and the Rufus Buck gang. Fresh from the Jesse James territory, Parker looked upon lawbreakers with such rage that there were times when hangman George Maledon ($100 per) was the most prosperous working stiff among Fort Smith's three thousand souls. Mass hangings—six was the Judge's high, although Fort Smith had a gallows built for twelve—were not uncommon. The ghastly sessions, always held at convenient hours, drew large crowds. The legal "necktie party" was the best show in town, but the angry man who produced it made himself unpopular—even with his own wife. Mary O'Toole Parker was a compassionate woman. She felt deeply for the wretches crushed into the two common cells in the basement prison putrid with the smell of urinal tubs, disease, sweat, and tobacco juice. She dared to take things to the doomed to comfort them.

The Judge disdained this kind of softness. "The good ladies who carry flowers and jellies to criminals mean well but that is mistaken goodness," S. W. Harman quoted him in *Hell on the Border*, the contemporary account of the Parker regime. "Back of this sentimentality are the motives of sincere pity and charity, sadly misdirected. They see the convict alone, perhaps chained in his cell; they forget the crime he perpetrated and the family he made husbandless and fatherless by his assassin work."

There was no sentimentality nor coddling nor delay in the Fort Smith court. The Judge's piercing blue eyes often glared down on evil-doers from 8 A.M. until far into the night. No case was too small for speedy, sure handling whether it involved tax-evaders, bawdy-house brawlers from Chippy Hill, sex criminals, or murderers. The Judge brooked no legal red tape. Never too keen a student of the law's tricky refinements, he relied more on the Good Book's eye-for-an-eye than Blackstone's mumbo-jumbo. Thus he never failed to let a jury know which defendant Judge Parker deemed guilty, whatever the evidence.

"I have been accused of leading juries," he said once,

"I tell you a jury should be led! If they are guided they will render justice. They must know that the judge wants enforcement of the law." Parker's juries knew: over the years his "good men and true" brought in 8,600 guilty verdicts and 1,700 acquittals—a ratio of 5 to 1. In first-degree cases, although death was not mandatory, as it is today in many states, Judge Parker always prescribed the scaffold. Knowing this, his juries cut the ratio of murder convictions to 2 to 1.

Even at that more merciful pace, Parker was able to condemn 168 men and four women. Only 88—all men—made the fatal journey to the massive scaffold in the yard, even though in the first fourteen years no appeals could be taken from the verdicts of the "court of the damned." During that period, White House commutations spared 43 from the rope. After 1889, when the Supreme Court opened the door to appeals, reversals cheated the hangman much of the time. Of the 46 doomed persons who took their cases to Washington, 30 were adjudged the victims of unfair trials; 16 of them then won acquittals and the other 14 got off with prison terms.

As a result, the old men in the capital who were so finicky about the legal niceties drew fierce rebuttals from "The Hanging Judge." Looking back with tender longing on the years when he alone was the law all the way from western Arkansas to the Colorado line, embracing all of what is now Oklahoma, Parker bluntly charged that "the appellate court exists mainly to stab the trial judge in the back." He said there should have been no reversals at all "unless innocence was manifest . . . I would have brushed aside all the technicalities that do not affect the guilt or the innocence of the accused."

In 1891, Washington barred Judge Parker's public hangings as unwholesome spectacles. Thereafter Fort Smith's sinners went to hell in comparative privacy until finally, five years later, the axe fell the whole way: the Parker mill of justice was abolished altogether, closing the books on twenty-one grisly years in the history of American jurisprudence. The Judge wasted away and died within three months in the shadow of the gallows he made so infamous, a broken old man at fifty-eight. "I never hanged a man," he protested, still righteous in his last hours. "The law hanged them. I was only its instrument . . ."

Hon. Isaac C. Parker.

Will Rogers Said It

In his book on Judge Parker, *He Hanged Them High,* Homer Croy quoted this passage from a talk Will Rogers made in 1928 in the Fort Smith High School:

"I just got here this mornin' and I've been looking around. I find that Fort Smith ain't as big as it ought to be. That's because it got such a bad start in the early days—Judge Parker hung so many men that this town got behind other towns in size."

Judge Parker, in his later years.

"THEY NEVER EVEN TWITCHED"

George Maledon, hangman.

George Maledon said it, for as Judge Isaac Parker's Lord High Executioner he was a man with abounding pride in his craft. "I never hanged a man who came back to have the job done over," he chuckled. "There's no ghosts hanging around the old gibbet." This was understandable. The bearded little fellow had a sure touch and the best rope money could buy. He used Kentucky hemp, shipped all the way to Fort Smith, Arkansas, by riverboat from St. Louis, and he kept it at home and oiled it himself and stretched it with sandbags to thin it down to a single sturdy inch all around. That way it made a nice knot.

The hangman was a meticulous fellow. German-born, an ex-Union soldier and frontier sheriff, he was a stickler for discipline, order, and neatness. He kept his scaffold as clean as his living room. He slaved over the monster. He would clamber up the twelve steps time and again to inspect the "Gates of Hell," for the trapdoor ran along

the twenty-foot platform and the hinges needed careful checking. He would put his own weight against the supports to test the great oak crossbeam that held his nooses. Finally he would jerk the trigger arm and let a 200-pound sandbag drop and then he would know that the most awful contraption in the Old West was in sure working order.

On September 3, 1875, only four months after "The Hanging Judge" introduced assembly-line justice to the lawless frontier region under his jurisdiction, George Maledon had six men to send to eternity in one morning. People came by the thousands from miles around, but the festive circus atmosphere did not distract the hangman at all. He was the picture of cool concentration as guards led out the condemned, shackled hand and foot.

Sam Fooy, half-breed, was ready to die. He had killed a school teacher in a $300 robbery and he was repentant. Smoker Mankiller, a Cherokee with a most unfortunate name, conceded that "we all have to die at a certain time" but protested to the last that he had not done in his white neighbor. Mankiller's wrinkled old mother was in the vast audience, as well as his sobbing wife, with their baby cradled in her arms. Edmund Campbell, Negro farmer convicted of shooting down an Indian in cold blood, had nothing to say. James H. Moore, horse-thief and murderer, waved to a friend in the throng: "Good-bye, Sandy." Daniel Evans looked down from the high platform and observed morosely, "There are worse men here than me," but he had murdered an eighteen-year-old boy to steal his fancy new boots. John Whittington, who had clubbed and knifed a drinking companion, left a written proclamation assailing the Demon Rum. He had taken to heart Judge Parker's words: "There is but One who can pardon your offense; this is the Savior whose blood is sufficient to wash from your soul the guilty stain."

George Maledon waited patiently for the formalities of the last words. Then he slipped the black masks over the heads of the men awaiting Judge Parker's brand of rehabilitation, trotted down the twelve steps, grasped the trigger-release with his steady left hand and dropped the six into eight feet of air with one quick pull. Then he eased the jerk-knots off their necks and took the ropes home. He would oil them and use them over and over again.

An Ounce of Mercy

John J. Overton, guilty of fraud, stood before the bar in Fort Smith. A jail term seemed inevitable from the severe Judge Parker, but instead the defendant heard the words: "Go home and sin no more."

Overton was 98 years old.

Maledon and his ropes.

Soon there was another batch of six to go, but a reprieve left only five for Maledon's "dance of death." There would be six again, and five again, and parties of four, three, and two. Maledon took them as they came. They were all alike to him. He hated lawbreakers. The Judge called them "men of blood," "wild men of the plain," "refuse of humanity," "brutes," and "demons," and the hangman— his neighbor, friend, and faithful helper—always nodded eager assent. He enjoyed his chosen work and the price was right—$100 a man, minus the modest burial expenses he had to pay himself.

Before he retired, Maledon had sprung the trap on 60 men—88 stretched rope in Judge Parker's twenty-one-year reign—and had killed five trying to escape from the foul, stinking dungeon Fort Smith called a jail. He was just as handy with a .45 as with his Kentucky hemp.

A personal tragedy marred Maledon's life in 1895. His beautiful daughter, Annie, eighteen, died with a bullet in her spine in the break-up of an unfortunate romance with a married adventurer named Frank Carver. The man was convicted of the shooting but cheated the gallows with the help of J. Warren Reed, the brilliant counselor-for-the-defense who was Parker's most formidable adversary. It was a blow to the Judge. He had looked forward to seeing Carver swing for what he had done to Annie Maledon, who used to romp with the two Parker boys. He would have watched the hanging from the window of his chambers, shuddering with emotion but glad just the same.

Maledon grieved, too—for his daughter, for the Judge whose iron hand was being stayed by the legal busy-bodies in Washington, for the community that shunned a decent, God-fearing hangman and for the family that shrank from him (Mrs. Maledon would never let him clutter the living room with his collection of press clippings and tintypes of the men he had hung). After a while George Maledon moved away from Fort Smith, and he never went back. The glory was gone.

William H. H. Clayton was the prosecutor in Judge Parker's "Court of the Damned" at Fort Smith, Ark., for fourteen years. The severe jurist called him a "very close, prudent examiner of witnesses" and gave him much more leeway than courts allow today. Clayton in turn saw Parker as "a necessity the Almighty created" to administer justice in the lawless Indian territory. President William McKinley made Clayton a federal judge in 1897.

143

Maomi July. Sam Sampson, Rufus Buck. Luckey Davis.
Lewis Davis.

THIRTEEN DAYS OF TERROR

The Rufus Buck gang got off to a fast start on July 28, 1895. That day a deputy marshal was shot to death just for looking suspiciously at the boys. In the next thirteen days Buck and his four confederates, Lewis Davis, Sam Sampson, Maomi July, and Luckey Davis, left a trail of horror in the Indian Territory.

A widow named Wilson was the first victim. Overtaken in her farm wagon, she was raped by the young Indians. Rosetta Hassan suffered the same fate while her husband was kept at bay with a Winchester. Then a stock man named Callahan was held up. He got a chance to outrun the playful gang's gunfire, but a Negro boy with him was killed for the fun of it. A series of horse thefts and holdups followed.

The reign of terror ended on August 10 in a little grove outside of Muskogee. A posse of marshals and Creek Light Horse (Indian police) trapped Buck and his men while they were dividing their loot and took them in after a gun battle. U. S. Marshal S. Morton Rutherford, who had enjoyed the help of such manhunters as Heck Thomas, Bud Ledbetter, and Paden Tolbert, took the gang into Muskogee and had to wave his rifle at a lynch mob to keep the Indians in one piece for safe delivery to Fort Smith to face trial in the rape of Rosetta Hassan.

Henry Hassan testified that when the band descended on his home they demanded a hot meal and looted the place while Mrs. Hassan prepared it. After they were fed, the witness went on, Luckey Davis ravished his wife, the others following. Then, he said, the band marched him two miles and let him go with a warning that "if you ever appear against us our friends will kill you." When he got back, he found his terrified wife cringing in a cornfield.

As the jammed courtroom listened in horror, Rosetta Hassan related in stark detail how Luckey Davis, who was half-Negro, half-Creek, started the procession of assaults. She said that when Davis told her, "You have to go with me" (into the bedroom), she pleaded not to be taken away from her babies, only to be told: "We will throw the G—D—— brats into the creek."

On the bench, Judge Parker was so livid with rage he could hardly conceal it. The prosecutor, J. B. McDonough, didn't bother to sum up, and William M. Cravens, one of the five attorneys appointed by the state for the gang, entered the shortest defense on record. "May it please the court and the gentlemen of the jury," said Cravens, "you have heard the evidence. I have nothing to say."

The jury filed in and out again, not even sitting down to ballot. The verdict was guilty and the prisoners were doomed to the gallows. When the hangman was through with Rufus Buck, they found in his cell a picture of his mother and on the back of it this poem:

144

MY DREAM

I dreamt I was in Heaven
Among the Angels fair;
I'd ne'er seen none so handsome
That twine in golden hair.
They looked so neat and sang so sweet
And played the Golden Harp.
I was about to pick an angel out
And take her to my heart:
But the moment I began to plea,
I thought of you, my love.
There was none I'd seen so beautiful
On earth, or Heaven above.
Good by, my dear wife and Mother
Also my sister.

Yours truly
RUFUS BUCK

It was a rather stiff and formal way to sign such an endearing thing, but you could say that Rufus Buck loved all the women in the family.

The Doomed Man's Dream

Sam Fooy, awaiting the scaffold in Fort Smith, had a dream and set it down. The *Fort Smith Independent* printed it on September 8, 1875:

"I dreamed I was on the gallows before a great crowd of people. I was sick and weak and felt like fainting, and thought I could not face death. Just then a man stepped up from the crowd, came right up to me and said, 'Look here, Sam, don't you be afraid to let them jump you. Jesus is standing under the floor and he will catch you in His arms.' That made me feel strong, when the drop came, and I felt no pain. I just fell asleep and woke up in the beautiful garden. It had running waters and stars were dancing on the waves."

Sam Fooy, murderer, died at peace.

Ned Christie was a bright Indian youth who served in the Cherokee tribal legislature but then unaccountably went bad. Bandit, horse-thief, rum-runner, and killer, he ran loose in the Oklahoma Territory for seven years before Judge Parker's deputies finally caught up with him in 1892. The end came in a twenty-hour encounter that had comic overtones. Christie and two confederates were holed up in a log fort in Tahlequah. Marshals Heck Thomas and Paden Tolbert sent all the way to Kansas for an Army cannon and set out with sixteen men to assail the fortress. The first 2,000 rifle slugs did no damage at all and 30 rounds of artillery fire bounced harmlessly off the logs. Finally, the law 'n order force used dynamite to blow out a side of the place and force Christie into the open. He came out fighting and was shot to death. This photo was made afterwards, showing the outlaw propped against a photographer's board with his rifle cradled in his arms.

THE SAGA OF CHEROKEE BILL

When Crawford Goldsby was small, his mother told him, "Stand up for your rights. Don't let anybody impose on you." When he was eighteen, a Negro named Jake Lewis imposed on him during a dance at Fort Gibson, Oklahoma, and the boy dared him to fight. Badly beaten and resenting that kind of imposition, too, Crawford Goldsby got a gun and shot Lewis (not fatally). Then he ran away.

Roaming the Seminole and Creek Nations, he fell in with Jim and Bill Cook, later famous among the Oklahoma outlaws, and got to be called "Cherokee Bill." He had at least a partial claim to the first half of the nickname, because he was part Cherokee, part white, part Mexican, and part Negro. His parents, who had separated, represented quite a mixture.

In June, 1894, a posse rode into Fourteen Mile Creek, outside of Tahlequah, looking for Jim Cook on a charge of larceny. The Cooks and Cherokee Bill met them head-on and in the ensuing fight the boy put the first notch on his shooting iron. He killed Sequoyah Houston, one of the possemen.

After that the path was soaked with blood. George Brown died for whipping his wife, Maude, who happened to be Cherokee Bill's sister. Richard Richards, railroad station agent, was killed resisting the boy in a holdup. Samuel Collins, a conductor, lost his life trying to throw

145

Cherokee Bill's last photograph.

Bill off a train. Ernest Melton's brain was shattered by a rifle bullet when he peeked in while Cherokee and the band were robbing the Shufeldt & Son general store in Lenapah.

Between forays, Bill managed to promote a romance with Maggie Glass, half-Negro and half-Cherokee, and that was his downfall. Spurred by a $1,300 reward offered by Fort Smith's Judge Parker, manhunters set a trap for the trigger-happy youth at Ike Rogers' home. The unwitting bait was Maggie Glass, who often visited there.

Bill came to the Rogers place after dark on January 29, 1895, and sat down for an evening of cumbersome wooing—he had a Winchester slung across his knee because he didn't trust Ike Rogers or Clint Scales, a neighbor who happened to be on the premises.

The cautious boy sat through dinner and a game of casino against Scales with his rifle always at hand. When Rogers went to bed, Bill plunked down beside him, fully dressed. He did no sleeping that night. Every time his host stirred, Bill raised the Winchester. In the morning, Rogers found a chance to end the cat-and-mouse drama and nail his $1,300 prize. Bill stooped over the fireplace to get a light for a cigar and Rogers bashed him over the head with a firestick. Scales helped him subdue the enraged outlaw and they took him into Nowata and turned him over to Deputy Marshals W. C. Smith and George Lawson for the journey into Fort Smith.

Judge Parker's jury speedily convicted Cherokee Bill of the murder of Ernest Melton. When his mother and sister wept over the verdict, the husky boy reprimanded them: "What's the matter with you? I'm not a dead man yet by a long ways." And he wasn't. J. Warren Reed, his attorney, appealed and lost and appealed again while his resourceful

client managed to store up a six-gun in his cell in the new prison even after guards had seized one .45 found hidden behind a loose brick.

On July 26, 1896, Bill jammed his door with a wad of paper when the cells in his row were being shut. Guard Lawrence Keating, a father of four children, came to investigate, and the boy killed him when he wouldn't throw up his hands. There was supposed to be a mass break that night, but Cherokee's confederates lost their nerve when other guards opened fire. Trapped, Cherokee meekly gave up his weapon in response to appeals from Henry Starr—a prisoner himself at the moment, but due to come out and win considerable notice as a badman. Starr was afraid that too much blood would flow unless Cherokee gave up.

Judge Parker blamed Larry Keating's death on the United States Supreme Court. He told reporters that the high court's "flimsiest technicalities" had enabled sixty "murderers" in the Fort Smith jail to stall their executions —among them Cherokee Bill. He said he would try the boy in the new case without waiting for the verdict in the Melton appeal.

Again the silver-tongued Reed pleaded for "this poor Indian boy" and again the verdict was guilty. The jurors took only thirteen minutes. Reed again got a stay of execution but in the meantime lost his appeal in the Melton case. The Judge quickly set up a fresh date with death for Cherokee.

There were a hundred guests—Fort Smith executions were attended at the time by invitation only, the hanging carnivals of the past having been outlawed by Washington —and Bill remarked about the audience when he was led into the courtyard. "Hell, look at the people," he said.

Zeke Crittenden. Dick Crittenden. Bill. Clint Scales. Ike Rogers. Bill Smith.

"Something must be going to happen." Then he glanced at the sky and observed, "This is about as good a day as any to die." His mother was on the long bench behind the trapdoor on the gallows. "Mother, you ought not to have come up here," Bill said, tenderly, and she replied, "I can go wherever you go." A guard then asked the boy whether he had anything more to say. "No," Cherokee answered evenly, "I came here to die, not to make a speech."

And so he died, on the end of a rope. He was only twenty, but it was said that he had managed to kill thirteen men in his two-year run. Another corpse was charged to his account later. Ike Rogers, the man who captured him, was shot to death alighting from a train at Fort Gibson and the general belief was that Cherokee Bill's little brother, Clarence Goldsby, was the executioner. If he was, he got away with it.

CAPTAIN BUNCH

There were outlaws who were handsome, daring, cold-blooded, cunning, and shrewd—but only a few, like Captain Eugene Bunch, the Southwestern outlaw, really possessed any education.

Bunch, known to outlaw history as "Capt'n Gerald," was a former school teacher who sought to augment his meager salary by holding up trains in Louisiana, Texas, and Mississippi. The "Wanted" posters described him as "soft-spoken," and several newspaper accounts called him "handsome and daring." He was all three, and the ladies found him enormously attractive.

The career of "Capt'n Gerald" was comparatively brief. In November, 1888, he climbed aboard a train outside New Orleans and courteously explained to the Southern Express messenger that if he didn't open the safe he would have his brains blown out. All of this was in a "soft voice."

The messenger complied and Bunch escaped with $10,000 in bonds and currency. Bunch made his way to Texas, holding up two more trains and netting several thousand more dollars. In the larger cities like Dallas he moved in the best circles and the ladies took to their hearts this brown-eyed, mild, almost melancholy man. He posed as an editor of a Richmond newspaper, carrying off his role so well that he edited a Texas newspaper for six months. It may be significant that the paper folded.

Somewhere along the line Bunch met the daughter of a former governor of Texas and began a torrid affair with her. When Bunch left for Mississippi for another train-robbing spree, she refused to stay in Texas and followed him.

Bunch robbed three more trains. One newspaper solemnly wrote, "It is reported that he has given money to a family in dire need." Thus was born a legend. Bunch had now become the Robin Hood of the canebrakes.

The reputation he acquired on the outlaw trail attracted other bandits. In 1889 Bunch abandoned his lone wolf tactics and rounded up a gang of five hard-riding killers and gunfighters, all on the run from the law in other states.

Charles O. Summers, a Pinkerton man, and T. V. Jackson, a detective for the Southern Express, trailed the gang to Jefferson County, Mississippi. Posing as a reporter-artist for the *New York Police Gazette* "to cover the fights," Summers got enough evidence to arrest a farmer who was the horse-holder for the gang. The farmer confessed and led the two detectives and a posse to the gang's hideout, a small island deep in a swamp. The possemen in bateaux poled their way through the tangled brush, and crept ashore to surround the island completely.

Bunch and two of his gang were trapped while eating. The two were killed and Bunch tried to make a break. A rifle bullet smashed his hip and he went down. He rose to one knee and fired, the ball taking off the tip of Jackson's hat. Summers fired and Bunch fell over dead.

In his pocket were found three letters from his sweetheart, the daughter of the ex-governor. They were written in code, but ironically, at the bottom of one was written: "If you don't understand, write or wire me . . ."

Cherokee Bill got his early training as a desperado under Bill Cook whose gang made quite a seamy name for itself in the Oklahoma Territory before it fell afoul of the Fort Smith authorities. Cook eventually drew a 45-year prison term.

This was Thurman Baldwin, also known as Balding, and also known as "Skeeter." He was in the Bill Cook gang in the Indian Territory. When his felony conviction was chalked up in Fort Smith, Isaac Parker doomed him to 30 years but conceded that the punishment did not fit the crime. The Judge said "it was not his intention that the prisoner should be imprisoned that length of time, his idea being that it was necessary to impose severe sentences to deter others." Skeeter served ten years. How much this deterred others, or even whether it made a law-abiding citizen of Skeeter, has been lost to history.

John Brown set a record all his own in Judge Parker's legal mill in Arkansas. Charged with slaying Deputy Marshals Josiah Poorboy and Thomas Whitehead in the Cherokee Nation, he was convicted three times, and three times the United States Supreme Court reversed the decision and saved him from the gallows. He spent five years in the Murderers' Row of Parker's dungeon-like prison. When he saved the government the expense of a fourth trial by pleading guilty, he was let off with a short sentence.

Henry Starr, a nephew of Belle Starr by one of her several marriages, killed Floyd Wilson, an on-again, off-again Parker deputy, and was doomed to the gallows but beat it on appeal. Convicted again, he won a pardon from President Theodore Roosevelt and went right out and stuck up a bank in Bentonville, Arkansas. A posse fired after Starr, Kid Wilson, and three confederates but the band got away—$11,000 richer. The next month—July, 1903 —Starr was seized in the Café Royal in Colorado Springs. In the Spaulding House nearby, his child bride was found sleeping snugly with $1,460 in cash and $500 in gold under her pillow—what was left of her husband's share of the Bentonville proceeds. Starr, who was twenty-two, got off with a five-year term. When he came out, he was killed trying to hold up another Arkansas bank.

Kid Wilson was picked up in a house of shame in Colorado Springs the same day that Henry Starr—co-leader of the $11,000 bank stickup at Bentonville, Arkansas—fell into police hands. Wilson, twenty-five, wanted in a string of robberies, drew a twenty-four-year term. He refused to tell reporters anything about his background. "My kinfolks have never done anything to place me where I am," he said, "so I prefer to say nothing of them."

OUTLAW IN A DERBY HAT

For a moment it seemed as if legend had made a mistake. Here was Marion Hedgepeth, the little-known, terrible gunfighter and outlaw of the West, dressed in a conservative blue suit, white shirt with a diamond stickpin—and a derby hat! In none of his pictures, even those taken when he was wandering about the West, his gun for hire, was he dressed in the traditional wide-brimmed hat, neckerchief, or buckskin jacket.

But despite his banker's appearance, Hedgepeth was a fighting machine with an incredibly fast draw. William Pinkerton, who chased him for years, told of the day in Colorado when Hedgepeth killed another outlaw who already had his six-shooter out of his holster when Hedgepeth began his draw.

As Pinkerton said, with a sigh of relief, when Hedgepeth died, "With his death passes one of the really bad men of the West. He was one of the worst characters I ever heard of. He was a bad man clear through."

There is little known of Hedgepeth's early life. He was born in Prairie Home, Cooper County, Missouri. When he was about fifteen he ran away. By the time he was twenty, Hedgepeth had been a cowboy in Wyoming, a holdup man in Colorado, and a killer in both states.

He was probably one of the most debonair of western outlaws. He was just six feet tall, dark-complexioned with wavy black hair. As the "Wanted" posters said, his shoes were usually polished.

In 1890 he was the leader of the "Hedgepeth Four." His followers were Albert D. Sly, alias "Bertie," James Francis, alias "Illinois Jimmy," and Lucius Wilson, alias "Dink." Charles Francis Burke in his *Great American Train Robberies* described the gang as "the most amazing criminal aggregation ever brought together in the United States."

On November 4, 1890, the gang held up the Missouri Pacific at Omaha, Nebraska. Their loot was small, only $1,000. A week later they stopped the Chicago, Milwaukee & St. Paul Express, blowing the express car to bits with dynamite. The express messenger miraculously survived, while the gang gathered up $5,000.

Eight days later at Glendale, Missouri, where ten years earlier Jesse James had killed two men in cold blood, Hedgepeth led his men aboard the St. Louis & San Franstation. It was their biggest strike; $50,000 in cash.

William Pinkerton, his operatives, and the St. Louis police finally trapped Hedgepeth and his gang through a bizarre set of circumstances, which started when a small child found some of the express envelopes and two six-shooters buried in a shed. A canvass of the neighborhood disclosed a man and a woman, recently moved in, had vanished the day of the robbery. An express wagon had been seen in front of the house and through the driver Pinkerton's men nabbed the gang.

Marion Hedgepeth.

In 1892, Hedgepeth went on trial in St. Louis. It was the biggest criminal trial in Missouri since Frank James. Flowers from admiring women, who fought with the bailiffs to get into the courtroom, filled his cell. While in jail, Hedgepeth became acquainted with "Mr. Holmes," a chemist who had been arrested for obtaining money under false pretenses. Under Hedgepeth's shrewd questioning, Holmes disclosed he was Herman Webster Mudgett, alias H. H. Holmes, America's Blue Beard, who had murdered scores of women. Hedgepeth gave his information to the authorities, hoping for a short term. Holmes died on the gallows. Hedgepeth received twelve years.

"That's what a life of graft got me," he said as he entered the penitentiary at Jefferson City, Missouri.

For twelve years committees, composed mostly of women, fought to have Hedgepeth freed. At last, in 1906, Hedgepeth was pardoned by Governor Folk.

The following year he was arrested for "blowing" a safe in Omaha. He received ten years but was released after serving two. Dying of tuberculosis, he was no longer the handsomest outlaw in the West.

But he was still a gunslinger, and a few weeks after his release he gathered together another gang, only a weak imitation of the old Hedgepeth Four, and went on a crime rampage through the West. Hedgepeth fought off police and posses and seemed to bear a charmed life. His name was again in the headlines.

On New Year's Eve, 1910, as the church bells were

ringing in the new year, he entered a saloon on Chicago's west side. He was filling his sack with jewelry and money from the loaded till, when a detective walked in with a drawn gun. He gave Hedgepeth a chance to surrender, but the outlaw fired from his hip. His shot went wide. The detective fired, the slug spinning Hedgepeth about. But he still possessed the raw, primitive courage of the outlaw who had once terrorized the West. Already dying, he got to his knees and, holding his Colt in both hands, traded shots with the detective. One went through the law officer's coat. Hedgepeth was hit again in the chest. He died still firing his revolver.

A typical official notice of escape and offer of reward.

150

THE SONTAG BROTHERS

In 1892, investigating train robberies in the vicinity of Kosota, Minnesota, and Racine, Wisconsin, the Pinkertons identified the robbers as George and John Sontag, "who owned a quartz mine near Visalia, California."

At a conference in Chicago, William Pinkerton notified the American Express Company, the Wells Fargo, and Southern Express Company that the pair had been traced to Visalia, and to alert their express messengers. A short time later, in August, 1892, a train was held up at Collis Station, a small town in Fresno County. After shattering the express car with dynamite, the thieves got away with $5,000 from the Wells Fargo safe.

Pinkerton wired the Wells Fargo office from Chicago that the robbers were probably the Sontag brothers. A posse went out to bring them in, and a gun battle followed in which two deputies were hurt. The train robbers fled to the hills and were joined by a sharpshooting farmer named Chris Evans. A few days later the trio was trapped in a barn. George Sontag was captured, but his brother John and Evans shot their way out, killing a deputy sheriff.

For nine months Pinkerton men, Wells Fargo detectives, local sheriffs, and Indian trackers trailed the two outlaws. Several pitched battles were fought and seven men were wounded. The dogged hunt for the robbers continued up and down the San Joaquin Valley. The train robbers de-

George Sontag.

Chris Evans.

John Sontag.

151

clared open war against the Pinkerton and Wells Fargo detectives and stopped several stage-coaches to see "if there are any detectives aboard we can kill."

In June a posse discovered the robbers' hideout. After an exchange of shots in which two deputies were killed, the posse was reinforced. There ensued an eight-hour battle, later known as "The Battle of Sampson's Flats," fought from tree to tree. Both bandits were wounded and

finally captured. John Sontag died that night. When he heard of his brother's death, George staged a revolt in Folsom Prison and was shot down scaling the walls.

Evans was sentenced to life imprisonment. The Pinkertons warned the local authorities that he would try to escape, a prediction that Evans made good on December 3, 1893. In February of the following year he was recaptured and returned to Folsom.

John Sontag and the sheriff's possemen who captured him.

"TERRIBLE" FRED WITTROCK

The *Police Gazette* and the big city newspapers were Fred Wittrock's undoing. In his small store in St. Louis he avidly read the accounts of Jesse James and his gang, and brooded over his own simple, unexciting life. One day he sold his store, bought a six-shooter and a piece of black cloth for a mask, and launched the career of "the terrible Fred Wittrock," as he once described himself in an interview.

In November, 1886, this mild little man held up the St. Louis and San Francisco Express outside St. Louis and stole $10,000 from the Adams Express Company safe.

He made an impressive figure with his black mask, deep growling voice, and unwavering six-shooter. He had gained entrance to the car by cleverly presenting forged credentials, stating he was the railroad's night superintendent.

Wittrock had the usual failing of many of our outlaws; he liked to see his name in the headlines. In a letter to the *St. Louis Globe Dispatch* he gave "the inside story" of the robbery and directed the reporter to a baggage room in St. Louis, "where the outlaw's tools can be found." Police and the reporter found a six-shooter, mask, black-jack, money envelopes, and an old song sheet. On the sheet

Fred J. Wittrock, alias J. M. Cummings.

was Wittrock's address, a St. Louis boarding house.

He was arrested twenty-four hours later by detectives who had watched the boarding house from a room across the street. He surrendered meekly. The most interesting thing about the arrest was the weather. It was 10° below zero, and the detectives, wrapped in blankets, had to take turns rubbing a peep-hole in the frost on the windows to keep watch for Wittrock.

The Burrows Brothers

Like Jesse James, Rube Burrows, leader of the Burrows gang of the Southwest, became the darling of the legend-makers and the ballad-singers after his death in 1888. He was a tall, handsome Texan with a thick black beard, flashing black eyes, and a laugh men later recalled as "booming and kind."

There are the usual stories told about Rube; of the wintry day he gave a shivering maiden his coat after she had been driven from the family hearth for having allowed a salesman to seduce her; of the time the gang drove away the miserly banker who was ready to claim the widow's mortgage, etc.

Despite the legends and the ballads, Rube and his brothers were only what a law officer called them—"desperate men, who had no love for tilling the soil like honest men." In brief, they were thieves and killers.

In January, 1888, the five-man gang, led by Rube, their undisputed leader, held up the Fort Worth and Denver Express outside of Bellevue, Texas. The loot, including the cash taken from the passengers, was $3,000. The Texas and Pacific Express was next, bringing in only $2,000. This time the manhunters had a clue—one of the masked robbers wore a new black raincoat.

A Pinkerton detective found a country storekeeper who had sold a black raincoat to a neighborhood farmer a few days before the robbery. The farmer was arrested and confessed he was working with the Burrows gang.

Thousands of "Wanted" posters were distributed throughout the countryside near Nashville, Tennessee, where Rube and his brothers were reported hiding out. An alert conductor saw the brothers on a train near Nashville, and after comparing their descriptions with the details on the poster, summoned the Nashville sheriff. Jim was caught, but Rube shot his way out of the trap.

"Give us Burrows a gun apiece and we will not be afraid of any man alive," Jim boasted in the Little Rock jail.

Jim died in prison a year later of consumption, which seemed to be an occupational disease with many American outlaws. Curiously, those men, identified with the open spaces of the West, died the fastest in prison.

Harry Tracy, the vicious tiger of the Wild Bunch, best summed it up: "My life has been rough . . . but there was always a horse under me and the range. I'll die before I let them put me back behind bars . . ." And he did.

Rube Burrows was killed, after Jim's death, in a gun duel with a fast-moving Southern Express Company detective.

Rube Burrows.

Jim Burrows.

Leonard C. Brock,
alias Waldrip, Jackson, etc.

W. L. Brock,
associate of Rube
and Jim Burrows.

153

All previous reward circulars issued by this Agency, referring to this robbery are annulled.

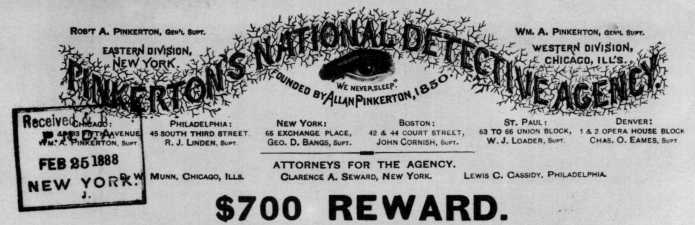

ROB'T A. PINKERTON, GEN'L SUPT.

EASTERN DIVISION, NEW YORK.

WM. A. PINKERTON, GEN'L SUPT.

WESTERN DIVISION, CHICAGO, ILL'S.

PHILADELPHIA: 45 SOUTH THIRD STREET. R. J. LINDEN, SUPT.

NEW YORK: 66 EXCHANGE PLACE, GEO. D. BANGS, SUPT.

BOSTON: 42 & 44 COURT STREET, JOHN CORNISH, SUPT.

ST. PAUL: 63 TO 66 UNION BLOCK, W. J. LOADER, SUPT.

DENVER: 1 & 2 OPERA HOUSE BLOCK CHAS. O. EAMES, SUPT

D. W. MUNN, CHICAGO, ILLS.

ATTORNEYS FOR THE AGENCY.
CLARENCE A. SEWARD, NEW YORK.   LEWIS C. CASSIDY, PHILADELPHIA.

$700 REWARD.

REUBEN HOUSTON BURROWS, alias **RUBE BURROWS,** charged with highway robbery, having, with his brother, **JAMES BUCHANAN BURROWS, and others,** wearing masks on the night of **FRIDAY, DECEMBER 9, 1887,** boarded the north bound train on the St. Louis, Arkansas & Texas R. R. at Genoa Station, Ark., and compelled the messenger of the **SOUTHERN EXPRESS COMPANY** to surrender the keys of his safe, which they rifled of $3,500. **James Buchanan Burrows,** and three others of the robbers, **have since been arrested.**

In an attempt to arrest **Reuben Burrows and Jim Burrows in Montgomery, Alabama,** on January 23, 1888, **Reuben Burrows** shot Mr. Neil Bray, a compositor on the *Advertiser,* who had been called on and was aiding the officer in his arrest.

DESCRIPTION.

REUBEN HOUSTON BURROWS is about 32 years of age, 6 feet in height, weighs about 160 pounds, blue eyes which do not look a person full in the face, round head, wears 7¼ hat, full forehead, face broad under the ears but thin near the mouth, short, inclined to pug-shaped nose, swarthy or sandy complexion, light sandy hair, thin light moustache, uses Hair Vigor to darken hair; left arm is a little shorter than the right, caused by having been broken at bend of arm; rather a lounging gait, carrying his hands in his pockets in a leisurely way.

Usually wears dark clothes and woolen shirts, a No. 8 boot, but no jewelry. Does not use tobacco; drinks, but not to excess; does not gamble, but can play the game of seven-up; is somewhat of a country story teller, relating stories of snake, dog and cat fights, etc. Is a good horseman, carries a 45-calibre pistol and is a good shot.

He was born in Lamar county, Alabama, is married, and has two children who are now with his father in Alabama. His wife is residing with her father, Mr. Hoover, at Alexandria, Alabama. He resided for 14 years in Wise and Erath counties, Texas; has worked for the Mexican Central R. R., and is a member of the Masonic fraternity.

The **Southern Express Company,** and the **St. Louis, Arkansas and Texas Railroad Co.** have jointly offered a **reward of Five Hundred Dollars ($500),** and in addition **the Governor of the State of Arkansas** has offered a **reward of Two Hundred Dollars ($200)** for the arrest, delivery to the authorities of the State of Arkansas, and conviction of **Reuben Houston Burrows.**

Send information to

Or to any Superintendent of

Pinkerton's National Detective Agency,

At Either of the Above Listed Offices.

WM. A. PINKERTON, General Superintendent Western Division, Chicago, Ill.

C. T. CAMPBELL,

Sup't Texas Express,

TEXARKANA, ARK.

Chicago, February 20, 1888.

$7,500 REWARD

Murderers and Train Robbers.

The Southbound Express train on the Mobile & Ohio Railway was robbed on the morning of Sept. 25, 1889, by three masked men, who are the same parties who robbed the Illinois Central train on Dec. 15, 1888, and murdered Chester Hughes, a passenger, in so doing.

No. 1.—Reuben Houston Burrow, alias Charles Davis, is described as follows: About 34 years old, 6 feet 1 inch tall, weight about 170 lbs., light complexion, dark sandy hair, long drooping mustache, possibly chin and side whiskers of recent growth, inclined to be sandy. The eyes are blue, small and deep-set, giving the brow a protruding appearance; nose short and appears stubby. Teeth sound and upper front teeth project slightly outward. Lower jaws prominent and protrude noticeably backward under ears. Hair on top of head very thin. Head round. When spoken to generally throws head backward displaying Adams apple in replying to questions. Speaks abruptly and rather quickly. Right arm little shorter than left arm. Wears 7¼ hat and 7½ boot. He neither smokes nor chews. Has a habit of telling funny stories and also of quoting and ridiculing the Bible. Has small scar scarcely noticeable on forehead over left eyebrow, made by bird shot. Has a small mole on the right cheek bone. When last seen wore dark colored coat, gray jeans pants, and reddish brown slouch hat, with narrow leather band and leather binding, known as a cowboy's hat. Is very restless and always watchful.

No. 2.—Joe Jackson, alias Henry Davis. About 30 years old; 5 feet 8 inches high; weight about 165 lbs. to 170 lbs.; black hair, black whiskers and mustache, whiskers generally worn full but are thin on side of face. Dark complexion; eyes, black and round. Has noticeable scar on left side of cheek or neck, also scar high up on forehead, which he keeps concealed by wearing his hair banged over it. Manner reticent and avoids looking at one when talking. Frequently complains of rheumatism in lower limbs, and occasionally, especially in wet weather, limps, but the limping is caused by gunshot wounds and not from rheumatism. His body and limbs are covered with gunshot wounds. He is compactly built and has round face. When last seen, wore dark rough suit, with cutaway coat and dark slouch hat.

No. 3.—About 30 years old; weight, 145 lbs.; 5 feet 9 inches high; rather slim in build; black hair and black eyes; black mustache and whiskers, of recent growth; dark complexion, face rather long. When last seen, wore dark mixed clothing and black slouch hat.

These men are all coarsely dressed, and might be taken for farmers or country laborers. They carried two small dark satchels and rubber overcoats, and one or more Winchester rifles; also small bundle. All wore heavy pistols and leather belts with cartridges. Numbers one and two are generally found in company with each other, and pass as brothers, though they do not personally resemble each other.

The following rewards are offered for the arrest and delivery of the men who committed the robberies above named, and for their delivery to any one of the undersigned:

By the Mobile and Ohio Railroad and Southern Express Company, $2000.00.

By the United States Government, $1000.00 each.

By the Illinois Central Railroad Company and the Southern Express Company, $1000.00.

By the State of Mississippi, $500.00.

By the State of Arkansas and the St. Louis, Arkansas & Texas Railway Company, $500.00.

By the State of Alabama, $500.00.

Total reward, $7,500.00.

Wire or write information to D. McLaren, Supt., Mobile & Ohio Railway, Mobile, Ala.; G. W. Agee, Supt., Southern Express Company, Memphis, Tenn.; A. G. Sharp, Postoffice Inspector, Chattanooga, Tenn.; J. G. Mann, Supt., Illinois Central Railroad, New Orleans, La.; H. C. Fisher, Supt., Southern Express Company, Nashville, Tenn., or the Governors of the above named States.

The Daltons: Angels and Outlaws

Mother Dalton, small but spirited, brought forth fifteen children and ruled her small army with a firm hand and an iron will. Her brother's boys, the Youngers, had gone bad. She never asked why. She knew what was good—work, school, church, and play—in the proper mixture, of course. Let other striplings romp the plains in their fancied warfare: cowboy and Indian, desperado and marshal, Redleg and bushwacker. No. The Daltons would collect in the rambling Colonial farmhouse in Cass County, Missouri, and listen to the religious hymns Mother extracted from the rickety piano. Louis Dalton, an easy-going 200-pound giant, saloon-keeper turned farmer because Adeline Younger Dalton wanted it that way, might complain about all the discipline but he would get nowhere. The line drawn by the lady of the house was straight and narrow. "She was a stern umpire of our morals," Emmett Dalton remembered years later, looking back on the great grief Mother came to know when four of her sons turned outlaw after another, Frank, had lost his life as a peace officer.

Virginia-born Adeline Younger was only sixteen when she became Louis Dalton's bride. All her children were born in Missouri, but in 1882 the Daltons followed the homesteaders into the Indian territory in Oklahoma. For a while they lived near the border of lower Kansas and the little town of Coffeyville, where in time Bob, Grat, and Emmett Dalton were to come to grief.

The "law" in the Territory was Isaac C. Parker, the "Hanging Judge." A marshal on the Parker staff in Fort Smith, Arkansas, Frank Dalton died in a gun battle with a trio of whiskey runners. Grat picked up Frank's star and Bob and Emmett, still in their teens, followed him into the service.

The freshly-arrived Daltons didn't wear their badges

Julia Dalton, widow of Emmett Dalton, is shown here on the Universal lot in Hollywood posing with the four stars of *When the Daltons Rode*—Andy Devine, Frank Albertson, Broderick Crawford, and Brian Donlevy. What's wrong with the picture? Only three Daltons rode together as outlaws—Grat, Bob, and Emmett. Bill turned outlaw later but in the movies Mother Dalton's four bad boys usually combine forces. Julia Dalton posed for this picture a few years after her husband died in Los Angeles in 1937. She waited almost fifteen years for Emmett when he went to prison after the Coffeyville bank raid.

very long. They left the Fort Smith Marshal's office to serve on the Indian Police in the Osage Nation, and then they tried the other side of the law. The trio always blamed the switch on the Federal authorities, saying they quit in disgust because they couldn't collect their fees. But Bob was fired for taking a bribe, and there were also stories that the boys had been caught doing a little rustling on the side while hunting down cattle-thieves. When Grat turned in his star, he went to California, where two other brothers, Littleton and Bill, had settled. Then Bob and Emmett appeared on the "Wanted" lists for sticking up a faro game in a New Mexico saloon. Emmett insisted that they only did it because gamblers had cheated them in the place. When the trail got hot, Bob followed Grat to California, while Emmett went back into the territory and scooped a king-sized dugout from the ground as a point of rendezvous and refuge against the time when his big brothers could come home. The dugout was within a day's ride of the Dalton homestead, then at Kingfisher, Oklahoma.

*　　*　　*

Nearing Los Angeles on February 6, 1891, Southern Pacific Train No. 17 ground to a sudden stop when four of its "passengers" broke out arms and covered the crew. Wells Fargo messenger Charles C. Haswell peered out of the Express car door into the darkness to see what had happened. He saw four men, their faces masked with bandanas, leap from the engine and tender and head his way, so he ducked back inside and doused the lights. In a moment there was a pounding on the door and a harsh voice commanded, "Open up and be damned quick about it." Haswell foolishly pressed his face against the glass pane to make out his callers and a piece of buckshot grazed his forehead. Then he got his shotgun and opened up, hitting one of the bandits, possibly two, before he drove them off. Back in the tender, fireman George Radcliff lay dying, shot in the abdomen by one of the raiders before they headed for the treasure in the brave Haswell's car.

Bill and Grat Dalton were arrested and tried in the profitless stick-up. Bill was cleared. Grat, convicted, drew a twenty-year sentence but escaped. Bob Dalton, also wanted, was never caught.

Presently Mother Dalton's three bad boys were reunited in their Oklahoma sod hutch, their feet solidly set on the outlaw path. Emmett blamed it all on the "false" charge in the California train holdup. "They've put the runnin' iron on our hides," he quoted Bob in *When The Daltons Rode,* the book he wrote in 1931 with Jack Jungmeyer. The railroad had put up a $6,000 reward for Grat and Bob.

"Posting a 'dead or alive' reward for a man performs some dark alchemy in his spirit," Emmett observed. "It places him beyond the pale. He becomes fair game for every pot-shooting hunter. Like a harried beast he goes to bay, mustering his primitive faculties to meet the outward thrust. In quite a real sense he belongs thereafter to the living dead . . ."

Handsome Bob Dalton, first a deputy marshal and then an outlaw leader, posed for this picture in the Indian Territory in 1889, two years before he was killed. Emmett Dalton said the woman in the photograph was Eugenia Moore, Bob's sweetheart.

"IT'S THE DALTONS!"

In the case of the Daltons, the "living dead" managed to get around pretty well in the short time left to them.

Jesse James rode roughshod over the West for sixteen years, and the law never laid a hand on him. Frank James was never taken: he came in after traitor Bob Ford, the "dirty little coward" of song and ballad, cut Jesse down.

Cole, Bob and Jim Younger, the Daltons' celebrated cousins, rode with Jesse's Middle Border raiders for a decade before the brave townsmen of Northfield, Minnesota, cut them down with gunfire in 1876.

The Dalton boys, by comparison, were fly-by-night desperadoes. Their reign of terror across Oklahoma in its homesteading days spanned only about eighteen months.

But it was a busy eighteen months, and it was a formidable band. Bob Dalton, in his early twenties, was the leader. Besides Grat, his older brother, and Emmett, baby of the family, not yet twenty-one, Bob could call upon the substantial services of seven badmen: George (Bitter Creek) Newcomb, Charley (Black-Faced) Bryant, Bill Powers, Charley Pierce, Dick Broadwell, William McElhanie, and Bill Doolin, who in time would head a gang

Emmett Dalton in the early 1930's.

of his own with Bill Dalton, the fourth and last bad boy in Mother Dalton's otherwise spotless brood of fifteen.

The terrified trainmen's cry—"It's the Daltons!"—first sounded on the Oklahoma plain in the spring of '91. The Santa Fe's Texas Express was stuck up at Wharton at 10 P.M. on May 9. Bob Dalton and Newcomb boarded the cab while the train was in the station and ordered the engineer to pull up at the stockyards on the edge of town. Emmett Dalton and Bryant then took over the guard detail in the cab while Bob and the others raided the express car. The whole thing was so orderly and efficient that few of the sleeping passengers (the Daltons boasted that they never robbed passengers) were aroused. There was no gunplay, unless you count the shot Bob threw at the messenger's feet when he seemed hesitant about opening the safe. The Daltons said they got $14,000. The newspapers used a higher figure and the railroad's was considerably lower, as was the custom of the time.

Black-Faced Charlie, so called because his face bore the burns of some close gunplay, didn't live long enough to enjoy his share of the proceeds. "Me, I want to get killed in one hell-firin' minute of smoking action," he said once when the Dalton men were fighting off a posse at Salt Creek—and he went in "one hell-firin' minute," taking a lawman along for the last ride.

Bryant rode into the town of Hennessey for some fun and frolic only to be arrested by Deputy U. S. Marshal Ed Short and loaded aboard a train for Wichita, Kansas, the nearest Federal court district. Once under way, Short elected to go to the smoker and let the express messenger guard Bryant. He handed the man the outlaw's own six-gun. The messenger put the weapon in a pigeonhole over his desk and went back to his normal labors. Bryant, hardly hampered by his handcuffs, seized the gun and started to back toward the door just as Short came back. Each man fired until he dropped. When the train drew into the next station, the Marshal and his captive were laid out on the rough board platform. "Take off my boots . . . and send word to my mother," Short pleaded with his last breath. Black-Faced Charley made the same standard-form request before he, too, passed from the Western scene.

Down to nine, the Dalton band functioned just as efficiently. At Lelietta, just north of Wagoner, the robbers flagged down a Missouri, Kansas and Texas train and carried off $19,000. Emmett said the loot included $3,000 in silver which all but wore out Bill Doolin when it fell to him to lug it back to the hideout.

The next strike came at Red Rock, a way station on the Santa Fe in the Cherokee strip. The railroad had a tip on the raid and employed the device which you see in the movie oat-eaters all the time. The line sent a heavily-armed decoy train ahead to engage the Daltons. The raiders let that one pass and helped themselves to $11,000 when the right wood-burner chugged into Red Rock.

If the Daltons appeared rather well-informed, credit it to good intelligence work. Eugenia Moore, Bob's sweetheart, used to pose as a newspaper writer and pry information out of the railroads. She would also scout depots selected as target areas. This brand of cautious advance work saved the Daltons from a fearful ambush at Pryor Creek, outside Adair in the Indian territory. The "Katy" came through Pryor Creek on the run from Denison, Texas, to Kansas City. The railroad had an armed force of fifty men staked out there on the night of July 14, 1892, to await a bandit raid. The Daltons learned about it and elected to take the train at Adair instead. The Daltons wounded Deputy Marshal Sid Johnson (Bob and Grat had once been lawmen with him at Fort Smith), Territorial Police Chief Charley LaFlore, and L. L. Kinney, a railroad detective, before they got to the choo-choo's safe. Emmett said the haul came to $17,000.

Nobody in the band was hurt at Adair, but the consequences were heavy just the same. Reward offers mounted until there was a prize of $5,000 a head on the Daltons. The trail began to sizzle. One posse might have trapped the band except that Emmett's girl, Julia Johnson, heard about it and made the dangerous journey to the band's hideout to tip the boys off. The Daltons began to talk about quitting the outlaw dodge. Grat and Bob thought of going to South America, Emmett wanted to settle down with Julia. There would be one more foray. . . . That was the Daltons' one-too-many.

FEBRUARY 8, 1891.

From the *San Francisco Chronicle* of February 8, 1891.

FOR THE WOMEN, FAREWELL

Julia Johnson, twenty-one and pretty as a picture, picked out the notes on the wheezy organ through misty black eyes and her fingers weren't too sure as they caressed the yellowing keys. For the gangling youth across the room, awkwardly erect because there was a rifle balanced on his knees, it didn't matter. The halting melody that emerged from the old organ was a symphony sent from heaven and delivered by an angel. The boy looked at the girl in the blue gingham dress and his reverie took him back five years to a day full of spring. Julia was playing the organ in the little log church where the Daltons and the Johnsons worshipped. He could only glimpse her face in the mirror that hung above the instrument, but it was enough. Emmett Dalton lost his heart before the last few notes of the hymn wafted across the Oklahoma prairie; he would never love any other girl.

While his big brothers poked fun at him and Mother Dalton beamed with pride, a change came over the boy. He began to slick back his hair and grease his boots with

159

tallow and brush his Sunday pants spotless. And in the next few months the rough path between the Dalton place and Texas Johnson's farm in Bartlesville was pounded flat by the hooves of Emmett's pony. Mr. Johnson frowned on the Dalton clan, but Julia fell in love with her ardent suitor. They would sit under the peach tree in the yard hour after hour. Emmett would play a serenade on his harmonica. Or they would talk: Emmett was going to be a law officer like his brothers. And Emmett and Julia were going to be married as soon as he was on his own.

But that was long ago. That was 1887, and this was 1892 and the Dalton boys, train robbers, were the most hunted trio in the West. Even now, Emmett could only afford the luxury of a final hour with Julia because Grat and Bob Dalton and Dick Broadwell and Bill Powers stood watch outside against the posse that might ride down on them at any moment.

It was not a happy hour.

"I had an almost overwhelming desire to ask her a very important question," Emmett recalled years later. "Then I became conscious of the rifle in my lap—always the rifle, even while courting—and the words wouldn't come. Too late now. What had I to offer Julia, a man with a price on his head and no clear way to extricate myself from the compounding results of crime? . . . I rode away. An outlaw has no business having a girl, no business of thinking of marriage . . . what the hell! I shouldn't have come at all. Might as well go the limit now!"

Why had he come? The Daltons were planning their biggest and boldest venture—a twin hold-up of the two banks in Coffeyville, Kansas—and they wanted to say some farewells first. The train robbers had a squeamish feeling about their excursion into the richer business of bank stick-ups. Cole and Jim Younger, their cousins, were still in the Minnesota State Prison at Stillwater paying the hard price for their bloody raid on the First National Bank of Northfield with the James Boys in 1876, and Bob Younger had died in his cell.

After Emmett's visit with his girl, Bob Dalton had another kind of farewell with his sweetheart, Eugenia Moore. Word came to the outlaws' hideaway that Eugenia, who rode as the band's advance agent even while a fatal malady clawed at her insides, had died. Bob held an unorthodox memorial. He tore up Eugenia's picture, the one he had always carried, and he sat up all night under the stars, smoking and fighting his grief. Emmett sat with him but there were no words spoken at all.

Later, as their date with destiny approached, the Daltons made another perilous sixty-mile journey out of their hideaway along the South Canadian River into Kingfisher. Now they were going to see Mother Dalton but, as Emmett told it:

A little distance off we halted, debating, held by an odd restraint. Now at the last minute we couldn't bring ourselves to go into the lighted house.

It wasn't that we feared official vigilance which might very well have stood in the shadows about our mother's house. It was a reluctance to hurt her with a swift, futile visit. To arouse hopes which we could not fulfill, to have no comforting answer for questions of maternal concern—no, that would be too cruel. Better she should not know how close we were, her three outlawed sons. For a moment we saw her in the distant window, her flitting form, setting the house in order for the night. None of us dared look at the other. With one accord we spurred our horses. And at the sound I saw her turn her face to the window, listening intently, as if she heard the passing hoofbeats. Such was Bob and Grat's last outspoken salute to the grand old lady who bore them.

Months passed before a heartbroken Mother Dalton learned that her three bad boys, who once were peace officers and now were worth $5,000 a head to any one who could bring them in, had come to say good-by before taking the last long chance.

. . . and Crime Marched On

In 1910 a New York reporter asked Emmett Dalton how he would keep the city free of crime. "Guard the entrances to the town," said the reformed outlaw.

Father Knickerbocker's little village then had a population of 4,766,883, spread over an area of 359 square miles.

The Dalton formula for banishing crime from the metropolis was not followed.

DISASTER AT COFFEYVILLE

DALTONS!

The Robber Gang Meet Their Waterloo in Coffeyville.

LITERALLY WIPED OUT

A Desperate Attempt to Rob Two Banks

FOUR BAD ROBBERS KILLED

The Fifth One Wounded and Captured.

FOUR GOOD CITIZENS DEAD

Marshal Connelly Shot Down Whilst Doing His Duty.

A MOST TERRIFIC BATTLE.

The Outlaws Beaten at Their Own Game.

A REMARKABLE OCCURRENCE

The Whole Country Startled by Wednesday's Fight.

MOURNING FOR THE DEAD

Business Houses Closed and the City Draped in Honor of the Gallant Men Who Gave

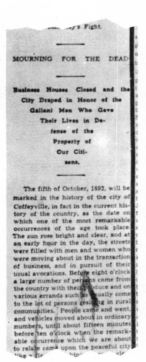

Monday's Fight.

MOURNING FOR THE DEAD

Business Houses Closed and the City Draped in Honor of the Gallant Men Who Gave Their Lives in Defense of the Property of Our Citizens.

The fifth of October, 1892, will be marked in the history of the city of Coffeyville, in fact in the current history of the country, as the date on which one of the most remarkable occurrences of the age took place. The sun rose bright and clear, and at an early hour in the day, the streets were filled with men and women who were moving about in the transaction of business, and in pursuit of their usual avocations. Before eight o'clock a large number of persons came from the country with their produce and on various errands such as usually come to the lot of persons residing in rural communities. People came and went, and vehicles moved about in ordinary numbers, until about fifteen minutes before ten o'clock when the remarkable occurrence which we are about to relate came upon the peaceful city like a flame ...

The six outlaws huddled around their campfire on Onion Creek in the Indian Territory. Using a stick, Bob Dalton sketched into the hard earth a drawing of the Plaza in Coffeyville, just across the Oklahoma-Kansas border. The map showed where the Condon Bank was, and the First National, only 50 paces away, and the hitching rack where they would tie their horses for a quick getaway. The Daltons knew the little town on Kansas' southeastern edge from their boyhood. Thus Grat and Emmett needed no refresher course, but Dick Broadwell, Bill Powers, and Bill Doolin had to pay close attention as their twenty-three-year-old leader outlined the plan of the first double bank raid in the West. The foray would eclipse anything ever attempted by Jesse James and the Youngers. Even after the haul was split six ways, there would be enough for everyone to put aside outlawry and start fresh.

At 2 A.M. the bandits swept their pockets clean. Into the flickering fire went anything that might identify them. Emmett burned the locket photo of Julia Johnson which he had treasured in his watch fob. Bob dropped in the last letter Eugenia Moore wrote him before she died. Then the fire was doused and the men turned into their blankets. They would sleep until dawn and ride over the prairie into Coffeyville for the biggest strike and the last. They would cover the fifteen miles in the leisurely manner of farmers on the way to markets in town. For the Daltons, it would be a sentimental journey: for they would pass the homestead where they lived when they were young.

* * *

From the *Coffeyville Journal* of October 7, 1892.

The Condon Bank today.

The C. M. Condon and Co. Bank, as it appeared in 1892.

Only five horsemen made Coffeyville on the fateful morning of October 5, 1892. Bill Doolin's horse pulled up lame on the way in. He said he would go back a ways, steal a fresh mount, and rejoin the band, but he never did. It meant one less hand to dip into the spoils, so the others went ahead. The town was just beginning to stir when they jogged down Eighth Street into the bright and sunny Plaza shortly after nine-thirty. The storekeepers were filling their shelves against the morning rush. Draymen were waiting in their wagons for the first calls. And there was something else: workmen were tearing up the street for repairs and the hitching rack near the banks had been torn down.

The Daltons should have known about that. In their train stick-ups, with Eugenia Moore riding ahead as scout, their careful planning had paid off handsomely. Twice they had foiled sure ambushes. Now a simple detail presented a problem. Bob Dalton swallowed his dismay and directed his band into the alley—*Death Alley,* it would be called later—that ran behind the city jail, one block below the Condon bank. The outlaws dismounted and tied their horses to a fence rail. Each man whipped a Winchester from his saddle boot and felt for his single-action .45s—one on the hip and one in a shoulder holster.

Bob and Emmett were wearing false beards and Grat had grown heavy chin whiskers, but Aleck McKenna thought he recognized the Daltons as the heavily-armed quintet passed his stable on the way out of the alley, so he kept an eye on them. He saw Grat veer left into the Condon bank with Broadwell and Powers as Bob and Emmett crossed swiftly to the First National. Then, through Condon's big plate glass window, McKenna saw a Winchester raised toward the cashier's counter and he started to shout: "The bank's being robbed! The bank's being robbed!"

The cry resounded in the Plaza as others picked it up. The Daltons heard it too, but they went about their desperate business.

Charles T. Carpenter, Condon's vice-president, was alone behind the counter when the trio led by Grat came in. His hands flew skyward as one bandit covered him and

the other two went into the office and threw down on T. C. Babb, the bookkeeper, and Charley Ball, the cashier. "Open the safe and open it quick," Grat barked. Ball looked into the Winchester a few feet from his head and lied, "It's a time lock. Won't open until 9:45." This angered Grat. "Open it or I'll kill you," he shot back. Ball hauled out a sack loaded with $4,000 in silver—there was $40,000 in the safe—but again said that he couldn't get to the currency until 9:45. It was then 9:42. The oldest of the Daltons was just as cool as the nervy little cashier. "That is only three minutes yet," he said, "and I will wait." He said he didn't want the silver. At that moment gunfire began to sound in the Plaza. The next three minutes would be crucial—especially for Charley Ball.

Isham's Hardware Store, 1954.

John J. Kloehr.

162

Across the street, things were going more smoothly for the bandits. Teller W. H. Sheppard, bookkeeper Bert S. Ayres and J. H. Brewster, a customer, stood at bay while cashier Thomas G. Ayres stuffed $21,000 in bills into the grain sack Bob Dalton had flung at him. Ayres had started by dumping a trayful of silver into the bag, only to be reprimanded by the outlaw leader, "Keep that silver out," Bob told him, sharply, "It's too heavy to bother with. The vault! The big stuff!" When the safe was emptied, the raiders started to herd their captives out ahead of them but a slug smashed into the door as they opened it, for now there were guns trained on both banks. The men of Coffeyville had armed themselves with rifles from the stocks of the stores in the Plaza; they were going to fight for the money earned by their toil. The fire was so heavy that Bob slammed the heavy door and elected to go out the back way, which meant covering an extra block to get to the alley. Sheppard was taken along to be used as a shield. As they emerged, Lucius M. Baldwin, a clerk, came toward them with an upraised pistol. Bob called out to him to stop but the youth thought it was a party of citizens, because Sheppard was walking ahead of the Daltons, so he kept coming.

"You look after that money sack," Bob told Emmett, "I'll do the fighting. I have got to get that man." Then he aimed his rifle and put a slug into the onrushing Baldwin's left breast. The youth dropped his gun—unfired—and sank to the ground, dying. He was the first casualty of the West's deadliest street battle. In a moment there would me two more—George W. Cubine, the bootmaker who served the Dalton boys when they were small, and Charles T. Brown, his partner. When Baldwin fell, the bandits abandoned Sheppard and started to run, Bob with his rifle

Bob and Grat Dalton, dead or dying, being held upright by officers.

at ready and Emmett clutching the grain bag with its vast riches. Coming into Union Street on the way to the alley, Bob spotted Cubine standing in the doorway of Rammel's drug store with a Winchester cradled in his arms. The merchant was facing away from Bob; the outlaw's first shot tore through his back and into his heart. Brown, a courageous old man, picked up Cubine's rifle and Bob's deadly fire finished him off. He fell alongside his partner.

Ready for the undertaker: The bodies of (*left to right*) Bill Powers, Bob Dalton, Grat Dalton, Dick Broadwell.

163

Cashier Ayres was hit a moment later. He had armed himself at Isham's Hardware Store opposite the First National and taken up a position in the doorway. Like Cubine and Brown, he never figured that the outlaws would take the long way around and come up behind him. Bob Dalton's fourth shot of the bloody morning crashed into his cheek below the left eye and put him out of action.

Bob and Emmett made the alley almost at the moment that Grat got there with Broadwell and Powers. Charley Ball's ruse had given the townsmen just enough time to start pouring fire through the glass window. Clutching a paltry $1,500 swept from the counter drawer, Grat ordered a retreat when one of his men was hit in the arm. In the next three minutes *Death Alley* got its name. Powers was hit. Then Broadwell. Then Bob. Then Emmett, twice. Grat took a slug flush in the chest and fell dead. The heaviest fire came from the big Isham store across the Plaza and from an array of citizens barricaded behind wagons in front of the Boswell & Co. hardware store but there was some at close range, too: City Marshal Charles T. Connelly, a school teacher turned to law 'n order, elected to shoot it out right in the alley and Grat got him before he himself fell.

Powers, hit again as he started to mount his horse, went down after Grat. Broadwell, badly shot up, managed to get away but plunged dead from his pony before he had gone a mile. Emmett, blood pouring from his hip and right arm, made his saddle, and never dropped the bulging grain sack either. But then he turned around to play out the high point of the Coffeyville drama. Instead of bolting out the back way of the alley to freedom with his $21,000 haul, the twenty-year-old outlaw forced his mount to the side of the brother he worshipped. Bob lay dying against a pile of rocks "Don't mind me, boy," the bandit chieftain gasped. "I'm done for. Don't surrender! Die game!" At this moment John J. Kloehr, the town liveryman, and Carey Seaman, the barber, stepped into the alley from behind an outhouse. Their shotguns roared as Emmett reached down to lift his dying brother. The boy fell with eighteen buckshot in his back just as Bob breathed his last. Then someone cried, "They are all down," and the firing ceased.

Only ten minutes had passed since the five bandits had tied their mounts to the fence behind the jail to write their outlaw saga. Now the double-bank raid was over and little Coffeyville was stained with blood. "Strong men wept great tears of grief, whilst the women and children cried and wrung their hands in agony," said the town's newspaper, *The Journal,* describing the aftermath of the battle. Coffeyville counted four brave citizens dead—Baldwin, Cubine, Brown, and Marshal Connelly—and three wounded, Tom Ayres, drayman Charley Gump, and T. A. Reynolds, a clerk at Isham's. On the other side there were four dead outlaws and a fifth, Emmett Dalton, badly wounded.

It was one of the most magnificent forays in all the West's lawless time, just as the Daltons had planned. It gave Mother Dalton's three strays massive stature despite their brief journey on the outlaw trail. It entitled them to go down in the books with their much more formidable kin, the Youngers, and with the James Boys. It was at once their crowning glory and their crowning failure, and there was a stern moral in it for the dwindling desperado legions on the fringes of the gallant frontier towns that were coming of age in '92: the day was over when you could thunder in off the trail and fill your grain sack with bank currency and ride gaily away, just like that. It was all but over before Coffeyville. Law 'n order was taking hold but the Daltons wouldn't believe it.

EMMETT DALTON PAYS THE PRICE

Emmett Dalton lay near death in the Farmers' Hotel in Coffeyville. He had rifle slugs in his right arm and hip and eighteen buckshot in his back and shoulders. If he lived, and if the lynch talk in the streets stopped, he faced an eternity behind bars. He didn't care one way or the other; he was too sick. But the girl alongside the iron bed did care.

"You're going to get well," Julia Johnson said.

"And you, what are you going to do?" the boy asked.

"I'm going to stay near you as long as I can. Afterwards—well, I'm going the whole way with you, no matter what happens."

The boy began to rally. Three days later Adeline Younger Dalton arrived from Kingfisher, Oklahoma.

"The thing she often must have contemplated had befallen at last," Emmett Dalton wrote years later. "The inevitable had happened. Her eyes looked old with unutterable pain as she sat beside my bed. Three of her boys were now dead by gunshot, dead by violence: Frank, the intrepid and respectable marshal, Bob and Grat, the bandits.

"What lay in her Spartan heart I was then too sick fully to comprehend . . . mother of officers and outlaws."

Ben and Bill Dalton, two more brothers, also came to the bedside. Bill was to go over the line now. Last of the bad Daltons, he would team up with Bill Doolin, who had dropped out of the Coffeyville raid at the last moment, and keep the tarnished family name on Western lips for a few more years.

Five months passed before Emmett was able to stand trial. He was charged with the killing of George Cubine and Lucius Baldwin, two of the four citizens who fell in the Dalton's double bank stick-up. While his own narrative described his brother Bob as the one who had shot Cubine and Baldwin, Emmett pleaded guilty to second-degree murder in Cubine's death. He was sentenced to a life term in the Kansas State Penitentiary at Lansing. When he went into "the iron corral" in March, 1893, hauling his 200-pound frame on crutches, he had just turned twenty-one. Outside, Julia Johnson would wait no matter how long it took.

Emmett Dalton quickly adjusted himself to what he termed the "snub-nosed halter" and the "short paths" of prison life. He worked in the tailor shop, fitting uniforms for the guards and stripes for the inmates. Thus he learned a trade, but he learned something more important. "A cell is hell," he wrote, "but it is also a place to compel reflection in those who have not been given to reflection. It cramps the body, but it may also serve to expand the mind."

The man who came out in 1907, pardoned by Governor E. W. Hoch, bore little resemblance to the wild youth who had followed his big brothers into law enforcement and crime with equal ardor. The man who came out became a churchman, a moralist inveighing ceaselessly against

Emmett Dalton is shown here in Hollywood in the early '30's, with Thomas H. Rynning, who made a big name in his own right in the West—on the right side of the law. Rynning was a cowboy, soldier, Indian fighter, Rough Rider, captain of the Arizona Rangers and prison warden. He handled his share of badmen but the Dalton he's shown with in this photo had long since turned to legitimate pursuits.

crime, and a crusader for prison reform—with Julia Johnson at his side all the time. She had waited almost fifteen years. Why? Emmett Dalton couldn't explain it himself. He said it was for "inscrutable reasons known only to the good Lord and the good women who bother about men like me."

While they were still digging pellets out of his big frame thirty years after Coffeyville, Emmet Dalton thrived as a free man. He became a building contractor and in 1920 settled in Los Angeles, where he dealt in real estate, wrote movie scenarios, and did some small crime-doesn't-pay bits before the cameras himself. In 1931 he went back to Coffeyville on what he and Julia called their second honeymoon. A reporter went with him to the cemetery that held the remains of Grat and Bob Dalton.

"I challenge the world to produce the history of an outlaw who ever got anything out of it but that," Emmett said, pointing to the grave of his brothers, "or else to be huddled in a prison cell. And that goes for the modern bandit of the skyscraper frontier of our big cities, too. The machine gun may help them get away with it a little better and the motor car may help them in making an escape better than to ride on horseback as we did but it all ends the same way. The biggest fool on earth is the one who thinks he can beat the law, that crime can be made to pay.

It never paid and it never will and that was the one big lesson of the Coffeyville raid."

Death stilled the rhetoric on July 13, 1937. The only survivor of the carnage at Coffeyville died peacefully at his home amidst the sprawling movie studios where even then cameras were grinding out totally unreasonable facsimiles of the Dalton story. Julia survived him—a woman of great dignity and, as Emmett always said, great patience.

As Emmett Dalton Recalled It . . .

"One thing I must say to the credit of the old-fashioned badman. He seldom shot his victim in the back. He had a certain pride at arms, a code of craft, a certain punctilio in his deadly dealings. His reputation didn't hang on potting someone in the rear or on the run—which requires no guts at all. When he came a-smokin' it was in the face of his challenger. . . . In this respect the Western gunplay was more like the older duello. It was entirely unlike the savage behavior of the modern city gangster or mountain feudist who places his victim 'on a spot' without a chance, to be mowed down in the dark with machine guns or rifles spitting from ambush . . ."

—From Emmett Dalton's
When the Daltons Rode

and As It Often Was . . .

Jesse James, unarmed, was shot in the back of the head by Bob Ford, standing a few feet away.

Wild Bill Hickok was shot by Jack McCall in the back of the head as he studied a poker hand.

Sheriff William Brady and his deputy, George Hindman, were cut down by Billy the Kid and his band from behind a 'dobe wall.

John Wesley Hardin was shot from behind by Old John Selman.

Morgan Earp was killed by assassins firing in the dark.

And the way Emmett Dalton himself told it, Bill Dalton was chopped down by police guns while playing on his porch with his crippled daughter.

Did any of them have a chance?

One Expert's View

Around the turn of the century a reporter asked Emmett Dalton what he thought of the "modern badman." The answer was crisp: "Why, I think the bandits we see today aren't worth the powder to blow 'em sky high with."

BILL DOOLIN AND HIS OKLAHOMBRES

It is said that fate was with Bill Doolin the day he was riding with the Daltons on the dusty road to Coffeyville. Not far from the town Doolin's horse pulled up lame and Bill was forced to turn back, thus escaping the rifles and six-shooters of the outraged citizens, who shot the Daltons out of their saddles.

Legend aside, it was always known that Bill Doolin had a large amount of common sense, and this rather than a horse's lame leg probably accounted for his turning back on the Coffeyville road. Doolin was no coward but also he was no fool and the fantastic scheme of Grat and Emmett Dalton to steal the doubtful glory that belonged to the Jameses and Youngers by robbing two banks at once didn't set right with Doolin.

When he heard the news of how the gang was wiped out, Doolin saddled up and rode back to Oklahoma to form what was one of the last of the organized outlaw gangs in the West. The Daltons rode for only fifteen months, but Doolin managed to rob and run for four long years.

Discounting the maudlin memories of senile old men, Doolin was a likable man. Unlike Jesse, the Youngers, Butch Cassidy, and many of the western outlaws, he never whined that "they forced me" to take to outlawry. He had had his share of hard knocks and back-breaking work, and when he came to the fork in the road of his life he made no pretense; outlawry and the road agent's life had its dangers but it also had its compensations. The posse could shoot hell out of your carcass, but it was also nice to be able to walk into the Guthrie saloon and order the boys to belly up to the bar while you decorated the mahogany with money which had once belonged to a bank or express company.

There is also a factual story to bolster the opinion of many frontier marshals that Doolin was a thief but never a bushwhacker. When the chips were down and his chief killer, Red Buck, had Bill Tilghman, one of the greatest of western marshals, in his sights from under a blanket, it was Doolin who stopped him.

"Bill Tilghman is too good a man to shoot in the back," he said in a voice which had enough iron in it to tell Red Buck that if he wanted to kill Tilghman he would first have to kill his chief.

Before the human flood tide flowed into the Cherokee Strip, Bill Doolin worked for O. D. Halsell, a Texas cattleman who owned the HX Ranch on the Cimarron, thirteen miles northeast of the future site of Guthrie. He hired Doolin, a tall, lanky Arkansas boy who knew how to use an axe, to build corrals and sheds. In two years Bill Doolin was as at home on a horse as he was swinging an axe. Halsell got to like the tall, blue-eyed boy and entrusted him with much of the ranch business.

Bill Doolin being brought back by Bill Tilghman to stand trial after his capture at Eureka Springs, Arkansas.

DOOLIN JOINS THE DALTONS

But ranch life became boring and Doolin joined the Daltons. In 1892 he participated in the Red Rock train robbery, where the gang robbed two trains at once. After the Coffeyville massacre he organized his own gang, bringing in as first in command Bill Dalton, who had not been a regular member of his brother's gang; Bitter Creek Newcomb, a strikingly handsome man; the killer George Weightman, alias "Red Buck"; Little Dick, a savage gunfighter raised by a foreman of the HX Ranch, who had found him wandering on the prairie; Jack Blake, alias Tulsa Jack, as fast with the gun as he was with cards; Dan Clifton, alias Dynamite Dick, a train robber and cattle rustler; Charley Pierce, a Pawnee, Oklahoma, race-horse owner; Arkansas Tom, a slim, fast-moving Missouri gunfighter; and "Little Bill" Raidler, a short muscular man, whose hair, parted in the middle, and mustache gave him the appearance of a jolly bartender. The newspapers

Dan Clifton, alias Dynamite Dick, a member of Doolin's gang.

claimed Bill was "educated" and knew "all about bank business." Bill certainly did; he had robbed quite a few with the Daltons.

They came from all parts of the West. They knew Hell's Fringe, the Oklahoma badlands, as well as they knew the backs of their own hands. From their pictures they might have been cast from the same mold. They were all superb riders, good shots, knew cattle, were fond of liquor, women, and horses. Most of them, with the exception of the murderous Red Buck, were friendly until they were crossed; then they shot to kill. Their simple philosophy was that they were outlaws only because they wanted to be. They were the frontier's quick and the dead, and they knew it.

The gang had convenient hangouts; one was a place known as Rock Fort, a fortified dugout in a sea of wild, unsettled land. There was a bullet-scarred tree nearby where the gang practiced shooting. On the days when they were getting ready to "draw a bank," it must have been a scene Hollywood would have loved; the outlaws galloping wildly across the prairie, six-shooters blazing at the splintered oak tree—now an imaginary posse—and slipping over to one side of their horses as they practiced "dodging a bullet," and snapping a shot back at the tree as they hugged the necks of their mounts.

The small town of Ingalls, ten miles east of Stillwater, with its small clapboard houses, was their favorite hideout. They didn't have to hide here; the natives were friendly and a network of informers and spies sounded the alarm if the marshals were coming. The backdrop for the frontier town was the Pawnee country, along the Cimarron, wild, unsettled, with many unknown trails, caves, and gullies.

THE BATTLE OF INGALLS

On September 1, 1893, a posse of marshals creaked into Ingalls hidden in the back of a covered wagon. The town lay quiet in the breathless heat. Doc Bragg's fourteen-year-old son, Dick, ambled along Main Street to the town pump. An elderly man appeared riding a mule. Then Bitter Creek Newcomb saw the first marshal, Steve Burke, and rifles and six-shooters crashed as one.

Glass shattered and the air held a strange hissing sound. After a furious battle, the gang finally pulled out with Newcomb held behind one of them and leaking blood. Three marshals lay dead in the middle of Main Street and the wooden walls of the saloon where they had fought was "riddled" with bullets, as the *Stillwater Gazette* said the same day.

"The Battle of Ingalls" led to the gang's final extermination. Three of the West's great marshals, Tilghman, Chris Madsen, and Heck Thomas, were assigned the job of running Doolin and his boys to their death or arrest. A special fund was allotted and spies were sent out to seek information as to where the gang was holed up.

Grim as it was, there was rough frontier humor to the chase. Once the posse surrounded a hideout and used dynamite to persuade the outlaws to come out with their hands up, but to Tilghman's chagrin, the men he wanted were not among the motley lot of rustlers and crooks. The sensitive frontier grapevine had hummed a warning and the gang had pulled out an hour before the house was surrounded. The chase ended at a lonely Indian cabin, where, as Mrs. Tilghman recalls in her excellent biography of her husband, the owner came out and said he was expecting them.

"The others said you would be along," he said. "We got dinner ready."

Doolin and his gang had eaten breakfast, it developed, and then informed the Indian the "other boys" would appear shortly, and they would pay the bill—as Chris Madsen did.

"It was a mean trick," Doolin later said when he was captured. "I'll pay Madsen back when I make a draw on a bank."

In the spring of 1894 Doolin married the daughter of a minister, who himself performed the ceremony in the parlor of his ministry. Romance never hindered Doolin's drawing on a bank, and 1894 was the big year. In Southwest City they robbed and killed the former state auditor, J. C. Seaborn, with Doolin receiving a bullet in his head during a gun battle. A Texas raid netted them $40,000, which was brought back to Oklahoma in a saddle blanket. The next strike took place at Canadian, Texas, where a sheriff was killed. When Little Bill Raidler and Bitter Creek Newcomb wanted to see the Chicago World's Fair, they robbed the express office at Woodward and journeyed to the Fair in style.

But the pressure was telling. The posses were riding herd on them, with Tilghman, Madsen, and Heck Thomas, all fast and accurate shots, in the lead. In June, 1894, the blazing guns of the deputies belatedly cut down Bill Dalton and he joined his brothers in death. Tulsa Jack was killed in a train robbery in the spring of 1895, and in the following July the handsome Bitter Creek Newcomb and Charley Pierce were killed.

DOOLIN SAVES TILGHMAN'S LIFE

It was in January of the following year that Doolin saved Tilghman from being shot in the back. The marshal had stopped at the Rock Fort dugout on a bitter, snowy night. As he stepped inside the dugout, he saw only the curtained wall bunks and an old man sitting at the far end of the room, a rifle cradled on his knee. After a brief exchange of words, Tilghman turned to warm his hands at the fire. Six Winchesters were immediately trained on his back from behind the curtained bunks.

Marshal, district attorney, and deputies. *Front right,* Caleb R. Brooks, U. S. District Attorney; *second row, left,* E. D. Nix, U. S. Marshal. All others are deputies. 1895.

A long, taut silence followed. Finally Tilghman said a good-night and went out. As he closed the door, Red Buck leaped out of the bunk with a curse. But Doolin grabbed him and refused to let him shoot down the law officer.

That year the gang broke up fast. Tilghman took to the trail again, this time searching for Little Bill Raidler. He found him hiding at a ranch on Mission Creek, in the eastern Osage Country. Bill came up the path to the log

William (Bill) Tilghman aiming his Winchester during the foray that resulted in the capture of Dick West, alias Little Dick, of Doolin's gang.

hut, just as the copper October sun was staining the sky. Suddenly Tilghman was standing in the doorway shouting to him to surrender. Raidler jumped to one side, drawing at the same time. The six-shooter leaped into his hand and barked.

Tilghman's hat was plucked off his head as though yanked by an invisible string. The shotgun he held roared. Raidler was thrown backward as if kicked by a mule, but he kept working his gun, the slugs splintering the frame and side of the building before he slumped to the ground. Tilghman bandaged his wounds with clean rags and rode with him the thirty miles to Elgin, Kansas, where the critically wounded man was put in a baggage car. Hour by hour Tilghman changed the dressings and held the outlaw's head as he gave him medicine.

Raidler recovered to stand trial. He was sentenced to ten years but pardoned when he developed locomotor ataxia from his wounds. It was Tilghman's recommendation which resulted in his parole.

Tilghman captured Doolin at Eureka Springs, Arkansas, where the outlaw was enjoying the springs. Tilghman went in alone and took Doolin in a bath after a fierce struggle. It is no legend that when he was packing Doolin's things he found a small silver cup.

"That's for my baby boy, Bill," Doolin said with the strange familiarity that existed between many of the old-time outlaws and marshals.

"I'll see that he gets it, Bill," Tilghman said, and put the cup in the valise.

At Guthrie, five thousand people crowded about the station fighting for a chance to see the pair. As crowds will do, they ignored the brave lawman for the thief. They cheered Doolin more than his captor.

Doolin pleaded not guilty and was held over for trial at the Guthrie federal jail. He escaped, freeing thirty-seven other prisoners. Forty years later it was learned that Doolin hid out at the New Mexican ranch of Eugene Manlove Rhodes, where he saved his famous host from being killed by a mad horse. He returned to his wife and baby boy only to be killed by Heck Thomas outside of Lawson, as he walked down a road in the moonlight leading his horse and cradling a Winchester in one arm. Behind came a wagon, driven by his wife.

The shotgun blast killed Doolin instantly. The body was put across a horse and Heck Thomas led the horse and the dead man back to Lawson, followed by the outlaw's weeping widow. There is one last ironic touch; on the back of the wagon was a chicken coop and a plow, mute symbols of the life Doolin, the outlaw, had scorned so often, but had at last tried to embrace.

Four great marshals: Heck Thomas, Bud Ledbetter, Chris Madsen, Bill Tilghman.

DOOLIN'S DESPERATE WOMEN

Jennie Stevens was sixteen and Annie McDougal was seventeen when they decided to join the Doolin gang. It all started, *The Guthrie Daily Leader* said, after an admiring cowhand at a dance spotted some of the gang stamping about in their high-heeled boots.

"Know who they are?" he asked. When the girls shook their heads, he whispered: "That's Bill Doolin and some of his boys."

To the young girls Red Buck, Charley Pierce, Bill Doolin, and the others must have had an air of frontier glamour that night. After Red Buck had swung them about in his wild fashion, the girls made a pact; they would leave home that night and become famous outlaws.

But the best of plans will go awry. When Annie, wearing the hired man's pants, rode off to join the gang, her horse had to buck and throw her. There is an amusing account of that night in *The Guthrie Daily Leader*. Annie had been on her way to a rendezvous with one of the cowboy-outlaws who was nesting with the gang in Ingalls. He was ready to take on Annie as his light o' love, but this disgrace-exhibition of riding disgusted him so much he rode off and made Annie walk ten miles to the nearest farmhouse to be driven home. The outlaw turned up the next day and "asked for the return of all his tokens, and the heartbroken girl turned them over."

However, a few nights later she again stole the hired man's pants, saddled a milder mount, and rode to Ingalls, where her outlaw-lover agreed to give her another chance. When Jennie rode into town, her friend introduced her to another dashing young puncher and romance blossomed.

As the *Leader* said: "Soon they were eating with them (Doolin's gang) and in the corral they shook out oats and fodder for their horses."

After the gang was broken up, Marshals Tilghman and Burke started out after Annie, who was now "Cattle Annie," and Jennie, who had been dubbed "Little Britches." Both girls were now traveling in the company of one Wilson, "the rounder from Pawnee," who had been in trouble several times for selling whiskey to the tribes and lifting a stray cow or two.

According to the *Daily Oklahoman,* the marshals located the girls in a farmhouse near Pawnee. As they rode up to the gate, Little Britches leaped out of a rear window onto her horse in the best Hollywood fashion, and galloped across the prairie in a cloud of dust.

"I'll get her," Tilghman shouted to Burke. "You get the other one."

Tilghman started out after Jennie. It was now a case of being torn between chivalry and duty. The kindest of men, he didn't want to shoot the girl, although he had a Federal warrant in his pocket charging her with consorting with the Doolin gang and several other crimes. Little Britches didn't make it easier. She had a Winchester and turned in her saddle to take some shots at Bill, who said

Cattle Annie and Little Britches.

later they were uncomfortably close.

Tilghman decided at last to end the chase. He unstrapped his Winchester and brought the girl's horse down with one shot. The young female desperado tried to leap clear but her boot caught in a stirrup, pinning her under the horse.

As Tilghman swung out of his saddle, she was reaching for her six-shooter, which was inches away from her finger tips. When he bent down to pick up her weapon, she tried to blind him by throwing dust in his eyes.

Jennie was full of fight. After breaking the gun and removing the bullets, Tilghman pulled her free of the dead horse. Then the battle started. She clawed, kicked, and bit. Once she raked his face with her long and dirty nails. Finally Tilghman turned her over his knee and paddled her bottom. She had an ample rear where the levis stretched tight. When he had finished, all the fight was taken out of Jennie. Instead of a tough young lady outlaw she was a weeping, dirty-faced teen-ager who wished she were home with Mother.

With Little Britches riding behind him, still sniffling, Bill rode back to the farmhouse. There Burke was having his own troubles. He knew Cattle Annie, older and

171

tougher, was a good shot and had a Winchester. He had reached a window when Annie looked out. Burke leaped up and grabbed her. With a shriek of rage she fell on the marshal. Like Tilghman, Burke soon found he had a wildcat on his hands. Annie also clawed, kicked, and bit. When Tilghman rode up, he found Burke, one of the most fearless marshals in western history, holding the girl in a bear hug. He was hatless, minus some of his hair, and with his face all scratched up.

Burke and Tilghman took the girls to Perry, where a matron scrubbed them up and dressed them in attractive clothes. From under the men's clothing, dirt, and grime, emerged two demure and rather attractive girls. Tilghman

made a plea for them before Judge Brierer, who sentenc them to short terms at Farmington.

Marshal Nix accompanied the pair on the journey ea to the penitentiary. Cattle Annie and Little Britches imm diately became celebrities. When they arrived in Bosto a huge crowd jammed the station to see "Oklahoma girl bandits."

After serving two years they were released. Cattle A nie, older and much wiser, married and settled down nea Pawnee. Little Britches remained in Boston, where sl worked as a domestic. Then she went to New York Ci "to do settlement work." Two years later she died of co sumption in Bellevue Hospital.

He Used Trains Instead of Horses

The Wild West, strangely enough, did not have a monopoly on colorful outlaws. The man whom peace officers of his day called "the nerviest outlaw in the country" was Oliver Curtis Perry, the New York train robber.

Perry, a former Wyoming cowboy and said to be a descendant of Oliver Hazard Perry, hero of the Battle of Lake Erie in 1812, robbed his first train on September 29, 1891. Using a small saw, he cut a hole into the express car of New York Central's crack train No. 31, en route from New York City to Albany. Perry burrowed into the mound of packages and as the train neared Albany, crawled to the top of the pile and ordered the bewildered messenger to turn over several thousand dollars in cash and jewels. He stopped the train by hanging between the cars with one hand and cutting the train's airhose with his saw.

Perry robbed two more trains: the American Express car on the New York Central outside Syracuse, New York, on February 21, 1892, and the New York Express Company car, New York Central, at Lyons, New York, on September 20, 1892. In the second robbery he missed $100,000.

The Lyons robbery was the most spectacular. At the height of a hailstorm Perry slid down a rope attached by a hook to the top of the express car, kicked in the window, and fought a savage battle with Daniel T. McInerney, the messenger.

Before he was pistol-whipped into unconsciousness, McInerney managed to give one feeble tug at the signal rope. Conductor Emil Leass peered through the glass door of the car to see Perry squatting over the beaten messenger, as he tried to open the tumbler of the safe which contained $100,000 in gold and jewelry.

Near Jordan, New York, a trainman jumped from the train and ran several miles to the village, where word was sent to Port Byron to stop the train. But when the train was stopped and searched, no trace could be found of Perry.

Oliver Curtis Perry.

Further on at Lyons, a posse was organized. There wa a crowd of fifty heavily armed men at the depot waiting t board a special train to return to Jordan and begin th search for Perry, when the conductor noticed Perry o the fringe of the crowd, acting as though "he was a mem ber of our party." Perry had simply taken a seat in th Pullman and, while the train was searched, walked out t the platform with the other passengers.

THE LOCOMOTIVE CHASE

Just as the conductor pointed at him and raised a shout, [P]erry leaped into the cab of a nearby freight engine and [o]pened the throttle. The posse followed on another track.
[It] was a weird chase; both locomotive funnels steaming [bl]ack smoke as they roared down the rails, the possemen [cl]inging to the sides of their engine as it inched close to [P]erry's. As they came abreast, the posse opened fire. [P]erry, one hand on the throttle, answered every shot. [S]uddenly he jumped on the airbrakes and shot the engine [i]n reverse. The possemen did the same thing. It was now [a] race backward, the rifles of the manhunters and Perry's [si]x-shooter cracking in the cold air.

Several times Perry threw his engine forward, then in [re]verse. But he couldn't outwit the other engineer. Finally, [tw]o miles outside of Newark, New York, on what was [th]en known as the "Blue Cut," he abandoned his engine [an]d took to the woods.

The possemen followed. When he reached the first [fa]rmhouse, Perry commandeered a horse and buggy. So [di]d the possemen. Now the chase continued in buggies [an]d carriages. They raced along the lonely backroads ex-[c]hanging shots. No one was hit.

The chase continued for twenty-five miles. Perry rode [hi]s horses into the ground, commandeering new ones at [fa]rmhouses. So did the possemen, who were now joined [b]y Sheriff Jerry Collins of Wayne County and a number of [ir]ate farmers.

Soon there were no more horses to steal and Perry took [re]fuge in a cedar swamp. The possemen waded in after [h]im, struggling through grass as high as a man, and in [w]ater at times shoulder-high.

Finally the exhausted outlaw took a stand behind a pile [o]f stones. Sheriff Collins came up shouting, "Do you want [t]o fight it out, Perry?"

From a Pinkerton release, dated New York, April 16, 1895.

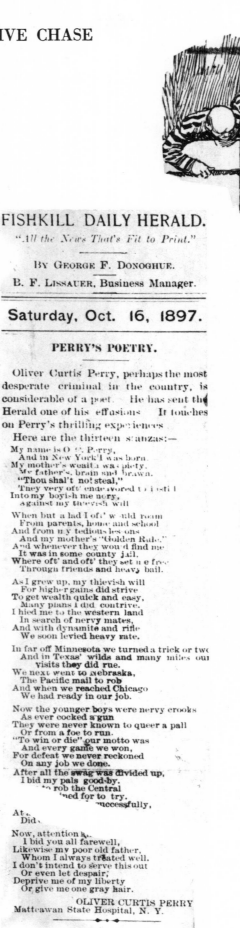

FISHKILL DAILY HERALD.
"All the News That's Fit to Print."

By George F. Donoghue.

B. F. Lissauer, Business Manager.

Saturday, Oct. 16, 1897.

PERRY'S POETRY.

Oliver Curtis Perry, perhaps the most desperate criminal in the country, is considerable of a poet. He has sent the Herald one of his effusions. It touches on Perry's thrilling experiences.

Here are the thirteen stanzas:—

My name is O. C. Perry,
And in New York I was born.
My mother's wealth was piety,
My father's, brain and brawn.
"Thou shal't not steal,"
They very oft' endeavored to instil
Into my boyish memory,
against my thievish will.

When but a lad I oft' would roam
From parents, home and school
And from my tedious lessons
And my mother's "Golden Rule."
And whenever they would find me
It was in some county jail,
Where oft' and oft' they set me free
Through friends and heavy bail.

As I grew up, my thievish will
For higher gains did strive
To get wealth quick and easy,
Many plans I did contrive.
I hied me to the western land
In search of nervy mates,
And with dynamite and rifle
We soon levied heavy rate.

In far off Minnesota we turned a trick or two
And in Texas' wilds and many miles our
visits they did rue.
We next went to Nebraska,
The Pacific mail to rob
And when we reached Chicago
We had ready in our job.

Now the younger boys were nervy crooks
As ever cocked a gun
They were never known to queer a pall
Or from a foe to run.
"To win or die" our motto was
And every game we won,
For defeat we never reckoned
On any job we done.
After all the swag was divided up,
I bid my pals good-by.
...o rob the Central
...ned for to try.
...ccessfully,
At...
Did...

Now, attention ...
I bid you all farewell,
Likewise my poor old father,
Whom I always treated well.
I don't intend to serve this out
Or even let despair;
Deprive me of my liberty
Or give me one gray hair.

OLIVER CURTIS PERRY
Matteawan State Hospital, N. Y.

From the *Fishkill Daily Herald,*
October 16, 1897.

173

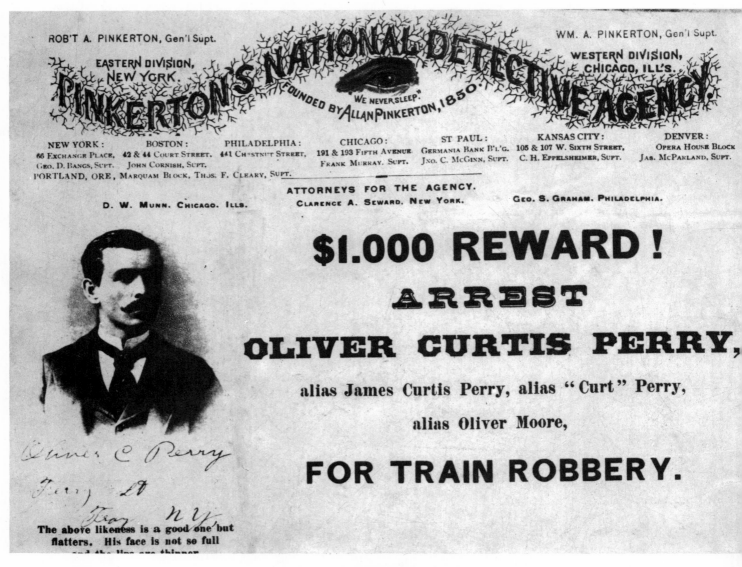

From a Pinkerton circular.

There was a long, taut silence. Then Perry called back, "No, I guess it's all up with me. I'm out of bullets."

He came from behind the rocks, threw his empty gun to one side and walked to Collins, who was holding out a pair of handcuffs.

Perry's attempted train robbery and his capture made sensational headlines throughout the country.

George Bangs, the Pinkerton superintendent, who had chased and captured many outlaws and killers, paid Perry this tribute:

"His last attempt at robbing that train by sliding down the rope is the most daring train robbery attempt in criminal history. I would call Perry the nerviest outlaw I ever heard of. There are few western badmen who possess his courage."

The New York World reporter was surprised to find Perry a courteous, literate man: "He is a soft spoken man with nothing ruffingly (sic) about his appearance. He speaks in an almost girlish voice."

Perry was sentenced to forty-nine years in Auburn Prison, New York. But a year later he was transferred to the State Hospital for the Criminal Insane at Dannemora, New York.

PERRY ESCAPES

On the night of April 10, 1895, Perry escaped. There is evidence that a young woman who had become infatuated with the outlaw had sent him a saw hidden inside a Bible. Perry sawed the bars of his cell and, after releasing several other convicts, he slid eighty feet down a drain pipe to freedom.

He found his way to New York, but as he said later, every policeman seemed to be looking for him. He stole aboard a New Jersey-bound ferryboat and was captured

From another Pinkerton circular.

sick, starved, and huddling over a small fire under the Palisades in Weehawken, New Jersey. His captor was a town policeman, who didn't realize how big his catch was until Perry told him.

Perry was returned to Dannemora Prison. In the 1920's he contrived a weird machine in his cell to put out his eyes, because he had "brought discredit" to the woman who had slipped in the saw to him and who now begged to marry him.

Perry drove two nails into a piece of wood, so spaced that one would fit over each eye. Then he sharpened the nails and weighted the piece of wood and hung it over his bunk, suspended by a thin cord.

Next he dulled his senses with a narcotic he had smuggled into the prison. While the drug was taking effect, he lay down on his cot, turned his face upward toward the instrument of torture, then set fire to the string.

The weighted wood dropped like a plummet, piercing each eyeball. A week later he was declared hopelessly blind.

As he wrote his lawyer: "I was born in the light of day, against my will of course. I now assert my right to shut out that light. In plain words I wanted to tear out my eyes."

In 1902, a reporter covering the transfer of inmates from Dannemora Prison saw a line of convicts marching across the yard. The last one was a bent-over, feeble man, looking about seventy years of age. It was Oliver Perry, "New York's nerviest outlaw," who was to write before his death: "I was only a lad without schooling so I had to take bold strokes with big chances . . ."

Perry spent twenty-five years in solitary confinement. For five years he tried to starve himself to death but was forcibly fed.

On September 10, 1930, he died, at the age of sixty-four.

THE APACHE KID: Murder for Revenge

The Apache Kid was a model youth until the age of twenty. Then it fell to him to kill a man. Under tribal law, it was simply an execution: his father had been murdered; his own duty was clear. The Kid was a sergeant of Apache scouts in the San Carlos Agency under Al Sieber, Arizona's celebrated Indian fighter. Though Sieber reminded him that the white man's law would not let him take justice in his own hands, the Kid slipped away with a few comrades and his quarry was found stabbed to death in a creek the next day.

The avenging band then surrendered to Sieber, but turned and fled when an Apache in the crowd started some gunplay. Two years later, weary of running, the Kid brought his men in to face a court martial. When they were convicted, President Grover Cleveland granted them a pardon—a tacit concession that the white man's law had its imperfections. The civil authorities thereupon indicted the band for slaying a whiskey salesman on the San Carlos Reservation before the surrender. The Kid

The Apache Kid (*fourth from left, standing*) and other Apaches photographed after their arrest in 1889, and before their escape.

and eight others were found guilty and sentenced to seven-year terms.

On November 1, 1889, Sheriff Glen Reynolds and

175

The Apache Kid when he was a sergeant of scouts.

Deputy William H. Holmes set out with them from Globe on the first leg of a journey to the prison at Yuma. Two days later the stage driver, Eugene Middleton, staggered

in with word that the prisoners had overwhelmed Reynolds and Holmes in the Pinal Mountains and shot them to death. Middleton had been left for the buzzards with a bullet in his neck.

From that day on Arizona witnessed the worst one-man reign of terror, rape, and robbery it had ever known. The ex-scouts with him were taken fast, but the Kid's great cunning kept him free—even with the substantial lure of $5,000 reward held out by the territorial legislature. Prospectors were robbed and killed in their mountain cabins, white settlers were attacked on their lonely ranches, and even the Indians paid a price in night raids on their reservations. The Kid's true toll couldn't be counted, because after a while he was blamed every time a lone rider struck. Between forays, he hid out in the Sierra Madre across the border in Mexico.

The terror ceased in 1894. One night Edward A. Clark, a prospector and former chief of the Wallapai Scouts, killed a squaw and wounded a man with her when they tried to steal a mare from his camp north of Tucson. The man got away, leaving a trail of blood. Clark always insisted it was the Apache Kid and that he had crawled into a hole somewhere to die. It would have been a fittingly romantic fade-out, because the Kid had killed Clark's partner five years before. But the authoritative *Lone War Trail of Apache Kid,* by Earle R. Forrest and Edwin B. Hill, says that the long-hunted desperado more likely got back into Mexico and lived out his days there.

Let's leave it this way: the Kid vanished into folklore, a good boy gone very bad once his hands dipped into the blood of his father's murderer. He was one western badman who at least had an understandable motive for departing from the straight and narrow.

The gambling room of the Orient Saloon, one of the most famous of its time.

176

V. Cattle Crisis and the Long Grim Aftermath

HOLE IN THE WALL

RANCHMEN RECALLED the winter of 1881-1882 as mild, with excellent grazing. The herds were in fine condition and, with the price of beef soaring from $30 to $35 a head, the ranchers were contented. Some realized a $300 profit on cattle purchased three years earlier.

But in 1883 a drought swept across the overstocked ranges from Texas to the Canadian border. The next summer the crash came. Since they could not feed or water the cattle, ranchers rushed to sell them, creating an oversupply which ruined the price. Cattle now went for $8 a head, and when the market kept going even lower, steers were offered at any price. Disaster had struck the West.

Fortunes vanished overnight. The big ranchers discharged most of their hands. Small ranchers gave up the struggle and abandoned their homes. The range was strangely silent.

With only their bedrolls, six-shooters, and horses left, the cowboys roamed the range, seeking food and work. Many times, in the gallant tradition of the West, the horse and not the man was fed first. Desperate in the face of starvation, a man with a gun would be likely to take matters into his own hand—his gun hand.

During the winter of 1886-1887, some of the jobless and homeless cow-punchers reached the barren, empty valley in the northern section of Wyoming, called Hole In The Wall, which for years had been a rendezvous for rustlers, horse-thieves, and renegade redmen. It was approximately fifty miles south of Buffalo, and about one day's riding to Casper in the north. East of the Hole were the excellent grazing lands of the Powder River country.

It was a desolate place, which evidently had been a prehistoric lake. In the course of the centuries the waters ate their way by a narrow stream through one end and formed an outlet. As age after age passed, the outlet be-

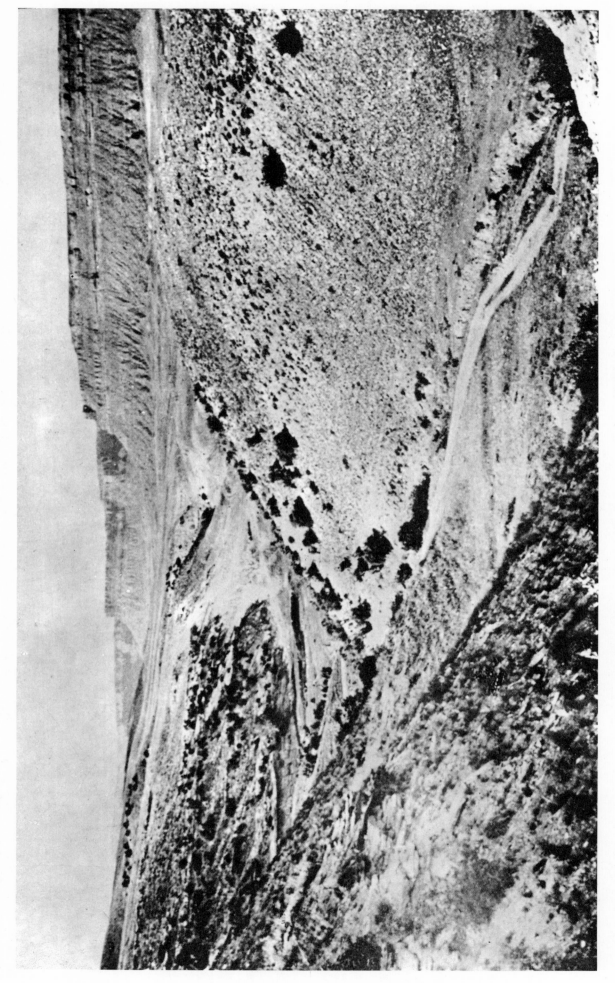

Hole in the Wall. The outlaws congregated around the creek bottom, shown in center.

The Robbers' Roost country, showing the Robbers' Roost Ranch.

came a deep gorge. The waters of the lake sank lower and lower until the late '80's, when the chain of little lakes and swift streams became, in the springtime, raging torrents. In receding, the waters of the huge lake left a basin hemmed in by rugged mountains and a sheer thousand-foot-high red wall in the north. There were numerous caverns and passages where anyone familiar with the place could hide out for days.

The valley itself is sloping and grassy, fed by mountain streams. Unlike the plains, it has no moaning wind, but only an eerie stillness. In the summer there is the smell of hot rock and sweet grass, the tule grass gleaming like polished brass in the strong sunlight. In the winter there is a white silence. The main entrance to the mountain stronghold is the narrow gorge, Hole In The Wall.

In the spring of 1887, Hole In The Wall was fast becoming a sizable community. Word soon seeped out to the lonely campfires beyond the red wall of the food and companionship to be found in the valley. The growth of the Hole community was rapid, as outlaws, rustlers, and jobless cow-punchers who had taken to the running iron for their living came in. This fortress in the hills soon became as impregnable as any medieval castle.

From this valley the outlaw trail ran south, a trail as marked as the Wilderness Road or the Natchez Trace or the Sante Fé—for those who rode it. It wound through deserts, over mountains, and beyond the plains of Mexico, with stations like those of the Underground Railway on the way.

The second principal station was Brown's Hole, later the headquarters for the Wild Bunch and the outlaw command. Geographically, Brown's Hole surrounds the point where the eastern boundary of Utah and the western boundary of Colorado join the southern boundary of Wyoming. Parts of it lie in all three states. Green River enters the lush valley from the West through a deep and rugged canyon and follows the base of the Diamond Mountains. After thirty miles it roars through the Lodore Canyon, a narrow slit in the sandstone walls. The valley extends for thirty miles with an average width of five miles. Steep and precarious trails lead to the valley floor. Tax collectors seldom appeared. The only link to the outside world was a small store on the Utah end.

Robbers' Roost, the most southerly of the stations, is located in the extreme end of Wayne County in southeastern Utah, about three hundred miles south of Brown's Hole. There are only three entrances into Robbers' Roost: one from Green River, one from Hanksville, and one from Dandy Crossing, all in Utah.

It is an ugly and, except for three or four springs, an arid spot. Unlike Hole In The Wall or Brown's Hole, it is not a great scoop in the earth but rather an elevated plateau on the summit of the San Rafael Swell. It is bounded on its eastern side by the Green River. To the south are the five black peaks of the Henry Mountains towering in the distance.

There were hundreds of riders who knew these outlaw hide-outs. Black Jack Ketchum, Bob Lee, Elza Lay, George Curry, the Logans of Missouri, David Lant, Harry Tracy, Camilla Hanks, and the leader of them all, Robert LeRoy Parker, perhaps the most likeable of America's outlaws.

There were women, too: gum-chewing Laura Bullion, alias Della Rose, and Etta Place, the beautiful and mysterious Etta. Laura knew the places better than Etta. She acted as a horse-holder for the gangs and, in one of her letters to her mother in Fort Worth, tells how she dreaded hiding out in Hole In The Wall. Even for an outlaw's girl, the loneliness and primitive savagery of these places were terrifying.

Cabin on the Hole in the Wall Ranch.

THEY HANGED KATE HIGH

Cattle Kate's chief bid for a niche in frontier history is that she ran a range bawdy-house where cattle were taken in for trade and she was hanged by a group of irate ranchers, one of the incidents which helped touch off Wyoming's long-smoldering Johnson County cattle war.

The hanging of Kate is still a touchy subject in Wyoming. A friend of the author's, on tour of the state, asked to see the gully "where Kate was hanged." He was ignored and later, in private, requested not to mention the incident again. Some of our inquiries also were ignored, except by one man, who wrote back, "All I know is she was hanged for rustling."

Kate's story begins back in 1888 when Jim Averill, of Sweetwater, said to have been a graduate of Cornell University, wrote to the editor of the *Casper Daily Mail*, protesting against the power of the cattle barons. Jim could turn a phrase and his letter was enthusiastically received by *Mail* readers. He followed up with several more blistering letters, and soon his name was on everyone's tongue in the Sweetwater Valley section. By the spring of 1888, Averill was undisputed leader of the small ranchers in their opposition to the big stockmen, who had put through the Maverick Bill (by which all unbranded cattle were to be the property of the Stockmen's Association).

Cattle Kate Watson.

Cattle Kate ready for action.

In 1888 Jim had a plan. His post-office-saloon had an all male clientele who on more than one occasion had hinted they would like to see a female on the premises. Jim remembered a girl named Ella Watson in Rawlins who might be suitable, so he sat down and wrote a flowery letter asking Ella to join him. He received a prompt reply. Ella would love to.

Two weeks later she rode up in a wagon loaded down with her furnishings. The *Cheyenne Mail Leader* described her as "of a robust physique, a dark devil in the saddle, handy with a six-shooter and a Winchester, and an expert with a branding iron."

The *Rock Springs Miner* tells us Ella came from Smith County, Kansas, the daughter of a well-to-do farmer. At eighteen she was married, but left her husband "because of his infidelity." She then worked in Denver, Rawlins, and Cheyenne. When she rode up to Jim's cabin she was twenty-six. Her father referred to her as "a little girl, between one hundred and sixty to one hundred and eighty pounds!"

James Averill.

Ella's place, contemptuously called "a hog ranch" by the big stockmen, was an instant success. Woman-hungry cow-punchers came from long distances to see Ella. If they were short of cash they brought cattle—preferably someone else's. To the people of Sweetwater, she was soon "Cattle Kate," and they treated her place with rough humor, the common attitude on the frontier toward commercialized sex.

Jim branched out. With his foreman, Frank Buchanan, he rounded up unbranded mavericks and fixed Kate's brand on them. The herd was then taken to a relay point and shipped to the market. Meanwhile his pen grew sharper. The cattlemen began to grumble. They were beginning to resent his attacks.

The blizzards of 1888 wiped out the herds. Kate's corral, however, was filled with cattle. In the spring when the herds were being rebuilt, Jim and his men swooped out of the night and began their operations as before, using, of course, Kate's corral.

As the profits rolled in, Jim took to smoking cigars and wearing a gold watch-chain, while Kate bought print dresses in Cheyenne and managed to stuff her man-sized feet into dainty slippers. Finally, with trade increasing beyond what she felt she could handle alone, Kate brought another girl to Sweetwater from Denver. But Jim almost spoiled that arrangement. One winter's night he got drunk and tied the girl to a wagon. There were some mutterings among his constituents when she was found half-frozen, but Jim was apologetic and gave the girl a handsome bonus.

In June a stockman found some of his cattle in Kate's corral. "Where did you get them?" he demanded.

Kate looked him in the eye. "Bought them," she snapped.

When the stockman showed signs of arguing, Kate ran into her cabin and came out with a Winchester. The stockman left, promising to return.

In July, Jim and his men drove off twenty calves of a big stockman, killing the mothers so they wouldn't be trailing behind them. Unfortunately, the stockman had picked these calves out for himself. When his hands rode up with the news, he went into a towering rage.

The "hog ranch" was the first suspect. A spy was sent there on a Saturday. He reported back that Jim and Kate were sitting in the living room, drinking and laughing. Kate's corral held the rustled calves. The rancher rounded up his men. The time had come, as the *Cheyenne Weekly Mail* had predicted, "when men would take the law in their own hands."

The *Cheyenne Leader* reported the posse riding up to the cabin and finding the couple "sitting before a crude fireplace, the room clouded with tobacco smoke, a whiskey bottle and glasses on the table and firearms within easy reach."

This report, however, does not jibe with a later coroner's jury report, which is more accurate. Kate was taken first, by surprise. She tried to make a run for it, but two men cut her off and brought her back to face the posse's leader. "You're going to Rawlins," she was told.

She hesitated only a moment. "I can't," she pleaded. "I haven't got on my good dress."

"Get up into the wagon," was the order, and buxom Kate was "helped" up. One of the men cut the corral fence, and the bawling calves were freed.

A mile east the arresting party stopped at Averill's place. Jim was told a warrant had been obtained for his arrest. He, too, was "helped" into the wagon. But Jim and Kate were not frightened. They laughed and joked and taunted the grim-faced riders.

At the mouth of a small canyon they were ordered down. The party, walking awkwardly across the boulder-strewn canyon in their high-heeled boots, marched Kate and Jim to the Sweetwater River. It was a scorching day and the sweaty men were in no sober frame of mind when they arrived under a split cottonwood.

The possemen said afterwards they didn't "mean" to hang the pair but only wanted "to frighten them." First they threatened to throw Kate in the river. But she laughed and pointed to the shallow water. "Hell," she snorted. "There ain't enough water in there even to give you hogbacks a bath."

Meanwhile Frank Buchanan, Averill's foreman, had arrived on the scene. He began sneaking up the canyon, hiding behind the boulders. He caught one of the possemen in the sight of his Winchester and let go. The bullet screamed across the canyon. Rifles and six-shooters barked in return. Gunpowder filled the still air. Finally

Buchanan was forced by overwhelming numbers to retreat.

Back at the cottonwood, a rope hissed over its stoutest branch. A noose was placed around Averill's neck.

"Jump," someone said.

Jim grinned. He still thought they were fooling. Kate's neck also was put into a noose. She began fighting like a tigress. Someone pushed Averill off a boulder. Another rancher helped Kate into eternity. The posse-men were amateur executioners and had forgotten to tie the hands of the condemned pair. As the *Casper Mail* said, "The kicking and writhing of those people was awful to witness."

It took them a long time to die. At last they swung motionless, their eyes bulging from their sockets and a bloody foam at their lips. The riders slowly rode away.

On Monday morning the bodies were cut down. A coroner's jury was called and six of the seven executioners were arrested, but each of the defendants was allowed to sign another's bail bond!

"Is human life held at no value whatever?" the *Casper Mail* thundered indignantly.

Kate's father, Thomas, came to Rawlins and claimed his daughter's body. "She never branded a hoof or threw a rope," he said sadly.

A dark, mysterious stranger, well-armed, rode in and said he was Jim's brother. He was seen standing over his brother's grave, and after rounding up five witnesses, vanished, much to the relief of the possemen nervously fingering their six-shooters.

Next Frank Buchanan vanished. Some said his bones were found later. A fourteen-year-old witness died mysteriously of "Bright's Disease," an ailment rather peculiar in a young child. In time the indictments were dismissed for lack of evidence and the case died. Kate's cabin fell into ruin. According to report, it was finally bought for $14.19, in a strange last twist to the story, by the leader of the posse, who turned it into an ice-house!

A letter from Jim Averill.

BANDITTI OF THE PLAINS

One of the most controversial books in the history of the western frontier is Asa Mercer's *Banditti of the Plains,* a hard-hitting account of the infamous "invasion" of Johnson County, Wyoming, by a small army of gunmen hired by the powerful stockmen. Published in the winter of 1893, the book, from its first day, had a violent life. Copies were burned, and Mercer himself was arrested on ridiculous charges, after a smear campaign equal in intensity to those of our own time.

It is significant that, although Mercer named some of the most powerful people in the state, charging them with crimes ranging from murder to insurrection, he was never sued for criminal libel. He pointed an accusing finger at state officials, insisting they had given their blessing to the raid, but those officials remained silent. Mercer even accused the President of the United States of being in sympathy with the stockmen, but the White House never answered the charges, repeated in many eastern newspapers.

Mercer, a small, intense, emotional man, was a spokesman for the frontier long before the Johnson County war took place. He was born in 1839—and in early manhood had been an editor, author, lawmaker, and even an immigration agent. After receiving a B.A. from Franklin University in Ohio, the restless Mercer traveled to Washington. He landed in Seattle shortly after the Confederate guns had silenced Fort Sumter.

His quality was soon recognized by Territorial Commissioner Daniel Bagley, who appointed him president of the University of Washington. Actually he had received a title and little more. His salary was $200 a term and his students numbered not more than ten.

The population of Washington included ten men to every woman, and in the interest of a better balance of the sexes, Mercer visited Lowell, Massachusetts, recruiting eleven young marriageable women to come to Washington. Ten settled down and married, only one going back to Lowell.

Encouraged, Mercer decided to repeat the experiment on a larger scale. Bagley and the leaders of the state enthusiastically endorsed his second plan. Ben Holladay, one of the biggest shipping magnates of his day, bought the 1,600-ton steamer *Continental* for $80,000 and offered to transport five hundred brides to Washington for $500 per head.

Despite a vigorous campaign in Greeley's *Tribune,* only forty-six "chaste ladies" showed up. After ninety-six days they reached Washington, where they were given a roaring reception. They were soon married to eligible bachelors, who virtually stormed the boarding house where the young women were staying.

After a period of editorship and statesmanship in the northwest, Mercer went to Texas, then to Wyoming, where he published *Banditti of the Plains.* The reaction came promptly. The book plates were destroyed and Mercer was charged with sending "obscene matter" through the mails, a completely ludicrous accusation. Copies of the book were destroyed—even the one in the Library of Congress disappeared.

The rest of Mercer's life was an anticlimax. He wrote other pamphlets and books, but gradually he slipped into obscurity. He died in 1917 at the age of seventy-eight.

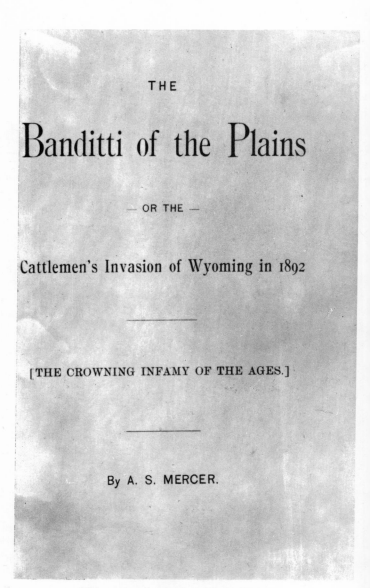

THE

Banditti of the Plains

— OR THE —

Cattlemen's Invasion of Wyoming in 1892

[THE CROWNING INFAMY OF THE AGES.]

By A. S. MERCER.

Title page of *Banditti of the Plains.*

INVASION OF WYOMING

The plot of Asa Mercer's *Banditti of the Plains*—the hackneyed one of cattle barons versus homesteaders—has been used by western fiction writers and Hollywood innumerable times. But Mercer's thrilling account outdoes Hollywood.

It would take a whole book to go into the economic and sociological aspects of this fantastic chapter of our western history. But we can say this: what Sherman's march to the sea represents to Georgians, the "invasion" represents to citizens of Wyoming. The issue of who was at fault will probably never be settled.

The invasion had its inception in the disastrous winter of 1886-1887. Heavy snowfalls and sub-zero temperatures wiped out whole herds. Spring found many of the big ranchers penniless. Rustling, meanwhile, had become so widespread that the population of the infamous Hole In The Wall country, near Casper, was doubled.

The leader of the homesteaders, nesters, grangers, rustlers—what you called them depended on what side you were on—was Nathan Champion, a powerfully built man, just under six feet tall and weighing about one hundred and ninety pounds. He had a jutting forehead, a fleshy nose, sandy hair, and blue eyes. He was an expert with a lariat, a good man with a six-shooter, and well-liked by the small ranchers in the Powder River country.

Even to this day Nathan Champion remains a controversial figure, saint to some and sinner to others. The

Sheriff W. H. (Red) Angus.

Cheyenne in the 70's.

185

Chicago Inter Ocean in 1893 called him "King of the Rustlers," but in the memoirs of the men who knew him he was pictured as the leader of the homesteaders, who was killed only because he defied the cattle barons.

After the catastrophic winter, an economic depression spread across the cattle country of Wyoming. The large herds were almost depleted; many ranchers were bankrupt and completely wiped out. To add to the troubles of the cattle barons, squatters or nesters were occupying the land, homesteaders were staking out claims, and jobless cowpunchers who had obtained a few dollars from their former employers for branding stray mavericks had decided to branch out for themselves. After all, it was the unwritten rule of the range that the maverick belonged to the longest rope . . .

And finally there was this: the free range was fast disappearing under the plow and the barbed wire. The old days were going and the cattle barons, in their lush Cheyenne Club, refused to accept it.

After the terrible winter of 1886-87 had passed, the Red Sash Gang, so called because of the sashes they wore around their waists, controlled much of Johnson County. In one year there was only one conviction for rustling. Numerous other cases were dismissed when either judge or jury winked at the evidence.

The stockmen, now realizing that to survive they must take firm, drastic action, issued a warning that all mavericks belonged to the Stockmen's Association. The homesteaders, who were branding the mavericks as their own cattle, laughed at the sudden uplift of morality among the big ranchers. As they said: "We are only doing what the big ranchers did themselves years ago . . ."

After the hanging of Cattle Kate and Jim Averill, Tom Waggoner, who owned a horse ranch forty miles southwest of New Castle, was kidnapped by three men and lynched in a place called, to this day, Dead Man's Gulch.

In November, 1891, six Regulators raided a small cabin on the Powder River where Champion was living. But the cow-puncher's aim with a rifle was too good and he drove them off.

A few weeks later the raiders bushwhacked Orley E. (Ranger) Jones, as he drove home from Buffalo. Riflemen shot him from his seat on the buckboard at a crossing of Muddy Creek, fifteen miles south of Buffalo.

Two days later John A. Tisdale, a popular young rancher, was murdered eight miles south of Buffalo. The killers had hidden in ambush in Haywood's gulch and killed him as he drove home. The Christmas gifts he had bought for his three children were found strewn about his body.

The murder of Tisdale, who had been Teddy Roosevelt's foreman on the Elkhorn Ranch in North Dakota, created a furor in the territory. There were many rumors but nothing could be proved. Frank Canton, one of the deadliest gunmen in the West, was accused of the killing. In his autobiography he claims he was arrested at his own request "to refute the slander" and the charges were dismissed.

Canton was one of the more sinister figures of his time. He was a slender, cold-eyed Texan who wore a long cape-like coat and was an excellent gunfighter. One man who knew him recalled later: "He only thought of guns and killings . . . they seemed to be on his mind all the time . . . he couldn't sleep. He was always jumping up and saying . . . 'Do you hear them? . . . get on your guns . . .' but it wasn't anything—just the wind or the horses . . ."

View of Buffalo, Wyoming, showing a freighting outfit in the early days.

In the spring of 1892, the cattlemen took the law in their own hands. Mercer claimed that an "extermination fund" estimated from $50,000 to $100,000 was voted to hire an army of gunfighters to invade Johnson County, and to launch a nationwide publicity campaign against the homesteaders, charging "a reign of terror exists that can only be overcome by the use of arms . . ."

Powerful forces worked behind the scenes in Washington. Later it was charged that President Harrison had given his official approval for the "invasion." There is no documentary evidence of this but it must be pointed out that Harrison never officially condemned the actions of the stockmen. Certainly he must have known about the proposed "invasion" from the nation's leading newspapers.

In Cheyenne, rifles and six-shooters began to arrive in crates. Stockmen in the Panhandle sent word they were ready to send in reinforcements.

On April 1, 1892, the Wyoming militia was ordered to join the invasion against the Hole In The Wall community. The obvious strategy was to prevent any local sheriff from acting and to cloak the gunmen with an air of officialdom.

On the afternoon of the same day, a meeting of stockmen in Denver passed a resolution condemning the "thieves and outlaws" and promising to protect the stockmen's interests. They were now on the record as a law unto themselves.

Major Wolcott, a cocky little martinet, was in charge of the invaders. A special train highballed out of Cheyenne bound for Casper, Wyoming, with Wolcott telling the engineer, "Put us out at Casper and we will do the rest."

The 200-mile run was made without incident. Wires were cut, isolating Casper. On the morning of April 8, a Friday, the army set out with ammunition wagons and chow carts. Champion's K.C. Ranch was the first target. On Monday morning the house was surrounded. Two trappers who had stayed the night came out for water and were captured. They told the mercenaries that only Champion and his partner, Nick Rae, were inside.

Rae made a run for it and was riddled with bullets. Champion, his six-shooter blazing, ran out and dragged his dying partner back into the house. The firing went on all day. Later a rancher came riding up to help Champion but was driven off by shots. He rode off wildly to rouse the other ranchers. But it was too late, for now the besiegers had decided to fire the house. A wagon filled with straw was set aflame and rolled down a hill. The tinder-dry house soon caught fire and became a roaring torch. Champion, game to the last, came running out firing both guns, but there were too many for him and he went down under a hail of lead.

Someone pinned a card, "Rustlers beware," on his body, and the raiders moved off. A reporter who had accompanied the "army" found a bloody little notebook, with entries Champion had made as he fought off the stockmen's mercenaries. It is a moving little "diary," ending

Major Frank Wolcott.

Frank M. Canton.

187

with, "The house is now all fired. Goodby boys if I will never see you again . . ."

The invaders now set out for their major goal—the town of Buffalo, about fifty miles north. They were jubilant as they told each other how they were going to wipe out the "rustlers' stronghold," while the Texas Kid, a young gunslinging cow-puncher, listed Nick Rae as his number one victim, and made a record of the blood money he had earned for the killing—fifty dollars.

But the rancher who had been driven off while trying to reach the K.C. Ranch had alerted Buffalo. Sheriff Red Angus, a friend of the homesteaders—and the rustlers—set out in Paul Revere fashion to rouse the Powder River country. Bob Foote, a tall, fierce-eyed old man with blazing eyes and a spade beard, reminiscent of John Brown's, rode up and down the main street of Buffalo, stirring the community to give battle to the enemy.

The *Big Horn Sentinel* quoted his harangue: "Citizens . . . an armed body of assassins has entered our country, and with bullet and fire have destroyed the lives and property of our people . . . this murderous gang is now marching on our village . . . men, citizens, as you love your home and families I call upon you to shoulder arms and go to the front to battle the approaching foe . . . come to my store and get whatever you need for this battle. It is free. Your manhood and mine demands action! Fall into line . . ."

It was a thrilling scene: the old man riding his big black bay up and down the dusty street, the fresh breeze twisting his beard, as he made a speaking trumpet of his hands to call his neighbors to arms.

One of the local ministers also rode into town, calling to his churchmen to resist the stockmen. The little village rallied. Men ran to Bob Foote's store and caught the Winchesters he was throwing out of a box, while another man filled their arms with cartridge cases. Tobacco, slickers,

food, and blankets were loaded in wagons. Anyone who didn't have a rifle strapped a bowie knife to his belt or shouldered a pitchfork.

Meanwhile Major Wolcott kept prodding his invaders along. "On to Buffalo, men," he shouted as he rode up and down the column . . . "We'll wreck that damn nester's hole . . ."

The column at last reached the T A Ranch on Crazy Woman Creek. After a short rest they set out again. When the ranch was only two miles behind them, they were confronted by the motley army of nesters, rustlers, and townspeople lined up on the crest of a small hill. A shout went up when they saw the invaders. Screaming curses and threats, they boiled over the hill and down on the gunfighters.

Wolcott's men took one look at the angry mob, holding aloft pitchforks, clubs, and rifles, then turned and raced back to the T A Ranch, leaving behind their wagons of weapons, ammunition, dynamite, and clothes.

At the T A they holed up in the large barn and, with augers, made firing holes which remain to this day. The Buffalo people erected their own barricades and dug in. Their rifles and six-shooters soon began to splinter the tough logs of the barn.

The battle raged on. Once when Ben Morrison, the well-known stockmen's detective, was seen at a window in the barn, one of the homesteaders who knew him jeered: "Want a drink of water, Ben?"

"Nope, I'm on ice already," was the answer, accompanied by a shot.

The nesters and rustlers completely turned the tables on the invaders, even adopting their tactics of cutting the telegraph wires so word couldn't get to Cheyenne—or anywhere else.

After two days and nights, during which the invaders went without food and water, one of their men managed

Dugout used by Champion and Nick Rae,
T. A. Ranch near Buffalo.

Barn in which Wolcott and his invaders were besieged.
near the shack on the K. C. Ranch.

to sneak through the lines. A wire was set up in Casper and a report of what was happening to Wolcott and his men sent to the Cheyenne Club. A message was flashed to the Washington homes of Wyoming Senators Carey and Warren. President Harrison was summoned from his bed at midnight and immediately dispatched an order to the Secretary of War to act under the orders of Governor Amos W. Barber of Wyoming.

On April 10 the *Casper Wyoming News* declared that although "there has been offered a very liberal inducement for couriers, everything so far failed to induce horseback riders to go into the Powder River country." The whole countryside, the paper said, "is a walking arsenal."

In discussing the purpose of the invaders, the newspaper noted wryly, "If their motive is to kill off all personal enemies on this trip, about half the population must be on the list."

In Cheyenne Governor Barber, in an interview with a Colorado newspaper correspondent, described how the invading party was "organized quietly in Denver, as it is felt that the preliminary arrangements could not be safely made in Wyoming, so widespread is the influence of the rustlers."

Then the chief executive of the state, in answer to the question of whether there was no other way to protect the interests of the cattlemen, grimly replied, "None . . . They (the cattlemen) must maintain their positions with rifles or let the robbers hold full sway . . ."

Back at the T A Ranch, Red Angus left for Fort McKinney to try to get help. He left in charge Arapaho Brown, who looked like a wizened copy of Buffalo Bill. While Red was racing across the prairie, Brown thoughtfully looked over the possessions abandoned by the mercenaries. There was plenty of dynamite and Brown summoned a council of war. By this time there were more than five hundred homesteaders, rustlers, and townspeople spread out in a firing line, all sights trained on the bullet-splintered barn. Then Brown called a vote on his proposition: to return the dynamite to its rightful owners—but with a lighted fuse. It was carried unanimously.

Bales of hay and logs were piled on a large wagon. Then a second wagon was nailed to the first and loaded with dynamite. The plan was for several volunteers to grab hold of the tongue of the second wagon and push both down the hill to the barn. The hay and barricades in the first wagon would protect them from the gunfighters' rifle fire as they advanced. When they reached the barn a fuse was to be touched off.

From inside the barn Wolcott and his men watched Arapaho Brown in tattered buckskins, and twelve volunteers, execute a dry run with the Ark of Safety, as Brown called the wagons. As twilight of the third day thickened, the mercenaries could see the smoke of the Dutch ovens rising in the air. The odor of boiling coffee came to them. Mouths watered and empty stomachs rumbled.

At last Wolcott announced: "We'll move out at dawn."

The night was still. The campfires of Arapaho Brown's

Arapaho Brown.

army winked along the Crazy Woman River. Somewhere in the hills wolves sang at the moon.

Back at Fort McKinney, Colonel Van Horne ordered his three troops of cavalry to mount. Just before dawn the cavalrymen streamed out of the gate, bound for the T A Ranch, about thirteen miles away.

As the first streaks of pink appeared in the east, Arapaho Brown summoned his volunteers. All along the line rifles were loaded and sighted at the black hulk of the barn. The wagon was started on its way and lumbered through the tall grass. In his sniper's post on the hill, "Dead Center Dave," a tough old frontiersman, loaded up his buffalo gun, aimed, and pulled the trigger. The crash of the heavy gun echoed across the quiet land.

Inside the barn, our writing friend, the Texas Kid, cursed and fired back. The Winchester's bark was sharp. Dead Center Dave screeched a Sioux war cry and fired again.

The Ark of Safety creaked through the grass. All along the firing line, rifles and six-shooters blazed away. The dynamite wagon was near the peak of the hill and was about to start down, when the notes of "Boots and Saddles" sounded in the clear dawn.

It was strictly Hollywood, but true; the fours thundered through the waist-high grass, the Stars and Stripes stiff in the morning breeze. Red Angus, riding at Colonel Van Horne's side, raised his hat and whooped. It was a signal they had won. Men stood up and whooped in return. Six-shooters and rifles were fired in the air. And from the barn the Regulators, or White Caps as they were called, crept cautiously into the barnyard, fingering their guns. They licked their cracked lips and wiped their powder-stained faces as they stared at the soldiers.

Red Angus insisted that Van Horne and his men arrest the invaders, and this was done. It was an ignominious defeat for Major Wolcott and his glorified gunfighters as they marched past the grinning homesteaders, rustlers, and townspeople, who leaned on their rifles and squirted their boots with tobacco juice.

Lengthy court trials and much whitewash ended in the dismissal of the mercenaries. The cattle barons swore to return to Johnson County "and clean out those rascals," but they never did.

"HANDS UP"

THE "HANDS-UP" POSTER

Like that other famous poster, "I Want You," of World War I, this picture creates a very effective optical illusion: the masked man appears to be pointed at your eyes, regardless of your position. Move right, left, up, or down, and the focus is still directly on you.

This poster, used extensively by the Pinkerton National Detective Agency, was made from a painting by "The Cowboy Artist," a character well-known in the West during the 1880's and early 1890's. The story behind the picture helped to make it famous: A highwayman had held up and robbed a faro bank. A stranger was arrested and brought to trial. There was no real evidence against him, but a dozen witnesses identified him as the masked bandit. On cross-examination, however, each testified that the bandit stood pointing his gun and looking *square at him*. Since only one of the witnesses could be right, all the testimony was thrown out of court and the innocent stranger was freed.

VI. The Wild Bunch

THE TRUE STORY of the Wild Bunch is a composite of all the lurid melodramas of the West, complete with all the elements that are now standard: wild rides across the plains, battles with posses, good men versus bad men, beautiful and mysterious women, train and bank robberies, the mysterious deadly-with-a-six-shooter stranger who kills, then disappears. But also there are many exploits and adventures of the Wild Bunch not yet known to television, not yet copied by the fictioneers.

Unlike the stories of the Jameses and Youngers or Sam Bass, there are official documents and reports by which the story of the Wild Bunch can be checked. Until four years ago, two Pinkerton operatives who had chased the gang all over the West were still living. One, Frank Dimaio, who followed two of the leaders into the jungles of South America, is alive today.

There is no doubt that the Wild Bunch was the largest, toughest, and most colorful of all western outlaw gangs. Certainly it was the first such aggregation to have an orderly organization. Shortly after the turn of the century, when the Pinkertons had killed or arrested most of the gang, the *Denver Daily News,* on June 29, 1903, in a special article, summed it up:

"The operations of the Wild Bunch were at one time so bold that during his term of office, former Governor Wells of Utah suggested that the governors of Colorado, Wyoming, and Utah unite in concentrated action to wipe out this gang. The operations of the freebooters extended from the Montana lines outward to the conjoining of Sweetwater, Wyoming, Unitah County; Utah and Routt County, Colorado.

The Wild Bunch varied in number at times from a mere handful of riders to a small army of outlaws. Sometimes they seemed to separate into different bands; in fact, these were interchangeable. Yet they never failed to join ranks to fight the common foe, the Pinkertons or the regional sheriffs and posses.

The undisputed leader was Butch Cassidy. His second-in-command was Harvey Logan, the deadly Kid Curry. Logan at times led his own combination, separate from Cassidy. Elza Lay was what Cassidy called "the educated member" of the Bunch. The more successful bank and train holdups were blueprinted by this slim, handsome man.

In the beginning the Wild Bunch riders came from all parts of the West for mutual protection and combined plunder. Hunted from place to place for individual crimes ranging from cattle-rustling to murder, they "rounded up" Hole In The Wall. From this natural fortress they defied the law, thundering forth from time to time to prey upon stage-coaches, express trains, small banks, and even country towns.

Then followed dashing rides across the plains for hundreds of miles to Hole In The Wall and immunity from arrest. As the *Chicago Inter Ocean* of October 6, 1904, said in a fifteen-column story about the Bunch, "they formed, as nearly as such a thing can be, a trust in outlawry, and it is significant that the forces of law and order slowly, surely, inevitably closed in on them and one by one hunted them down and made them pay the penalty."

Before Cassidy, Kid Curry, and the Sundance Kid appeared, the leader of the Hole In The Wall was "Laughing Sam" Carey, one of the notorious bandits of the Wild West. The *New York World* commented that "Carey is not the jovial, laughing, good-natured individual his name would indicate. On the contrary he is grim-faced with a long string of murders to his credit."

Carey was an evil-looking character with a long knife scar under his right eye, the mark of a wound inflicted by a fellow "with whom he had a disagreement." The demise of the fellow was hastened when the top of his head was blown off by Laughing Sam's revolver, fired almost point-blank.

Carey robbed and murdered his way through South Dakota, Wyoming, and Montana. The bank raid on Spearfish, South Dakota, was his idea, and it turned into another Northfield, with Sam emerging as the only survivor. Badly wounded, he managed to reach Hole In The Wall, where one of the outlaw "surgeons" dug out bullets from his back, shoulder, and arm.

Carey's riders included the Taylor brother who murdered the Meeks family in Carrollton, Missouri, H. Wilcox, the train robber, and Bud Denslow, who made a specialty of robbing the Union Pacific.

However, after the Johnson County war the real Wild Bunch appeared. Besides Cassidy, Lay, and the Missouri Logans—Harvey and Lonnie—there were Bob Lee, the Logans' first cousin; Tom Ketchum and his brother, "Black Jack," who led his own band in New Mexico; Bill Carver, sneering and cold-blooded; George L. Curry, alias Flat Nose Curry; Ben Kilpatrick, the Tall Texan, handsome, fast on the draw, with a roving eye for the ladies; Camilla Hanks, the stumpy little man with the deaf right ear who could rob a train "as slick as a whistle," according to Kid Curry; Tom O'Day, a restless young gunfighter who died in a Texas street before he was thirty.

There were many other riders. Some stayed a few weeks, then left to ride south on the outlaw trail. Although there were many actors in this lurid western melodrama, there was only one star—Butch Cassidy, the Gay Desperado.

Will Roberts.

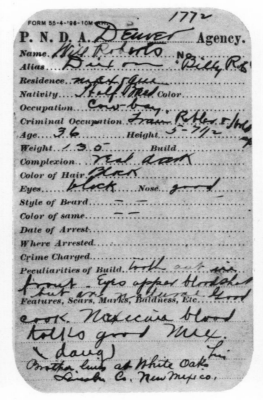

Elza Lay.

Jesse Linsley.

William Cruzan.

Shown here and on the following pages are pictures from the Pinkerton National Detective Agency's files on outlaws. A detailed record and description appears on the reverse side of almost every picture. This Pinkerton file was, in effect, the first rogues' gallery of outlaws. These pictures and data have never been published before.

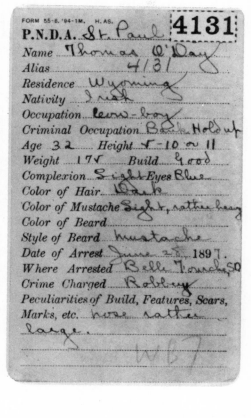

Tom O'Day.

O. C. Hanks.

Ben Kilpatrick.

The Tall Texan

Ben Kilpatrick, the Tall Texan, was the ladies' man of the Wild Bunch. He was tall, handsome, with deep brown eyes, wavy brown hair, and a luxuriant moustache. He is described in the wanted posters as "soft spoken," and a detective who arrested him in 1899 recalled to author Horan in 1949 that when he broke into his room, Kilpatrick, stretched out on the bed, looked up and said simply: "Howdy! Looking for someone?"

As a gunslinger he was only fair. But as Cassidy said, he had nerve and was absolutely fearless. The authors have his letters to his mother written in prison, and they show that he possessed more than passable intelligence.

James Lowe.

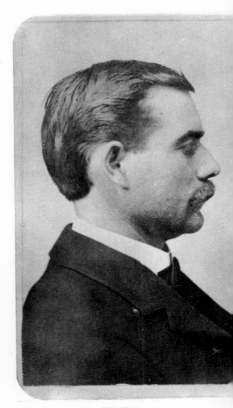

John Arnold.

Harry Longbaugh.

The Sundance Kid

Harry Longbaugh, the Sundance Kid, was, of all the Wild Bunch, Butch Cassidy's closest associate. The Kid and Butch, together with the mysterious Etta Place, spent many years traveling together— in New Orleans, New York, and South America, as we shall see.

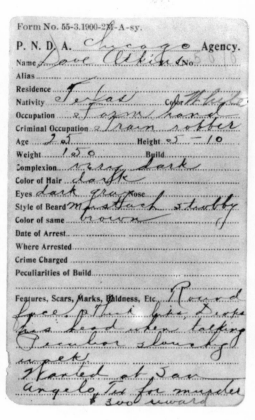

Dave Atkins.

P.N.D.A.　　　No. _9_

Name　James Lowe

Alias
Residence　Kansas City
Nativity　Am　Color　W
Occupation　Laborer
Criminal Occupation　Train Robber
Age　32 (10)　Height　5 - 3 3/8
Weight　133　Build　M. St
Complexion　M. Ruddy
Color of Hair　Dk. Blonde
Eyes　Grey　Nose
Style of Beard
Color of Same
Date of Arrest　Feb. 9 - 10
Where Arrested　St Louis, Mo.
Crime Charged　Train Robbery
Peculiarities of Build

Features, Scars, Marks, Baldness, Etc.
Faint cut left side ridge nose
"　"　R　"　"

Form No. 55-3.1900-2M-A-sy.

P.N.D.A. Chicago Agency.
Name　Dave Atkins　No.
Alias
Residence　Texas
Nativity　Texas　Color　White
Occupation　Farm hand
Criminal Occupation　Train robber
Age　25　Height　5 - 10
Weight　150　Build
Complexion　very dark
Color of Hair　dark
Eyes　dark gray　Nose
Style of Beard　Mustach stubby
Color of same　brown
Date of Arrest
Where Arrested
Crime Charged
Peculiarities of Build

Features, Scars, Marks, Baldness, Etc. Round
face, thin lips, drops
his head when talking.
Peculiar slouching
walk.
Wanted at San
Angelo, Tex for murder
$300 reward

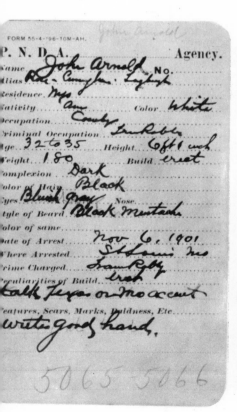

Bob Lee.

P.N.D.A.　　　Agency.
Name　John Arnold　No.
Alias　Rob Cunningham Lightpft
Residence　Miss
Nativity　Am　Color　White
Occupation　Cowboy
Criminal Occupation　Train Robber
Age　32 to 35　Height　6 ft 1 inch
Weight　180　Build　erect
Complexion　Dark
Color of Hair　Black
Eyes　Black gray　Nose
Style of Beard　Black Mustache
Color of same
Date of Arrest　Nov 6, 1901
Where Arrested　St Louis Mo
Crime Charged　Train Robbery
Peculiarities of Build　erect
talk Texas or Mo accent
Features, Scars, Marks, Baldness, Etc.
writes good hand.

5065 5066

FORM 55A-3.'95-M. H.　　Chicago　1670

Name　Bob Lee　No. 4431
Alias　Bob Curry
Residence　Dodson Mo.
Nativity　American　Color　White
Occupation　Gambler & Hold up
Criminal Occupation　Train Robber
Age　34　Height　5 Ft 9 in
Weight　175　Build　Heavy
Complexion　Dark
Color of Hair　Black
Eyes　Brown　Nose　Broad & flat at
Style of Beard　nostrils
Color of same　Black
Date of Arrest　Feb. 28. 1900
Where Arrested　Cripple Creek Colo.
Crime Charged　Train Robbery
Peculiarities of Build

Features, Scars, Marks, Baldness, Etc.
Small scar on left cheek
about one inch from
base of nose

Butch Cassidy (Robert Parker).

Frank Elliott ("Peg Leg").

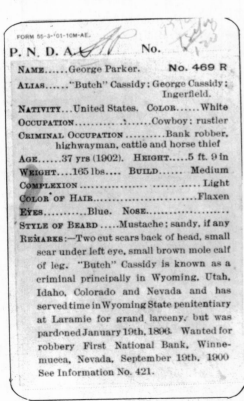

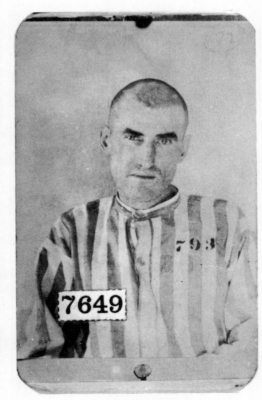

Joe Chancellor.

Arrayed against Cassidy and his Wild Bunch was another sort of bunch, the Pinkertons
—not only the Pinkertons themselves, but a remarkably able, well-trained and experienced force of operatives.

R. A. Pinkerton.   W. A. Pinkerton.

Pinkerton operatives Charles A. Siringo and W. O. Sayles.

Tom Horn.

He Went in Alone

One of Tom Horn's little known exploits is the capture of Peg Leg, a vicious member of the Wild Bunch who formed his own gang in the 1880's. Peg Leg Watson, alias McCoy, made the mistake of holding up an Adams Express car and thus getting the Pinkertons on his trail. Horn, who worked as a Pinkerton man for a short time, went after Peg Leg.

"He didn't give me much trouble," Horn said simply in his autobiography. But the *Denver Post* and J. McParland's report from the Denver Pinkerton office tells how Horn trapped Peg Leg in his cabin, then after warning the outlaw he was coming, walked across the yard and into his house, his rifle cradled in one arm. It took cold courage to walk across that open yard and "go in alone," as McParland said.

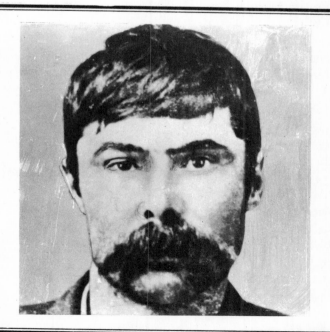

Tom O'Day: A Bad 'Un

On November 23, 1903, Tom O'Day, alumnus of the disbanded Wild Bunch, was captured by Sheriff Frank K. Webb, of Casper, Wyoming, with a herd of twenty-three stolen horses. He was convicted and Judge Craig, when sentencing him, commented on the passing frontier, saying:

"In the early days of Wyoming it was the custom to rustle stock, and if a list could be compiled of all the men who had gotten a start in life by this method, it would make a large catalog. But those days are past, and Tom, you ought to have quit when the rest of the boys did. If I were to sentence you for all the crimes you have committed, you would be in there for the rest of your life, but your sentence today shall be only for the crimes you have committed this time. After you serve it, try to live an honest life. You will find it pays . . ."

KID CURRY: TIGER OF THE WILD BUNCH

He was slightly under six feet tall, with a fleshy, prominent nose, dark brown hair, thick mustache, and fierce black eyes. His even teeth were tobacco-stained. He had long arms and the typical bowlegged walk of a cowboy born to the saddle.

He was a quiet man, almost aloof. He spoke in monosyllables when with strangers, but even among his friends he was decidedly reserved. A heavy drinker, his favorite was Mount Vernon. He wore a single-shot Colt (Peacemaker) with a pearl handle and probably could outshoot most gunfighters he met.

His name was Harvey Logan, the infamous Kid Curry of the Wild West. He was the tiger of the Wild Bunch and one of the frontier's really bad men.

He had a cavalier way with women, whether they were common whores or ladies who lifted their skirts aside when he passed. As one of them said later:

"Harvey treated me like a lady. He gave me a brooch after the robbery (Winnemucca) and he always held my arm when we walked down the street. I thought he was a gentleman through and through."

Logan might have been a gentleman through and through, but he was deadly when the blood lust was upon him. His dossier in the Pinkerton National Detective Agency files lists eight men he killed, at least two in cold blood. On one occasion he rode two hundred miles out of his way to kill a rancher who, he said, "informed on me."

Logan had three brothers, Lonny, Johnny, and Henry, who was the only one who lived a respectable life and died in bed. Born in the 1870's, they were orphaned at an early age and raised by their aunt, Mrs. Lee, who lived in a small cottage in Dodson, Missouri.

Harvey, the oldest, was the leader. In an interview with a detective after Lonny's death, Mrs. Lee said they were always "well-mannered boys who regularly attended a Bible school every Sunday." But in their teens, she added, they displayed signs of restlessness and were always reading Ned Buntline's wild tales and talking about the West with an old trapper who lived on the edge of town.

Harvey was nineteen, Lonny eighteen, and Johnny sixteen, when they left home to "become cowboys." Henry stayed behind but also left the next year, subsequently to become the owner of a small country store.

On the edge of Dodson, the Logans were joined by Bob Lee, their first cousin. They reached Wyoming and joined the rustling gang led by Flat Nose George Curry, described in his dossier as "the largest rustler in Wyoming." Curry's swagger delighted the boys and under his patronage they became rustlers on a small scale.

It is curious to discover that Harvey, in his admiration of Curry, adopted his name and became "Kid Curry." Butch Cassidy was to show in the same way his admiration

Harvey Logan, alias Kid Curry.

for a well-known rustler, Mike Cassidy, who worked o his father's ranch in Utah.

About 1888 the Logans, with Bob Lee, drove a her of stolen cattle to Montana, where they bought a smal run-down ranch five miles west of Landusky. A thrivin mining town, it was named after its first citizen, Pik Landusky, a scar-faced old miner who had, with a viciou temper, the strength of a bear. The old miner had fou stepdaughters. One, Elfie, who, Charlie Siringo later r called, "whispered in my ear" the secret hide-outs o Harvey Logan, fell in love with Harvey. They met fr quently and secretly at the Logan ranch. When Pik learned that his daughter was pregnant, he went gunnin for Harvey, who had left for Hole In The Wall aft receiving a letter from George Curry. Landusky returne home, swearing vengeance. It would come his way—b with tragic results.

The Logans returned to Johnson County and joine Nathan Champion's Red Sash gang. After the "invasio of Wyoming and Champion's death, they fled back to the run-down ranch in Montana with other rustlers and ou laws and took over the town. We don't know how or what terms, but Logan and Landusky declared a truce. was an uneasy one, with both men ready to draw whe ver they met in the dry goods store, where whiskey was served over a makeshift bar by a one-legged owner, who knocked out the more obstreperous drunks with his crutch.

Christmas Eve, 1894, was celebrated in wild fashion. The Logans came riding into town, six-shooters blazing at windows and signs. The rougher citizens greeted them with cheers and whoops, while the God-fearing ones shuddered behind their closed doors. All day the gang "hur-ahed" the town. In the dry goods store-saloon Pike Landusky was beginning to get drunk and angry.

Harvey Logan swaggered in, guns on his hip, with Lonny and another rustler from Hole In The Wall named Jim Thornhill. When he passed the old miner, Harvey Logan turned and, for no known reason, smashed Lan-dusky in the face. The miner went down but bounced back to his feet, raging like a wild bull.

Lonny and Thornhill held back the other customers with guns while Pike and Logan began battering each other. It was a brutal brawl with no holds barred. Lan-dusky was fifty-five and hampered by a long, heavy coat, while Logan, in his twenties, had on only a jacket and sweater. He soon had old Pike begging for mercy. But Logan was possessed by the homicidal rage which often seemed to grip him. Again and again he smashed the miner's head against the floor. Pike managed to open his coat and get at his six-shooter. That was just what Logan

wanted. In a moment his gun was in his hand. Pike died on his knees.

While Lonny and Thornhill still held off interference, Harvey stole a buckboard. The three backed out of the saloon, jumped in the wagon, and galloped out of town. At the ranch they hastily gathered up some belongings and rode for the one retreat where they knew they would be safe—Hole In The Wall.

Curry welcomed them with open arms. Champion was dead and the stockmen, although they were making threats to come back and "finish the job," were obviously licked. The herds were plentiful and the running irons hot. The Logans, Bob Lee, and Jim Thornhill joined Curry in Hole In The Wall.

Back in Montana a rancher named Jim Winters sup-posedly had informed on the Logans and when Harvey—now known as Kid Curry—heard of it, he vowed revenge. In January, 1896, he and his brothers rode back to Mon-tana "to get Winters," as Kid Curry boasted. But the plains grapevine had carried the threats back to Montana and when the Logans rode up, Winters killed Johnny with a blast of gunfire.

After a short gun battle the Logans were driven off. "I'll get Winters even if I have to ride to hell to do it," Kid Curry swore. It was to be a long ride, but he would make it.

HE SMELLED LIKE A SKUNK

In 1897 Butch Cassidy, then using Powder Springs, Colorado, as his hangout, organized the Train Robbers' Syndicate. The title was facetious, but the goal of the syndicate was exactly what the title implied—to rob trains, particularly the Union Pacific.

In 1897 J. P. McParland, who headed the Denver office of the Pinkertons and who probably knew more about outlaws than any law officer in the West at the time, gave the syndicate official recognition when he outlined it in a report to William Pinkerton, adding, "The organization known as the Train Robbers' Syndicate is composed of outlaws and former cowboys, headed by George LeRoy Parker, alias Butch Cassidy, a cowboy, rustler, and gam-bler. It is also composed of members from the Logan and Curry gangs. From reliable sources we have received, they intend to make railroads and express companies their principal victims. We must use every facility to break up this gang."

William Pinkerton summoned his district officers at Denver and a campaign was mapped out. Charlie Siringo, the famous cowboy-detective, was selected to infiltrate the ranks of the syndicate. Soon a cool-eyed stranger with six-shooters strapped down in gunfighter style drifted into Powder Springs. The gang welcomed him as Charles L. Carter, a Texas gunfighter. Curiously, whenever they were ready to pull a train robbery, the railroad changed the

Bill (Tod) Carver.

schedules. When suspicion finally swung to the stranger, Carter, he was already gone. The syndicate was dissolved and Cassidy's men turned to robbing banks.

On one of their bank raids, Bill Carver, a Wild Bunch rider, had a brush with a skunk and came off second-best. It happened in 1900, when the Wild Bunch was near the end of its days but still pulling off bank robberies with much success. Harry Longbaugh, the Sundance Kid, Butch Cassidy, and Bill Carver were heading for Deadwood to rob the bank there. On the way they ran into an old friend from Hole In The Wall who advised them the people of Deadwood were "riled up" because of the many attempts to rob the bank and were all armed waiting for the next raid. Cassidy called off the Deadwood raid, and since their friend then advised them the Winnemucca Bank "was an easy one," shifted the operations to Nevada.

They rode to a ranch near town "to watch" things for a few days. On the morning of the bank raid, Cassidy, Carver, and the Sundance Kid were on their way to join Kid Curry and some of the other members of the Wild Bunch. Carver seemed to be the handyman of the outfit that day. "He was carrying the blanket rolls which hid a 30-40 carbine tied with a strap. He (Carver) wore hobnailed shoes and looked like a tramp," an eyewitness later reported.

On the way they cut through a barbed wire fence. Inside the field Carver, who had the wire cutters, spotted a large skunk. He drew and fired, but missed. The skunk didn't. While the rest of the gang whooped and hollered in glee, Carver ran after the skunk, finally killing it. He stamped back to his horse, which immediately shied away.

After several attempts, he managed to mount. Butch and the Sundance Kid, holding their noses, motioned him away. Carver, cursing, was made to ride in the rear. In town they pulled off the bank robbery with ease. But even the bank clerks held their noses when Carver approached with a burlap bag.

"Carver could hardly stand the smell himself," a report by a Pinkerton informant stated. "The clerks kept sniffing and at one point Carver said, 'Dammit, I can't help it. He got me first.'"

The gang rode all that day and cached their money after an even split. They changed their clothes and rode off into different directions. As the informer added: "The first thing Carver said when he reached town, was where could he change and take a bath? Even though he had changed his clothes, he smelled like a skunk."

THE ROSE OF THE BUNCH

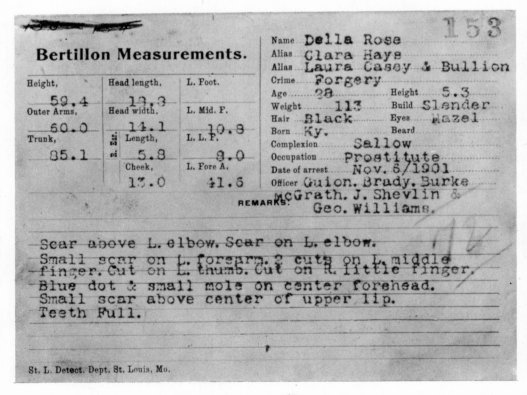

This Pinkerton rogues' gallery picture of Laura Bullion, alias **Della Rose** of the Wild Bunch, is an early example of the Bertillon method.

The Frenchman, Alphonse Bertillon, invented the method which bears his name, in 1883. It was first introduced in the United States by the city of Chicago and the Pinkertons in 1886. As it began to show impressive results, city after city adopted it. Strangely enough, however, it wasn't until the spring of 1896 that Sing Sing Prison first used the Bertillon system.

Bertillon's discovery was that there were twelve measurements on the human body which did not change in an adult. These measurements, plus distinctive scars, markings, fingerprints, etc., plus use of photographs, resulted in the identification of millions of criminals the world over. The criminal files and the listings of rogues' galleries are vastly improved today, but the core of Bertillon's original system is retained.

Note the slight discrepancy between Laura's two height measurements. There were many such mistakes made in the early rogues gallery pictures, probably due to the fact that more than one arresting officer contributed to the "pedigree."

ETTA PLACE, "ASSOCIATE OF OUTLAWS"

She was tall, slender, soft-spoken, well-mannered and well-poised. She could ride, and shoot both a Colt and a Winchester. Some say she was a "soiled dove," from Fanny Porter's bordello in Fort Worth, Texas, but Frank Dimaio, the detective who chased the Wild Bunch in the Argentine, said as late as 1949 that he believed she was a young school teacher from Denver who fell in love with the handsome Harry Longbaugh, the Sundance Kid of the West. Her name was Etta Place, and she played the leading feminine role in the long, melodramatic story of the Wild Bunch of the Wild West.

Her dossier in the Pinkerton files describes her as an "associate of outlaws." She first appeared on the scene in 1899 when the Bunch rode into Fort Worth for "some fun." This, of course, meant holing up at Fanny Porter's place. It was there that Kid Curry met Annie Rogers, who was the best Fanny could offer. Annie liked the solemn, reticent outlaw, and traveled with him for the next few years. It was she who said, testifying before a Grand Jury, "He never failed to treat me like a lady." When he was flush after a train or bank robbery, he inevitably bought her some trinket.

Fanny herself never found any fault with "the boys," as she called them. The Sundance Kid was the most exuberant of the gang. Once, while roaring drunk, he shot down a glass chandelier in Fanny's place, but the next day he sheepishly dug down into his store-bought jeans and paid Fanny.

Laura Bullion, or Della Rose, as she was known, was the only one besides Etta Place who actually rode with the gang. The authors have several of her letters, intercepted by the postal authorities, which show her to be literate. Her home was near Austin, Texas, and evidently she and her lover, the Tall Texan, had known each other in their childhood. Laura had six brothers—two of them apparently rustlers—and three sisters. Her mother, a hardworking ranch widow, admitted in one letter she could not cope with her brood. "I can't stand another minute of it," she wrote Laura.

But it was Etta Place who was the mysterious beauty of the Wild Bunch. She traveled around with Butch Cassidy and the Sundance Kid, but what her relations were with them, or each of them, and what became of her, remained quite unknown until recently in spite of much conjecture. The story is here revealed for the first time in the "Robin Hood of the Pampas" section of this book.

Harry Tracy.

MAD DOG OF THE WILD BUNCH

Only Harry Tracy could match the cold-blooded quality of Kid Curry of the Wild Bunch. Tracy, believed to have been born in Poughkeepsie, New York, appeared in the Hole In The Wall country in about 1896 as a fugitive from a murder charge in Utah. He was sullen, tight-lipped, and with deep-set icy blue eyes. He soon demonstrated he was handy with a six-shooter and even the tough boys inside the Hole kept their distance.

In the winter of 1898 Swede Johnson, a semi-illiterate cattle rustler, rode into the Hole and was welcomed by Tracy and his partner, Dave Lant. Like Tracy, Johnson was a fugitive from a murder charge in Thompson Springs, Utah. The gang accepted him on Tracy's recommendation but regretted it months later.

In March, Johnson killed seventeen-year-old Willy Strang after the boy had playfully knocked a water-dipper from the outlaw's hand. Johnson persuaded Tracy and Lant to ride with him and the trio left the Hole that afternoon, after making arrangements with their pal Jack Bennett to have supplies brought to them.

The murder of the boy aroused the law-abiding citizens. Led by Valentine Hoy, they rode out after the three killers. A gun battle took place in a canyon and Hoy was killed just as Bennett appeared on the scene with the supplies. Bennett was captured and tied to his saddle.

Meanwhile posses from three neighboring states began gathering at the nearby Bassett ranch as the body of Hoy was lowered down the mountain by ropes, than transported

Old Bassett Ranch.

along the narrow trails by horses, then by buckboard. The dead man's brothers were in an understandable rage when they saw the riddled body. Bennett was strung up from the corral crosspieces. While he died at the end of the rope, the posses set out to where Tracy, Lant, and Johnson were holed up.

The three were caught on their way to Powder Springs. The shooting was fierce as the sounds of the battle echoed and re-echoed in the small canyon on Diamond Mountain. Lant and Johnson surrendered, but Tracy, dodging from rock to rock, answered shot for shot. All day and into the twilight in the sub-zero temperatures, the fight went on.

At last there was a long silence. "Come out, Tracy, with your hands up," one of the possemen shouted.

Tracy shouted his terms and after some haggling he came from behind a rock. His lips were chattering and he was almost frozen but he was still the arrogant outlaw.

Three states—Utah, Colorado, and Wyoming—fought over the trio. Lant and Tracy went to Colorado and Johnson to Wyoming. However, bars could not hold Tracy. He broke out of the Aspen, Colorado, jail twice. Once he was recaptured but the second time he made good his escape.

Dave Lant.

2-Bar Ranch, showing gate similar to the one on which Jack Bennett was hung.

Grave of Jack Bennett on Old Bassett Ranch.

203

BUTCH CASSIDY, Top Gun of the Wild Bunch

Of all the outlaws of the Wild West, probably Robert (not George) LeRoy Parker, known to frontier history as Butch Cassidy, is the most likable. Not much is known of his family or his background, and the authors believe this is the first time that certain important elements of the famed outlaw's life have been revealed. Much of the detail was given to author Horan, after the publication of his *Desperate Men* in 1949, by R. Moroni Gillies, of New Castle, Utah, a cousin to Butch. The most startling bit of information supplied by Mr. Gillies is the fact that Butch was married and the father of two children. The family Bible has Butch born on April 6, 1866, the first of thirteen children. He was christened Robert LeRoy Parker, not George as has been popularly believed. A brother Dan, born November 21, 1867, later became an outlaw.

Family records show that Butch Cassidy's grandparents crossed the prairie by ox team in 1854, when his father was ten and the girl who was to become his mother was nine. They were married in 1865. In 1882 Maximilian Parker, the outlaw's father, bought "Old Jim Marshall's Place" on the Sevier River, twelve miles above Circleville (Circle Valley), and moved his large family there. The ranch was an old outlaw's hangout and soon the two boys, Robert and Dan, joined the rustlers and the gunfighters—with Robert adopting the name of the man he adored, Mike Cassidy, a tough, hard, and fast-shooting outlaw.

"During their teens," Mr. Gillies wrote, "they spent much of their leisure time at my father's house. Mother said they were wild and constantly counselled them to go straight. But they wouldn't listen; Cassidy was their idol and they followed him."

Tom McCarty.

Mike Cassidy.

The Parker home near Circleville, Utah.

Bill McCarty.

Under Mike Cassidy's tutelage, young Parker became a rustler. Cassidy was also quick on the draw and taught Robert the rudiments of the gunfighter's trade. Kid Curry and Harry Tracy were the real killers of the Wild Bunch, but although it has been overlooked, Butch also was handy with a gun. Oldtimers in Circle Valley have told stories of seeing young Cassidy, in his teens, practicing his marksmanship by drawing and firing at a playing card nailed to a tree. He seldom missed and the bullet holes were in dead center of the card.

One of the favorite hiding places of the older Cassidy was Bryce Canyon. When his stolen herds got too large, he moved them to another hide-out in the Henry Mountains near the Colorado Mountains. Young Parker was his second-in-command when they drove their stolen steers to Robbers' Roost. Mike Cassidy knew every foot of the way and it was from him that his protégé learned the out-of-the-way canyons and valleys of the badlands.

The outlaws living in Robbers' Roost had a unique way of getting rid of stolen cattle. The gangs split up into small groups and were assigned a few cattle which they drove to a rendezvous. The second day the stolen cattle would be left on some isolated ranch. From here they were driven to another "station" on the rustlers' trail. These stations were ranches subsidized by the gangs. They had perfect alibis; they were gone only one day from their home; they had not stolen any cattle, only moved "some strays" off their land.

Cassidy's stolen herds were usually sold at Green River or to some dealer in Colorado. That summer Mike Cassidy was in a gunfight and, after wounding a rancher, left hurriedly for Texas. Young Cassidy left the following week.

He next appears in Telluride, Colorado, where he worked for a few months as a mule driver. There he met the McCarty brothers, and as one of their riders, participated in his first bank robbery.

Like the Jameses, the McCartys were a blood brotherhood. Bill is said to have ridden under Jesse James, but that is doubtful. His name does not appear in any of their memoirs, nor is it mentioned in the Pinkerton dossiers. Tom McCarty married a sister of Williard Christiansen, son of a Mormon bishop. This bishop's son was to become known in the West as Matt Warner, Butch Cassidy's friend, expert bank and train robber, and saloon operator. Warner eventually went straight and when he died in 1937, he had earned a fine reputation as a law officer.

On November 3, 1887, Cassidy, riding with the McCartys, held up the Denver and Rio Grande, five miles east of Grand Junction, Colorado. The express messenger, however, refused to open his safe. The gang took a vote and decided to let him live and forget about the safe.

On March 30, 1889, Tom McCarty, Butch, and one other member of the gang robbed the First National Bank of Denver. Tom McCarty told the bank president he had just overheard a plan to rob the bank.

"My God," the bank officer gasped. "How do you know about this plot?"

"Because I planned it," McCarty said. "Hands up!"

In this raid they obtained $20,000 in bank notes. The gang rode off to Star Valley, which lies partly in Wyoming and partly in Utah. Matt Warner, with an eye out for business, opened a saloon in this outlaw hangout and it was surely one of the most colorful in the West. The back of the bar was wallpapered with stolen bonds and bills. In the center was a $10,000 note which the gang knew they never could cash.

On June 24, 1889, the gang rode out of Star Valley to rob the San Miguel Bank at Telluride, Colorado. Cassidy, who knew the town, undoubtedly planned the robbery. It went off without a hitch and $10,500 was dropped into a sack. They lost the posse which set out after them and the gang spent some of their split in Warner's saloon.

From 1890 to 1892 Cassidy worked on various ranches as a cowhand. He was an expert with the branding iron, lariat, and gun. Men liked him. He had a friendly grin, a wonderful sense of humor, and unlike the outlaws of the Middle Border, he was not vicious and was not a cold-blooded killer. Not until the last battle with the Bolivian army, many years later, is there evidence of any killing by Cassidy.

In 1892 he rode into Rock Springs, where he worked for a time in a butcher store. It is curious that, though an experienced top-hand with many outfits, he would accept such a menial job. But he was on "the dodge" and perhaps thought wearing a butcher's apron might help him hide from the detectives. It was this job which tagged Cassidy with the nickname, Butch.

Cassidy's stay in Rock Springs was short. A quarrel with a drunk led to his arrest. He was arraigned and fined. He left, outraged at being jailed for such a minor charge. He next appeared in the hills, selling what could be called today a protection racket. For a fee he would "protect" the ranchers from rustlers. If no fee was paid, the rancher would find his cattle missing. Al Rainer, a small-time rustler, was his partner.

A flu epidemic swept the Wind River community that winter and more than one resident recalled how the blue-eyed cattle rustler and outlaw was the hero. A Mrs. Simpson, who lived near Wind River, told how Butch rode fifty miles to bring vital medicine to a sick family.

Spring of 1894 found Cassidy and Al Rainer driving a herd of stolen horses to Star Valley. Sheriff John Ward, of Unitah County, Wyoming, traced the two thieves to a hide-out by trailing the daughter of a local rancher who had come to the small town of Afton, Wyoming, to pick up their mail.

The girl told them where Rainer was working in a saw-mill while Cassidy was in their cabin. After a short fight, Rainer was taken and tied to a tree. Sheriff Ward and a deputy went in after Butch. He went for his guns, hanging on a chair, and managed to yank out his six-shooter and fire at Ward. The bullet went over the law officer's head. The deputy fired and a bullet grazed Butch's scalp, knocking him out. Handcuffs were slipped on his wrists, and he was taken into custody for the first and last time.

Cassidy's trial in Lander, where he was known and liked, attracted a large crowd. Strangely enough, the prosecuting attorney was the son of the Mrs. Simpson who liked to tell how Butch Cassidy rode fifty miles to bring medicine to her neighbors. Before the trial opened, a friend of Cassidy's produced a forged bill of sale for the thirty horses, but the man whose name was forged showed up in court denouncing the forgery and the document did Butch more harm than good.

After a short trial Cassidy was found guilty and sentenced to two years. Rainer was acquitted. The night before he was to depart Butch asked permission to leave—unescorted. "I give you my word I'll be back tonight." he told the warden. It is difficult to imagine a modern warden even thinking twice about such a request, but the warden

Matt Warner, in 1937.

Matt Warner (*standing, right*); Jack Egan (*standing, left*); Mid Nichols (*sitting, left*); Mark Braffett (*sitting, right*). Photograph taken in Price, Utah, in 1902, two years after Warner had reformed after serving his term in prison.

MOST DESPERATE PLOT UNEARTHED

OCT 6

Connection of the Montpelier Bank Robbery with the Murders Near Vernal Last Spring.

THERE MAY BE A BATTLE.

How Cassady and His Gang Proposed to Liberate Their Pals.

WARNER, WALL AND COLEMAN

Looted the Bank to Get Defense Money.

Prepared to Take Their Friends From Custody By Force of Arms as a Last Resort—The Arrest of the Desperadoes Confidently Expected This Morning—They Are Located Near Ogden at This Time—A Story of Daring and Crime That Recalls the Deeds of Jesse James—Clever Work of the Detectives and Officers in Bringing the Facts to Light—The Indicted Men Now on Trial at the Junction City.

The identity of the three men who on August 13 last, in broad daylight robbed the Montpelier bank in Idaho of $7,160 and then escaped into the mountains, has been discovered.

They are George Cassady, alias "Butch," Ellsworth Lay and Bob Meeks. All are notorious outlaws and desperadoes of the first water, especially the former two who are leading stars of the old McCarthy gang of cattle thieves, train and bank robbers.

The bandits are now camped in the mountains seven miles out of Ogden, and unless the officers change their plans, they will be run down and captured today.

MAY BE A BATTLE.

Should the officers go into the mountains a bloody conflict is looked for. The robbers, it is believed, have been reinforced by half a dozen members of their own gang and all are armed prepared for any emergency.

Coupled with the discovery of the identity and approximate whereabouts of the Montpelier bank robbers the most startling and sensational revelations have been made and compared with them the execution of the robbery itself is completely overshadowed in point of interest.

THE BANK ROBBERY.

It has now come to light that the robbery was committed for the purpose of securing money with which to defend the notorious Matt Warner and his almost equally notorious associates, Walter Wall and E. D. Coleman, whose trial for the brutal murder of Richard Staunton and David Melton near Vernal last May is now pending in the Second judicial district at Ogden.

Matt Warner, now in the Ogden jail awaiting trial for one of his many crimes, and George Cassady who engineered the looting of the Montpelier bank, are both leaders of the old McCarthy band of outlaws. They have been associated in many daring bank robberies. Either would lay down his life for the other if liberty was at stake and to secure it they would stop at nothing.

THE GANG ORGANIZED.

When Warner was taken charged with the murderous tragedy, Cassady resolved to secure his release. First he organized a plan to break into the jail at Vernal and liberate the murderers, but the plot was fustrated by the removal of the prisoners to the new jail at Ogden. But this did not stop Cassady's efforts.

Realizing that all attempts to liberate his men by force would be futile, Cassady took it upon himself to furnish money with which Warner could secure the best legal assistance obtainable. The Montpelier bank robbery was planned. It was successfully executed and over $7,000 was realized. First the defense enlisted the services of D. V. Preston, an attorney from Rock Springs who has previously defended Cassady in criminal cases. Then the services of Judge Powers and D. N. Straup were enlisted and finally F. L. Luther, of Uintah county, completes the list of legal representatives for the defense. In connection with this it is boldly asserted that $1,000 of the stolen money has already found its way into the pockets of an attorney associated in the case.

A DESPERATE PLAN.

But the members of Warner's gang are not relying solely upon the skill of lawyers to secure the release of their partner. A bold plot to set him free at the point of pistols has been discovered. Cassady, at the head of a gang of desperadoes, has planned to be present at Warner's trial. When the opportunity should present itself, Sheriff Wright and his deputies were to be overpowered—shot down like so many dogs, if necessary, and the prisoners liberated.

And this is not all. The outlaws have a perfect organization. They have threatened to kill anyone who dares to take the stand and testify against any of the three men now charged with the murder of Staunton and Milton, and sufficient evidence has come to light to demonstrate the seriousness of the situation. Enough has been revealed to show that within the borders of this state exists an organization of thieves and cut-throats paralleled only by the notorious bandit organization headed by the James boys during the palmy days of yore.

It was thought that three years ago when two of the McCarthy boys were killed while attempting to rob a bank in Alta, Colo., the chiefs of the had been done away with and the power of the organization had broken, but leaders even more than any of the McCarthy's ever

An account of a Cassidy-Warner exploit.

of that day did. To the West of 1894, a man's word was his bond, even if he was an outlaw.

Cassidy appeared back at the jail that next morning. Where he went and whom he visited no one knows. He turned in his guns and became No. 187 on July 15, 1894. He was twenty-six.

On January 19, 1896, he was released. His first stop was Hole In The Wall. Butch was given a rousing reception. His new partner was Elza Lay, a melancholy-looking young man with a wispy mustache.

Bob Meeks, another outlaw, joined them, as did several other bandits and gunslingers who drifted into the valley. A hideout was built high on Diamond Mountain, protected on three sides by cliffs. Today it is known as Cassidy's Point.

Matt Warner still owned his saloon and the whiskey flowed. It was there Butch heard of the end of the McCarty gang in Delta, Colorado, in a burst of gunfire similar to the end of the Jesse James gang in Northfield and the Daltons in Coffeyville.

In the fall of 1896 Warner was arrested for the Montpelier bank robbery and when Butch heard about it he ordered the boys to saddle up and ride into town and free him. But Warner insisted it was too dangerous and the "most desperate plot" was called off.

In April, 1897, Cassidy and Lay held up the mining camp at Castle Gate, Utah, and took $8,000 from the paymaster. Back at Star Valley the success of the robbery was greeted with a wild party at Matt Warner's saloon.

Butch Cassidy was now emerging as undisputed leader of the lawless, homeless, restless cowboys who had turned from the lariat to the running iron of the rustler and the mask and gun of the highwayman.

MANHUNTERS

It is worth repeating here that in the days of Jesse James and later the Wild Bunch, there were no FBI men, seven-state police alarms, nor such things as extensive fingerprint collections in Washington. There were only the Pinkertons, the regional law officers, and the federal marshals. There were some good law officers among the latter two classes, but many were cowards or thieves themselves, working hand in glove with the outlaw element which ruled the community.

It was the Pinkertons, hired by the American Bankers' Association, the Adams Express, and many of the railroads, who brought the fight to the outlaws. When you read their simple reports, you have to marvel at the persistence with which they chased a band of horse-thieves over 3,000 miles, or traveled by horse, train, steamer, and then mule into the jungles of South America to track down their quarry.

The Pinkertons lost several men fighting the outlaw gangs. The battle against Jesse James and the Youngers cost them two of their best operatives. One was killed in a gunfight with the Youngers, the other shot down in Clay County. Some of the men who have become giants in western folklore were on their payroll. Tom Horn, big, rangy, and deadly, wore a Pinkerton badge. Charlie Siringo, the famous range detective, was a Pinkerton man for years. James McParland, who knew many of the outlaws by their first names, directed most of the operations from the Denver office, with the guidance of William Pinkerton from Chicago and New York. Men like Pinkerton operatives Frank Murray and George W. Bangs worked for months on train robbery cases, seldom quitting until they had the culprits.

What was the routine of a man chasing American outlaws? How did he operate? William Minster, who captured

A page from the daily log of a Pinkerton operative.

N. K. Boswell, chief of range detectives.

George Bangs.

Bill Miner, the famous old outlaw said to have originated the phrase, "Hands Up," in the West, recalled his schedule for author Horan in 1949:

"When the outlaws were raiding the trains and banks we mostly slept in the office. If a bank or train was held up, the Adams people would notify us and the main office, or office nearest us. We would get instructions by wire and ride off within the hour. Our horses were always saddled, our Winchesters strapped to the blanket rolls. We knew most of the sheriffs or their deputies and this helped us round up posses when we reached the scene of the crime. Sometimes we rode for days and weeks on the trail, across states and halfway across the country after these gangs."

The Pinkertons had the first outlaw rogues' gallery. This gallery was founded by Allan Pinkerton when he started his agency shortly before the Civil War. His iron rule, followed by all his detectives, was to get pictures of the criminals they caught or chased, and then a list of their

Frank Murray.

Charles A. Siringo.

James McParland.

209

aliases, nicknames, hangouts, and criminal associates. As the years went on, the picture file and pedigrees gradually developed into a rather thorough and dependable "Index of Outlaws."

In the Pinkerton files today is the original picture of the Wild Bunch taken with their derby hats, all looking like salesmen of the 1890's. A Pinkerton man working with a Union Pacific detective found the photographer who took the famous picture and, between the railroad and the agency, they blanketed the West with copies.

When the Bunch split up and the leaders came to New York City, a Pinkerton man made a studio-by-studio check. At last he found at De Young's, the famous society photographer, the picture of the Sundance Kid and Etta Place. This clue led to the Manhattan boarding house where they lived under false names. From there the Pinkertons traced them to South America.

The detectives of those days were rugged men. They rode well, were excellent shots, and had great stamina and cold courage. William Pinkerton, years later, recalled how he and a railroad detective walked through a swamp, waist-deep at times, to capture the Farrington brothers. Charlie Siringo recalled in his memoirs how he rode thousands of miles after Harvey Logan, lived with moonshiners, swam swollen rivers, escaped assassination by minutes, posed as a gunfighter to infiltrate the outlaw bands, then persuaded Elfie Landusky, the buxom daughter of Pike Landusky, killed by Logan, to tell him where her lover was hiding.

There were also brave men hired by the stockmen's associations of Wyoming and other states, such as N. K. Boswell, chief of the range detectives. Like the Pinkertons and the honest law officers of the West, they did much to stamp out rustling and horse-stealing.

And, of course, there were the famous Texas Rangers, whose exploits without peer have set the standard throughout the world for mounted police forces.

Big Nose George Curry

Big Nose George Curry, who had taught the Logans all they knew about rustling and outlawry, finally wound up as a pocketbook. This is the way it happened.

After joining Cassidy and the Wild Bunch in several robberies, he returned from New Mexico to Hole In The Wall country, where he again engaged in stealing cattle. Curry had been spotted by the manager of a cattle company changing a brand. The sheriff of Vernal, Utah, was summoned, and rounding up a posse, he began chasing Curry. It was a running gunfight for six miles. At last Curry was brought down with a shot through the head, at Castle Gate, Utah. The sheriff found the name Tom Dilly in Curry's pocket and thought he had killed a minor cow thief. But the dead man's picture was circulated and positively identified as Curry.

As late as 1949 there were old time cowpunchers in the Green River country who insisted that Curry was never killed but had joined Butch Cassidy and the Sundance Kid in South America. The proof of Curry's death is in the check the Union Pacific sent to the sheriff for killing the outlaw. It was an old reward of $3,000, dead or alive. And railroads are notoriously cautious with a dollar.

Curry wound up as a pocketbook when strips of skin were removed from his chest by particularly gruesome souvenir hunters, and made into pocketbooks and moccasins.

Big Nose is not to be confused with Kid Curry, whose file appears opposite.

Complete Criminal File
Harvey Logan:

Harvey Logan, alias Harvey Curry, Kid Curry.

Nativity:	Dodson, Mo.
Occupation:	Cowboy, train robber, horse and cattle thief, holdup man and murderer.
Age:	37 . . . 1902
Eyes:	Dark
Height:	5 ft. 7½ inches
Weight:	145 to 160 pounds
Color:	White
Build:	Medium
Other features:	Prominent nose; dark brown hair, darker mustache, long arms.
Marks:	Gunshot wound on right wrist. Slightly bowlegged.
Personality:	Reserved manner. Drinks heavy, and has bad habits.
Record:	Killed Pike Landusky, of Landusky, Montana, Dec. 25. 1894. Robbed the

Belle Bourche Bank, S. D., June 27, 1897. Escaped from the Deadwood, S. D. jail, Oct. 31, 1897. June 2, 1899, held up the Union Pacific at Wilcox, Wyoming. June 5, 1899, shot and killed Sheriff Hagen, Conners County, Wyoming. May 16, 1900, killed Sheriff John Tyler of Moab County, Utah, and Deputy Sam Jenkins. June, 1900, killed the Norman brothers. July 26, 1901, killed James Winter. July, 1901, killed Sheriff Scarborragh, Apache County, Ariz. March 27, 1901, killed Oliver Thornton, of Painted Rock, Texas. Dec. 13, 1901, wounded three deputies at Knoxville, Tenn. Captured, but escaped. June 7, 1904, held up the Denver & Rio Grande RR at Parachute, Colorado. June 8, 1904, he killed himself near Glenwood Springs.

Shackles, tanned skin, and death mask of Big Nose George Curry (George Parrott).

211

Express car blown up in holdup at Wilcox, Wyoming, June 2, 1899.

IT WENT UP WITH A BANG

On April 25, 1898, the governors and deputies of Utah, Wyoming, and Colorado forgot the man they had said they were determined to capture dead or alive. And Butch Cassidy, the man in question, forgot their feud to stare at the headlines which told the country that the *Maine* had been sunk and that the United States declared war on Spain.

In a burst of patriotism Butch and his men rode into Powder Springs and held a meeting to determine which of them could enlist. But cooler heads prevailed. Among them were too many murder charges. Butch led most of his men back to the outlaw hangout, but some of them did go to war.

It is more than legend that some of the former Bunch riders were tough soldiers. One veteran officer recalled vividly to the authors how they swaggered their way through the war. "They were absolutely fearless, dead shots and the most prodigious whiskey drinkers I have ever known," he said. "They were best with the mules getting supplies through the jungle. Moros tried to ambush them but it was too bad for the Moros. They were often found dead along the trail with a forty-five slug in their heads."

After his initial burst of enthusiasm, Cassidy turned once again to train robbery. The Union Pacific, his favorite target, was again the victim. On June 2, 1899, the first section of the Overland Flyer was stopped at Wilcox, Wyoming. With Cassidy were George Curry, Harvey Logan, and Elza Lay. Like Jesse James, they stopped the train by putting a red lantern on the track. As the train

ground to a halt near a small wooden bridge, two men jumped into the cab and ordered W. R. (Rhinestone) Jones to uncouple the express car and move the train across the bridge.

Jones refused. One of the outlaws, Harvey Logan, smashed the engineer across the bridge of the nose.

"Pull this train up," Kid Curry snarled.

"I'll be damned if I do," shouted the plucky Jones.

Logan slashed Jones across the cheek. As the engineer was flung back, the Kid began beating him with the revolver barrel. The other bandit, believed to be Elza Lay, jumped in between them. "That's enough. Leave him alone," he said. Then he took the throttle and drove the train across the bridge. Behind them the bridge blew sky-high as a dynamite charge exploded.

Cassidy and his men surrounded the Adams Express car. He shouted to Woodcock, the messenger, to come out. Woodcock replied, "Come in and get me."

Cassidy then slipped a stick of dynamite under the car and touched it off. The blast blew out one side of the car. Woodcock was tossed the length of the car and was barely conscious when Logan came up and cocked his six-shooter at him.

"Let him alone, Kid," Butch said. "A man with his nerve deserves not to be shot."

The bandits then blew the safe apart with dynamite. "It went up with a bang," one of them recalled later. But they were amateurs and blew apart the bonds and currency. Their victims probably didn't see the joke, but undoubtedly those outlaws made an amusing picture as they scurried about the tracks gathering up the $30,000 in bonds and money.

A few hours later a special train was dispatched to the scene from Cheyenne, 120 miles to the west, carrying officials and detectives of the railroad, Pinkerton detectives, and a posse of men and horses. Another train with flatcars carrying ten horses and heavily armed men moved out of Laramie a few hours later.

At Wilcox, the rendezvous point, the posses divided, one covering the Northwest, the other the Southwest. Curry, Lay, and Logan were trailed to the River Platte, Casper, Wyoming, which they crossed on a Sunday morning. There the manhunters were joined by a posse from Converse County. Thirty miles north of Casper, at Teapot Creek, the three fugitives were cornered. The gullies and mountain passes echoed with gunfire. After retreating for ten miles, the outlaws took a stand behind a rock formation that served as a fort.

The leader of the posse was Sheriff Joseph Hazen, a young and courageous law officer. He led his men in a frontal attack, but Kid Curry killed him—with one shot, he later boasted. His body was dragged behind some rocks by the infuriated possemen, who began an advance, this time determined to wipe out the trio.

Curry, Lay, and Logan knew what the outcome would be if they were captured. Shouting curses and threats, Logan darted back and forth from rock to rock, answering shot for shot. For two miles the gunfight raged. At twilight there was a temporary lull. In the thickening blue light, Logan ordered the horses abandoned. They retreated still another mile into a small box canyon.

Clouds covered the moon and while the posse camped at the canyon's mouth, Logan and his men took a vote and decided to try to break out of the dead-end canyon. Slithering among the rocks like raiding Comanches, they passed the sentries, shifting the bags of money from one to another as they worked their way past the guards.

They traveled all that night on foot, scarcely stopping to catch their breath. On the north fork of the Powder River they found a rancher friend, who supplied them with horses and food and ammunition.

The posses kept after them, but lost them in Lost Cabin country. Somewhere in the vast, wild country, Logan, Lay, and Curry joined up with Cassidy to split the money. The Bunch then rode 300 miles to Brown's Hole and Robbers' Roost.

At the Roost, Kid Curry temporarily separated from Butch to drive a herd of stolen horses north with George Curry. Butch, Lay, and some of the other members of the gang rode south into Arizona and New Mexico. That was the longest ride the Wild Bunch ever made.

In Alma, New Mexico, they got jobs as hands on the WS Ranch, one of the largest in that section. It is significant that all rustling stopped when Butch appeared.

NOTICE OF REWARD

FOR

UNION PACIFIC TRAIN ROBBERS.

Satisfactory evidence has been obtained that Louis, "Bob" and Harvey Curry are three of the parties who held up and robbed Union Pacific train at Wilcox, Wyoming, on Friday, June 2nd, 1899. Descriptions are as follows:

Louis, or "Lonny," Curry; thin, long nose, slightly turned up at end, which makes a "dish" in the nose; age 28 years; height five feet seven inches; weight, 155 pounds; hair, dark brown, thin and curly; eyes, hazel, slightly sunken in head; mustache, dark brown, small and curly at ends; scar over right eye, not noticeable at a distance; sometimes wears a beaver overcoat; upper portion of head, square; No. 7 shoe.

"Bob" (R. E. Curry; 36 years of age; height, five feet, nine inches; 175 or 180 pounds; hair black, straight and thick; eyes, hazel; mustache, black, heavy and drooping over mouth, not curled at ends; full round face; square jaws; cheeks, red; good complexion; when freshly *shaved*, beard shows very black through skin; shoulders, round; heavy body; well proportioned and stout built all through; No. 8 shoe; fingers short and thick, show marks of work; face slightly "dished;" bull-dog appearance; at front view good looking at times; complexion helps out; nose very small, broad and flat at nostrils, looks like negro's; face is such that rule laid on it would touch nose, forehead and chin; small bunch of hair, looks like a mole, near base of nose on left cheek; mustache hides mouth, even when he smiles; wears hat pulled down over right eye; wears flannel shirt and gold cuff buttons with initials "T. M." on them.

Harvey Curry, called "the kid," description not known.

Louis and Harvey are brothers but they are not related to "Bob."

Louis Curry was proprietor of the "Club Saloon" at Harlem, Choteau County, Montana, until January 7th, 1900, when he hurriedly sold out and left that place with "Bob," both heavily armed. It is surmised that Harvey will join them. They are supposed to have in their possession a part of the $3,400.00 unsigned currency of the First National Bank of Portland, Oregon which was stolen at the time of the Wilcox robbery. Five Hundred Dollars of which they tried to have redeemed through that bank. This currency consists of bills described as follows:

	Bank numbers in lower left hand corner.	Treasury numbers in upper right hand corner.
22 $50 notes,	A3705 to A3726 inclusive.	A744372 to A744393 inclusive.
22 $100 "	A3705 to A3726 "	A744372 to A744393 "
2 $20 "	A5641 to A5642 "	T130922 to T130923 "
2 $10 "	A5641 to A5642 "	T130922 to T130923 "
2 $10 "	B5641 to B5642 "	T130922 to T130923 "
2 $10 "	C5641 to C5642 "	T130922 to T130923 "

The reward offered on June 19th, 1899, by Union Pacific Railroad Company, Pacific Express Company, and United States Government, aggregating Three Thousand Dollars for each robber, is still in effect.

UNION PACIFIC RAILROAD COMPANY.
PACIFIC EXPRESS COMPANY.

OMAHA, NEBRASKA, January 12th, 1900.

ROUGH ON CROOKS

In Hardin, Montana, Lonny Logan, handsome and less evil than his brother, Harvey, was beginning to feel the pressure of the manhunters. Charlie Siringo, the cowboy detective, on his adventurous mission to track down Curry and Harvey Logan and their herd of stolen horses, had been stationed by William Pinkerton in Helena, Montana, and ordered to get Lonny also.

Siringo had just left Landusky, where he had "made myself in solid with Elfie Curry," Harvey's light o' love, in an effort to find out where Kid Curry was hiding. He had ridden into Landusky in his favorite role as Charlie Carter, the killer from New Mexico, but Lonny had already gone back to his saloon in Hardin.

One day Lonny heard that the slim-mustached "killer" named Carter, riding a white horse, was inquiring about him. This was enough for Lonny. He had an idea who it was. He sold his saloon for $1,500, rode out of town, and headed for Arkansas. At Little Rock, Bill Sayles of Pinkerton's met Siringo, who had followed Lonny's trail. They joined forces and again Logan got wise and fled.

Logan, described as "dark, good-looking, with a tiny mole on his right cheek and soft hat pulled over his right eye," hid out with a gang of horse-thieves in Bear Paw Mountains, near Perry, Montana, but the detectives were relentless. They closed in on the mountain hide-out only a few hours after Lonny had left upon being warned that "Carter" was looking for him.

In the frontier towns the news kept following Lonny that Siringo and Sayles were on his heels. He avoided the towns and kept to the mountains. He became lean, hungry, and grew a beard. The chase led to Hole In The Wall country, where Lonny discovered that the gang were in New Mexico and the local deputies were beginning to ride in and arrest those who remained.

Lonny stayed a week. There didn't seem any place to hide. In the spring of 1899, he rode back to Montana, then swung east to Missouri, to seek refuge in the only hiding place now left: the wooden house on the outskirts of Dodson, where he had grown up.

Mrs. Lee, described later by the *Kansas City Post* as "an estimable old lady who never knew what type of life her nephews led," welcomed Lonny. For several weeks he found a peace he had never known before. Then he made one mistake; he cashed one of the stolen notes from

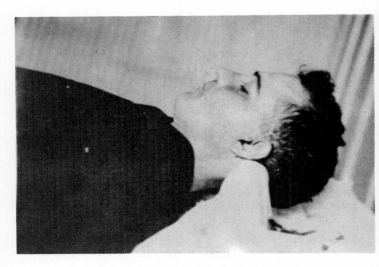

Lonny Logan on time for his funeral.

the Wilcox robbery, given him by Harvey.

Shortly afterward a wire was sent by the Pinkerton office in Denver to Sayles: "Wilcox notes found in Dodson, home of Logans."

Sayles saddled up. On the morning of February 28, 1900, at 8 A.M., Sayles and a posse raided the house. Lonny saw them coming through the snow and bolted out the back door. He fired once and Sayles fingered a torn sleeve.

Lonny dived behind a mound of snow and began firing. The posse blazed away in return.

"You're surrounded, Logan—surrender!" Sayles called.

A shot answered him. For twenty-five minutes the posse and the outlaw kept up a steady fire. Suddenly there was a lull.

"Here he comes," cried a posseman.

Logan had leaped upon the mound of snow. Then he charged, his six-shooter working. The posse fired as one man. Lonny spun around, almost torn in two by the Winchester and revolver bullets.

The body was brought back to Kansas City in a carriage and the *Post* laconically told the story with the headline: "Tough Here On Crooks."

Back inside the old farmhouse, the "estimable" old white-haired lady wept as she told a reporter how she had brought up the young orphans. "I never knew . . . ," she said. "I always thought they were good boys . . ."

THE STRIKE AT TIPTON

It was 8 P.M. on the evening of August 29, 1900, when Train No. 3, Union Pacific, passed the station at Tipton, Wyoming, and approached Table Rock. It was an upgrade, and as the engineer slowed his train down, four figures ran out of the darkness and swung up on the coal tender.

A few minutes later, the conductor heard a gruff voice order: "Pull back that throttle."

He turned to find a masked man pointing a .45 Colt at his stomach. The throttle was pulled and the train ground to a halt. Conductor E. J. Kerrigan swung down from the first coach.

"What's going on here?" he asked.

"Uncouple the express and mail cars," he was ordered.

Ignoring the bandits, Kerrigan turned and walked up the steps. Kid Curry shoved his Colt in his back.

"Dammit, get down, and do as I told you!"

Kerrigan turned. "This train is on an upgrade. I must set the brakes on each car or we'll crash downhill."

"Let him go, Kid," Cassidy said.

Logan waved his gun and Kerrigan went through the coaches, setting the brakes and urging all the passengers not to look out the window. One deaf man put his head out, asking about the delay. A gun flashed, a pane shattered, and he pulled his head back in.

"Outlaws!" he gasped.

"Exactly, sir," Kerrigan said calmly and went out.

At gun-point, Kerrigan then uncoupled the cars. The conductor, with Deaf Charlie Hanks covering him with a gun, pulled the express and mail cars a mile distant. Hanks guarded the engineer and Kerrigan, while Logan, Cassidy, and Bill Carver "commenced operations on the express car."

By an amazing coincidence, Woodcock, who had been blown out of his car by Cassidy in June, 1899, at Wilcox, was the messenger this time. When Cassidy heard the news, he turned to Kerrigan. "Tell Woodcock to open the door or this time we'll blow him and the car sky-high."

Kerrigan stood next to the heavy door, pleading for fifteen minutes with Woodcock not to risk his life.

"Tell Cassidy that the first man who enters this car will be killed," was the messenger's reply.

Kerrigan reported to Cassidy and the gang held a conference. Cassidy told Kerrigan he admired Woodcock's courage and he didn't want to hurt him. "Try again," he said. This time, with the outlaws keeping their word not to rush the door, Woodcock opened it a slit and admitted Kerrigan.

Somehow the conductor managed to persuade Woodcock it was useless to try to fight dynamite. Woodcock at last opened the door and the gang entered the car.

Three charges of dynamite blew open the safe. Cash, watch movements, and watches were dumped into a bag. Kerrigan offered his own watch but Cassidy shook his head. "We don't want anything from the railroad boys." The total loot was $5,014 in cash and a few hundred dollars' worth of watch movements.

Interior of express car blown up at Tipton.

$4000 REWARD

By Union Pacific Railroad Company.

Second Section Train No. 3 Held Up by Four Masked Men,

ABOUT TWO AND ONE HALF MILES WEST OF TIPTON, SWEETWATER CO., WYO., AT 8:30 P. M. AUGUST 29, 1900.

$8,000.00 REWARD!

In ADDITION to the reward of $1,000 EACH offered by the Union Pacific Railroad Company for the capture of the men, dead or alive, who robbed Union Pacific train No 3, near Tipton, Wyo., on the evening of August 29th, 1900, the Pacific Express Company, on the same conditions, hereby also offers a reward of $1,000.00 for each robber.

THE PACIFIC EXPRESS COMPANY.

August 31st, 1900.   Green River, Wyo., September 1st, 1900.

Dear Sir:—

Our money loss is $50.40, damage to car safe and express freight will amount to $3000.00. Robbers used Kepauno Chemical Co., Giant Powder, dated September 15th, 1899. Ashburn Mo. Works, forty percent.

Yours truly,
(signed) F. C. Gentsch, Gen'l Supt.

Tipton Reward notices and a note typed at the bottom of one of them.

After the Tipton robbery the Union Pacific's management decided that it must be the last. Chief Special Agent T. T. Kelliher was ordered to organize a posse of the best trackers and marksmen in the West.

Within a week George Hiatt, H. Davis, Si Funk, Jeff Carr, and the famous Joe Lefors clumped in their high-heeled boots into Kelliher's office to receive their instructions. These were simple: shoot to kill, wipe out the Wild Bunch if they tried to hold up a Union Pacific train again. (In Frank H. Spearman's novel, *Whispering Smith,* Joe Lefors was the prototype of the hero and Kid Curry was the desperado Harvey Du Sang.)

Besides the super posse, a special train was outfitted with stalls, a loading ramp for horses, a dining car (with a place for hay), berths, a fast engine, and a veteran engineer. The six manhunters were equipped with the best horses money could buy in the West and given specially manufactured high-powered Winchesters and field glasses. The train was held on a siding on day and night notice, and the posse was never far away. The horses were always well fed and "ready to run."

Butch Cassidy heard of the elaborate preparations to wipe him out, and promptly left the area. He recognized that train robbery was just about finished and he decided to quit while he was ahead, and free.

217

There was to be one last train robbery. On the way back north, Kid Curry persuaded Butch they should try another strike. Cassidy reluctantly agreed.

There had been some minor changes in the Bunch. Deaf Charlie Hanks was now one of the riders, and Laura Bullion, alias Della Rose, also was with the Bunch. She had once been Bill Carver's girl, but after Bill had been killed in a gunfight in Sonora, Texas, Laura joined up with Ben Kilpatrick, the Tall Texan, and he brought her into his gang. The Tall Texan, she explained later, had been introduced to her by one of Carver's friends "as a gent who would take care of me."

Laura was a good rider and, with her hair piled under a wide-brimmed sombrero, she could pass as "a young cow-puncher," the "Wanted" posters said.

At 2 P. M. on July 3, 1901, Logan climbed aboard the blind end of the baggage car and Harry Longbaugh, the Sundance Kid, boarded one of the coaches of a Great Northern railroad train when it stopped at Malta, Montana.

Near Wagner, Logan, armed with two six-shooters, crawled over the tender into the locomotive and ordered the engineer to halt the train. Longbaugh slid out of his seat to run up and down the coaches, firing his guns and shouting, "Keep your heads in," to the passengers.

At Logan's command the train was pulled across a bridge where Cassidy and Hanks, who had been hiding at a ranch seven miles away, were waiting. Laura Bullion was at the ranch caring for the extra horses for the getaway.

Butch forced a fireman to carry his bag of explosives and then set off the charge that shattered the Adams Express car. This time the haul was fairly large, $40,000 of incomplete bank notes of the National Bank of Montana, at Helena, and $500 in incomplete bank notes of the American National Bank.

The notes, in tens and twenties, lacked the signature of the president and cashier of the banks to which they were consigned, and as usual after the loot was divided, each member of the gang forged the signatures.

A hundred-man posse swept out of Malta, but Butch and his men—including Laura Bullion—were riding madly across the state, their destination Fort Worth, Texas, and Fannie Porter's gaudy brothel. For Butch it was to be his last grand fling in the States.

From a reward notice, dated St. Paul, August 5, 1901.

Photograph of GEORGE PARKER.   **Description.**

NAME, GEORGE PARKER, alias "BUTCH" CASSIDY, alias GEORGE CASSIDY, alias INGERFIELD.

AGE, 36 years (1901).   HEIGHT, 5 ft., 9 inches.

WEIGHT, 165 lbs.   BUILD, Medium.

COMPLEXION, light.   COLOR OF HAIR, flaxen.

EYES, blue.   MUSTACHE, sandy, if any.

NATIONALITY, American.   OCCUPATION, cowboy, rustler.

CRIMINAL OCCUPATION, bank robber and highwayman, cattle and horse thief.

MARKS, two cuts scars back of head, small scar under left eye, small brown mole calf of leg.

"BUTCH" CASSIDY is known as a criminal principally in Wyoming, Utah, Idaho, Colorado and Nevada and has served time in Wyoming State penitentiary at Laramie for grand larceny, but was pardoned January 19th, 1896.

Description of HARRY LONGBAUGH.

NAME, HARRY LONGBAUGH, alias "KID" LONGBAUGH, alias HARRY ALONZO.

AGE, 35 to 40 years.   HEIGHT, 5 ft. 9 inches.   WEIGHT, 165 to 170 lbs.
COMPLEXION, dark (looks like quarter breed Indian).   COLOR OF HAIR, black.   BUILD, rather slim.
EYES, black.   MUSTACHE, if any, black.   NOSE, rather long.
FEATURES, Grecian type.   NATIONALITY, American.   OCCUPATION, cowboy, rustler.
CRIMINAL OCCUPATION, highwayman and bank burglar, cattle and horse thief.

HARRY LONGBAUGH served 18 months in jail at Sundance, Cook Co., Wyoming, when a boy, for horse stealing. In December, 1892, HARRY LONGBAUGH, Bill Madden and Harry Bass "held up" a Great Northern train at Malta, Montana. Bass and Madden were tried for this crime, convicted and sentenced to 10 and 14 years respectively; LONGBAUGH escaped and since has been a fugitive. June 28, 1897, under the name of Frank Jones, Longbaugh participated with Harvey Logan, alias Curry, Tom Day and Walter Putney, in the Belle Fouche, S. D., bank robbery. All were arrested, but Longbaugh and Harvey Logan escaped from jail at Deadwood, October 31, 1897, and have not since been arrested.

GEORGE PARKER, alias "BUTCH" CASSIDY, HARRY LONGBAUGH and a third man were implicated in the robbery of the First National Bank of Winnemucca, Nevada, on September 19, 1900.

Photograph of O. C. HANKS.   **Description.**

NAME, O. C. HANKS, alias CAMILLA HANKS, alias CHARLEY JONES, alias DEAF CHARLEY.

AGE, 38 years (1901).   HEIGHT, 5 ft., 10 inches.

WEIGHT, 156 lbs.   BUILD, good.

COMPLEXION, sandy.   COLOR OF HAIR, auburn.

EYES, blue.   MUSTACHE, sandy, if any.

NATIONALITY, American.   OCCUPATION, cowboy.

CRIMINAL OCCUPATION, train robber.

MARKS: Scar from burn, size 25c piece, on right forearm. Small scar right leg, above ankle. Mole near right nipple. Leans his head slightly to the left. Somewhat deaf.

Raised near Los Vegas, New Mexico, where he is wanted for murder. His mother lives near Corpus Christi, N. M. Arrested in Teton County, Montana, 1892, and sentenced to 10 years in the penitentiary at Deer Lodge for holding up Northern Pacific train near Big Timber, Montana.

Released April 30th, 1901.

The GREAT NORTHERN EXPRESS COMPANY will give $5000 reward for the capture and identification of the men implicated in this robbery, or a proportionate amount for one, two or more and $500 additional for each conviction.

Persons furnishing information only, which may lead to the arrest of one or all of the robbers will share in the reward.

In addition to the above there are large outstanding rewards offered for the arrest of some of these men, individually, by banks, railroads and express companies robbed by them, and by Governors of States, where individual members of this gang have committed murders and other crimes.

These rewards offered aggregate upwards of $10,000.

BANDITS ON BICYCLES

It was Lillie, a slim young "soiled dove," last name unknown, who told how Butch Cassidy and the rest of the Bunch spent their last days in Texas riding bicycles past Fannie Porter's brothel to the cheers of the staff and customers.

Lillie was a disgruntled girl when interviewed by William Pinkerton. After the Wagner robbery, Pinkerton personally led his men in the field. ("I rode a hundred miles today with Sayles," he wrote McParland. "I am determined that these men must be placed behind bars.")

Lillie said she first met the Bunch in Idaho after the robbery. "The boys had six or seven bags of gold," and other bank notes in a large trunk. But as Lillie told it, some smarter crooks managed to steal some of the loot. Kid Curry, in a murderous rage, went gunning for the culprits but they skipped town.

Next stops for the Bunch were Fort Worth and San Antonio. Cassidy went under the name of Jim Lowe, an alias he used on several occasions, while Logan took the name of Bob Nevilles. Logan was evidently drinking heavily, in the "hook shops," but the rest of the gang went in for city clothes, and on one occasion visited a Fort Worth photographer and had a group picture taken.

This picture, which eventually led to their downfall, is shown above. It is the original print and still bears the name of the photographer, who gave the copy to a railroad detective and a Pinkerton man who were looking for the gang. Butch said later, "We were passing the place (studio) and thought it would be a good joke to have our pictures taken."

Cassidy was the "athletic type," Lillie said, and took to bicycle-riding as the craze swept across the West in 1901.

Left to right, standing, William Carver ("He smelled like a skunk."), Harvey Logan (Kid Curry); *sitting,* Harry Longbaugh (The Sundance Kid), Ben Kilpatrick (The Tall Texan), Robert Leroy Parker (Butch Cassidy). *From the original photograph by John Swartz, 705 Main St., Fort Worth, Texas.*

That must have been quite a scene: the notorious outlaw riding up and down the street in Fort Worth's red-light district, his black, iron-hard derby perched cockily to one side, a daredevil grin on his face, as the women cheered and the other outlaws whooped their delight.

Harvey Logan soon tired of Lillie and sent her away with $167 in gold coins. Fanny Porter, it seemed, liked to forget business after hours and on several occasions got drunk with Kid Curry. Logan, all the evidence indicates, was not a sociable drinking partner. He seldom spoke, only drank steadily, while his black eyes smoldered with hatred toward society.

Once, after an all-night drinking party, he and Lillie fell inside the door of Fanny's place. She met them at the doorway but stepped aside when she saw Logan's face. He was in a killing mood and when the Kid said he was going to sleep in her bed, the madam showed him to her gaudily decorated bedroom, where Kid Curry slept on the snowy sheets with his boots and his derby on—and his gun in his hand.

The outlaws foolishly spent some of the forged bills in Fort Worth and soon the detectives were asking questions. Butch was tipped off. The last time Lillie saw Cassidy and Logan, they were dressed in what she described as "cowboy clothes" and "said they had to leave." As an afterthought, she said sadly: "If I had known who they were I would have taken them for all they had."

Somewhere along the way, Kid Curry and Butch Cassidy parted company for the last time. Butch realized that the Wild West was gone. The open range was gone, the days of the cowboy-outlaw were over. The Pinkertons, the telegraph, the steady creep of civilization across the plains had spelled the end.

With the Sundance Kid and the Kid's sweetheart Etta Place, Butch shook the dust of the West from his boots and looked to the frontier of another land—South America.

Fannie Porter.

THE TALL TEXAN SURRENDERS

"And your name, sir?" Victor Jacquemin, teller of the Merchants' Bank of St. Louis, asked the tall, handsome man.

"Benjamin Arnold, of Fort Worth, Texas," the stranger said, smiling. "I'm a cattleman and this is Mrs. Arnold."

The sharp-featured, slim woman, with deeply tanned hands and face, smiled back.

"Pleased to know you, sir—and Mrs. Arnold," the teller said, then pushed the two hundred dollars across the counter. The couple, described by teller Jacquemin as "well-dressed and well-spoken," thanked him and left.

Jacquemin pushed the bank note (of the National Bank of Helena, Montana) to one side, while he waited on others. A half-hour later he picked it up automatically and glanced over it. A gear clicked in his mind. He went to another drawer and pulled out a "Wanted" poster. There were the grave-faced men in derby hats staring at the camera, and above it: "Wanted for Train Robbery." The list of stolen bank notes was included. Jacquemin ran his finger down the list. The note he had taken was listed as stolen in the Wagner train robbery. He studied one of the men in derby hats. Mr. Arnold was Ben Kilpatrick, alias the Tall Texan . . .

Jacquemin hurried to the president's office. In less than an hour he was being interviewed by a St. Louis detective and a Pinkerton operative. He and a St. Louis jeweler positively identified Arnold as Kilpatrick, and Mrs. Arnold as Laura Bullion.

The Union Station was surrounded but the outlaws never showed. That next day the Pinkertons papered the city with posters and alerted all detectives and patrolmen. On November 8, 1901, a detective spotted a carriage racing down Twentieth and Chestnut Streets.

He caught a glimpse of the "tall and ruddy complexioned man I knew to be the outlaw, Kilpatrick." The officer hired another carriage and followed the first one "to many saloons on Chestnut, where he had a few." The detective shadowed Kilpatrick to 2005 Chestnut Street, a boarding house. He called for help and with several other detectives they surrounded the house and kicked in the door of the Texan's room.

Ben leaped for his holster but the detectives overpowered him. In his pocket was found a key for a room at the Laclede Hotel, St. Louis. A check of the register showed it had been occupied by Mr. and Mrs. J. D. Rose, both identified, of course, as Laura Bullion and the Tall Texan.

Laura was found talking to expressmen about removing her luggage, a large valise and two small bags. The *St. Louis Times* described her as "soft-spoken, well-dressed, slender woman with a graceful figure, who protested gently that she was innocent."

The next day Laura broke down and confessed she was Della Rose, who rode with the Wild Bunch. In the valise was found $7,000 of the Wagner train robbery money.

Chief of Detectives Desmond of St. Louis, one of the finest law officers in the West, told reporters, "I wouldn't doubt she took part in the holdup of the train at Wagner. I wouldn't put it beyond her. She is cool, absolutely fearless, and in male attire would absolutely pass for a boy. She has a masculine face and that would give her assurance in disguise. . . ."

The Pinkertons brought the teller and jeweler to the jail and they positively identified the pair as the ones who had passed the forged and stolen bank notes.

Laura told Desmond the whole story of her life, a drab account of a young, motherless girl on the frontier. She had shifted for herself, dancing in Wyoming and Texas gambling halls. At seventeen she was the girl-friend of Bill Carver, the train robber.

Kilpatrick endured the "sweating" for three days. Desmond questioned him for hours, day and night, but Kilpatrick doggedly insisted he was J. Rose, a Texas gambler. Finally, when they were both staggering with exhaustion, Kilpatrick wearily waved his hand.

"All right, I'm Kilpatrick. I'll tell you the whole story tomorrow."

"Kilpatrick known as the Tall Texan who robbed the train at Wagner?" Desmond said.

"Yes," Kilpatrick said, and went to sleep.

The next day he signed a complete confession. On December 12, 1901, he pleaded guilty to a twelve-count indictment and was sentenced to fifteen years in the federal penitentiary in Atlanta. The following day Laura Bullion was sent to the Tennessee penitentiary for five years.

The authors have all of their prison correspondence, intercepted by the warden's office, as requested by the Pinkertons. In the guise of writing his "dear mother," the Tall Texan was coolly plotting an escape attempt with the aid of some of the other members of the Wild Bunch at liberty. But before it could materialize he was put into solitary.

Laura's letters were legitimately to her family. Her mother, who evidently knew Kilpatrick, sent them both small packages, along with the gossip of the family who worked a ranch in northern Texas. The letters give a fascinating insight into everyday life on the last frontier at the turn of the century. Children are born on kitchen tables, men are bushwhacked on lonely roads, feuds break out, barbed wire is cut, and men go gunning for the culprits. And as a high spot is the figure of Laura's mother, harassed by rustler-sons and a train-robber daughter, and complaining about the chore of baby-sitting!

Harry Longbaugh.

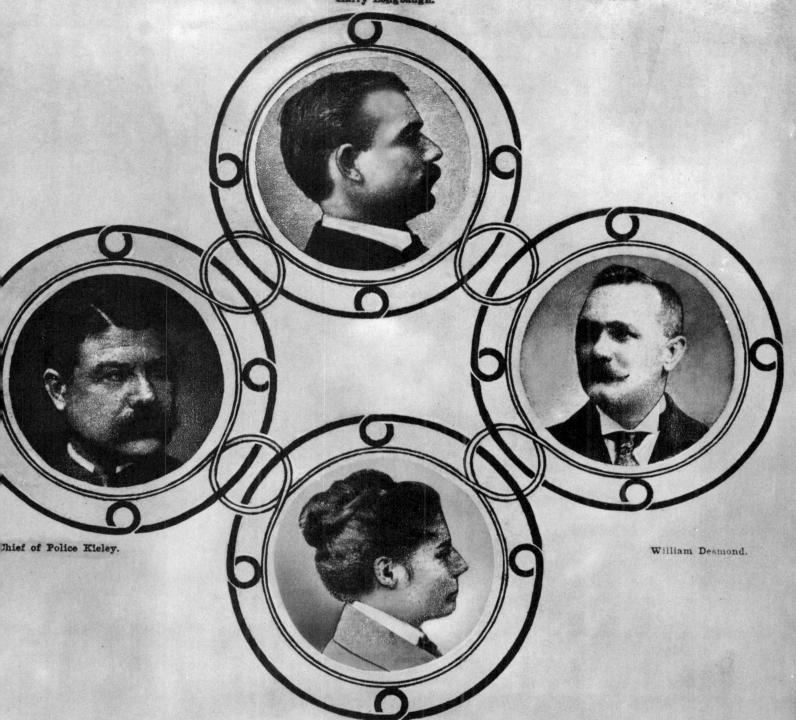

Chief of Police Kieley.

William Desmond.

Della Rose, Alias Laura Bullion.

RRY LONGBAUGH IDENTIFIED AS "THE LONE TEXAN"

(By Associated Press.)

Louis, Nov. 15.—A telegram has been received by Chief of Detectives Desmond from Sheriff House of Concho county, Texas, stating that the picture of baugh, the train robber suspect held at the Four Courts, had been identified as that of Ben Kilpatrick, "the lone Texan," who is wanted there for murder lpatrick escaped at Sonora last April when Bill Carver was killed.

e woman prisoner, Laura Bullion is also well known there.

re of the stolen Helena national bank notes are turning up in circulation about San Angelo.

ief Desmond "sweated" Kilpatrick again today.

acknowledged that he had been reared in Paint Rock, Texas, and knew Sheriff House.

ou are wanted for murder down there," said the chief. "Now, whom did you kill?"

don't remember being in any trouble down there," replied the prisoner.

en he stopped talking.

To Chief of Police Mathew Kiely of St. Louis and William Deasmond, chief of detectives of that city, belongs the credit of having capture Longbaugh, one of the men who held up and dynamited a Great Northern train in Montana last July, and the woman who has cast her l h·s. The pictures of Longbaugh and the woman here given were taken under the snupervision of the officers whose likenesses appear ere sent to The Inter Mountain from the St. Louis police headquarters.

THE ESCAPE OF KID CURRY

From Texas to Knoxville, Tennessee, Harvey Logan, Kid Curry, left a paper trail of forged and stolen bank notes. Annie Rogers, voluble brunette prostitute, was traveling with him, and from the Pinkerton reports they hit every "hook shop" and brothel in the Southwest.

Logan was drinking heavily and becoming more vicious. The peak days of the Bunch were gone and he probably knew it. Manhunters were everywhere. In the fall of 1901, the Kid was one of the most wanted men in the country.

The week that the Tall Texan was sent to prison he wandered into a saloon in Knoxville and took off his coat to play a game of pool. The stakes were high and he became quarrelsome. A fight started and someone pulled a gun. As Butch Cassidy explained, the men in the Wild Bunch liked single-action .45 Colts because the barrel could be a deadly weapon. "Why fire a shot, kill a man and bring on the law, when you can break his nose?" he once said.

Logan used that technique effectively on the pool player who tried to gun him. The man went down with a smashed face. His companions tried to rush Logan but were bowled over like ten-pins. A carriage of deputies galloped up and began firing as they ran into the door of the saloon.

Two patrolmen went down badly wounded. Logan kicked open a back door only to fall thirty feet into a culvert. A patrolman fired and winged him in the shoulder. Ten miles out of Knoxville, bleeding badly, Logan crawled into some brush. He ripped his shirt apart and made a crude bandage, then continued walking. By dawn he had covered thirty miles and was on the outskirts of Jefferson City, east of Knoxville.

He was so weak from the cold and loss of blood he could barely crawl through the bushes. By noon one of the many posses hunting him with dogs surrounded the gully where he was hiding and forced him to surrender.

From Jefferson City a special train took him to Knoxville, where a mob of five thousand people waited to see "the notorious Kid Curry." At Central Police Station, a scholarly-looking man, wearing glasses, walked into the room where Logan was manacled to a chair. They stared at each other. Finally Logan said quietly, "Hello, Spence. How are you?"

Lowell Spence, Assistant Superintendent of the Pinkerton office in Chicago, nodded. "This is Harvey Logan," he said.

Logan stared after Spence as he walked out with the Knoxville chief. "Some day I'll kill that man," he said calmly. "He is very troublesome."

As Spence told author Horan in 1949, not long before he died, "I had no doubt that Logan meant that. Later he told me to my face that he would never be kept behind bars and when he was free he would look me up. 'I got Winters and I'll get you, Spence,' he said."

Kid Curry, the tramp.

In November, 1902, a jury convicted Logan. He filed an appeal but the state Supreme Court turned it down. Logan's lawyer said the outlaw "had a sharp mind" and actually helped in the preparation of his appeal.

When William Pinkerton was informed that Logan had lost his appeal, he lost no time in warning Knoxville. "There is not one good point about Kid Curry," he said. "He is the only criminal I know who does not have one single good point. He is desperate and will use any means to escape."

At a conference between Knoxville and federal authorities, it was agreed that Logan be taken to the escape-proof Columbus, Ohio, penitentiary.

On Saturday, June 27, 1903, Logan rose from his bunk in the Knoxville jail, stretched, and smiled at guard Irwin. He nodded at the river in the sunset. "Beautiful sight, isn't it?"

The guard agreed and turned slightly. Quick as a flash Logan snatched up a small noose he had made from the wire on a broom and lassoed the guard, yanking him against the bars. In a moment he had tied the guard's hands with canvas strips he had made. Next he took from under his bunk several pieces of molding tied together with strips of canvas and on one end a rusty handle bent into a hook. With this he began "fishing" for the cardboard box under the guard's desk containing a .45 Colt and a .38 Smith and Wesson. At first it seemed an inch too short but Logan flattened himself against the bars and dragged the box to him.

He next took the keys from the guard's pocket, unlocked his cell, then went to the door leading out to a corridor where Bell, the second guard, was stationed. He rapped the bars and the other guard appeared. He started to run but Logan's voice rasped like a saw through ice. "Move and I'll kill you," he snarled.

Bell froze in his tracks. Under Logan's guns he opened the door. Logan used him as a human shield to make his way to the courtyard where Sheriff Fox's horse was kept.

THE KNOXVILLE SENTINEL. SATURDAY JUNE 27. 1903

BANDIT LOGAN WAS LAST SEEN FIVE MILES FROM CITY SATURDAY

He Was Riding Leisurely Along a Byroad Having Left the Pike---Spoke to No One He Met

Logan pulls the wire.

From the *Knoxville Sentinel* of June 27, 1903.

The guard, on Logan's orders, "saddled up the mare." The Wild Bunch rider, guns in hand, galloped down Prince Street, waved to a little girl playing on her porch, then vanished.

One witness said he saw Logan riding down the street at 5:02 P.M. By 6:30 P.M., posses were thundering out of town. But Logan led a charmed life. Ten farmers saw him riding along the main roads, guns stuck in his belt, yet seemingly not bothered by anything like mere posses.

Back at the jail, guards Irwin and Bell said they were both "surprised" by Logan and were forced to let him go under the threat of death. But there were many discrepancies in the escape, still unsolved. R. W. Austin, United States marshal, who was passing the jail at 5:15, an hour after the outlaw had lassoed guard Irwin, made a public statement.

"I saw Sheriff passing in a leisurely manner, and I said, 'Hello, Sheriff, how is Logan?' He replied, 'He is gone.' I replied, 'Why, you must be joking.' He answered, 'No, it is a fact.' "

Back at the jail the amazed Austin found that despite his orders Logan had been allowed to walk in the corridor, and two weeks earlier had obtained a map of the country "south of the river." But the crusher for Austin came when he found out—an hour after Logan's escape—that no posse had been organized to go out after him!

It was the marshal himself, according to his version, who gathered together the posses to comb the mountains for Logan. "I phoned all over the country, calling to my aid all the United States marshals and deputies, and sheriffs. Both the sheriffs of Blount and Sevier Counties stated they would start at once and did with posses. I was in frequent communication with all parts of the country, sending out descriptions of him and using the telegraph to contact many points."

Half a century later, the evidence shows how carefully Logan planned his escape. After his appeal was turned down, he had staged many berserk outbreaks, smashing furniture and ripping apart his canvas bed top. In one rage he had smashed a sink with his broom. Later he unwound the fine wire and made a lasso. He kicked apart a bucket and hid the rusty handle as a hook.

Lowell Spence took out after Logan. He trailed him through the Great Smokies and as far north as Colorado. There in a lonely graveyard he was to write finis to the career of the Tiger of the Wild Bunch.

THE TALL TEXAN CHECKS IN

In March, 1912, Ben Kilpatrick, the Tall Texan of the Wild Bunch and one of Black Jack Ketchum's best riders, checked in his chips in an ignominious end. He didn't die as he galloped across the plains pursued by a posse, or in a melodramatic gun duel with a sheriff. Instead the handsome Texas outlaw was killed in an express car by a Wells Fargo messenger half his size, who slugged him across the head with an ice mallet. Then the messenger, thirty-one-year-old David A. Trousdale, picked up Kilpatrick's Winchester and killed Ben's partner and former cell-mate, Howard Benson, of San Angelo, Texas, as he walked into the express car.

In an interview with a correspondent for the *New York Herald*, Trousdale said: "They thought they were such smooth workers at the game. But it made me sore the way they acted, so I decided to take some of the conceit out of them. By a ruse I made the bigger one (Kilpatrick) look the other way; then I struck him on the head with the ice mallet. I picked up his rifle and killed the other one as he walked out of the mail car toward me."

He added: "I am more worried about what to do with the vacation and the reward the company has given me than I am about killing those two."

The Tall Texan had been at liberty only a year before he was killed. He was released on June 11, 1911, from Atlanta, over the protests of the Pinkertons, who wanted him tried for the murder of Oliver Thornton in Paint Rock, Texas, and other train robberies. After their release Kilpatrick and Benson rode to Sanderson in the alkali section of southwestern Texas, where the Devil's River flows to the Rio Grande. They camped out in Devil's River Valley an outlaw hangout, to plan their first robbery. The hangout was as notorious as Hole In The Wall or Robbers' Roost. The *St. Louis Star* said of it:

"For many years it has been known to convicts from the Texas Penitentiary that if they could reach the Devil's River country after escaping there would be small danger of being recaptured. It is probable that no other portion of the West harbors so many notorious characters as this particular section. In fact, some of them boast that should they be arrested it would be impossible for the arresting officer to take them out on account of the intervention of friends."

The outlaws selected the Pacific's Sunset Flyer as the first victim. On the afternoon of March 14, 1912, Kilpatrick and his companion forced their way into the Wells Fargo car, with Benson telling Trousdale, "I'm a Union Pacific detective. We just got wind of a robbery attempt on you."

Trousdale went for his gun, but Kilpatrick aimed his Winchester. "Don't try it, young fellow," he warned.

While his companion went into the mail car the Tall Texan started toward the safe. That's when Trousdale picked up his ice mallet and killed him. Minutes later he killed Benson.

THE WILD WEST, NEW YORK, NEW YORK

On the bitterly cold morning of February 1, 1902, Mrs. Taylor opened the front door of her fashionable boarding house at 234 West 12th Street, New York City. Two men, both handsome and ruddy-faced, and a tall, slim woman, stood on the steps. The smaller of the men took off his derby and introduced himself as Jim Ryan, his companions as Mr. and Mrs. Harry D. Place.

They inquired for the best rooms and Mrs. Taylor, impressed with their fine clothes and courtly western manners—"We're cattlemen, ma'am," Mr. Ryan said—showed them a suite of two rooms. At Ryan's request, she moved another boarder who had a room facing the street.

When Mrs. Taylor left, Butch Cassidy, alias Jim Ryan, and Mr. and Mrs. Harry Place, alias Harry Longbaugh, the Sundance Kid, and Etta Place, took off their coats and the "hardware" under them, their single-action .45 Colts.

Butch Cassidy had finally realized his ambition to come to New York. It was to be the first stop on the long trip to the Argentine. They carried with them a valise with more than $30,000 in it, the profits of the Wagner, Tipton, and Wilcox robberies. "We thought it would be enough for a good time in New York and a stake in South America," Butch said later.

He paid a week's rent in advance and the outlaws and their lady went out on the town. Every morning they hired a carriage and rode around the city looking at the sights. They ate at the finest restaurants, saw the best shows.

One of their most important excursions was to Tiffany's. There they examined, a clerk later testified, a tray of fine gold watches. Finally Etta selected one, a small open-faced gold watch which she pinned on the front of her dress. The bill was $60. Butch paid it in cash. Unlike the Tall Texan and Lonny Logan, Cassidy and the Sundance Kid had cashed most of their forged notes earlier before moving on. Now there was no danger of being traced by the railroad detectives or the Pinkertons.

New York City must have been a world of incredible wonders for these three people who knew only the drab saloons and brothels and the lonely vast open spaces of the country where they had hid out for so long. The first subway was being built, automobiles were chugging down Broadway, Lillian Russell's six white horses "and many carriages" were a daily attraction; there were the Flatiron Building, the glittering lights of Broadway, and Monk Eastman's trial.

The Wild Bunch loved to have their pictures taken and this weakness once again led the manhunters to them. On February 3, two days after their arrival, the Sundance Kid and Etta went to the studio of De Young, who served the Four Hundred, at 826 Broadway, near Grace Church.

De Young remembered Etta Place and Harry Longbaugh. They were dressed formally. The Sundance Kid

Harry Longbaugh and Etta Place. *From the original photograph by De Young's, Broadway and 17th St., New York.*

was in tails and a high hat, while Etta Place was dressed in a long, shimmering gown of velvet. The photographer later said he thought they were distinguished "and perhaps Western society."

They had three pictures taken together, and then the Sundance Kid had his picture taken alone, as did Etta. If the photographer noticed the bulge under the Kid's left arm where his holster was, he did not say so.

While in the East, the Sundance Kid traveled up to Buffalo, New York, to be treated for an old case of gonorrhea, at the Pierce Medical Institute. He went alone and Butch and Etta continued to view the city.

Mrs. Taylor said they were a quiet, reserved trio at all times. Etta Place seemed very proud of her watch and showed it to the landlady.

"It is a gift from my husband," Etta said.

When the Sundance Kid returned from Buffalo, they booked passage on the S. S. *Soldier Prince*, under the names of Ryan and Mr. and Mrs. Harry D. Place.

There is no doubt that after he escaped from Knoxville, Harvey Logan tried desperately to join Butch Cassidy in South America. In one intercepted letter, Kilpatrick, the Tall Texan, wrote Laura Bullion, "The Kid is trying to reach C. I wonder why we didn't hear from him."

Kid Curry never reached Butch. After the escape he fled to Montana, then to Colorado, where he formed a new gang composed of former rustlers and outlaws. They hid out near Parachute, Colorado, and on the afternoon of July 7, 1903, rode out of their hideout and tried to rob a train. They blew open the safe but got only a few dollars.

The telegraph wires hummed with the news and posses formed. The chase lasted for two days and nights. On the afternoon of the second day, the possemen cornered the gang in a small canyon. One deputy winged a man as he jumped from behind a rock, and saw him fall.

In a lull they heard a voice call out: "Are you hit?"

A weak reply came back: "Yes, and I'm going to end it here."

There was a single shot before the battle started up again. Two of the gang made their escape, the third was found behind a rock, his .45 Colt in one stiffened hand. He wore a ragged sweater, old trousers, and battered black

Annie Rogers and Harvey Logan.

The Sundance Kid in formal attire.

hat. His face was sunken in and he looked "as if he had been sick." There was a bullet hole in his left temple.

The body was strapped on a horse and brought to Glenwood Springs. Several townspeople identified the corpse as that of Tap Duncan, "who worked for a Texas outfit." The body was then buried in the local graveyard and the sheriff sent out a routine wire, describing the dead man and the robbery.

When the wire reached Denver, Detective McParland announced the dead man was Harvey Logan, alias Kid Curry. William Pinkerton sent a wire to the sheriff asking him to disinter the corpse and have the local photographer take a picture. This was the procedure followed by the Pinkertons in every case where an unknown outlaw was killed in the commission of a crime. Copies of the picture would then be sent to all branches for identification.

The announcement created a stir. McParland was laughed at, especially after the Cody, Wyoming, bank was robbed, with Logan identified as the leader of the gang. Pinkerton realized there was one man in the West who positively could identify the body: Lowell Spence, who was in Colorado on Logan's trail.

"To end the endless questions, have Spence look at the body," was Pinkerton's order.

Spence was accompanied to Glenwood Springs by chief agent Canada of the Union Pacific. The body was exhumed, tied to a flatboard in the cemetery, and propped up.

Spence took one look. "That's Kid Curry," he said.

But Canada and the other deputies wouldn't believe him. To clinch the identification, Spence took the picture and physical description of the dead man to Knoxville. There Federal authorities checked their records and confirmed that they tallied with that of Logan. The guards, jailers, and others who had "daily contact" with the famous outlaw unanimously agreed that the corpse was "that of Kid Curry." In Federal Court the case was marked "closed by virtue of suicide."

In 1949 Mr. Spence, then eighty-seven, recalled those days. "The deputies in the West had seen Kid Curry perhaps only once," he said. "But I had seen him daily in Knoxville and in the courtroom for hours at a time. His scars, and body defects tallied along with his picture. It was impossible not to recognize him."

Lowell Spence.

Harvey Logan, "in death."

BUTCH CASSIDY: Robin Hood of the Pampas

For nearly half a century western historians have wondered what eventually happened to Butch Cassidy when he fled to South America with Harry Longbaugh, the Sundance Kid, and the beautiful Etta Place. From time to time, at the turn of the century, strange stories drifted back to the West by returning outlaws whom the law no longer wanted. They told how Butch led a large outlaw gang, hiding out in the jungles and robbing banks and gold trains.

The men who built the Bolivian Railroad also had stories to tell of him when they returned to the States. In 1920, Arthur Chapman, author of the famous *Out Where the West Begins,* told part of the story in *Elks Magazine.* However, as he explained to Sylvester Vigilante, then in the American History room of the New York Public Library, "It's one of the great stories of the West, but I don't think anyone will ever piece it together."

Vigilante, who has made a lifetime study of outlaws and the western frontier, and who had heard bits of the story himself, agreed at the time.

Now, for the first time, the entire story of what Cassidy did in South America, how he lived, how he died, and what finally happened to the tantalizing Etta Place, can be told here. In 1950, author Horan visited the fabulous Frank Dimaio, the Pinkerton detective, nearly ninety, living in Dover, Delaware, and in a series of interviews, and from Dimaio's own reports in the Agency, obtained the first-hand story of how Dimaio chased the outlaw trio in South America. Then from several correspondents, and finally from Percy Seibert, the man for whom Cassidy and the Sundance Kid worked and perhaps the only man Cassidy trusted, he obtained the missing pieces.

The story can well begin on a spring day in 1907, when a lonely rider on a saddle mule came up the trail from La Paz, Bolivia, to the Concordia Tin Mines, southeast of La Paz. Clement Rolla Glass, manager of the mine, standing in front of the gleaming white administration building, shaded his eyes from the thin mountain sunshine to watch the rider approach.

The towering ranges of the Santa Vela Mountains dwarfed both mule and man. The clatter of the hooves on the stony path which wound up the mountainside sounded very loud when a rider came up. High above the camp, the tram car—18,000 feet high—was silent. Only a few half-breeds moved listlessly about the camp. Since the panic of 1907 the Concordia had shut down, lock, stock, and barrel. But with things easing up in the States, the rough, happy-go-lucky men who mined the camp were drifting back. They were a hard lot, and many were wanted back in the States for murder and outlawry. They had names like "Buffalo Irish," "Little Tex," "Johnny Mac," and so on. Last names were not asked.

Glass said later that he spotted the rider as a man from the western part of the United States. When pressed for an explanation, he replied simply, "He looked like one. I could spot them a mile away."

The rider came close. He was of medium size, with close-cropped blond hair, blue eyes, sun-blackened face. When he asked for a job, Glass in return asked if he knew anything about mules and livestock.

The rider said he did. Glass then told him he was hired. "One hundred and fifty and grub." He pointed to a small white house on the side of the mountain.

"That's the bunkhouse," he said.

As the man turned away, Glass asked his name. The stranger rubbed his chin. "Let's say Santiago Maxwell."

"Good enough," Glass replied. "Chow time is at six."

As you have probably guessed, Maxwell was Butch Cassidy.

About a week later, another rider on a mule came up the trail. He was taller than Cassidy, slim, and whistling shrilly. Under the name of Brown he, too, was hired. Of course he was Harry Longbaugh, the Sundance Kid.

Soon after—it was apparent to Glass they knew each other—Cassidy and Longbaugh were sent to La Paz to buy $200 worth of mules and feed. Cassidy came back with the stock and handed $25 in change to Glass.

As they walked away, Glass realized that something about them was troubling him. As he said later: "In a country where every man went armed, Cassidy and Longbaugh never openly sported firearms."

As the hot days dragged on, the Pampas grapevine buzzed with the news that a strange trio, two men and a woman, had robbed several banks in the Argentine. First

Frank Dimaio.

230

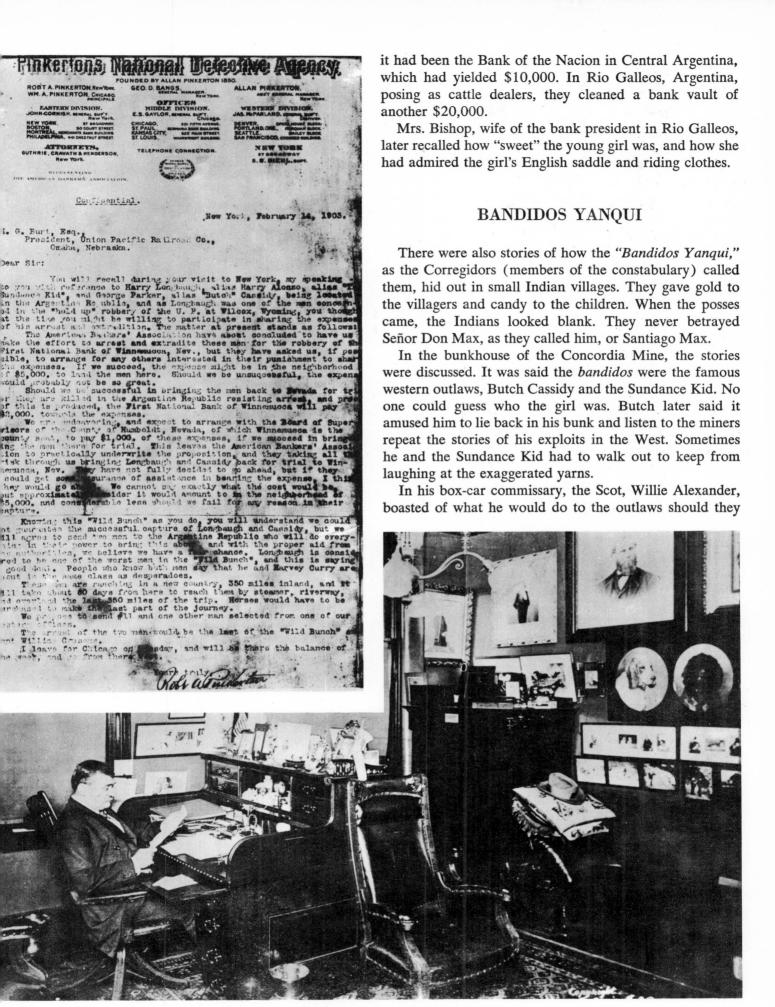

it had been the Bank of the Nacion in Central Argentina, which had yielded $10,000. In Rio Galleos, Argentina, posing as cattle dealers, they cleaned a bank vault of another $20,000.

Mrs. Bishop, wife of the bank president in Rio Galleos, later recalled how "sweet" the young girl was, and how she had admired the girl's English saddle and riding clothes.

BANDIDOS YANQUI

There were also stories of how the *"Bandidos Yanqui,"* as the Corregidors (members of the constabulary) called them, hid out in small Indian villages. They gave gold to the villagers and candy to the children. When the posses came, the Indians looked blank. They never betrayed Señor Don Max, as they called him, or Santiago Max.

In the bunkhouse of the Concordia Mine, the stories were discussed. It was said the *bandidos* were the famous western outlaws, Butch Cassidy and the Sundance Kid. No one could guess who the girl was. Butch later said it amused him to lie back in his bunk and listen to the miners repeat the stories of his exploits in the West. Sometimes he and the Sundance Kid had to walk out to keep from laughing at the exaggerated yarns.

In his box-car commissary, the Scot, Willie Alexander, boasted of what he would do to the outlaws should they

William A. Pinkerton in his Chicago office.

231

Percy Seibert, who employed Cassidy.

ever come to his place. The miners listened. When Willie went on like this, he got so excited he forgot to keep tabs on the drinks.

On a November night, 1908, Glass was aroused by one of the half-breeds, named Pedro, who babbled out a story of how he had overheard the two new workmen discuss robbing the La Paz gold train. They were the American bandits from the Argentine.

Pedro was an alcoholic, but Glass recognized genuine fear in his face. With his heart "in my throat," as he later said, he armed himself with a Colt and a Winchester and, followed by the shaking Pedro, walked up the rocky mountain trail to the bunkhouse.

Outside he took a deep breath. A. Basil Reece, his assistant, was in La Paz. It was all his responsibility. If these two dangerous men killed him . . .

He kicked at the door. "Maxwell . . . Brown . . . open up."

After what seemed an eternity, the oil lamp was lighted and the door opened.

Maxwell—Cassidy—sleepy-eyed, stared at him in the lantern light.

"Mr. Glass . . . what the hell . . ."

Glass swung his Winchester at Cassidy. "I know who you men are, Maxwell," he said. "You're the robbers from the States who stuck up the banks in the Argentine. Now get out of my camp."

The quiet struck like a clock. Cassidy grinned. H turned to the Sundance Kid and made a motion. Glas suddenly realized he had been the target for a single-actio .45 Colt poking through a blanket.

Cassidy kicked the door closed. He lit a cigarette. "Sure Mr. Glass, we're the Hole In The Wall fellows. I'm Cassid and this is Longbaugh, the Sundance Kid."

Longbaugh leaned over and said, seriously, "Glad t know you, Mr. Glass."

Both outlaws laughed heartily.

Glass said he thought they were making a fool of him "I don't know who you are," he said. "If you think you'r coming here and planning to rob this camp . . ."

Cassidy shook his head. "Why should we rob the Con cordia, Glass?" he asked, "You have treated us fairly an that's all that counts with us."

"Pedro overheard you," Glass said.

"Pedro doesn't understand English," Butch replied. "I we were going to rob the Concordia, would we talk abou it in Spanish?"

Glass, who recognized the logic, was forced to agree "We're not going to pull any jobs here, Mr. Glass," Butcl said. "And nobody else is."

As Glass started to go out, Cassidy stepped in front o him, his hand on the door knob.

"I'm still Maxwell and the Kid is still Brown. Is tha fair, Mr. Glass?"

Glass nodded. He said Butch's grin was infectious.

"I won't betray you men," he said, "but if you try any thing at the Concordia . . ."

Cassidy again swore he would keep faith with Glass and the mine superintendent went out. He would alway recall how he stood in the chilly darkness listening to the rush of the night wind as it moaned about the mountains His hand was trembling when he put the Colt back int his belt and went down the narrow trail back to the ad ministration building.

Glass never betrayed Cassidy and Longbaugh. The continued to work at the Concordia for some time, while far to the West, Pinkerton detective Frank Dimaio wa wandering up and down the coast seeking a clue to thei whereabouts.

Dimaio, in the last years of his life, told how the Agency chased Cassidy and Longbaugh from New York to the Argentine. In 1902 an operative had tracked them acros the country to New York. In South America, where he hac finished another investigation, Dimaio learned that they had opened a bank account in the River Platte Bank fo $30,000 and had filed a government land claim in Cholio Province of Chubut, in the 16 de Octubre District.

Cassidy brazenly demanded assurance from the ban president, he later boasted to Glass and Seibert, that the bank was burglar-proof. "We have heard there are many bandidos down here," he told the bank president with a grave face. The president, later interviewed by Dimaio confirmed the story.

Dimaio then contacted a dentist living in Buenos Aires who had a ranch next to Cassidy's place. The dentist was dumbfounded when he heard who his neighbors were. He described them as "perfect gentlemen" and Mrs. Place as "a good housekeeper and fine rider." They had a small herd, he said, some sheep and horses, and had been making additions to the place. Cassidy said of this that he and the Sundance Kid had really tried to go straight but "circumstances" changed his mind.

These were the circumstances. The Sundance Kid, gay and handsome, had an eye for the ladies. Etta, Butch later said, was more of a housekeeper than a mistress. Longbaugh became friendly with a rancher's wife and one day was caught in her bedroom by her irate husband. Longbaugh, always fast on the draw, jumped for his holster and shot the man in the shoulder.

"The damn fool had a gun and might have killed me," he explained.

They didn't leave at once, but shortly after the shooting of the rancher Cassidy received a mysterious cablegram from Buenos Aires. After he read it, he passed it to the Sundance Kid and Etta. That afternoon they rounded up their herd, approximately 200 steers, and made what was perhaps one of the first South American cattle drives, from Chubut to La Paz, Bolivia. How they crossed the jungles and the mountains is not known.

The Concordia Tin Mine.

233

The barracks where Cassidy and the Sundance Kid lived at the Concordia Mines (first white house on the left).

Butch Cassidy and the Sundance Kid on the pampas in Bolivia. Cassidy is sitting on the mule and Longbaugh is tending to his mount. On the right is Don Carlos Mexia, son of the Mexican Minister to Paris and London and former Prosecuting Attorney of Mexico City. The Mexia family was one of the oldest in Mexico. The picture was taken about the time when Cassidy was introducing American-type outlawry to South America.

THE WILD WEST COMES TO SOUTH AMERICA

It was not long afterward that Butch introduced out-lawry, Wild West style, to the pampas of South America. Bank after bank was robbed. Posses were no problem. The local Corregidors had little stomach for riding after the fast-shooting *bandidos*.

Then, in 1907, something happened to Etta Place, which solves the mystery of the disappearance of the beautiful, hard-riding female outlaw. It was nothing glamorous, but a rather humdrum incident. Etta was stricken with an attack of acute appendicitis. It was decided that she had to return to the States for an operation. Etta, by this time, was becoming weary of always riding and hiding—the hide-outs in the abandoned Jesuit monasteries of the Bolivian jungles had no appeal at all to her—and was only too happy to return to the States.

Longbaugh and Cassidy drew straws to see who would have to go back to the States with her. Butch won. Longbaugh, the loser, took her back to Denver—after a gay stopover in New York. He brought her into the hospital on a Saturday and promised to return that night.

But the Kid found some old friends and, after a drinking party, shot up a saloon, winged a bartender, and in general "hurrahed" the city. He woke up in a boarding house, still drunk, and after bellowing for coffee, took his single-action Colt and fired several shots at the ceiling.

"That brought them on the run," he recalled, grinning.

The Sundance Kid, realizing what he had done, took the first train back to New York. A few months later he met Cassidy at a rendezvous in the Grand Hotel, La Paz, Bolivia.

We now pick up their story at the Concordia Mine, on Christmas morning of 1908. Christmas was one holiday that was celebrated with gusto. The bells of the small church of Our Lady of Guadalupe filled the clear morning with silvery sound. Americans, Irishmen, Welshmen, Englishmen, and Spaniards stood in the Plaza, as was the custom, and shook hands all around.

Cassidy was there and Glass introduced him to a new arrival, Percy Seibert, of New York. Young Seibert, then twenty-five, had made an impressive record in the back country of South America as Commissary General of the Bolivian Railroad Commission for the Study of Railways. He had just returned from the States, where he had been on a buying tour for the Bolivian Supply Company, a company allied with the Concordia Tin Mines.

Now one of the most decorated Americans in South American history, Mr. Seibert recalls his first meeting with Cassidy. "I noticed this young man," Seibert said, "on the outside of the circle of men. I was going from man to man, being introduced and shaking hands. But he moved away from me clockwise. Finally I caught up with him and when I asked his name, he just grinned and shrugged

and said, 'Oh, Jim Maxwell.' So Butch Cassidy became Jim Maxwell, or Santiago Max, as the Indians called him."

Later, on the trail, Glass asked if he knew who the fellow with the light hair was. When Seibert said he didn't, Glass replied, "He's Butch Cassidy. The Sundance Kid is also here. They work for us."

"Why, I saw them back in the States at Coney Island the day I left," Seibert said.

Glass swung his mule about. "Are you crazy, Perce?" he said. "They're right here."

Seibert shook his head. "I mean I saw them for ten cents in Coney Island in a movie. It was about Cassidy and the Wild bunch holding up the Rawlins, Wyoming, Express."

In his downtown office in Manhattan, Seibert recalled how he and Glass laughed. "By a strange coincidence," he said, "I had wandered into a Coney Island movie and spent the afternoon watching Butch Cassidy and the Sundance Kid ride across the western plains after the robbery. Then a few weeks later I was shaking the same outlaw's hand!"

In the months which passed, Seibert saw much of Cassidy and Longbaugh. Cassidy, when he found he could trust Seibert, told him he had regrets about his life but knew it was too late to turn back.

"I tried to make a deal with the state (Wyoming) but it fell through," he said. "There's no turning back now."

Butch also explained the absence of a gun on his hip: "Too conspicuous to wear, even down here. The Corregidors (constables) won't be looking for a man who doesn't wear hardware."

However, Cassidy and the Sundance Kid (also known in Bolivia as the Sundie Kid) were always armed, each carrying a concealed single-action .45 Colt. Butch explained: "It has a long and heavy barrel and can be used as a weapon. I'd rather crack a messenger across the nose than kill him. All the messenger has is a bump on the head. Hell, it isn't his money anyway . . ."

Butch's philosophy about banks and express companies was common in the early West. In the popular mind of that time they represented big business which foreclosed on farms and homes and were hated by small ranchers and farmers.

Cassidy was a hard worker. He had little use for women but liked his Mount Vernon liquor. Once or twice a week he would drift down to Seibert's office and "yarn."

"Butch was friendly but was always alert," Seibert recalls. "He never failed to sit on a sofa between two windows. When he leaned back he casually let his holster lay across his hip. It was the unconscious instinct of a man who has been hunted for life."

In Seibert's estimation, Cassidy was a friendly, happy-go-lucky man who could be a deadly enemy but a faithful friend. He possessed a magnetic personality which attracted not only the lawless, but also law-abiding men.

Seibert gives a vivid example of this. After the Sundance Kid had shot the rancher in Chubut, the wounded man contacted the authorities in Buenos Aires. A posse was sent to Chubut, but before they had set out someone in a high government office had cabled the warning to Cassidy. When the posses came up they found the ranch deserted.

Cassidy's only regret was that a man had been killed during a holdup of the Compañia National Store in Argentina. The manager had gone for his gun and the Sundance Kid had killed him.

Cassidy said that the Indian villages were their favorite hide-outs and never once were they betrayed. Of Etta Place, who had ridden with them on every holdup, he had one wry observation: "She was the best housekeeper in the Pampas," Butch said, "but she was a whore at heart."

A SHOOTING EXHIBITION

On one occasion at the Concordia Mine, Butch and the Kid gave an exhibition of fast drawing and fast shooting. They had gone down the trail to "yarn" with Seibert and Mr. Glass. As the afternoon wore on, the talk drifted around to weapons. The debate between Cassidy and Glass over the respective merits of a six-shooter and a Winchester grew hot.

At last Butch turned to Longbaugh. "Let's show him, Kid." Longbaugh jumped up, spun the chamber of his six-shooter and said, "Let's go, Butch."

Cassidy looked around and selected four empty bottles. He tossed two to Longbaugh and kept the other two. Outside, both outlaws settled into a semi-crouch, then threw the bottles high up in the air.

"I never saw anything like it," Seibert recalled. "I never

Left to right: James K. Hutcheon, Scotch transportation contractor who knew Butch and the Sundance Kid very well; Hutcheon's foreman, name unknown, another of Hutcheon's foremen, named McCarthy, who made his headquarters in Eucalyptus and who also knew Cassidy; Edmund Maget, a Swiss clerk who worked for the Caracoles Tin Company at Eucalyptus; James Cunningham, the Caracoles Tin Company accountant; Adam Hutcheon, cousin of James Hutcheon and Mrs. P. A. Seibert.

The Grand Hotel, San Vicente. Note stage-coach.

saw two guns drawn faster and I was with men skilled in firearms all my life. Before I knew it the Colts were in their hands and they were shooting. The four bottles crashed in splinters. They repeated this trick several times. Sometimes Butch missed but the Kid always hit the falling targets. However, against Mr. Glass, they weren't too good in firing at fixed targets. As Butch said, "I guess we're better when our targets don't stand still."

Cassidy and Longbaugh worked at the Concordia from 1907 to 1909. One night Butch Cassidy paid Seibert a visit.

"Guess it's time to pull out, Perce," he said.

Seibert nodded.

"Thanks for everything," he said, and went out. Later it was learned they had ridden across the Andes to Tirapati, Peru, to hold up the Inca Gold Mining Company coach but Fred Brown, the superintendent who had a third sense, sent out an empty box on one stage, then sent out the small fortune of the mine in another stage much later. Butch, of course, got the empty box.

They rode again at Eucalyptus Station, where they got $10,000 in gold. Cassidy's fame began to spread. Other outlaw fugitives from the States began to drift into his camp but Butch wanted no part of them. Dick Clifford was one and another lanky Texas gunfighter called Dey, who later returned to Texas with a valise filled with gold. When a pastor on the New York-bound boat happened to see the valise and its contents, he remarked on the large amount of money.

"Ah, yes, Reverend," (as the *New York World* quoted him) Dey replied, "the Lord has been uncommonly good to me lately."

There are many stories of Cassidy's loyalty to friends in South America. In 1909 he met one of the managers of the Concordia on the trail. Later that night Cassidy rode up and called him out in the darkness to tell him he and Longbaugh were going to rob the payroll train that morning.

This is the corral outside San Vicente, from which Cassidy stole the mules
for his last holdup.

"Good Lord, Butch, that certainly would embarrass me," the man said.

"That's what I thought, seeing people saw us together coming into town," Cassidy said. "Forget it. There won't be any holdup."

In 1908 Cassidy also prevented the kidnapping of a Mr. Andrew Penny, who owned the Penny Duncan Mine. Penny was in his office in Oruro, and Butch rode into the Concordia to tell Glass about the plan he had found out. He then told them he would "take care of things" and rode back into the jungle. The kidnapping plan, later confirmed by local police, was never carried out. Meanwhile in Oruro, Penny had hired Fred Stanford, the best gunfighter he could find. A tin plate was nailed across the balcony and Sanford sat behind it with two Winchesters and boxes of ammunition waiting for the kidnappers but they never appeared. We can only guess how Butch "took care of things."

Another time Glass himself was the selected victim and

Butch rode two days and nights to warn the mine super-intendent. Then as before, he spread the word in the other outlaw hideouts, that Glass was his friend and his gun was ready to defend him. The kidnappers again called off their plans.

THE LAST HOLDUP

The last robbery Cassidy and the Sundance Kid pulled off was the Alpoca Mine holdup. A mule train with the money from the mine, en route from Alpoca to Tupiza, was held up by the two outlaws on a jungle trail.

Butch made the mistake of stealing the big silver-gray mule of the mine superintendent. When they rode into a barrio in the village of San Vicente, near Grande River, fifteen miles west of the holdup scene, the hotel owner, also the local Corregidor, spotted the stolen mule and sus-pected a robbery. While his wife prepared supper for the

238

pair in the patio of the hotel, he rode to contact a small company of Bolivian cavalry ten miles east of La Paz.

The soldiers rode up and the *capitan* ran into the patio shouting to the *"Bandidos Yanqui"* to surrender. They were his last words. The Kid killed him. Another soldier raised his rifle and Butch's shot spun him around.

The soldiers surrounded the patio and began shooting from the walls. As twilight deepened into dusk, the firing continued. Night fell and the cavalry men threw torches of brushwood into the patio. The flames cast wavering shadows on the walls while a pall of gunpowder smoke hovered over the miniature battlefield.

Cassidy and Longbaugh had put their Winchesters and extra ammunition across the patio and the Kid made one mad dash to try to get them. He picked up the rifles and ran back. Halfway across the patio he was shot several times and died in the dust. Butch saved the last bullet for himself. As the dawn pinked the east, the soldiers heard one shot. They later found the outlaw dead behind a barricade of tables and chairs.

Butch, the Sundance Kid and the soldiers shoot it out. At the time of the Aramayo Mining Company holdup, Butch and the Sundance Kid were employed by James K. Hutcheon as foremen of his wagon trains which transported for the Aramayo Company. As Mr. Seibert recalls, Hutcheon, who liked Cassidy and Longbaugh, did not know of their lawlessness until after they had died in this siege. He knew them as Santiago Maxwell (Cassidy) and Enrique Brown (Longbaugh). They also went under the name of "the Lowe Brothers."

Only a short time before Cassidy and Longbaugh pulled their last and fatal holdup, a Reverend Wenberg, a Norwegian missionary, who had met Cassidy in northern Bolivia, ran across him in the lobby of a hotel in Tupiza, Bolivia.

"Why, Mr. Maxwell," he said. "How are you?"

Cassidy gave him a cold stare. "I am fine," he replied, "but my name is Lowe." And then walked away.

As he later said, he was sorry he had to snub the missionary, but he did it so the authorities would not link them together after the news of the Aramayo Mine Company holdup reached the large cities.

BLACK JACK KETCHUM: Let 'er Go!

Black Jack Tom Ketchum was probably the only American outlaw who maintained any self-discipline. Ketchum, when he found that he had committed an error of judgment, whether it was in connection with pretty girls or just hitching his horse, would methodically beat himself on the head with the butt of a six-shooter, muttering meanwhile, "You will, will you? (bang) Now take that (bang) and that (bang)!"

One day about the turn of the century, after returning to Clayton, New Mexico, from a cattle drive, Ketchum was handed a letter written by a pretty young lady named Cora, "who had promised to wait." The letter was brief. Cora had run off with a cow-puncher named Slim who had even watched when Ketchum had kissed her good-bye.

Cora's clinching last line was: "No more than you got out of sight then we went to Stanton and got married."

Colonel Jack Potter, who told the story in *Sheriff and Police,* then described Ketchum going down to the bank of the Perico River with his twisted saddle rope and administering a severe beating to himself "while cursing all womankind."

After the cowhands saved Ketchum from beating himself to death, he pulled up stakes for Wyoming's Hole In The Wall country. The Pinkerton files describe him as "one of the leaders of the Hole In The Wall gang," but Tom Ketchum and his brother Sam never shared leadership of the Bunch with Cassidy. They had their own gang of robbers and outlaws who made New Mexico their stamping ground. Occasionally they used Wild Bunch riders in their robberies.

W. H. Reno, special agent of the Colorado and Southern Railroad Company, who chased the Ketchum gang, described their robberies and capture in a letter written on September 12, 1899. A copy of this letter is in the possession of the authors.

The gang had held up Train No. 1 at Twin Mountains, New Mexico, three times. On July 11, 1899, Tom Ketchum, G. W. Franks, and William McGinnis (Elza Lay) held up the train at this point for the fourth time.

Reno and a posse captured them near Cimarron, New Mexico, in a place called Turkey Canyon, about thirty-five miles from the Atchison, Topeka & Santa Fé Railway. In the fight, Sheriff Edward Farr, of Huerfano County, Colorado, and W. H. Love, of Cimarron, were killed, and Ketchum was shot through the right shoulder and captured a few days later. Lay also was captured but Franks escaped.

On August 16, Sam Ketchum was shot by conductor Frank Harrington while trying to hold up the same train at the same spot. He gave the name of Frank Stevens but he was soon identified. His shotgun-shattered arm was amputated but Sam died of blood poisoning.

Reno said in his letter that Ketchum "has committed a

Black Jack Ketchum in his earlier days.

Black Jack.

number of murders" and had been identified by Captain John Boyd of Jerome, Arizona, as the killer of two men at Camp Verde, on July 2, 1899. Before his death, Sam cleared up for law officers the identity of the famous Black Jack. At the ranch where he was captured he proudly told the manhunters, according to the *Illustrated News*: "I'm the brother of Tom Ketchum, the original Black Jack."

But Reno and a Captain Thacker, who headed the posse, could not agree. Both brothers, they insisted in an exchange of letters, were called Black Jack.

Tom Ketchum was convicted of Farr's death and sentenced to the gallows. Elaborate preparations were taken to guard the county jail after reports reached Governor M. A. Otero of the Territory of New Mexico that "outlaw bands are reporting ready to storm the jail and rescue their comrade."

It was a big story and the *New York Times* of April 25, 1901, found space for it. Their correspondent reported that Ketchum had watched the erecting of the scaffold from his cell window.

"Very good, boys," he called down when it had been finished, "but why don't you tear down that stockade so the boys can see a man hang who never killed anyone?"

When the priest came in, Ketchum refused him with a wry smile. "I'm going to die as I lived, padre," he said. "Have someone play a fiddle when I swing off."

He "leaped" up the gallows steps, according to the *Times* reporter, and helped the hangman adjust the noose.

Ketchum, a tall and handsome man, made an impressive picture on the gallows with the noose around his neck and the wind ruffling his thick black curly hair. "I'll be in Hell before you start breakfast, boys," he said cheerfully as the black cap was put over his head. There was a brief silence. Then a muffled voice called out: "Let 'er go."

The hangman dropped his hand. The trap sprang. There was a last gruesome touch. In an amateur slip, the weights had not been properly adjusted. The terrific jerk tore Ketchum's head from his shoulders.

Black Jack in irons, linked with Chacon, another outlaw.

The hanging of Black Jack.

TOM HORN: HIRED KILLER

There are two sides of the coin in the life of Tom Horn: one side is clear and brilliant—the other corroded with evil. Horn was a brave, loyal scout, a peace officer and soldier, but he was also a hired killer who dry-gulched his victims in a businesslike manner at so much a head.

The gallows finally claimed Horn. On November 20, 1903, he died for the murder of Willie Nickell, a fourteen-year-old boy.

Horn's record as an Indian scout is impressive. More than any other man, Tom Horn was responsible for the capture of Geronimo. After Al Sieber, the famous Indian scout, had been shot up by the Apache Kid, Horn trailed the old Medicine Man for hundreds of miles to persuade him to meet with General Miles.

Horn never knew fear. It is said he was recommended for decoration for bravery under fire—we can find no documentary evidence to support this—and tales about him during the Spanish American War, in which he served as a mule-skinner, are numerous.

Horn had an excellent physique. He was over six feet in height, straight as an arrow shaft and without an ounce of fat on his frame. He was a top ranch hand and in July, 1888, won prizes at the rodeo at Globe, Arizona, and later the world's championship for steer roping and tying.

He was born in Memphis, Missouri, in 1861, to a thrifty, hard-working farm family. But young Tom was a wanderer. In his teens he ran away. He was later employed by the Overland Mail Route, drove a team, herded mules, and worked on big ranches in Arizona. When his wander-lust overcame him, he pulled foot for California. There he met Al Sieber, who took him back to Arizona as a Mexican interpreter.

Horn lived with the Apaches and got to know them well. A stretch of mining followed but he and Sieber soon gave up the pick and shovel work. When Geronimo left the reservation, Horn and Sieber went back into the scouts. Later Horn was the intermediary for the army in the Indian peace talks.

Horn also served as a Pinkerton operative with a specialty for tracking down and arresting train robbers. After making the spectacular arrest of Peg Leg McCoy, a notorious outlaw, Horn walked into the Pinkerton office in Denver and resigned.

"You have a fine organization but I have no more stomach for it," he reportedly said.

Horn next appeared in the Hole In The Wall as an exterminator of rustlers. Greed and the love of power no doubt prompted Horn to soil his record as a law officer, Indian scout, and honest cowhand by turning hired killer. He liked to be seen in the company of the cattle barons, to enjoy their fine cigars, imported wines and whiskeys, and to have them slap him on the back and listen respectfully as he spun his tales of his adventures. And there was also the intoxicating feeling of being able to swagger

Tom Horn, with rope he made in jail.

Richard Proctor, Deputy Sheriff of Laramie County. He helped arrest Horn for the Nickell murder.

down the streets of Cheyenne, blood-money jingling in his pocket, to push his way into a saloon and see men cringe under his cold eyes.

Horn was a skilled butcher. He took great pride in his assassinations. As the testimony in his murder trial shows, he would wait patiently for hours in a driving rain or drizzle, chewing on raw bacon, for the one perfect shot. He never left any evidence behind except a small rock under his victim's head—his trademark. It was murder, executed neatly and precisely: the solitary crack of a rifle shot, then silence and death.

When Horn appeared in Hole In The Wall, dead men began to be found on trails or by their lonely camp fires. Word soon drifted about the outlaw camps that Tom Horn was gunning for them. Known rustlers began to disappear. However, Horn rode into the Hole when the great days of the Wild Bunch were over. Only the small-time stragglers were left.

Young Willie Nickell was shot down from ambush by Horn, who supposedly had been gunning for his father, a sheep man. The case remained unsolved until Joe Lefors, a deputy United States marshal, entered it. He became friendly with Horn, who was drinking heavily, and led him to boast of his killings, while hidden witnesses and a secretary took notes.

Horn denied he made the confession but a jury convicted him and he was sentenced to the gallows. The decision rocked the West. Horn had powerful friends among the cattlemen and wagers were made he would never hang.

An elaborate escape plan in which dynamite was to be used to blow out one side of the jail, was discovered. Later Horn tried to break out with another prisoner but was recaptured. Finally the militia was called in to patrol the streets of Cheyenne and Horn went to the gallows, his lips still sealed, his "employers" unknown.

Tom Horn in his jail cell.

THE HUNT FOR HARRY TRACY

The last main act in America's outlaw melodrama opened on the morning of June 9, 1902, when a column of prisoners marched across the yard of the Salem, Oregon, Penitentiary to be lined up against the wall and counted by guards Farrell and Girard. All were accounted for and the guards began to walk to the head of the column.

Near the middle of the column Harry Tracy, who had fought off the tri-state posse with Dave Lant and Swede Johnson, eagerly studied the lid of a tool-box as he entered the prison foundry. When he saw the chalk marks on it he nodded to Dave Merrill, behind him, then made a lunge at the box and opened it. Before the guards knew what had happened, Tracy had grabbed up a rifle, killed Farrell with one shot through the head. Merrill scooped up a sawed-off shotgun from the box and clubbed down a lifer who tried to help the guards.

The prisoners poured out into the yard, shouting and yelling, as Tracy and Merrill scaled one wall, using a ladder conveniently left in the yard. Once over, they engaged the guards on the outer wall. Tracy killed one on the northwest corner, then toppled another from the wall. A third, shot in the shoulder, fell inside the yard. Tracy picked him up and used the wounded man as a human shield as he broke through the outer gate. On the edge of the woods he cold-bloodedly killed the wounded guard, then vanished into the thick brush with Merrill. Behind them the sirens of the prison wailed like frenzied banshees. Telegraph and telephone wires hummed with orders. One of the greatest manhunts in American history had begun.

The first day of their escape, Tracy and Dave Merrill, brother of the dance-hall girl Tracy had married before he went to prison for robbery, hid out in the woods. On

AL JENNINGS:
A PALE IMITATION

As the memoirs of the peace officers and the old frontier newspaper files attest, the fight to root out outlawry on the western frontier was a grim and deadly war of extermination with none of Hollywood's or television's phony glamour. But occasionally there was comic relief such as the "Al Jennings gang." Burton Rascoe, in his biography of Belle Starr, aptly describes their outlaw career as "the shortest and funniest on record."

As road agents they lasted 109 days, during which time they commenced but abandoned two attempts to hold up trains and made one actual holdup in which the five-man gang got sixty dollars apiece and the conductor's nickel-plated watch.

Four of the gang, including Frank and Al Jennings, were arrested single-handedly by U. S. Marshal Bud Ledbetter. Frank served seven years in prison, Al Jennings five. Both men returned to the quiet pursuits of decent, peace-loving citizens. Al Jennings was defeated in the race for the governorship of Oklahoma, then took up lecturing. It was on the basis of a lurid story of his career as a western outlaw in the *Saturday Evening Post* that he gained his reputation. To put it mildly, as western badmen and outlaws, the Jennings gang was a pale imitation of the real thing.

June 10 they entered Salem, robbed two men of their guns and clothes, and headed for Portland. For transportation they robbed two deputies of their carriage "and then bade them a cheery good morning."

On June 11 they abandoned the carriage near Gervais. A fifty-man posse cornered them in the forest but they blasted their way out.

A cordon was thrown around the countryside with "every man who owns a gun" ordered to join the manhunt. But Tracy and Merrill again broke out, this time robbing two deputies of their arms.

The governor of Oregon now ordered the state militia to join the posses. Two hundred and fifty soldiers marched to Gervais but that night Tracy and Merrill crawled through their lines.

On June 14 the outlaws reached the outskirts of Portland, stole two horses, made a farmer's wife cook them breakfast, and forced an old boatman to row them across the Columbia River to Washington. Dinner that night was eaten at another farmhouse—at gun-point. The bloodhounds were baying when Tracy led Merrill back into the forest. Two hundred and fifty men ambushed them but again the outlaws shot their way free.

On June 29 they fought their way through a roadblock. Later they were seen walking along the Northern Pacific railroad tracks about fifty miles from Tacoma. The rewards now totaled eight thousand dollars with the governor ordering all soldiers and posses to "shoot to kill."

On the morning of July 8, Tracy walked alone into the office of a fishing company on Puget Sound. As Tracy explained later, he had fought a weird duel in the woods with Merrill, after he had read in a farmhouse a newspaper account of how Merrill, a few years earlier, had been given a lighter sentence for betraying him to the police.

They had stood back to back in the dripping woods, then walked slowly away from each other. At the count of ten they were to turn and fire. Tracy turned and killed Merrill at the count of eight. As he explained, "I knew he was going to turn at nine, so I killed him, instead of him killing me."

Tracy captured the whole fishing camp on Puget Sound. The chef was made to cook his breakfast, after Tracy had insisted the workers be fed first. As men who were there recalled the scene, he sat at a long table, haggard and deadly-looking. He had a ragged mustache, cold, deep-set eyes that looked out from under the rim of a battered black hat. He leaned on a Winchester with two six-shooters stuck inside his belt.

After breakfast Tracy ordered that the skipper of the large gasoline launch tied up at the pier be brought to him. When the captain appeared, Tracy told him he was taking over the boat. At gun-point he ordered the captain and his crew down to the launch.

"Where to?" the captain asked.

Tracy sat back with a grin. "Seattle," he said.

It was an amazing voyage that afternoon on Puget Sound. Now Tracy was being hunted both on land and sea. Hundreds of law officers, soldiers, and deputies scoured the countryside while tugs and Coast Guard vessels searched the Sound. Meanwhile the gasoline launch chugged leisurely along with Tracy demonstrating his excellent marksmanship to the crew by shooting at driftwood, and telling stories of his "duel" with Merrill. When they were in sight of McNeil's Island, Tracy motioned with his rifle.

"Run the boat over there," he said.

"In God's name, what for?" the captain asked.

"I want to pick a few guards off the walls," he said calmly.

Only after the captain had pointed out that they would be fired upon and innocent men would be killed, would Tracy agree to let the captain change his course. The trip ended near Seattle, where Tracy tied up the captain and crew. He waved good-bye, after telling them he was going into Seattle "to break up a saloon."

Later that day in a driving rain he encountered a twenty-one-man posse, fought them to a standstill, killing a deputy sheriff and wounding three others in a weed-choked yard before two cabins.

A few days later he forced Mrs. R. H. Van Horn to cook him a meal, after asking her politely to be quiet and not make an outcry.

"I will today—but not tomorrow," she said.

When a butcher boy delivered the family meat, Mrs. Van Horn managed to mouth the word "Tracy" and the boy gave the alarm. When the outlaw left that night, a posse had his wagon surrounded. In the darkness someone shouted, "Throw down your arms, Tracy."

Tracy leaped off the wagon, firing at the same time. Two men died on their feet, each with a bullet through his brain. Then Tracy pumped a slug into the heart of another deputy. In a moment he vanished into the darkness.

The manhunt dragged on all summer. Again and again Tracy fought off posses and law officers. He hid in the swamps for weeks at a time, only to reappear on the road, tipping his battered hat to some farm woman and saying, "Please make me a meal."

In August he reached Lincoln County, exhausted and vicious as a wounded wolf. A posse spotted him helping two men build a barn in Lincoln County and moved in. The sun was in his eyes and Tracy's aim was bad. A chance rifle shot tore open his leg.

He hobbled into a wheat field, which the possemen surrounded. All night they waited. Then at dawn a single shot was heard. They found Tracy dead with a bullet hole in his head. One of the most famous manhunts in the Northwest had ended.

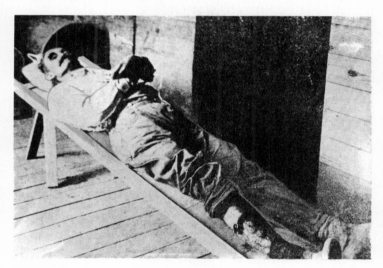

The end.

Picture Credits

The numbers refer to pages

Alfreda, Sister M., St. Gertrude's Monastery, Cottonwood, Idaho, 136.

Arizona Pioneers' Historical Society, 67 top, 112 left, 113 bottom, 114 top, 125 top left, top right, 137, 175 bottom, 176 top, 241 top.

Associated Press, 44 top, 69 top right, lower right.

Bucks County Historical Society, Doylestown, Pa., *The New Doane Book,* 10.

California State Library, 151 lower left.

Coates, Robert M., *The Outlaw Years,* The Maucaulay Company, N. Y., 14.

Colorado, State Historical Society of, 24 top left.

Cottle, Tom, 148 upper right, lower left, lower right, 168.

Croy, Homer, 133 top.

Decker, Peter, 188.

Denver *Post,* 243.

Denver Public Library, Western Collection, 242 top.

Elks Magazine, April, 1930, 239.

Frink, Maurice, *Cowland Cavalcade,* and Wyoming Stockmen's Association, 181 bottom.

Gard, Wayne, *Frontier Justice,* University of Oklahoma Press, Norman, Oklahoma, 21 bottom, 23 top.

Haley, J. Evarts, University of Oklahoma Press, 125 bottom.

Horan, James, 232

Houghton, Mifflin Company, 107 bottom, 108 lower right.

Huntington Library, 23 bottom, 78 top.

International Newsreel, 158.

Kansas State Historical Society, 52 upper right, 105, 106 top and bottom, 107 top.

Kelly, Charles, *Outlaw Trail,* published by the author, 177, 178, 179, 202 bottom, 203 lower left, lower right, 204 lower right, 205 top left.

Lake, Stuart N., copyright, 110, 111.

Life photographer Stackpole, Peter, 56, 68 lower right.

Mazzulla, Fred M., 46 top, 181 top, 182, 183.

Mercaldo Archive, The, 21 top, 22, 29 top, 30, 31, 34, 37, 41, 46 lower left, 47, 48, 50 top, 53, 55, 63, 87, 92 bottom, 93, 98, 100 top, 108 lower left, 113 top, 115 top and bottom, 128 top, bottom, 134, 161, right, 176 bottom, 185 bottom, 240 top, 241 bottom.

Missouri Historical Society, 42 bottom, 43 top.

Montana Historical Society, 125, 129 lower left.

National Archives, 43 bottom, 57, 62 bottom, 103, 127, 131, 141 top, 152 top, 163 bottom, 240 bottom.

National Park Service, Department of the Interior, 90.

Nebraska State Historical Society, 101 bottom.

New Mexico, Museum of, 59, 60, 64, 65 lower left.

New York Historical Society, 12, 72.

New York Public Library, 15, 28, 52 upper left, 184.

Oklahoma Historical Society, 116 bottom, 132 top, 133 bottom, 143 bottom, 148 upper center, 170, 171, 187 bottom, 244.

Oklahoma, University of, Library,
　Division of Manuscripts, 132 bottom,

Tilghman, William, collection, 27, 48 upper left, 135, 145, 148 upper left, 163 top, 167, 169 top.

Wenner, Fred, collection, 116 top.

Pearson, A. Company, Inc., 39 top.

Pinkerton National Detective Agency, 29 bottom, 32, 33 top right, bottom, 36, 39 lower left, lower right, 46 lower right, 71, 73, 74, 75, 76, 77, 80, 82 bottom, 85 bottom, 149, 150, 151 upper right, lower right, 152 bottom, 153, 154, 155, 159, 172, 173 left, 174, 175 top, 190, 192, 193, 194, 195, 197 top center, top left, center, lower left, 198, 199, 200, 201, 203 top, 204 top, 208, 209 top right, lower left, lower center, lower right, 214, 218, 219, 220, 221, 227, 228, 229, 230, 231.

Rasch, Philip J., 55, 58 top right.

Remington, Frederic, *Century Magazine,* 1888, 1890 and *Collier's,* 1890, 91, 94, 95, 96, 97, 99.

Reynolds, J. E., 24 top right, 78 bottom.

Riggs Studio, 141 bottom, 142, 143 top, 144, 146, 147.

Rose, N. H. Collection of Frontier Photographs, 38 lower left, lower center, lower right, 45, 49, 54 bottom, 58 top left, 66 bottom, 69 top left, 70, 86, 88, 101 top, 104 top, 104 bottom, 109, 112 right, 117, 118, 119 lower left, 119 lower right, 120 top left, top right, lower right, 121, 123 top left, 124, 126, 138, 139 bottom, 157, 162 right, 245.

Seibert, Percy, 233, 234, 236, 237, 238.

Sann, Paul, 44 bottom, 66 top, 67 bottom, 161 center, 162 left, 164.

Texas, University of, 85 top, 123 top right.

Tilghman, Mrs. Zoe A., 169 bottom.

Union Pacific Railroad, 211, 212, 213, 215, 216, 217, 224.

Universal Studios, 156, 159.

Walter, George W., *The Loomis Gang,* Prospect Books, Prospect, N. Y., 18, 19, 20.

Warner, Matt, *The Last of the Bandit Raiders,* Caxton Printers, Ltd., 204 lower left, 205 top right, 206.

Wayside Press, *Captain Lightfoot: The Last of the New England Highwaymen,* Topsfield, Mass., 16, 17.

Wells Fargo Bank, History Room, 114.

Wells Fargo Historical Museum, 79 top, 83.

White Studio, New York City, 139 top.

Wichita City Library, 100.

Wilstach, Frank, *Wild Bill Hickok,* Doubleday & Company, 50 bottom.

Wyoming State Historical Department, 210.

Wyoming, University of, Library,
　Archives and Western Department, 51, 185 top, 186, 187 top, 188, 197 top right, 242 bottom.
　　Condit collection, 180.
　　Union Pacific collection, 54 top, 79 bottom.
　　Wyoming Stock Growers Association collection, 209 top left.

Yale University Press copyright, *Pageant of America, The,* 61.

Young, Cliff, 35, 38 top, 84.

Bibliography

Abbott, E. C. and Helena Huntington Smith, WE POINTED THEM NORTH: *Recollections of a Cow Puncher*, Farrar & Rinehart, Inc., New York, 1939.

Aikman, Duncan, CALAMITY JANE AND THE LADY WILDCATS, Henry Holt & Co., New York, 1927.

——DEADWOOD THE DREADFUL, *American Mercury*, November, 1927.

Applegate, Frank G., THE APACHE KID, "Folk-Say: *A Regional Miscellany*," University of Oklahoma Press, Norman, 1931.

Arnold, Oren, THUNDER IN THE SOUTHWEST: *Echoes from the Wild Frontier*, University of Oklahoma Press, Norman, 1937.

Bartholomew, Ed, WILD BILL LONGLEY: *A Texas Hard-case*, The Frontier Press, Houston, 1953.

Bechdolt, Frederick Ritchie, TALES OF THE OLD TIMERS, The Century Company, New York and London, 1924.

Bennett, Estelline, OLD DEADWOOD DAYS, J. H. Sears & Co., Inc., New York, 1928.

Botkin, B. A. (ed.), A TREASURY OF AMERICAN FOLKLORE, Crown Publishers, New York, 1944.

——A TREASURY OF WESTERN FOLKLORE, Crown Publishers, New York, 1951.

——(Ed.), FOLK-SAY: A REGIONAL MISCELLANY, University of Oklahoma Press, Norman, 1930.

Breakenridge, William M., HELLDORADO, Houghton Mifflin Company, Boston and New York, 1928.

Briggs, Harold Edward, FRONTIER OF THE NORTHWEST, Appleton-Century Co., New York and London, 1940.

Buel, J. W., Edited by J. Brussel, THE TRUE STORY OF WILD BILL HICKOK, Atomic Books, Inc., New York, 1946.

——HEROES OF THE PLAINS, Historical Publishing Co., St. Louis, 1882.

Burke, Martha Jane (Canarray) LIFE AND ADVENTURES OF CALAMITY JANE BY HERSELF, Originally published in 1896 and reprinted in FRONTIER AND MIDLAND, 1936.

Burt, Maxwell Struthers, POWDER RIVER: *Let 'Er Buck*, Farrar & Rinehart, Inc., New York and Toronto, 1938.

Burns, Walter Noble, TOMBSTONE: *An Iliad of the Southwest*, Doubleday, Doran & Co., Inc., Garden City and New York, 1929.

Calamity Jane, WHITE HORSE EAGLE, WIR INDIANER. 1. As told to Edgar von Schmidt-Pauli, Verlag fur Kultur-Politik, Berlin, 1929. 2. [WE INDIANS, Translated from the German by Christopher Rede Turner, T. Butterworth, Ltd., London, 1931.]

Campbell, Malcom, MALCOLM CAMPBELL, SHERIFF, Wyomingana, Inc., Casper, 1932.

Casey, Robert J., THE BLACK HILLS AND THEIR INCREDIBLE CHARACTERS, The Bobbs-Merrill Company, Inc., New York, 1949.

——THE TEXAS BORDER and Some Borderliners, The Bobbs-Merrill Company, Inc., New York, 1950.

Clum, John P., NELLIE CASHMAN, *Arizona Historical Review*, Vol. 3, January, 1931.

——IT ALL HAPPENED IN TOMBSTONE, *Arizona Historical Review*, Vol. 2, October, 1929.

Chapman, Arthur, "GETTING THE DROP" AND LIVING, New York *Herald Tribune Magazine*, January 3, 1932.

——BUTCH CASSIDY, *Elks Magazine*, Vol. 8, April, 1930.

Coe, George W., (with Nan Hillary Harrison), FRONTIER FIGHTER, The University of New Mexico Press, Albuquerque, 1934.

Connelley, William E., WILD BILL AND HIS ERA, The Press of the Pioneers, New York, 1933.

Coolidge, Dane, FIGHTING MEN OF THE WEST, E. P. Dutton & Co., Inc., New York, 1932.

Coursey, Oscar William, BEAUTIFUL BLACK HILLS, Educator Supply Company, Mitchell, South Dakota, 1926.

Crawford, Lewis Ferandus, REKINDLING CAMP FIRES: *The Exploits of Ben Arnold (Connor)*, Capital Book Company, Bismarck, South Dakota, 1926.

Croy, Homer, HE HANGED THEM HIGH, Duell, Sloan and Pearce, New York, 1952.

Culley, John Henry, CATTLE, HORSES & MEN OF THE WESTERN RANGE, The Ward Ritchie Press, Los Angeles, 1940.

Cunningham, Eugene, TRIGGERNOMETRY, The Press of the Pioneers, Inc., New York, 1934.

Currie, Barton W., AMERICAN BANDITS: *Lone and Otherwise*, *Harper's Weekly*, New York, September 12, 1908..

Dalton, Emmett and Jack Jungmeyer, WHEN THE DALTONS RODE, Doubleday, Doran and Co., Inc., Garden City, New York, 1931.

Davis, Clyde Brian, THE ARKANSAS, Farrar & Rinehart, Inc., New York, Toronto, 1940.

Douglas, C. L., FAMOUS TEXAS FEUDS, The Turner Co., Dallas, 1936.

Duffus, R. L., THE SANTA FE TRAIL, Tudor Publishing Co., New York, 1930.

Dykes, J. C., BILLY THE KID: *The Bibliography of a Legend*, The University of New Mexico Press, Albuquerque, 1952.

Eisele, Wilbert E., THE REAL "WILD BILL" HICKOK, William H. Andre, Denver, 1931.

Farber, James, TEXAS WITH GUNS, The Naylor Company, San Antonio, 1950.

Fergusson, Erna, MURDER & MYSTERY IN NEW MEXICO, Merle Armitage Editions, Albuquerque, 1948.

Forrest, Earle R., ARIZONA'S DARK AND BLOODY GROUND, The Caxton Printers, Ltd., Caldwell, Idaho, 1952.

——and Edwin B. Hill, LONE WAR TRAIL OF APACHE KID, Trail's End Publishing Co., Inc., Pasadena, 1947.

Freeman, Lewis Ransome, DOWN THE YELLOWSTONE, Dodd, Mead, and Co., New York, 1922.

French, William John, SOME RECOLLECTIONS OF A WESTERN RANCHMAN: *New Mexico, 1883-1899*, Methuen & Co., Ltd., London, 1927.

Fulton, Maurice Garland (ed.), PAT F. GARRETT'S AUTHENTIC LIFE OF BILLY THE KID, The Macmillan Company, New York, 1927.

Gard, Wayne, SAM BASS, Houghton Mifflin Company, Boston, 1936.

——THE CHISHOLM TRAIL, University of Oklahoma Press, Norman, 1954.

——FRONTIER JUSTICE, University of Oklahoma Press, Norman, 1949.

Gardner, Raymond Hatfield, In collaboration with B. H. Monroe, THE OLD WILD WEST, The Naylor Company, San Antonio, 1944.

Glasscock, Carl Burgess, BANDITS AND THE SOUTHERN PACIFIC, Frederick A. Stokes Company, New York, 1929.

——THEN CAME OIL, The Bobbs-Merrill Company, Indianapolis, New York, 1938.

Graves, Richard S., OKLAHOMA OUTLAWS, State Printing and Publishing Company, Oklahoma City, 1915.

Haley, J. Evetts, CHARLES GOODNIGHT: *Cowman and Plainsman*, University of Oklahoma Press, Norman, 1949.

——JEFF MILTON: *A Good Man with a Gun*, University of Oklahoma Press, Norman, 1948.

HARDIN, JOHN WESLEY, THE LIFE OF, Smith and Moore, Texas, 1896.

Harman, S. W., HELL ON THE BORDER, The Phoenix Publishing Co., Fort Smith, Arkansas, 1898.

Harrington, Fred Harvey, HANGING JUDGE, The Caxton Printers, Ltd., Caldwell, Idaho, 1951.

Hendricks, George D., THE BAD MAN OF THE WEST, The Naylor Company, San Antonio, 1942.

Hendron, J. W., THE STORY OF BILLY THE KID, The Rydal Press, Inc., Santa Fe, 1948.

Henshall, John A., TALES OF THE EARLY CALIFORNIA BANDITS, III., BLACK BART, *Overland Monthly*, second series, Vol. 53, June, 1909.

Hodge, Frederick Webb, ed., HANDBOOK OF AMERICAN INDIANS NORTH OF MEXICO, Government Printing Office, Washington, 1907-1910.

Holbrook, Stewart Hall, LITTLE ANNIE OAKLEY & OTHER RUGGED PEOPLE, The Macmillan Company, New York, 1948.

——CALAMITY JANE, *American Mercury*, Vol. 64, February, 1947.

Holloway, Carroll C., TEXAS GUN LORE, The Naylor Company, San Antonio, 1951.

Hough, Emerson, THE STORY OF THE OUTLAW, Grosset & Dunlap, New York, 1907.

Hoyt, Henry F., A FRONTIER DOCTOR, Houghton Mifflin Company, Boston, 1929.

Hughes, Dan de Lara, SOUTH FROM TOMBSTONE, Methuen & Co., Ltd., New York, 1938.

Hungerford, Edward, WELLS FARGO: *Advancing the American Frontier*, Random House, New York, 1949.

Jackson, Joseph Henry, BAD COMPANY, Harcourt, Brace and Company, New York, 1939.

——TINTYPES IN GOLD, The Macmillan Company, New York, 1939.

Jennewein, J. Leonard, CALAMITY JANE OF THE WESTERN TRAILS, Dakota Books, Huron, South Dakota, 1953.

Jennings, Alphonse J., BEATING BACK, D. Appleton and Co., New York, 1914.

Jordan, Philip D., THE ADAIR TRAIN ROBBERY, *The Palimpsest*, Vol. 17, February, Iowa City, Iowa, 1936.

Keleher, William A., THE FABULOUS FRONTIER: *Twelve New Mexico Items*, The Rydal Press, Santa Fe, 1945.

Krakel, Dean F., THE SAGA OF TOM HORN: *The Story of a Cattlemen's War*, Powder River Publishers, Laramie, 1954.

Lake, Stuart N., WYATT EARP: *Frontier Marshal*, Houghton Mifflin Company, Boston, 1931.

Lloyd, Everett, LAW WEST OF THE PECOS: *The Story of Roy Bean*, The Naylor Company, San Antonio, 1936.

Lord, John, PICTURESQUE ROAD-AGENTS OF THE EARLY DAYS, *Overland Monthly*, second series, Vol. 70, November, San Francisco, Calif., 1917.

Martin, Douglas D., TOMBSTONE'S EPITAPH, University of New Mexico Press, 1951.

Masterson, William Barclay, FAMOUS GUN FIGHTERS OF THE WESTERN FRONTIER: WYATT EARP, *Human Life*, Vol. 4, Boston, Massachusetts, February, 1907.

Masterson, V. V., THE KATY RAILROAD AND THE LAST FRONTIER, University of Oklahoma Press, Norman, 1952.

McCarty, John L., MAVERICK TOWN: *The Story of Old Tascosa*, University of Oklahoma Press, Norman, 1946.

McDaniel, Ruel, VINEGAROON, Southern Publishers, Kingsport, Tennessee, 1936.

McKee, Irving, "BEN-HUR" WALLACE, University of California Press, Berkeley, 1947.

McNeal, Thomas Allen, WHEN KANSAS WAS YOUNG, The Macmillan Company, New York, 1922.

McReynolds, Robert, THIRTY YEARS ON THE FRONTIER, El Paso Publishing Co., Colorado Springs, 1906.

Mercer, Asa Shinn, THE BANDITTI OF THE PLAINS, Published by the author, Cheyenne, Wyoming, 1894.

Michelson, Charles, STAGE ROBBERS OF THE WEST, *Munsey's Magazine*, Vol. 25, New York, July, 1901.

Miller, Joseph (ed.), THE ARIZONA STORY, Hastings House, New York, 1952.

Myers, John Nyers, THE LAST CHANCE: *Tombstone's Early Years*, E. P. Dutton and Co., Inc., New York, 1950.

Nix, Evett Dumas, (As told to Gordon Hines), OKLAHOMBRES, St. Louis, 1929.

Noyes, Alva Josiah, IN THE LAND OF THE CHINOOK, State Publishing Co., Helena, 1917.

Otero, Miguel Antonio, THE REAL BILLY THE KID, Rufus Rockwell Wilson, Inc., New York, 1936.

——MY LIFE ON THE FRONTIER, 2 vols., The Press of the Pioneers, Inc., New York, 1935. (Vol. 2, University of New Mexico Press, Albuquerque, 1939.)

Patterson, W., CALAMITY JANE, *Wide World Magazine*, Vol. 11, August, 1903.

Pannell, Walter, CIVIL WAR ON THE RANGE, Welcome News, Los Angeles, 1943.

Poe, John W., THE DEATH OF BILLY THE KID, Houghton Mifflin Company, Boston, 1933.

Raine, William MacLeod, GUNS OF THE FRONTIER, Houghton Mifflin Company, Boston, 1940.

——45-CALIBER L W: *The Way of Life of the Frontier Peace Officer*, Row, Peterson and Co., Evanston, 1941.

——and Will C. Barnes, CATTLE, Doubleday, Doran and Company, Inc., New York, 1930.

——FAMOUS SHERIFFS AND WESTERN OUTLAWS, Doubleday, Doran & Co., Garden City, New York, 1929.

Rainey, George, THE CHEROKEE STRIP, Cooperative Publishing Co., Guthrie, 1933.

Rascoe, Burton, BELLE STARR, Random House, New York, 1941.

Ray, Clarence E., THE DALTON BROTHERS, Regan Publishing Corp., Chicago.

Raymond, Dora Neill, CAPTAIN LEE HALL OF TEXAS, University of Oklahoma Press, Norman, 1940.

Rice, Wallace, DEDICATION OF THE MEMORIAL TO JAMES BUTLER HICKOK, WILD BILL, *Journal of the Illinois State Historical Society*, Vol. 23, October, 1930.

Ridings, Sam P., THE CHISHOLM TRAIL, Cooperative Publishing Co., Guthrie, 1936.

Ripley, Thomas, THEY DIED WITH THEIR BOOTS ON, Doubleday, Doran & Co., Inc., New York, 1935.

Rister, Carl Coke, THE SOUTHWESTERN FRONTIER: 1865-1881, The Arthur H. Clark Co., Cleveland, 1928.

Rogers, Cameron, GALLANT LADIES, Harcourt, Brace and Co., New York, 1928.

Ryder, David Warren, STAGE COACH DAYS, *Sunset*, Vol. 59, San Francisco, September, 1927.

Sabin, Edward Legrand, WILD MEN OF THE WILD WEST, Thomas Y. Crowell Company, New York, 1929.

Scanland, John Milton, LIFE OF PAT F. GARRETT *and the Taming of the Border Outlaw*, Carleton F. Hodge, El Paso, Texas, 1952.

Shirley, Glenn, TOUGHEST OF THEM ALL, University of New Mexico Press, Albuquerque, 1953.

Siringo, Charles A., A LONE STAR COWBOY, Sante Fe, New Mexico, 1919.

——RIATA AND SPURS, Houghton Mifflin and Company, Boston and New York, 1927.

Sonnichsen, C. L., ROY BEAN: *Law West of the Pecos*, The Macmillan Company, New York, 1943.

——BILLY KING'S TOMBSTONE, Caxton Printers, Ltd., Idaho, 1951.

——I'LL DIE BEFORE I'LL RUN, Harper and Brothers, New York, 1951.

Stanley F., DESPERADOES OF NEW MEXICO, The World Press, Inc., Denver, 1953.

Sullivan, W. John L., TWELVE YEARS IN THE SADDLE FOR LAW AND ORDER ON THE FRONTIERS OF TEXAS, Von Breckmann-Jones Co., Printers, Austin, 1909.

Sutton, Fred Ellsworth, As written down by A. B. Macdonald,
——HANDS UP!, The Bobbs-Merrill Company, Indianapolis, 1927.

Taylor, T. U., BILL LONGLEY AND HIS WILD CAREER, Frontier Times, Bandera, Texas, 1925.

Thomas, T. J., BILL CARLISLE, TRAIN ROBBER, *Wide World Magazine*, Vol. 62, London, October, 1928.

Thorp, Jack, with Neil McCullough Clark, PARDNER OF THE WIND, Caxton Printers, Ltd., Caldwell, Idaho, 1945.

Tilghman, Zoe A., MARSHAL OF THE LAST FRONTIER, The Arthur H. Clark Co., Glendale, California, 1949.

——OUTLAW DAYS, Harlow Publishing Co., Oklahoma City, 1926.

Vestal, Stanley, QUEEN OF COWTOWNS: DODGE CITY 1872-1886, Harper & Brothers, New York, 1952.

——THE OLD SANTA FE TRAIL, Houghton Mifflin & Co., Boston, 1939.

Walker, Tacetta B., STORIES OF EARLY DAYS IN WYOMING, Prairie Publishing Co., Casper, 1936.

Warner, Matt, As told to Murray Edwin King, THE LAST OF THE BANDIT RIDERS, The Caxton Printers, Ltd., Caldwell, Idaho, 1940.

Walrath, Ellen F., STAGECOACH HOLDUPS IN THE SAN LUIS VALLEY, *The Colorado Magazine*, Vol. 14, Denver, January, 1937.

Walter, George W., THE LOOMIS GANG, Prospect Books, Prospect, N. Y., 1953.

Walters, Lorenzo D., TOMBSTONE'S YESTERDAY, Acme Printing Co., Tucson, 1928.

Webb, Walter Prescott, THE GREAT PLAINS, Ginn and Company, Boston, 1931.

——THE TEXAS RANGERS, Houghton Mifflin Co., Boston, 1935.

——THE GREAT FRONTIER, Houghton Mifflin Co., Boston, 1952.

Wellman, Paul I., DEATH ON HORSEBACK, J. B. Lippincott Co., Philadelphia and New York, 1934.

———THE TRAMPLING HERD, Carrick and Evans, Inc., New York, 1939.

Wells, Evelyn and Harry Austin Peterson, THE '49ERS, Doubleday and Co., Inc., New York, 1949.

White, Owen P., TRIGGER FINGERS, G. P. Putnam's Sons, New York, 1926.

———EL PASO, *American Mercury*, Vol. 2, New York, August, 1924.

———FIVE EL PASO WORTHIES, *American Mercury*, Vol. 18, New York, December, 1929.

———and Warren Nolan, THE BAD MAN FROM MISSOURI, *Collier's*, New York, January 14, 21, and 28, 1928.

Wilstach, Frank J., WILD BILL HICKOK: *The Prince of Pistoleers*, Garden City Publishing Co., Inc., New York, 1926.

Wright, Robert M., DODGE CITY, THE COWBOY CAPITAL.

Younger, Cole, THE STORY OF COLE YOUNGER, BY HIMSELF, Press of the Henneberry Company, Chicago, 1903.

UNPUBLISHED MANUSCRIPTS

Memoirs of Old Bill Miner, the stage-coach robber, as dictated to a friend while in prison. Owned by James D. Horan.

Memoirs of Mike M. Rice, Arizona Historical Society.

Memoirs of J. O'Shea, Arizona Historical Society.

"Chasing Train Robbers in the Old West," memoir of Pinkerton detective Minster, Pinkerton Archives.

Transcript of reminiscences of Frank Dimaio, retired Pinkerton detective. Owned by James D. Horan.

Percy Seibert's reminiscences of Butch Cassidy in South America (and pictures). Owned by James D. Horan.

Family reminiscences of Butch Cassidy by Moroni Gillies of New Castle, Utah, and an *interview with Lowell Spence* (the Pinkerton man who solved the mystery of the death of Kid Curry) November, 1949. Owned by James D. Horan.

Memoirs of Charles J. Eastman, Arizona Historical Society.

Fishback Manuscript, Arizona Historical Society.

Pinkerton National Detective Agency archives.

Index of Names and Places